# Research for Policy

Studies by the Netherlands Scientific Council for Government Policy

**Series Editors**

The Netherlands Scientific Council for Government Policy (WRR) is an independent strategic advisory body for government policy in the Netherlands. It advises the Dutch government and Parliament on long-term strategic issues that are of great importance for society. The WRR provides science-based advice aimed at: opening up new perspectives and directions, changing problem definitions, setting new policy goals, investigating new resources for problem-solving and enriching the public debate.

The studies of the WRR do not focus on one particular policy area, but on cross-cutting issues that affect future policymaking in multiple domains. A long-term perspective complements the day-to-day policymaking, which often concentrates on issues that dominate today's policy agenda.

The WRR consists of a Council and an academic staff who work closely together in multidisciplinary project teams. Council members are appointed by the King, and hold academic chairs at universities, currently in fields as diverse as economics, sociology, law, public administration and governance, health and water management. The WRR determines its own work programme, as well as the content of its publications. All its work is externally reviewed before publication.

**The Research for Policy Series**

In this series, we publish internationally relevant studies of the Netherlands Scientific Council for Government Policy. Many of the cross-cutting issues that affect Dutch policymaking, also challenge other Western countries or international bodies. By publishing these studies in this international open access scientific series, we hope that our analyses and insights can contribute to the policy debate in other countries.

**About the Editors**

Corien Prins is Chair of the WRR and Professor of Law and Information Technology at Tilburg Law School (Tilburg University).

Frans Brom is Council secretary and director of the WRR office. He also is Professor of Normativity of Scientific Policy Advice at the Ethics Institute of Utrecht University.

Gijsbert Werner • Arthur van Riel
Mérove Gijsberts • Marianne de Visser

# Financial, Staffing and Societal Sustainability of Dutch Health Care

## An Urgent Need for Clear Choices

Springer

WRR
THE NETHERLANDS SCIENTIFIC COUNCIL FOR GOVERNMENT POLICY

Gijsbert Werner
Netherlands Scientific Council for Government Policy (WRR)
The Hague, Zuid-Holland, The Netherlands

Arthur van Riel
Netherlands Scientific Council for Government Policy (WRR)
The Hague, Zuid-Holland, The Netherlands

Mérove Gijsberts
SCP
Netherlands Institute for Social Research
The Hague, The Netherlands

Marianne de Visser
Netherlands Scientific Council for Government Policy (WRR)
The Hague, Zuid-Holland, The Netherlands

ISSN 2662-3684 ISSN 2662-3692 (electronic)
Research for Policy
ISBN 978-3-031-58566-1 ISBN 978-3-031-58564-7 (eBook)
https://doi.org/10.1007/978-3-031-58564-7

Translation from the Dutch language edition: "Kiezen voor houdbare zorg. Mensen, middelen en maatschappelijk draagvlak" by Gijsbert D.A. Werner et al., © Wetenschappelijke Raad voor het Regeringsbeleid 2021. Published by Wetenschappelijke Raad voor het Regeringsbeleid. All Rights Reserved.

This work was supported by Wetenschappelijke Raad voor het Regeringsbeleid



This Springer imprint is published by the registered company Springer Nature Switzerland AG
The registered company address is: Gewerbestrasse 11, 6330 Cham, Switzerland

# Preface

In this book, the Netherlands Scientific Council for Government Policy (Wetenschappelijke Raad voor het Regeringsbeleid—WRR) argues that governments need to make sharper choices to ensure the accessibility and quality of healthcare in the future. While this study focuses on the Netherlands, given rising demand for healthcare across many countries, its conclusions are broadly relevant to researchers, policy makers, and practitioners grappling with questions surrounding the sustainability of healthcare systems.

Dutch healthcare generally performs well, but the growth in healthcare demand is unsustainable in the long term. We are using more and more expensive healthcare, pushing the boundaries of financial, personnel, and societal sustainability. Without changes, one in three people would need to work in healthcare in 40 years. Over the past decades, efforts have been made to improve the efficient organization of healthcare and to recruit more personnel. While we should continue these efforts, they will not be enough in the future. The challenge is too significant.

The WRR concludes that to limit the growth of healthcare, we need to make better choices regarding healthcare priorities. Three key considerations guide this approach. First, where can we achieve the most health gains for as many people as possible? Second, in which areas of healthcare should quality and accessibility be strengthened? Third, how do we sustain the financial, personnel, and societal dimensions of sustainability in the long term?

To make better choices about the sustainability of healthcare, the WRR recommends a three-pronged approach. Firstly, citizens should be prepared for healthcare scarcity and involved in the necessary decision-making, for example, through the establishment of a citizen forum. Secondly, politics must actively take responsibility for healthcare sustainability by setting priorities, including investing in sectors facing consistent challenges in quality and accessibility and focusing on prevention. Thirdly, we should clearly delineate collectively organized healthcare for all sectors more than we do now. This requires a clear distribution of responsibilities between the political sphere and implementing organizations.

This book was written by Dr. Gijsbert Werner (project coordinator), Dr. Arthur van Riel (staff member), Prof. Dr. Mérove Gijsberts (staff member), and Prof. Dr. Marianne de Visser (council member). In earlier stages of the project, Prof. Dr. Arnoud Boot (council member), Mr. Drs. Josta de Hoog (staff member), Dr. Peter de Goede (staff member), Aukje Muller (intern), Jasmin Palamar (intern), Lynn Colder (intern), and Lisa Janssen (intern) were members of the project group. Support was provided by Magda de Wit, Paul van den Berg, Mitra Javanmardi, and Dmitri Berkhout.

The text of this report was reviewed by Prof. Dr. Louise Gunning-Schepers (Professor of Health and Society), Prof. Dr. Patrick Jeurissen (Professor of Healthcare Affordability), Prof. Dr. Pauline Meurs (Professor of Healthcare Governance), Prof. Dr. Rob Baltussen (Professor of Global Health Economics), and Prof. Dr. Ronald Batenburg (Professor of Labor and Organizational Issues in Healthcare). We thank them for their valuable suggestions.

The Hague, The Netherlands

Gijsbert Werner

Arthur van Riel

Mérove Gijsberts

Marianne de Visser

# Contents

# About the Authors

**Gijsbert Werner** is a senior research fellow at the Netherlands Scientific Council for Government Policy (WRR—Wetenschappelijke Raad voor het Regeringsbeleid). He was the project coordinator of the team responsible for writing this analysis of financial, staffing and societal sustainability of the Dutch healthcare system. At the WRR, he also worked on reports on climate justice and global population ageing. Previously he worked as an evolutionary biologist studying the evolution of cooperation at the University of Oxford and VU University Amsterdam.

**Arthur van Riel** is a senior research fellow at the Netherlands Scientific Council for Government Policy and Professor of Historical Political Economy at the Erasmus University Rotterdam. An historian and economist by training, he worked as an advisor to successive Dutch Finance Ministers before joining the Scientific Council in 2012. His academic work has covered the political economy of the Weimar Republic, the role of political institutions and public policy in Dutch nineteenth century industrialization, the economy of the Dutch Republic, the evolution of private debt and the functioning of the European Monetary Union.

**Mérove Gijsberts** is senior research fellow at the Netherlands Institute for Social Research/SCP and professor by special appointment at the European Research Center of Migration and Ethnic Relations (ERCOMER) at Utrecht University. She temporarily joined the Netherlands Scientific Council for Government Policy to contribute to this book.

**Marianne de Visser** is a member of the Netherlands Scientific Council for Government Policy. She was chairing the committee which was engaged in the project on financial, staffing and societal sustainability of the Dutch healthcare system. Her academic work focuses on diagnosis and treatment of neurological and in particular neuromuscular diseases. Previously she has had various administrative functions at the (inter)national level.

# Chapter 1
# Introduction

## 1.1 Background

When people are asked what they consider important in life, one of the first answers is invariably "good health". That, after all, is essential to living a fulfilling life.[1] Good health enables you to do what you want, to enjoy yourself, to take charge of your life and to participate in society. Sooner or later, however, we all face health problems. When that time comes, we trust that care will be available: for ourselves and our loved ones, for young and for old and regardless of education or income. Moreover, we expect care to be good, close at hand and affordable. When we need it, we are often at our most vulnerable: uncertain, confused, afraid of pain or suffering, anxious about the future. And sometimes it is literally a matter of life and death.

A good and accessible healthcare system is important precisely at such times, when we are vulnerable. It not only helps the sick and their loved ones, it also gives healthy people peace of mind and confidence. Covid-19 has once again shown how much faith we as a society place in quality and accessibility of care: during the pandemic we proved prepared to take very far-reaching social and economic steps to guarantee those aspects of the system. This illustrates just how important we consider good health. The high quality and accessibility of care are thus core public values in our society, so it is essential that they be respected now and in the future. Not just in an acute crisis situation, but also—indeed especially—in the long term. That is what the Netherlands Scientific Council for Government Policy (*Wetenschappelijke Raad voor het Regeringsbeleid*, WRR) understands by "sustainable healthcare", the subject of this report. If that comes under pressure, to a greater or lesser extent it will endanger the underlying public values. Sustainability should therefore be regarded as a crucial factor: only when it is in order can we safeguard the public values of healthcare.

---

[1] Gfk (2017); CBS (2016).



G. Werner et al., *Financial, Staffing and Societal Sustainability of Dutch Health Care*, Research for Policy, https://doi.org/10.1007/978-3-031-58564-7_1

But the sustainability of healthcare *is* coming under increasing pressure. This is true not only in the Netherlands, but also in the countries around us. The cause lies in a variety of developments. These include the ageing population and the widening of treatment options as a result of technological innovation. Later in this report we look more closely at the specific ways a number of these trends are affecting the sustainability of healthcare. The broad picture, though, is that the need for care is growing faster than both the economy and—even more urgently in the short term—the labour force. A situation that is expected to persist for decades, giving cause for concern about the sustainability of healthcare. And presenting a challenge not just for that sector, but for society as a whole. After all, other domains are making their own calls on the scarce manpower and resources available. Education, the environment and housing all have their own public values to safeguard, too. So whilst sustainability is obviously a pressing issue within the healthcare sector, its impact goes far beyond that.

Pressure on sustainability can manifest itself in three different dimensions. Firstly, there is financial sustainability: can we keep on paying for it all? But just as important is the issue of staffing sustainability: are there enough people to care for everyone, now and in the future? And finally, but no less crucial, the question of whether the system can continue to meet our expectations and wishes as a society. We call this third dimension societal sustainability: does the healthcare system provide the quality of care Dutch citizens expect, and do they actually experience that quality when they use it? Are people prepared to show the solidarity needed to maintain good and accessible care for all? This is what determines a society's support for its healthcare system. To guarantee the public values of quality and accessibility, performance in all three dimensions must be maintained and balanced (Fig. 1.1).

This report is the result of a research project conducted by the WRR in response to a request for advice from the Dutch government,[2] which in turn was responding to questions from the House of Representatives.[3] This course of events was prompted by growing political and public concern about rising expenditure on healthcare, which in the longer term seems sure to exceed the rate of economic growth. This issue has implications not only for healthcare itself, but for all government policy.

This subject calls for a long-term perspective, so where possible we look ahead to likely developments between now and the middle of this century. It also requires a broad view; we therefore cover healthcare as a whole and across the board, from hospitals and care for the elderly to youth care and social support services. This also includes the prevention of illness, medical conditions or complications. This broad perspective stems from the idea that everyone needs different forms of care during the course of their life. To be able to speak of a sustainable healthcare system, public values must be safeguarded throughout people's lives. Our long-term and broad view also means that we do not look specifically at responses to acute health crises

[2] Minister van Volksgezondheid, Welzijn en Sport (2018a).

[3] Tweede Kamer (2017); Omtzigt and Slootweg (2018).

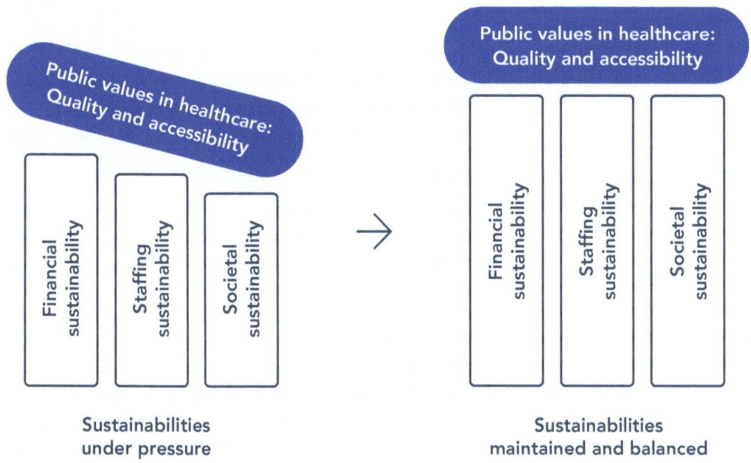


**Fig. 1.1** Three dimensions of sustainability as pillars of public values in healthcare. (The public values of quality and accessibility are guaranteed only if financial, labour and societal sustainability are all maintained and balanced)

such as the recent Covid-19 pandemic (see Box 1.1). Where possible, however, we do draw lessons or parallels from that episode if and when they are relevant to the broader issue of healthcare sustainability.

**Box 1.1: Covid-19 in This report**
The terms "Covid-19" and "coronavirus" do not appear as often in this report as some readers might expect. Although our document is being published in the chronic phase of one of the biggest global healthcare crises ever, we nevertheless mention it only indirectly. Why is that? The main reason is that we are looking at the long term. Our primary focus is a fundamental issue, sustainability, which was around long before Covid-19 came along and has not changed significantly in nature as a result of it. In our advice we try to look beyond the pandemic at a theme that will still exist now Covid-19 has become part of our daily reality. Although this does not mean that it plays no part in this report: where relevant we draw upon experiences during the crisis to illustrate the broader themes and issues we discuss. At a recent symposium organized in co-operation with the Council for Public Administration (*Raad voor het Openbaar Bestuur*, ROB) and the Health Council of the Netherlands (*Gezondheidsraad*), the WRR explored the preparation for acute health crises in more detail.[4]

[4] WRR et al. (2021)

Our broad perspective also means that, rather than homing in on specific sectors, we instead concentrate upon overarching trends and patterns in Dutch healthcare as a whole. This perspective is also relevant internationally, because developments influencing the sustainability of the system in thc Netherlands are also under way in other countries, especially in the Western world. And wherever useful we do take a closer look at a particular sector in order, say, to shed more light on a particular development or pattern. Problems associated with sustainability, for instance, are not equally prevalent in all subsectors of healthcare and the relevant public values—quality and accessibility—are better safeguarded in some domains than in others. The starting point of this report is that we can only talk of a sustainable healthcare system if the three dimensions of sustainability—financial, staffing and societal—are maintained and balanced in the long term. Only then can we as a society continue to guarantee good and accessible care for all in the future. And only then can we ensure that public values are upheld in other policy areas as well.

## 1.2 Public Values and Good Healthcare

Before examining the dimensions of sustainability identified above, we first discuss the public values associated with healthcare. Research shows that health is absolutely central to people's lives,[5] one of the most important factors determining our well-being. As to what exactly "health" is, however, perspectives vary. To a great extent, these depend upon context in which the question is asked.[6] For example, health may be seen the absence of constraints caused by illness.[7] Or more broadly as the ability to cope with life despite various challenges.[8] Or it can be about physical aspects of health, about mental aspects or about both. But whatever perspective they adopt, people generally agree that it is essential to stay—and to feel—healthy for as long as possible. Perhaps the most important underlying objective of care and prevention, then, is to maintain our health and to improve it where possible.

For people who do need care, two distinct aspects are key. Firstly, they must be able to access the care they require. And secondly, that care must be of good quality. These two concepts can be further refined and fleshed out, but in a general sense they jointly determine whether the care a person receives is *good*. So a healthcare system is a good system if it delivers quality and accessibility for everyone. This is why the WRR regards these two factors as the core public values of healthcare.[9]

[5] Kooiker (2011); Gfk (2017).

[6] Haverkamp et al. (2017).

[7] WHO (2005).

[8] Huber et al. (2011).

[9] The "triangle" of quality, accessibility and affordability is often used in healthcare policy, but we have adopted a slightly different categorization in this report. We consider personal affordability (can an individual pay for the care he or she needs?) as an aspect of accessibility (see also online Appendix 1 on the website of the WRR). Affordability at the macro level (can society bear the total costs of healthcare?) is the same as what we call financial sustainability in this report. We regard this, together with the other two dimensions of sustainability, as preconditions for sustainable healthcare.

In themselves, both accessibility and quality are abstract concepts. Both can be defined, operationalized and measured in many different ways in order to make them manageable. And both can be broken down into different sub-aspects. Accessibility, for instance, can be defined in financial terms: can people afford healthcare? Or geographically: is care available nearby? Or temporally: how long do people have to wait before they receive care? Likewise, we can explore a wide range of interpretations of quality. Examples include the safety of healthcare, patient autonomy, the professional and technical competence of the provider and their patient focus.

Moreover, in neither case does the concept itself tell us what standard we should aspire to. How accessible should care be? What level of quality is good enough? What we mean in concrete terms by quality and accessibility of care, and how far these concepts extend, is ultimately up to us all as a society to decide. The benchmarks we set in the form of targets and indicators (such as norms for acceptable waiting times) implicitly articulate a collective normative undertaking on our part, as a society, towards patients and potential patients. They express a minimum standard, a lower limit below which we believe healthcare should not fall. Where that limit lies, what level of quality and accessibility we want to offer, is to a large extent a medical question—but not one which can be answered on medical grounds alone because it also reflects practical, staffing, organizational and political considerations and limitations.

Accessibility and quality are important for people who need care, but not just for them. At some point in our lives, after all, we all become patients. Or have relatives who do. The certainty that we, and they, will be well looked after when that time comes is essential to our well-being even when we are in good health. An accessible and high-quality healthcare system is therefore very much in the general public interest.

## 1.3 Dimensions of Sustainability—Financial, Staffing and Societal

Why are there reasons to doubt the sustainability of healthcare? To answer this question we have to look to the future by drawing on a combination of historical developments, the current situation and forecasts. Which is precisely the purpose of in this report. As already mentioned, we distinguish three dimensions of sustainability: financial, staffing and societal. We briefly introduce each of these core themes below.

**Healthcare Spending Is Growing Faster Than the Economy**

At the political level, the financial dimension of sustainability is often the most visible. We are referring here to expenditure at macro level—what the nation as a whole spends on healthcare—rather than the costs incurred by individual users of the system. In 2019, we in the Netherlands spent more than €100 billion on care, or about €6000 per person.[10] Only the social security system laid out anything like as much (just over €80 billion).

Healthcare spending has been increasing across the board for decades, both per person and as a percentage of the total economy. And it is expected to continue rising for the foreseeable future, faster than the rate of economic growth. In a preliminary study conducted for this report, for instance, the National Institute for Public Health and the Environment (*Rijksinstituut voor Volksgezondheid en Milieu*, RIVM) predicts that annual healthcare expenditure will triple to about €15,800 per person by 2060 (constant 2015 prices).[11]

**Staffing Challenges in Healthcare**

Not only is healthcare placing an increasing burden on the nation's financial resources, but demand for staff is also growing. There is a high degree of uncertainty in the estimates, but subject to reasonable assumptions the healthcare workforce could account for more than 36 per cent of the active population by 2060.[12] In other words, unless something changes in the meantime more than one in three of the Dutch working population will in that scenario be employed in healthcare. Especially in care for the elderly and other labour-intensive parts of the sector, demand for personnel looks set to continue growing strongly. And the pressure is not limited to professional staffing: the demand for informal (and unpaid) carers is also expected to increase further as the population ages.

**Appreciation of and Concerns About Care**

Our third dimension is societal sustainability. This is the most difficult aspect to measure with precision, but we can chart relevant developments. In public surveys over the past decade, healthcare (along with education) has almost always been one of the three policy domains we as a society are most concerned about.[13] The Dutch are generally positive about the quality of care they receive, and about its providers in particular, but they also express worries about its accessibility for themselves or their loved ones. These concerns relate primarily to home care, youth care, mental healthcare and long-term social care for the elderly. High insurance premiums, excesses and additional payments are also mentioned frequently. Half of the population states that healthcare is already too expensive. Societal sustainability also requires that people remain willing to display the solidarity the system demands of them by paying premiums and taxes. When we look at this factor, on the one hand we still find broad backing for the general principle – 70 per cent of the Dutch support the idea that we should all contribute towards spending on care for the sick – but on the other we encounter some emerging bones of contention. For example,

[10] We have here adopted the RIVM perspective on healthcare spending. This definition comprises both personal and collective expenditure, including that on welfare and social care. Unlike the approach to care costs taken by Statistics Netherlands (CBS Zorgrekening), this disregards spending on childcare. The broad picture is the same in all the various versions.

[11] Vonk et al. (2020).

[12] For details, see Chap. 3 of this report.

[13] Den Ridder et al. (2019).

research shows that solidarity is waning when it comes to lifestyle-related illnesses and care for the elderly.[14] And although people say that more needs to be invested in healthcare, they are reluctant to see their own premiums and taxes raised to do that.

All things considered, what picture does this paint? At the macro level, as healthcare accounts for an increasing share of public spending it threatens to put pressure on other budgets. Moreover, we look likely to experience major staff shortages sooner rather than later. And while many people feel that more should be spent on care, they already consider their own contribution too high. Or even far too high. At the same time, all the forecasts point to even greater challenges in the medium and long term. This is the quandary facing politicians and administrators, a dilemma of wishes and ambitions. And the reason why the sustainability of healthcare is a major issue for the whole of Dutch society.

## 1.4 Sustainable Healthcare—A Matter of Choice

What does all this mean for our healthcare system in the future? We address this question in more detail later in our report, but here make a start by outlining five broad issues which lead us to an overall perspective.

Firstly, the wider picture raises concerns about the overall sustainability of healthcare. Pressure points are appearing in all three of the dimensions we have identified, and unless policies change it seems probable that these will only escalate in the long term. We therefore need to further investigate where and why the sustainability of healthcare is under pressure.

Secondly, although the three dimensions are conceptually and analytically distinct, in practice they are closely intertwined. By accident or design, any measures intended to address one of them are bound to affect the other two. Restricting wage rises or the number of jobs in the care sector would relatively quickly improve financial sustainability, for instance, but also undermine staffing sustainability because it makes working in the sector less attractive. So enhancing sustainability is often a trade-off between dimensions. Where a measure has a positive impact on one but negatively affects another, a balance needs to be found. Too much emphasis on one dimension can quickly backfire.

Thirdly, sustainability is not a binary phenomenon. In each of our dimensions a more or less sustainable situation can be achieved, but it is never possible to identify an exact moment when sustainability suddenly topples into unsustainability. After all, we can choose to allocate more resources to healthcare. Within reasonable limits and with some delay (training time), it is also possible to recruit more workers to the sector, although there is less room for manoeuvre here than in the financial dimension. Allocating more people or resources to healthcare is generally a legitimate and socially desirable choice.

[14] Holst et al. (2020); Kooijman et al. (2018).

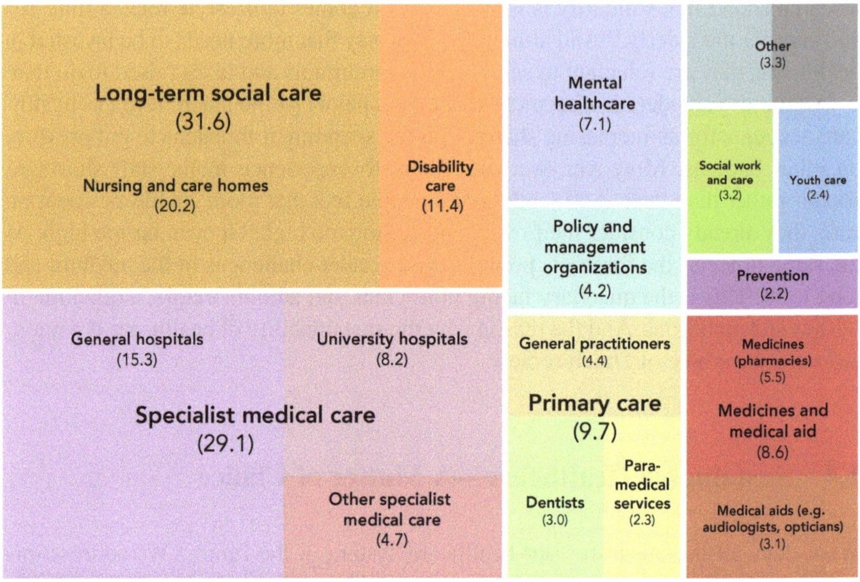


**Fig. 1.2** Costs by healthcare domain in 2019 (in billions of euros). (Distribution of total healthcare expenditure in the Netherlands by provider type, divided into ten categories. The area of each field is proportionate to the share of expenditure by that group of providers. Source: CBS Statistics Netherlands (Statline table 84053))

But—and this is our fourth observation—that is a choice with consequences. Given the sector's huge size, in terms of people and resources, it inevitably entails substantial and unavoidable trade-offs. And these are not confined to healthcare itself. As Fig. 1.2 shows, considerable sums of money (and, by extension, considerable human resources) are allocated each year to all the various domains making up the sector, but particularly to specialist medical and long-term social care. Any funding increase in one area is likely to come at the expense of another (most probably a smaller one). Similarly, we cannot use the people and euros deployed in healthcare for other public purposes. As demand in this sector rises, the more acute the trade-offs become. Already in recent years, a substantial chunk of the increasing overall prosperity of the Dutch population has been absorbed by rising healthcare costs. Forecasts suggest that this will remain the case, probably for decades to come. This limits scope for investment in other policy areas. A similar challenge applies when it comes to staffing: here too, the slowing growth of the working population inevitably means that an increasing commitment to healthcare will quickly translate into labour shortages in other sectors, public and private alike.

Fifthly, we note that real social costs would be involved in slowing the growth in use of the healthcare system in an insufficiently well-considered manner, let alone in achieving a net reduction in that use. The benefits of many forms of care are considerable. These include not only the direct health gains of people who are treated or cared for, but also the confidence that good, accessible care is available to us all—not to mention indirect advantages such as economic benefits.[15] Where the challenge of sustainability– or the policy response to it—leads to quality or accessibility in parts of the sector falling below the minimum acceptable standard, public dissatisfaction and even unrest may arise due to the gap between expectations and perceived reality. At this point the limits of societal sustainability come into view. And even if there is no general unrest, some—most likely vulnerable—groups may suffer. Which alone would undermine the core public values of healthcare.

This brings us to the overall perspective at the heart of this report. The WRR concludes that good healthcare for all requires better choices, precisely because the limits of its financial, staffing and societal sustainability are coming into view. Specifically, this means that the key task now before us is to better delineate the sector's future growth, in so doing steering it as carefully as possible towards those healthcare and preventive interventions which achieve the greatest health benefits[16] and safeguard public values most effectively. In other words, in order to guarantee the quality and accessibility of healthcare for everyone, better choices have to be made. This will be no easy task. It requires clear and sometimes uncompromising decisions, which can be difficult to make from a normative point of view. And these in turn require a long-term vision of the role and function of healthcare in our society that has broad public support. In this report we explain how we have arrived at these conclusions. We also discuss perspectives drawn from various scientific disciplines on making choices within and about healthcare, and explain why the processes involved could be better. Finally, we suggest concrete ways to make better choices. These rest on three distinct pillars: (1) strengthening public support for clearer choices; (2) making clearer political choices in favour of sustainable healthcare; and (3) strengthening practical ability to make better choices about the demarcation of collective healthcare. Government most certainly has a role to play in these tasks, but so too do healthcare institutions, providers and citizens themselves.

## 1.5 Report Structure

We have divided this report into three parts. In the first we look at the current state and organization of the Dutch healthcare system, at expected developments and at the sticking points and difficulties they are creating. Essentially, this is our problem analysis. In the second part we look at how issues of sustainability have been addressed in the past and ask whether these approaches remain adequate for the future. Finally, in the third part we outline our perspective that sustainability in healthcare is a matter of choice. How are choices in healthcare made now, why do they need to be better and how can that be achieved?

---

[15] Polder et al. (2020).

[16] By this we mean the number of years of healthy life expectancy that can be achieved. This is often measured in terms of "quality-adjusted life years" (QALYs). See also Chap. 8 and Broeders et al. (2018).

**Part 1—The System Now, Developments and the Implications for Sustainability**
In Chap. 2 we look at the changing context in which the Dutch healthcare operates and then discuss trends and developments that are influencing its use. And in the third chapter we home in on the expected consequences for staffing, financial and societal sustainability. In the final chapter of Part 1 we review the current organization of the Dutch healthcare landscape and how our system is performing in terms of quality and accessibility.

**Part 2—Existing Approaches to Sustainability**
In Chap. 5 we turn our attention to improving sustainability through more efficient organization of the sector. The purpose of this report is *not* to suggest specific ways to improve efficiency, but we do assess the potential to do so and ask whether this is proportionate to the extent of the sustainability challenge. We end this part of the report with a chapter devoted specifically to staffing sustainability (Chap. 6).

**Part 3—Making Better Care Choices**
In Chap. 7 we address choices in healthcare: how are they made now what are their effects? Chap. 8 then analyses barriers to better choices: why are they so hard to make, how can we explain this from different perspectives and scientific disciplines and what does all that mean for ways of doing things better?

In the final chapter we formulate three key conclusions concerning sustainable healthcare. Building on our three pillars to facilitate better choices, we then outline policy directions to make Dutch healthcare more sustainable in the future and propose starting points for better choices.

**Background Studies**
The analyses presented in this report are based in part upon four background studies undertaken and already published by partner organizations (Box 1.2). We have also conducted a series of in-depth interviews with academics, providers, policymakers and other stakeholders on the subject of healthcare sustainability. The full list of interviewees can be found at the end of this report. Finally, six detailed appendices are available online (only in Dutch), each dealing with specific aspects of this report.

**Box 1.2: Background Studies**
To support the insights and analyses in this report, a number of background studies have been undertaken by WRR partner organizations and published as separate papers. All are available in Dutch only.

- **Healthcare spending forecast 2015–2060**
- *Toekomstverkenning zorguitgaven 2015–2060*
- An RIVM survey of expected spending on healthcare over the next four decades, in a variety of scenarios.[17]

(continued)

[17] Vonk et al. (2020).

**Box 1.2** (continued)

- **Health effects and social benefits of healthcare**
- *Gezondheidseffecten en maatschappelijke baten van de gezondheidszorg*
- A study of the broad social and health benefits of healthcare, also by RIVM researchers.[18]

- **Sustainable care for the elderly—experiences and lessons from other countries**
- *Houdbare ouderenzorg—Ervaringen en lessen uit andere landen*
- A comparative study of the sustainability of long-term care for the elderly in a number of Western countries, by researchers from IQ Healthcare Radboud UMC, the Leyden Academy on Vitality and Ageing and Erasmus School of Health Policy.[19]

- **Dutch healthcare policy in an historical perspective, 1941–2017**
- *Het Nederlands zorgbeleid in historisch perspectief, 1941–2017*
- An historical analysis by researchers at Utrecht University of Dutch policy with regard to sustainability issues in healthcare since the Second World War.[20]



[18] Polder et al. (2020).

[19] Kruse et al. (2021).

[20] Bertens and Palamar (2021).

# Chapter 2
# Care in a Changing Context

Due largely to autonomous developments such as an ageing population, increasing prosperity and technological progress, the demand for care—and hence the sustainability challenge—is increasing across the board.

## 2.1 Driving Forces Behind Growing Use of Care

The scientific literature highlights a number of driving forces that influence the use of health and social care. Underlying many of these is the interplay of supply and demand: some of the forces in question mainly affect the demand for care, others its supply. Others still influence its cost. These forces interact to such an extent that they are often difficult to unravel or to quantify individually.

So what forces we are talking about? We distinguish between developments in demographics, prosperity, labour productivity, technology and system or policy.[1] The factors that determine growth in expenditure can be divided into three categories: demographic, economic and "other" developments,[2] with the latter including such determinants as technology, sociocultural developments, labour productivity and the influence of policy. In this report we look not just at the affordability of healthcare, but more broadly at its sustainability. In so doing, moreover, we differentiate between issues of staffing and societal sustainability. So, for example, demographic developments like the ageing population affect not only levels of spending on care but also—because the workforce is shrinking in relative terms—also the ability to recruit and retain enough personnel in the long term. Additionally, developments in the labour market can also touch upon societal issues. For instance,

[1] Polder (2018).

[2] Vonk et al. (2020).



G. Werner et al., *Financial, Staffing and Societal Sustainability of Dutch Health Care*, Research for Policy, https://doi.org/10.1007/978-3-031-58564-7_2

the quality of care for the elderly may be compromised in the future if the number of informal carers decreases. This demonstrates all the more that the driving forces behind the use of care not only interact between themselves but can also impact the three dimensions of sustainability.

In this chapter we discuss the most important developments likely to influence the future sustainability of health and social care. We divide these into five broad categories: demographic, population health status, economic, technological and sociocultural. Within each category we then identify specific trends, although several in fact straddle several categories. Some influence the supply of and/or demand for care (referred to collectively as the "volume of care"), whilst others help shape its price. As such, these are not so much policy trends within the care sector as "autonomous" developments at the societal level. Rather than covering all care-related trends and developments, moreover, we confine ourselves to those expected to have an impact upon its financial, staffing or societal sustainability: what we define as the "driving forces" behind the growing use of care. For each we discuss its relationship with the sustainability of care, focusing mainly upon its likely impact in the financial (and staffing) domains—simply because they are easier to quantify than societal sustainability. At the end of the chapter we look at the implications of the forces identified for various specific subsectors of health and social care. This exercise reveals that current and expected developments only make the issue of sustainability in this field more urgent.

Many of the driving forces we discuss in this chapter are not unique to the Netherlands. Indeed, they are playing a similar role throughout the Western world. Where relevant, we examine the extent to which the Dutch situation differs from that in other countries. Our primary focus here, moreover, is developments in the longer term. On this scale, the current Covid-19 pandemic is expected to have only limited effects upon the health status of the population as a whole. According to Statistics Netherlands (*Centraal Bureau* voor de *Statistiek,* CBS), the higher mortality rate caused by Covid-19 did have some effect upon life-expectancy figures in 2020 and 2021, but they are likely to return to pre-pandemic levels in the years to come—just as they did after the Spanish flu and the Second World War. In all probability, therefore, Covid-19 will not have a structurally negative impact upon the upward trend in life expectancy which has been observed for many years now.[3]

## 2.2 Demographic Developments

Demographic developments include changes to the composition and geographical distribution of the population. "Composition" refers to the relative sizes of various cohorts within the population, such as age groups or types of household (the proportion of one-person households, for instance), as well as those with a migrant

[3] CBS (2020a, b).

background (defined in the Netherlands as persons with at least one parent who was born abroad). The most striking ongoing change with regard to geographical distribution is population shrinkage in peripheral regions of the Netherlands and growth in urban areas. One thing that trends in both respects have in common—although not the only one—is that they substantially influence demand for health and social care.

**Population Growth Driven by Migration**

In their recent joint publication *Verkenning bevolking 2050* ("Population Study 2050"), the Netherlands Interdisciplinary Demographic Institute (Nederlands Interdisciplinair Demografisch Instituut, NIDI) and Statistics Netherlands analyse a number of scenarios to explore the possible make-up of the Dutch population in 2050.[4] The final picture will depend upon developments in migration, births and deaths. The study assumed that the country had 17.4 million inhabitants on 1 January 2020. If immigration, the birth rate and life expectancy remain high throughout the next 30 years, it predicts a population of 21.6 million in 2050. The uncertainty around population growth is considerable, however, especially when it comes to developments in the field of migration. The number of migrants entering (and leaving) the Netherlands can fluctuate substantially from year to year, e.g., due to the Russian war in Ukraine the number of immigrants has increased significantly over the first 6 months of 2022. According to the researchers, it is also quite possible that the population will hardly grow at all over the next three decades—or even shrink slightly (to 17.1 million inhabitants).[5]

The number of people with a migrant background living in the Netherlands looks likely to increase between now and 2050. On September 1, 2022 this group accounted for 5.2 million of the nation's 18.3 million inhabitants (25.2). Depending upon how migration patterns unfold in the future, their number will grow to between 5.3 and 8.4 million in 2050.[6] Meanwhile, the number of people with a Dutch background in 2050 will be between 11.2 and 13.4 million (compared with 13.1 million in September 2022). The exact figures will depend upon how the birth rate and life expectancy develop. In all the scenarios investigated, then, the principal driver of population growth in the Netherlands will be migration. Even if this is at the low end of the forecast range, the proportion of inhabitants with a migrant background will increase from 25 per cent in 2022 to 30 per cent in 2050. At the high end it will rise to 40 per cent.

Regardless of which of these scenarios proves most accurate, the make-up of the potential labour force is set to change in line with trends in the age composition of the population. As one would expect, population growth increases the overall size of the workforce. But how trends in this respect will impact the impending labour shortage in the health and care sector also depends upon a range of other factors,

[4] NIDI and CBS (2020).

[5] In an earlier Statistics Netherlands population forecast, the most likely scenario was growth from 17.3 million in 2019 to 19.6 million in 2060 (CBS, 2018a).

[6] NIDI and CBS (2020).

such as the future birth rate, the extent to which people choose to work in this sector and the scale and nature of inbound labour migration. We return to this topic in Chaps. 3 and 7.

Whilst the total number of Dutch residents with a migrant background is increasing, the composition of this group is changing noticeably. The proportion with roots in the western member states of the European Union (EU) or in "traditional" countries of origin (Indonesia, Suriname, the Dutch Caribbean, Turkey and Morocco) is on the decline.[7] Due to the eastward enlargement of the EU, the increased influx of labour and student migrants from regions like Latin America and Asia and higher numbers of asylum migrants arriving from the Middle East and Africa, diversity by origin is increasing.[8] The key question for us is whether this is leading to sustainability issues for health and social care at the macro level, or will do in the future. There are many different aspects to this quandary. For the time being, those with a migrant background are younger on average than those with a Dutch background. Combined with a phenomenon known as the "healthy immigrant effect" (people in relatively good health are far more likely to migrate),[9] this ensures that—despite their lower average socio-economic status—the immigrants entering the country tend to be healthier than the national average. However, this is not true for the total population with a migrant background.[10] This is due in part to its lower average socio-economic status, as well as to the so-called "immigrant health decline hypothesis". Confirmed time and again in longitudinal analyses, that states that the longer immigrants remain in a country, the poorer their health becomes.[11] For this reason, more migration could potentially generate more health problems in the future. Moreover, the average age of the migrant population is rising. At present, 4.2 per cent of people in the Netherlands aged 65 and over are of non-Western origin. In 2060 that figure will have reached 17.1 per cent—818,000 people in total.[12] In the major cities, however, the proportion will be significantly higher.[13] In Sect. 2.3 we look more closely at the health problems affecting elderly people with a migrant background and how these relate to sustainability issues.

**Ageing Population**

As a result of the postwar baby boom and then a sharp drop in the birth rate from the early 1970s onwards, the proportion of elderly people in the Dutch population

[7] Their share decreases from 60 per cent in 2020 to close to 40 per cent in the future variants with high migration, and to just under 50 per cent in the variant with the least migration (NIDI & CBS, 2020).

[8] WRR (2020a).

[9] Kennedy et al. (2015).

[10] Nielsen and Krasnik (2010).

[11] Antecol and Bedard (2006); Lubbers and Gijsberts (2019).

[12] Per Statistics Netherlands' definition of non-Western migrants (see CBS, 2018a).

[13] In Amsterdam, The Hague and Rotterdam, currently about a quarter of all over-50s are of non-Western origin (and approximately 60–70 per cent of them are of Surinamese, Moroccan or Turkish origin).

(compared with the proportion of young people) is increasing fast. This trend has been under way for some time, with the result that the number of over-65s is expected to rise from 3.1 million in 2020 to 4.8 million in 2040 (26 per cent of the total population). And the number aged over 80 will actually triple in those 20 years, from 0.7 million to 2 million. The combination of these two developments (a rising proportion of older people and a rising average age) is known as "double ageing". It is in fact a phenomenon occurring in all Western countries, with Japan, Italy and Spain as global leaders.[14] In the Netherlands it will continue until 2040, after which the share of elderly people in the population is expected to start decreasing slowly.[15]

What does this mean for the sustainability of health and social care? Expenditure in this sector is closely linked to age. For children and for adults of working age, average spending per person is low. But after the age of 75 it rises sharply (see Fig. 2.1).[16] This is due mainly to the fact that older people often have several disorders simultaneously (what we refer to as "multimorbidity"), which very quickly pushes up the cost of their care—both curative and long-term (see next section). For the group aged 65 and over, total annual healthcare expenditure looks set to rise from €37 billion to €167 billion between 2015 and 2060, an average yearly increase of 3.4 per cent.[17] And grow from 44 per cent of overall national spending on health

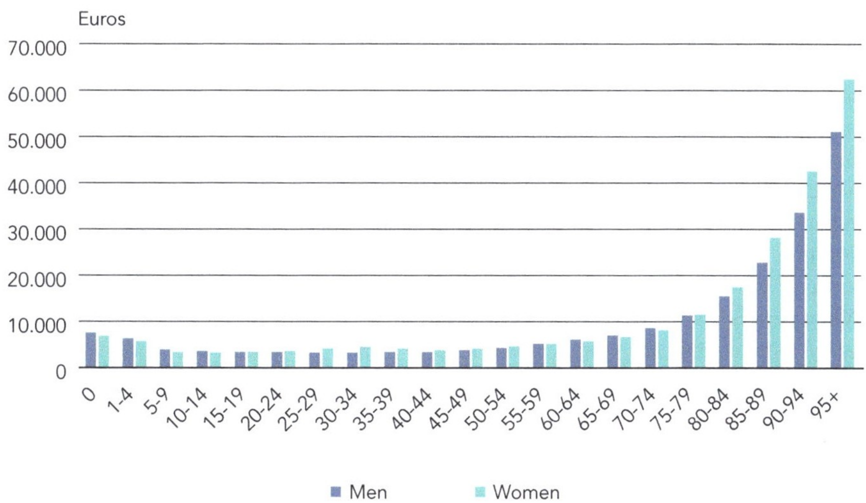


**Fig. 2.1** Care expenditure per resident of the Netherlands in 2017, by age and sex. (Source: Vonk et al., 2020)

[14] Verbeek-Oudijk and Putman (2016).

[15] CBS (2018a).

[16] In research and Statistics Netherlands data, elderly people are most commonly categorized are those aged 65 or over. However, health problems tend to start later in life—around the age of 75—and the costs of care also increase significantly from that age (see Fig. 2.1).

[17] Vonk et al. (2020).

and social care to 58 per cent. For women in particular, the costs increase rapidly with age; they live longer on average than men and so are more likely to be single and living alone, which means they rely more upon formal care provision. It is expected that in 2060 women aged 75 and over will spend considerably more, relatively speaking, on geriatric care services than on hospital treatment.[18] Ageing thus looks set to shift the principal cost burden towards long-term care—although that does not alter the fact that it also puts more pressure on GP services and emergency healthcare (because the elderly are prone to falls, for example). At present, more than 60 per cent of over-65s use specialist medical care. And particularly in the oldest age group (85-plus), use of district nursing services (40 per cent), home care (30 per cent) and long-term domiciliary or residential nursing care (33 per cent) is relatively high.[19]

However, the relationship between rising care costs and ageing in fact hides another phenomenon: the so-called "red herring effect".[20] For the most part it is actually high healthcare spending in the final year of life—at whatever age—which causes the sharp upward trend. So it is not so much age that explains the increased expenditure as the approach of death.[21] It is important to note here, though, that there are substantial underlying variations and so it is probably more meaningful to look at the costs of care over a person's entire life than just those in their last year.[22] Measured over complete lifetimes, people appear to vary far less in the amount spent on their care. This is an important observation, not least in the light of our consideration of the societal sustainability of health and social care (willingness to pay—see also Chap. 3 on solidarity).

What does all this mean when we look to the future? Since older people use it more than the young, demand for care is certain to rise as the population ages. Another related development is the increase in life expectancy. This is attributable in part to improving knowledge and skills within the care sector.[23] It is also another example of the red herring effect. If we fail to take longer life expectancy into account, we are in grave danger of overestimating the financial impact of ageing. When people live longer on average, after all, the costs of their care do not necessarily increase but are simply postponed to a later point in time. Ageing as such therefore appears to play only a modest role as a driver of increased spending, at least when looking at healthcare expenditure across the board. When it comes to

[18] Vonk et al. (2020).

[19] NZA (2018a).

[20] Zweifel et al. (1999).

[21] The older a person is when they die, however, the lower the costs of their care in the final year tend to be. This is because the intensity of treatment often decreases with advancing age. See Polder (2018).

[22] Polder (2018).

[23] Mackenbach (2020).

social care for the elderly, on the other hand, ageing has a significantly greater impact.[24]

In Chap. 1 we discussed the expected growth in health and social care expenditure between now and 2060. Ageing will remain an important factor here, even after the peak in about 2040, but its influence is set to decline from 2035 onwards.[25,26] On average, total costs will increase by about 2.8 per cent a year. About two-thirds of that will be down to factors other than ageing, which we return to later in this chapter.[27] This means that demographic developments will account for annual growth of some 1.2 per cent in overall care spending, with care for the elderly as an outlier: the increase there will be in the region of 2.5 per cent a year. Naturally, these forecasts involve some uncertainty. Demographic developments often turn out differently than expected, and economic growth and advances in medical science and care practices are also difficult to predict.

The ageing population has repercussions not only for financial sustainability, as just discussed, but also for staffing sustainability. On the one hand population growth looks set to level off in the future, favourably shifting the ratio of people in work to people in need of care, but on the other the phenomenon of double ageing, in particular, will increase the overall demand for care. Meaning that the sector will need more and more workers. Yet it is struggling to fill all its vacancies even now, and this has worsened as a result of the Covid-19 pandemic. At present, one in seven people in the Netherlands work in the care sector; to fully meet future demand, according to current estimates that will need to rise to one in three by 2060. So not only is the ageing population increasing demand for care, it is also placing huge demands on the labour market. We discuss this in more detail in Chap. 3.

[24] Polder (2018). The RIVM's care expenditure prognosis for 2015–2060 (Vonk et al., 2020) analyses historical spending patterns and attributes them to either demographic or "other" developments. The latter include growing prosperity (evolution of GDP) and technological, policy and sociocultural developments. The trend analyses are based upon care expenditure in real terms; that is, adjusted for inflation and expressed using the equivalent values in a base year (2015). The relative spends by age and gender from the RIVM's (2015) cost of diseases study (*Kosten van ziekten 2015*) were then applied to the Statistics Netherlands population forecast of 2018, which describes the expected evolution of the Dutch population between then and 2060 (CBS, 2018a). To the consequences of these demographic trends are added the growth in expenditure due to "other" developments, made up of two components: sector-specific and diagnosis-specific growth. In order to be able to express future spending on care as a percentage of GDP in the projections, an average annual real growth rate of 1.7 per cent is assumed for the next 25 years. That figure comes from the Netherlands Bureau for Economic Policy Analysis (CPB), based upon its 2014 Central Economic Plan (CPB, 2014).

[25] The RIVM bases its work upon the Statistics Netherlands population forecast of 2018. The population study mentioned previously (*Verkenning bevolking 2050,* NIDI & CBS, 2020) is of a later date.

[26] Despite rising care expenditure overall, the proportion of the total spent on care for the over-65s will hardly grow after 2040.

[27] Vonk et al. (2020).

### Geographical Shifts

Another relevant demographic development is population shrinkage on the "periphery" of the Netherlands: predominantly rural areas away from the Randstad conurbation in the west of the country. Certain specific regions are particularly badly affected: not only is their overall population declining but its age composition is changing at a faster rate than in the rest of the country.

Figure 2.2 reveals this shift at a glance. Between 2020 and 2035, the proportion of people aged 65 and over will increase particularly fast in the peripheral regions,[28] so that in large parts of the country more than half of the population will be in this age group. After 2040, as mentioned earlier, ageing should start to decline slightly and the regional differences will narrow again.[29]

This trend has a number of consequences for the sustainability of care. The most important is its impact upon staffing—and hence also societal—sustainability. It is in the regions most subject to shrinkage that the supply of care is coming under the greatest pressure, simply because fewer people—particularly of working age—live there. At the same time they are where the population is ageing most rapidly and so the demand for care is greater.[30] As a result, these parts of the country will face more and more acute staff shortages in the future—everyone from GPs to domiciliary and residential care workers.[31] Likewise, fewer informal carers will be available.[32] We discuss this latter point in more detail in Sect. 2.6.

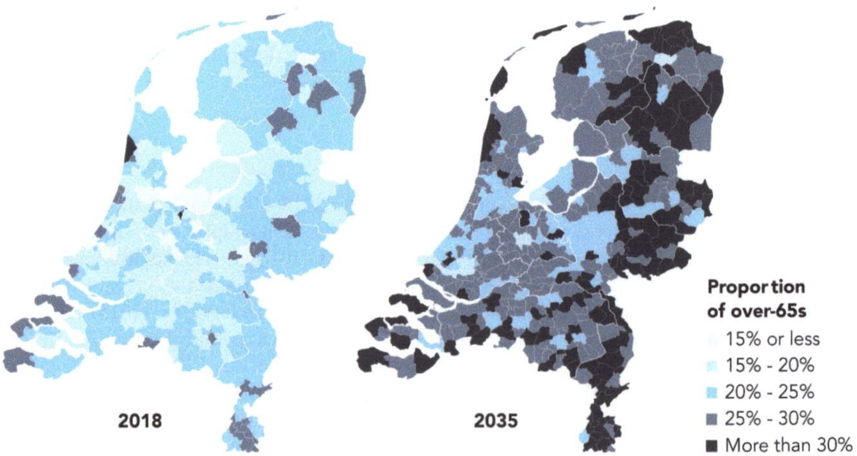


**Fig. 2.2** "Peripheral" ageing in the Netherlands, 2018 and 2035 (proportion of over-65s by municipality). (Source: PBL & CBS, 2019)

---

[28] PBL and CBS (2019).

[29] Also because, relatively speaking, ageing will then increase faster in the large cities (PBL & CBS, 2019).

[30] RIVM (2018a).

[31] See Nivel and Prismant (2019) (twenty factsheets on twenty Dutch regions).

[32] de Jong and Kooiker (2018).

**Key points—Demographic developments**

- The proportion of elderly people in the population is increasing and their average age is rising. This is pushing up health and social care costs, especially in long-term care.
- At the same time the supply of care personnel is decreasing due to the ageing population.
- These repercussions of these trends are being particularly felt in the peripheral Dutch regions, where the population is shrinking.

## 2.3 Developments in Health Status

The health status of a population can change for many reasons, and such changes often affect the demand for health and social care. One topical example is the Covid-19 pandemic, which struck the Netherlands in March 2020. This led to a sudden and massive spike in demand for acute care. But more gradual epidemiological changes also have their effects. A good example here is the ongoing decline in the proportion of smokers in the population, which in time will lead to fewer smoking-related conditions like lung cancer and cardiovascular disease.[33] Demographic and epidemiological developments often interact. For example, an ageing population is associated with a relatively higher incidence of age-related diseases such as dementia.

Overall, the outlook for the future is not unfavourable. Despite being older on average, the population as a whole will not feel unhealthier. It is expected almost 80 per cent of people in the Netherlands in 2040 will describe themselves as "feeling healthy"—the same proportion as in 2018—whilst about 87 per cent will experience no physical hindrance to their activities.[34] Moreover, average life expectancy is predicted to rise from 81.8 to 85.4 years over the next 20 years, and the number of years people spend in good health will also increase. For men that will go up from 64.2 to 68.5 years between 2018 and 2040, and for women from 62.7 to 66.4 years.[35]

Broadly speaking, we can identify a number of health-status trends likely to influence the future sustainability of care provision: more chronic diseases and multimorbidity (multiple disorders at the same time), more mental disorders, increasing use of child and youth care services, greater socio-economic inequalities in health and—as a residual category—future risks to health.[36] In two recent reports the Dutch National Institute for Public Health and the Environment (Rijksinstituut voor Volksgezondheid en Milieu, RIVM) presents its prognoses concerning the future

[33] RIVM (2018a, 2020a).

[34] RIVM (2018a, 2020a).

[35] Vonk et al. (2020).

[36] The RIVM's care expenditure prognosis (*Toekomstverkenning Zorguitgaven 2015–2060,* has a longer time horizon (up to 2060) than its public health prognosis (*Volksgezondheid Toekomst Verkenning*: up to 2040). RIVM (2018a); Vonk et al. (2020).

prevalence of various medical disorders and diseases, together with the associated costs. As the RIVM itself notes, like all forecasts these healthcare expenditure projections—and certainly those for 2040 and beyond—involve considerable uncertainties. After all, their assumptions are necessarily based upon past trends; actual developments often unfold in ways not expected. These uncertainties only increase as the time horizon lengthens.

**More Chronic Diseases and Multimorbidity**

One key prognosis with potentially major consequences for the sustainability of health and social care is the increasing prevalence of chronic diseases, and especially multimorbidity. It is estimated that 54 per cent of people in the Netherlands will have a chronic medical condition in 2040, whilst the number with two or more will have risen from 5.3 million in 2018 to 6.6 million.[37] Multimorbidity often leads to a greater need for care than the individual conditions would do separately, thus upping the overall burden on the system. It is also frequently associated with more complex care requirements, and hence with higher overall costs than individual diseases. In the Netherlands in 2013, for example, 48 per cent of spending under the Healthcare Insurance Act (Zorgverzekeringswet, Zvw) was accounted for by the "most expensive" 5 per cent of patients, with an average of 3.5 conditions each. The remaining 52 per cent was "spent" by the other 95 per cent of the population, with an average of 0.7 conditions each.[38]

In addition to chronic diseases like arthritis, diabetes or dementia, the elderly are often susceptible to falls, impaired vision, incontinence and suchlike problems. This kind of accumulation of ailments makes them vulnerable. Amongst those aged 85 years and older, 80 per cent have three or more chronic conditions at the same time (in the population as a whole, the proportion is 18 per cent).[39] In particular, the number of people suffering from dementia is expected to more than double over the next 20 years: from 154,000 to 330,000. In all likelihood this condition will cause the most deaths and the highest burden of disease in 2040. During the same period the number of cancer patients is forecast to rise from 547,000 to 970,000. And the number with cardiovascular disease from 1.9 million to 3.0 million.[40] These three diagnostic groups—cancer, cardiovascular disease and mental disorders (which includes dementia)—look set to account for the greatest burden of disease two decades from now.

The ageing population therefore requires more care, and in different forms. Lifestyle factors also play an important role. Unhealthy behaviours such as smoking, excessive alcohol consumption, lack of exercise and an unhealthy diet are responsible for 20 per cent of the burden of disease.[41] Of all these, smoking is the most significant determinant. However, the downward trend in its prevalence—except amongst the least well-educated—appears to be a continuing trend; the number of smokers in the

[37] RIVM (2020a).

[38] Wammes et al. (2017).

[39] RIVM (2020b).

[40] SER (2020).

[41] RIVM (2018a).

Netherlands is expected to fall from 22 per cent of the population in 2018 to 14 per cent in 2040. It is also expected that more people will meet the national targets for physical activity.[42] In other lifestyle-related areas, though, the picture is less encouraging. In particular, overweight and obesity rates look set to increase from 50 per cent of the population today to 62 per cent in 20 years' time.

Currently, 16 per cent of Dutch children are overweight and 3 per cent are obese. And their numbers are rising.[43] These conditions can cause numerous health issues: psychosocial problems, joint complaints, high blood pressure, diabetes and cardiovascular disease. One important risk factor here is the socio-economic status of the child's family.[44]

**More Mental Disorders**

Another current trend that seems likely to continue is the growing burden of disease attributable to mental disorders like depression and anxiety,[45] as well as psychosocial ailments like burnout and work-related stress.[46] In 2017, some 1.1 million adults in the Netherlands received mental health treatment. The vast majority of this was outpatient care by a general practice nurse.[47] Treatment is also available at general and specialist mental health clinics. Demand for all these services is increasing. This growth, together with the policy focus upon ambulatory care—even people with severe mental illnesses should be able to live and participate in the community as far as possible—is increasing pressure on provision for people with a chronic mental condition. In addition, social isolation and loneliness are likely to become more and more common, especially amongst people living alone; the number of lonely people in their twenties and over is forecast to rise by 875,000 between now and 2040.[48] Although loneliness occurs in all age groups, it increases with age. Research shows that, as well as reducing a person's quality of life, loneliness can pose risks to their health.[49] Finally, we have read a lot recently about a rise in mental disorders amongst young people being exacerbated by the uncertainty around the Covid-19 pandemic and by the restrictions imposed upon them. The epidemiological literature shows that it is not so much mental disorders as stress-related complaints that are on the increase, especially amongst schoolchildren and—to a growing extent—students in further and higher education.[50]

[42] RIVM (2020a).

[43] This categorization uses body mass index (BMI), an international standard to determine whether a person's weight is healthy for their height. A BMI of 18.5–25 indicates a healthy weight, 25–30 overweight, 30–35 severe overweight or obesity and over 35 morbid obesity.

[44] NCJ (2012).

[45] RIVM (2018a).

[46] Van Echtelt (2020); TNO (2019).

[47] The number of these patients tripled from 175,000 in 2013 to 535,000 in 2017.

[48] RIVM (2020a).

[49] Van Campen et al. (2018); Coalitie Erbij (2020); Holt-Lunstad et al. (2015).

[50] RIVM, Trimbos & Amsterdam UMC (2019).

**Increasing Use of Child and Youth Care Services**

One final trend worth mentioning is the substantial increase over the years in the number of young people in need of child and youth care services. This development, incidentally, dates back to well before their decentralization to local authorities in 2015.[51] As Fig. 2.3 shows, use of child and youth support provision (services without a child protection or juvenile rehabilitation component) has tripled since 2000.[52] At the turn of the millennium, one in every twenty children needed support; now it is one in eight. In 2019 a total of 443,265 under-18s received some form of child or youth care. These included 41,000 child protection and just over 9000 juvenile rehabilitation cases. If the trend is extrapolated to 2027, the total number using provision of this kind will reach approximately 520,000 (one in six).[53]

The Netherlands Youth Institute (Nederlands Jeugdinstituut, NJi) cites three main reasons for this upward trend: (1) factors related to child development and upbringing caused by problems at home (such as a divorce), pressure to perform, problematic social media use and so on, as well as the problemization of child development and upbringing by parents; (2) inability by local authorities to control intakes since they assumed responsibility for these services; and (3) high expectations with regard to the preventive effects of child and youth care, despite its modest

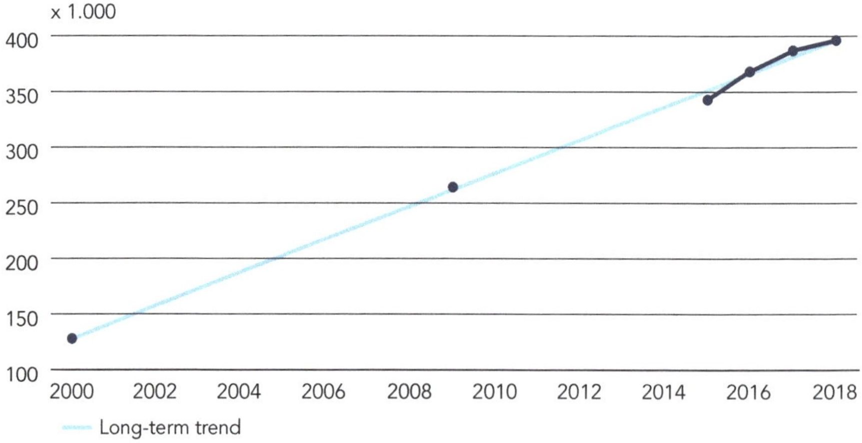


**Fig. 2.3** Use of child and youth support provision, 2000–2018 (ages 0–17). (Source: van Yperen et al., 2019)

[51] In 2015 local authorities were made responsible for child and youth care services on the grounds that they are closer to the target group and so better able to provide bespoke care. Moreover, bringing this provision under one roof would make fragmentation a thing of the past.

[52] Van Yperen et al. (2019). The figures for 2000–2009 are based upon Netherlands Institute for Social Research (SCP) estimates (Pommer et al., 2011) and those for 2015–2018 come from Statistics Netherlands (CBS, 2019a).

[53] Van Yperen et al. (2019).

development in practice. Because of these factors, use is often made of child and youth care provision even though the outcomes are limited.[54]

**Greater Socio-economic Inequalities in Health**

Socio-economic inequalities in health have long been a subject of academic study. Although overall life expectancy and the number of years people are expected to live in good health are increasing, the *differences* in health status between those in high and low socio-economic categories are substantial and have not changed significantly for decades. The better-educated and better-off are healthier than those with little schooling and less money. Measured by educational attainment, the disparities in terms of life expectancy, mental illness and lifestyle factors are considerable. Less well-educated women live an average of 5.4 years less than women with higher education, whilst the discrepancy for men is no less than 6.5 years. When it comes to years in good health, the gap is even wider: 14.2 years for men and 15.5 for women.[55,56] Similar differences are observed for mental disorders, such as depression and anxiety, with the less well-educated being affected more severely across the board. As for lifestyle factors, smoking is on the decline in all groups but more so amongst the well-educated than the less well-educated; they are diverging, then, and so are their respective chances of suffering smoking-related diseases. Meanwhile, the prevalence of obesity has increased in every socio-economic category but in the coming years the greatest rise is expected in those with the least schooling. The proportion of less well-educated people who feel healthy is forecast to decline over the next 20 years, from 60 to 53 per cent, but remain more or less stable for the better educated (from 86 to 85 per cent).[57] Not only have differences in health status by educational attainment not diminished over the years, then, but in some domains they have actually increased or are expected to do so in the future.

The question is what this means for the future sustainability of healthcare. The so-called "Matthew effect" appears to be at work here, meaning that the socially disadvantaged reap fewer benefits from health-promotion measures than groups that are already in a better socio-economic position. Although everyone has gained to some extent, on balance the disparities have been enhanced.[58] Despite seeming a paradoxical outcome, this effect is quite commonplace when measures target an entire population without taking into account its different challenges, skills, financial situations and opportunities. It is those distinctions which can cause an approach of this kind to exacerbate rather than mitigate inequalities.

Socio-economic inequalities in health can put the societal sustainability of the sector under pressure by undermining solidarity in its support, on "lifestyle" grounds. It makes a difference whether the inequalities are viewed as a consequence

[54] Van Yperen et al. (2019).

[55] Broeders et al. (2018).

[56] RIVM (2018a).

[57] RIVM (2018a).

[58] Broeders et al. (2018).

of personal choices (lifestyle) or as unavoidable.[59] People are less inclined to display solidarity if they believe that others' health problems are their own fault (see Chap. 3). With regard to lifestyle-related diseases in particular, a debate is currently raging in the Netherlands about personal responsibility and its limits. It is increasingly being pointed out that people's ability to make "healthy" choices and stick to them is often overestimated in surroundings full of negative stimuli.[60] Moreover, external factors such as the quality of housing, access to amenities locally, working conditions, debt problems or the situation at home can render "healthy" choices hard to make.

And what about the impact of socio-economic inequalities in health upon the sector's financial sustainability? It is undeniable that the composition of the population by educational attainment evolves over time. In 1930, for instance, approximately 80 per cent of the Dutch population had only basic schooling. But since then that percentage has dropped dramatically, and it continues to do so. This group, the less well-educated, thus forms a relatively small and shrinking part of the population as a whole. In and of itself, their decline should if anything make health and social care slightly more affordable (or at least no less affordable) since the overall health status of the rest of the population—a growing majority—is improving. In reality, however, the picture is not that simple: not only does the make-up of the broader category of those with low socio-economic status also change over time, meaning that it includes more and more people not classified as less well-educated, but the health issues facing the residual group are becoming ever more complex and persistent. Its health outcomes suggest that it is becoming harder for this group to overcome those issues. Moreover, its average age is increasing. This could limit the health potential of the group with low socio-economic status group in the future, by comparison with those now falling into this category, which might well push up the cost of care.

On top of that, the ethnic composition of this category is changing. Groups with a lower socio-economic status include a relatively large proportion of people with a migrant background, who are often in poorer than average health and sometimes also have particular care needs.[61] This applies especially to older first-generation immigrants, who are set to increase significantly in number (see 2.2). Statistics Netherlands analyses show that the costs of health and social care for people with a Turkish, Moroccan, Surinamese or Dutch Caribbean background are higher than for their peers of Dutch origin.[62] It is also important to note that, relatively speaking, this group of elderly migrants is significantly younger than its counterpart without a migrant background.

[59] Stronks and Gunning-Schepers (1993).

[60] WRR (2014a, 2017).

[61] Ruijsbroek et al. (2011); CBS (2020b).

[62] CBS (2020c).

This could mean that in the future, as they age, these groups in particular will further increase the cost burden on the healthcare system.[63] Which in turn might put its financial sustainability under pressure in certain regions, especially when it comes to forms of care with decentralized funding. The regions in question are those with a high concentration of members of groups with low socio-economic status, including people with a migrant background, where the increasing aggregation of problems such as poverty, debt and unemployment could well exacerbate health problems (context effects). Localities facing this combination of issues are spread throughout the country, but there are obvious clusters in the northeast of the Netherlands and in south Limburg, as well as in the major cities. Within cities, further urbanization and rising property prices seem certain to reinforce the divide between those neighbourhoods with mainly higher incomes and those where earnings are much lower. This could further increase health inequalities. These developments have the potential to put pressure on the societal sustainability of health and social care.

**Future Risks to Health**

As Covid-19 has made abundantly clear, situations can arise which put acute pressure on the sustainability of health and social care. In the case of the recent pandemic, its long-term consequences for sustainability are still not known. What is certain is that it has brought society face to face with the risks posed by massive outbreaks of influenza or zoonoses. We may well now be at an epidemiological turning point, entering a new phase in which novel infectious diseases mix with existing health problems.[64] Other risks faced by the healthcare sector include increasing antibiotic resistance and declining vaccination coverage.[65] These developments may eventually lead to further rises in the costs of care; for instance, because infections can no longer be treated effectively. Whilst the full magnitude of the effects of these phenomena is difficult to quantify, it is clear that they could contribute towards upping the pressure on both financial and staffing sustainability.

---

[63] Certain conditions are more prevalent in individuals with a non-Western migrant background. These include dementia, diabetes, cardiovascular disease and musculoskeletal disorders. Multimorbidity is also more common. About half of elderly people of Turkish or Moroccan origin in the Netherlands have four or more chronic diseases, compared with only roughly a quarter of those without a migrant background. In addition to poorer physical health, this group is also more prone to mental health problems (psychosis, depression, etc.). Moreover, elderly migrants score higher for general risk factors like loneliness, lifestyle-related disorders (less exercise), socio-economic vulnerability and smaller social networks. And they also have to contend with migration-specific risk factors, including language difficulties, poor health skills, homesickness and a desire to return to their country of origin. Because of this accumulation of risks, they can be said to be doubly vulnerable: as elderly people and as migrants. See, for example: Schellingerhout (2004); CBS (2020c).

[64] RIVM (2020a).

[65] The most recent figures show that vaccination rates are now rising again. Nevertheless, the targets for MMR (mumps, measles and rubella) and HPV (human papillomavirus) coverage are not being achieved (see RIVM, 2019).

Environmental and climate change are also engendering risks for the health and social care of the future. Some of these are already becoming apparent, such as the effects of air pollution or heat stress (during heatwaves). Three-quarters of total Dutch population growth up until 2040 will occur in the cities and towns of the Randstad conurbation.[66] So these are the places most likely to come under increasing environmental pressure, with less green space, more pollution and so on. But the effects of these developments are likely to be uneven. Socio-economically weaker neighbourhoods, for instance, already have to contend more often with poorer air quality and higher rates of heat stress due to their location and the design of their buildings. Again, this puts pressure on healthcare services in particular geographical regions. And again all these developments could potentially affect the sector's future sustainability.

**Key Points—Developments in Health Status**

- More and more people are suffering from cancer, dementia and cardiovascular diseases. In addition, lifestyle-related conditions are on the increase. This also applies to loneliness: it is expected that almost 6.7 million people will be socially isolated and lonely in 2040.
- In combination with an increase in the number of chronic conditions and multimorbidity (several conditions at the same time), this will lead to ever higher healthcare costs in the future.
- The use of child and youth care services and basic mental healthcare provision is increasing substantially, putting added pressure on the supply of care.
- Socio-economic inequalities in health remain a persistent problem in the Netherlands. This is putting financial sustainability under pressure, particularly in certain specific regions. Combined with weakening solidarity when it comes to lifestyle-related conditions, growing inequality is also straining societal sustainability.

## 2.4 Economic Developments

### Growing Prosperity

Economic factors primarily influence demand for health and social care and its price. As they become wealthier, societies tend to spend a larger proportion of their revenues on healthcare.[67] Growing prosperity enables this rising expenditure, at a

[66] RIVM (2018a).

[67] Economists call this "positive income elasticity". For the use of care at the national level, the income elasticity is usually greater than 1.This means that consumption of a good, in this case care, increases faster than incomes rise. With the consequence that more affluent societies on average spend more on care than less affluent ones. This effect does not necessarily extend to the individuals within a society, though: at the personal level, the income elasticity for care is often around 0

rate faster than overall economic growth. When the economy is expanding, more resources are available and people often expect the government to invest in healthcare. And it has the means to comply. This interaction indicates that the relationship between prosperity and spending on care is not autonomous. Governments and other institutions—and hence policy as well—play an important mediating role.[68]

So what is the exact relationship between growing prosperity, actual and expected, and the financial sustainability of the care sector? First of all, it is very strong in quantitative terms. In a 2015 review the OECD showed that greater prosperity is a key factor behind growth in spending on care in its member countries; statistically speaking, it explains 42 per cent of the increase.[69] But prosperity is also an important indicator when it comes to the sustainability of healthcare. This aspect is often measured by looking at care expenditure as a proportion of the economy as a whole, expressed as a percentage of gross domestic product (GDP). Comparing the results year on year indicates whether relative spending on care has been rising or falling. This indicator is also used in projections, but there it is heavily dependent upon the reliability of economic growth forecasts and that is far from guaranteed, especially in the longer term.[70] In its care expenditure prognosis for 2015–2060 (*Toekomstverkenning Zorguitgaven 2015–2060*), the RIVM uses the projections derived by the Netherlands Bureau for Economic Policy Analysis (Centraal Planbureau, CPB) from the 2014 Central Economic Plan,[71] which assumes an average annual real economic growth rate of 1.7 per cent for the period until 2060.[72] On this basis, the RIVM estimates that health and social care expenditure will rise from 12.7 per cent of GDP in 2015 to 19.6 per cent in 2060.[73,74] Expressed in 2015 euros, this would mean a tripling of spending per capita from just over €5100 to almost €15,800.[75]

(income has no effect upon use of care) or even negative (higher incomes use less care, relatively speaking). This effect is related to the average poorer health status of lower income earners in Western countries, combined with the collective nature of their care systems: for the individual, financial constraints (personal affordability) are hardly a determining factor at all in their use of care. For more details of the relationship between care use and income elasticity at different levels of analysis, see Getzen (2000).

[68] Vonk et al. (2020).

[69] OECD (2015a).

[70] Vonk et al. (2020).

[71] CPB (2014).

[72] The RIVM states that although growth may fluctuate considerably from year to year and that other studies assume a much lower rate in the medium term, average annual growth of 1.7 per cent is a prognosis reasonably in line with the historical development of GDP (Vonk et al., 2020: 52).

[73] This is the RIVM's perspective on care spending.

[74] See also Chap. 3, in particular Table 3.1, for an alternative estimate of expenditure on care as a percentage of GDP, based upon CPB estimates.

[75] Vonk et al. (2020).

**Labour Productivity**

Labour productivity is another driver of increasing expenditure on care. Its effect plays out through the price of that care. According to a well-known principle in economics, the relative prices of a sector's products and services rise when the increase in labour productivity in that sector is slower than in the economy as a whole. Called the Baumol effect,[76] this is a common phenomenon with services in which human interaction plays an essential role, like health and social care and education. Compared with other economic sectors such as manufacturing, care is labour-intensive. To keep it competitive in the battle for personnel, its rates of pay have to keep pace with national trends (see also Chap. 7). This steadily increases the payroll costs incurred by providers, and so ultimately leads to higher overall expenditure. In manufacturing by contrast, pressure to raise wages can often be offset through mechanization or automation, which make it possible to produce more with fewer people. This is far harder in care, which also has only limited opportunities to achieve higher productivity through broader efficiency gains. After all, time and concern for the patient are an integral part of the care "product"—and indeed determine its quality to a large extent.[77]

The possibilities to improve labour productivity in health and social care, as in comparable public services like education, are therefore more limited than in other economic sectors. By the nature of care itself, this factor remains more or less stable whilst the wages paid to its labour force evolve more dynamically, in line with the general trend. As a result, care becomes relatively more and more expensive over time.

This does not mean, though, that there have been no productivity gains at all. In hospital care especially, in times of limited resources some substantial improvements have been made by substituting human labour with technology. But in other parts of the sector, such as care for the elderly, this has proven far less possible.[78] In the case of the Netherlands, it has been estimated that the Baumol effect accounts for a yearly increase in health and social care expenditures of about 0.5–1 per cent.[79] This is slightly less than the effect of the demographic developments discussed earlier, but it is by no means insubstantial.[80]

**Key Points—Economic Developments**

- Growing prosperity is an important driving force behind increases in expenditure on care in the Netherlands, but also in other OECD countries. Demand for care tends to rise at a faster rate than economic growth.

(continued)

[76] Baumol (1967).

[77] Vonk et al. (2020).

[78] Blank and Eggink (2011); Blank and Van Heezik (2019).

[79] Pomp and Vujic (2008).

[80] Vonk et al. (2020). The RIVM does not specifically consider the Baumol effect as a separate factor in its prognosis, so we only know how it has evolved to date and have no future projections.

- The RIVM estimates that expenditure on care will rise from 12.7 per cent of GDP in 2015 to 19.6 per cent in 2060. This would represent a tripling of spending per capita, from just over €5100 to almost €15,800.
- Labour productivity does not improve as fast in the care sector (and other public services) as in the economy as a whole due to the labour-intensive nature of the work, particularly in long-term care. Due to this Baumol effect, wage costs increase and so total expenditure on care rises.

## 2.5 Technological Developments

The public debate sees regular hopeful claims that technological developments now and in the future can offer a solution to sustainability issues. In the policy world, too, a multitude of initiatives and plans to stimulate care-related technology reflect such expectations. One example is the huge European subsidy schemes promoting "e-health" in the hope of mitigating the effects of ageing upon healthcare spending.[81] Care providers, administrators and policymakers also hope that new technologies can reduce staff workloads by improving efficiency and saving time.[82] The Covid-19 pandemic has further fuelled expectations by, for example, increasing the use of video consultations.

Offsetting this optimism, however, are analyses identifying technology as one of the main drivers of rising spending in the sector. In many cases, after all, technological progress expands medical possibilities—as when a new drug is developed for an illness that was previously untreatable, for instance. Advances in areas like gene therapy, imaging equipment for the better targeting of radiotherapy and surgical robots are proceeding at breakneck speed. In such cases technological innovation broadens the range of possible care: we can now treat patients where previously that was not possible. But this often makes things more expensive. Technological developments thus primarily influence the supply side of care, but also affect its price.

Our core question in this section is which of these perspectives is most salient. Are the high expectations that technology can help keep care sustainable realistic? Or do technological innovations ultimately only lead to more care that is more expensive (more possibilities create more demand)? And going beyond the financial implications, how will all this impact staffing and societal sustainability?

First, though, what do we actually mean by "technology in care"? Technology is a very broad term that can cover a wide variety of phenomena and products. A study by the OECD defines technology in healthcare as referring to the procedures, equipment and processes by which such care is provided.[83] This broad perspective covers all kinds of developments, from electronic patient records and implants to medi-

[81] For example, Zorgvisie (2019).

[82] Wouters et al. (2019); ING (2019).

[83] Marino and Lorenzoni (2019).

cines and proton radiotherapy. But also solutions not specific to healthcare yet still influential in its provision, such as the information technology (IT) handling its processes and procedures. We therefore follow the spirit of the OECD definition, but extend it to cover social as well as health care whilst excluding innovations that are purely organizational or systemic in nature. Otherwise, strictly speaking the introduction of a new care system or the decentralization of home care to local authorities would also count as a "technological development". And although that might be defensible from a purely economic perspective, it would be out of line with everyday usage of the term "technology".

Moreover, various ways of classifying technological developments are possible, according to the role they play in the provision of care. Here we again follow the OECD, which in a 2017 report distinguishes between "biomedical technology" and "enabling technology". This distinction is similar to that sometimes drawn between "product innovations" and "process innovations".[84] The first of these categories, biomedical or product innovation, includes medicines, medical equipment and diagnostic tools, but also developments like genetic engineering, personalized medicine and so on. In other words, anything associated directly with the delivery of care to the patient or client. The primary focus here is usually improving the quality of care, with efficiency gains taking second place.

As for "enabling technology" (or process technology), the OECD includes such phenomena as e-health, robotics, artificial intelligence (AI) and big data.[85] That is, innovations related to the care delivery process in general terms rather than the care itself. In this domain the main emphasis is improving efficiency rather than quality, although technologies such as big data can certainly also impact actual care and its quality directly—the dividing line is not always clear-cut.

**Developments in Biomedical Technology and Sustainability**

Current developments in the field of biomedical technology are wide-ranging and fast-moving. We can only speculate about their future path, but it seems certain that product innovation will continue apace. There are a number of reasons why such advances drive up healthcare spending.[86] The first is their own price: a new technology is usually more expensive than an old one, especially in the early days (due to patents, for example, or because relatively few players are active in the market when a development is in its infancy).[87] Then there are factors that affect the volume of care, starting with the fact that there is no real brake holding back healthcare providers—and by extension patients—in the adoption of new technologies, treatments or diagnostic methods (here too there is a relationship with increasing prosperity; see previous section). Secondly, these technologies tend to be complementary in nature:

[84] ING (2019).

[85] There are many different definitions of e-health in circulation, which differ in scope. In the *Nictiz-NIVEL eHealth Monitor* it is defined as the application of both digital information and digital communications to support or improve health and healthcare (Wouters et al., 2019).

[86] SER (2020).

[87] Hult et al. (2018).

rather than replacing existing forms of care, they usually add new ones. Thirdly, they sometimes make it possible to minister to patients who were previously more or less beyond help, so that more care is provided overall. Take gene therapy for rare and hitherto often untreatable conditions, for instance, which has given new hope to countless sufferers. And fourthly, in many cases a new technology also increases the volume of care required because it extends life expectancy.[88] In short: when more is possible, more is done.

So whilst new technology certainly has important benefits—it can deliver significant health gains—its price and volume effects may also push up the cost of care and thus negatively impact the sector's future financial sustainability.[89] For staffing sustainability, too, its influence is generally more negative than positive. New technology only rarely directly replaces human care providers, but instead is more likely to increase the volume of care they deliver and generate greater demand for specialist personnel.

As for societal sustainability, in healthcare in particular it is true that if something is available then people will want to make use of it. So new or improved supply creates new demand. If a certain treatment is possible but withheld, for example, that can easily cause a public outcry. We experienced exactly this in the Netherlands in 2017 when it was decided not to include the proprietary cystic fibrosis drug Orkambi (*lumacaftor/ivacaftor*) in the basic statutory health insurance benefits package because its cost was deemed too high relative to the benefits.

This topic touches on normative discussions within the sector about how far medical professionals should go with treatment, as well as those concerning the true health benefits of certain medicines (see Chap. 8).

**Developments in Enabling Technology and Sustainability**

Developments in enabling technologies generally aim to achieve efficiency gains and so in principle could offset the effect of biomedical technologies, which usually make healthcare more expensive. We can distinguish between a number of types of benefit an enabling technology can provide. Firstly, facilitating communication and contact, as in the case of video telephony. Secondly, robotic or domotic support; take informal care robots that can perform household chores, for example, or automatic fall-detection devices. Thirdly, the ability to monitor more and more patients and other vulnerable people, such as the elderly, remotely or at home. Fourthly, the use of AI and big data to generate more (and better) diagnoses through machine learning and other ways of analysing large data files. And finally the development of electronic patient records, personal health environments and the like to give people better access to their own health and medical information.

Right from the outset, expectations were high. Enabling technologies would allow people to live independently for longer, increase staff productivity and improve the quality of care, whilst at the same time bringing down costs. The dream was an ideal combination of cheaper care and lower volumes, achieved in part by

[88] SER (2020).

[89] Polder (2018).

averting or delaying demand. But the reality proved different. It was soon realized that deploying more technological aids in care for the elderly, for instance, does nothing to reduce either staffing levels or costs[90]—a conclusion that still seems to stand.[91,92] Which, of course, does not mean that those aids cannot make life easier for patients.

As for the future, it is difficult to say what to expect. We do not know how fast advances in digitalization, e-health and AI will unfold, or how intelligently they can be used in the care sector. The question here is whether greater digitalization will lead to more efficient care provision. If so, technology could have a positive effect for staffing (and financial) sustainability. But it is also possible that, by lowering barriers, the use of technology actually leads to an increase in demand for care. Eliminating some of the hurdles experienced by patients is doubtless good for the accessibility of care, and possibly also its quality (demand might otherwise have been missed), but could well be bad for its sustainability. On the societal front, meanwhile, the key question is how accepting the public will be of ever-increasing digitalization and robotization.

One development which could make something of a difference is the fact that technological progress is making it increasingly possible to transfer some aspects of care to the home environment. This is known as "blended care". One example is certain treatments for cancer patients, such as chemotherapy. Another is home dialysis. For people suffering chronic medical conditions, self-management looks likely to become more and more important in the future.

New technologies like e-health applications will support this trend.[93] As a result of the Covid-19 pandemic, moreover, we have seen a substantial rise in the use of online video consultations by GPs and hospitals. Such developments could well impact staffing levels and patterns. But there are also constraining factors, including the nature of the sector's IT infrastructure, the degree of support amongst care professionals and the current financing model, which is heavily biased towards treatment volumes.[94] Similar barriers also exist in other countries. We discuss this issue further in Chap. 7, where we also identify the greatest opportunities and impediments associated with it.

### The Net Effect of Technology

All things considered, it is clear that technological developments in the health and social care sector have brought about health gains, some of them substantial. As discussed above, however, the same developments have also pushed up spending on care, not only directly through price rises and greater volume of provision but also indirectly by, for example, increasing life expectancy. Advances in enabling technologies do not appear to be cushioning, let alone reversing, the pressure on

[90] De Klerk (1997).

[91] Van Campen et al. (2016).

[92] Went et al. (2015).

[93] RIVM (2020a).

[94] See, for example, SER (2020).

financial sustainability, whilst innovations in biomedical technology are currently pushing it in a negative direction. Although the exact relationship between technology and healthcare spending is complex, on balance it thus appears that technological developments are exacerbating rather than alleviating the problems associated with sustainability.[95]

All in all, there seems to be a general consensus that technology contributes towards higher spending on care at the macro level. But that does not alter the fact that studies at the micro level sometimes present a different picture: in specific cases and viewed in isolation, certain innovations definitely are cost-effective.[96] One reason why this is not so across the board, meaning that cost increases are the norm, is that efficiency gains cannot always be monetized due to such factors as fill and waterbed effects (see also Chap. 6). Although the estimated amounts vary widely, the finding that technological developments are a strong net contributor to rising health and social care expenditure is common in Western countries. An OECD review of relevant literature reveals that an average of 35 per cent of growth in spending in this domain is driven by technology.[97]

**Key Points—Technological Developments**

- Care-related technological, medical and biomedical developments have led to major health gains but also drive up spending by raising both prices and demand.
- Increasing use of enabling technologies like robotics, domotics, home monitoring and e-health has the potential to improve staffing and financial sustainability.
- But these expectations have yet to be fulfilled, in the Netherlands and other countries. This is due in part to a number of constraining factors, including the IT infrastructure, volume-driven financing and limited patient and staff support.
- The net effect of technological innovation in the care sector is likely to be an increase in expenditure.

## 2.6 Sociocultural Developments

A final core determining factor for the future sustainability of the health and social care system is sociocultural developments. Here again we can identify a number of long-term trends likely to influence the demand for care, and hence its sustainability. Sociocultural phenomena can act upon both the demand and the supply side of

95 Polder (2018); see also Pammolli et al. (2008).

96 Pammolli et al. (2008).

97 Marino and Lorenzoni (2019).

care use, and in principle there are plenty that could make it either more or less sustainable. It is also impossible to predict what new developments might occur in this field, since they often follow in the wake of demographic or technological changes. Nevertheless, we have identified two that are expected to put the sustainability of care under particular pressure. The first is a direct result of a demographic trend, namely the growth of the elderly population in need of informal care. The second is primarily demand-based and concerns changing public perceptions of the sector's capabilities.

**More Elderly People Living Alone and Increasing Pressure on Informal Care**
One significant repercussion of the growing elderly population is that the number of one-person households is expected to increase. In 2020 the Netherlands had approximately 1.4 million over-75s, just over 1.2 million of them living independently. More and more, that means living alone.[98] According to Statistics Netherlands, the number of households in this category will double by 2050.[99] Although many older people are keen to stay in their own home for as long as possible, some have no choice because access to care and nursing homes has been steadily restricted in recent years.[100] Government policy emphatically favours them living independently if they can. Approximately 94 per cent of all senior citizens and 70 per cent of the over-85s therefore do so, often with support from district nursing services. Only a relatively small number, 115,000 (6 per cent of all senior citizens), were residents of a nursing or care home in 2019.[101] Remaining at home can be problematic, though, as it greatly increases the burden on the elderly themselves and their social network. Forecasts indicate that the number of socially isolated and lonely older people is likely to increase (see above). And whatever their situation, this group makes huge demands of both formal providers (day care and home care services) and informal carers.

A substantial proportion of the support provided to elderly people living independently is informal and unpaid.[102] For those with health problems in particular, it is often a cornerstone of their care.

This form of care offers a possible way to meet some of the future demand for people with basic nursing skills. This has already increased in recent years due to the ageing population and the decentralization of care services. More and more, informal carers are filling the gap. At present, 4.4 million Dutch people over the age of 16 provide some form of informal care, and for 750,000 of them this is both long-term (for more than 3 months) and intensive (more than 8 h per week). Almost two million combine the task with a paid job, whilst almost 9 per cent (380,000) feel heavily burdened by it.[103] Not only do survey results indicate that there is good reason to doubt the willingness of informal carers to increase their efforts—especially outside their

[98] De Klerk et al. (2019).

[99] CBS (2018a).

[100] Rli (2014); Van Dam et al. (2013); Verbeek-Oudijk and van Campen (2017).

[101] CBS (2019b).

[102] De Klerk et al. (2019).

[103] Kooiker et al. (2019).

own family circle[104]—but this group also forms an important cohort from which formal caregivers will have to be recruited. Another cause of limitations to the potential for informal care is the growing rate of labour-force participation (see also Chap. 7).

Above all, however, the demographic potential for informal support is rapidly diminishing. Moreover, we know from the regional population and household forecast compiled jointly by the Netherlands Environmental Assessment Agency (Planbureau voor de Leefomgeving, PBL) and Statistics Netherlands that this is particularly the case in regions with an ageing and shrinking population (see above). That potential is often measured in an international context using the so-called "oldest old support ratio", which compares the number of people in middle age (as an indicator of the pool of potential informal carers) with the number in the very oldest age group (as an indicator of the demand for care).[105] Fig. 2.4 shows that the gap between these numbers is steadily narrowing. For the Netherlands as a whole, the ratio in 1975 was 30:1 (that is, there were thirty times as many 50–75 year olds as people aged 85-plus). It currently stands at 14:1 and by 2040 is expected to be 6:1. In parts of the provinces of Groningen and Drenthe, the Achterhoek region and the upper Noord-Holland peninsula, as well as the entire provinces of Zeeland and Limburg (more or less the same areas we described earlier as the "periphery" of the Netherlands), the difference will be even smaller. At such levels the ability to satisfy informal care needs is compromised even under current circumstances, never mind if—as expected—there has been a structural increase in demand.[106] Incidentally, this is not only the case in the Netherlands—it is also an international trend in richer societies.[107]

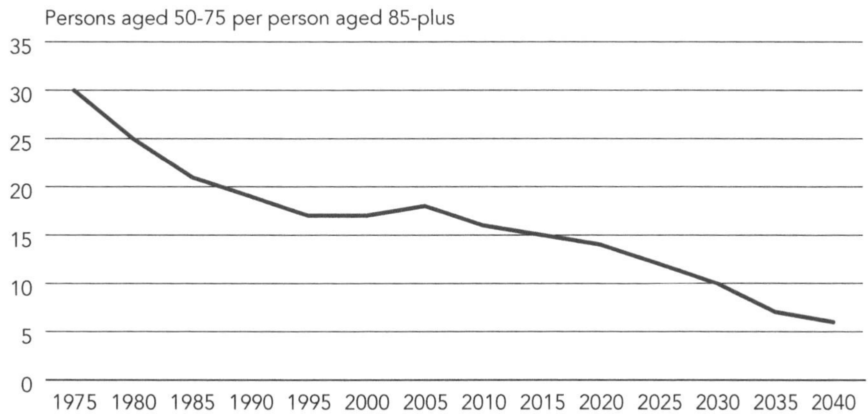


**Fig. 2.4** Oldest old support ratio (number of 50–75 year olds per person aged 85-plus), 1975–2040. (Source: PBL & CBS, 2019)

[104] Van den Brink (2017).

[105] Herrmann et al. (2010).

[106] de Jong and Kooiker (2018).

[107] Herrmann et al. (2010).

### Changing Public Expectations

A second sociocultural development can be summarized as "changing public expectations". As previously discussed, technological developments in the care sector are unfolding at great speed. One of the consequences of this is that expectations on the part of both patients and providers regarding the capabilities of healthcare are rising just as fast. This touches on the discourse surrounding the *medicalization* of care: the phenomenon that care-related issues are being drawn more and more into the medical domain.[108] As well as the demand side (a more assertive public), the supply side (care providers and the pharmaceutical industry) is playing a part in this process. And so too are changing norms and expectations in wider society.[109] One familiar example is the overhasty labelling of lively behaviour in children as a medical disorder, ADHD, to which medical solutions are then applied (for example, prescribing the drug Ritalin). The result has been a sharp increase in certain diagnoses, and consequently in the number of prescriptions issued.[110] Another example is the late-stage treatment of diseases like cancer, often involving very costly therapies, the effectiveness of which in terms of prolonging life and maintaining its quality is often questionable. Finally, there is the increasing focus upon the concept of "vitality", particularly in care for the elderly.[111] Such rises in expectations make it increasingly difficult to accept the news that a medical condition cannot be resolved or cured.

Related to this is the trend towards the ever-greater *personalization* of care. Diagnoses are becoming more specific and treatments more unique (and far more expensive).[112] On the supply side, this is straining the desire for an efficiently organized healthcare system based upon a certain degree of uniformity in treatment methods.[113] On the demand side, it is generating growing calls for greater freedom of choice. People are become increasingly assertive, demanding and individualistic, so that their preferences and perceived needs no longer fit neatly into standardized collective packages.[114] If someone cannot afford expensive uninsured treatment for a loved one, for example, they will try to raise the necessary money themselves through crowdfunding and shop around—at home and abroad—for a provider. In the Netherlands in 2020, €1.9 million was raised for gene therapy with the drug

[108] RVS (2017a); Van Dijk et al. (2016, 2020).

[109] Conrad (2005).

[110] Gezondheidsraad (2014).

[111] Giudici et al. (2019).

[112] We are referring here to "personalized medicine", "precision medicine" or "tailor-made therapy", defined by the Netherlands Organization for Health Research and Development (ZonMw) as the ability to use a patients' individual characteristics (such as their genetic blueprint or protein expression) or specific features of their disease (such as mutations in a tumour) to determine the treatment most likely to succeed for them personally (https://www.zonmw.nl/nl/over-zonmw/nationale-wetenschapsagenda/route-personalised-medicine/). One example is targeted therapies for breast, lung, skin and other cancers, designed after molecular analysis of the tumours.

[113] RIVM (2018a).

[114] Trappenburg (2005).

Zolgensma for a baby with the rare muscle disease SMA (spinal muscular atrophy).[115] There are numerous similar examples, and in principle this option is within everyone's reach thanks to developments such as digitalization and social media.

Initiatives of this kind are quite understandable at an individual level, but at the macro level they can lead to inequality in the use of care—the more assertive you are, the more you can achieve—as well as a decline in confidence in collectively-funded provision and hence put pressure on its societal sustainability (see Chap. 3). The developments discussed also impact the financial and staffing dimensions, although that effect is difficult to quantify in isolation.[116]

**Key Points—Sociocultural Developments**

- The ageing population is going to increase pressure on informal care. The number of elderly people living alone is set to double by 2050, and with it the problem of loneliness, whilst there will be fewer informal carers to help them.
- Public expectations of what the care sector can and should provide are rising. By fuelling developments like medicalization (bringing more and more care-related issues into the medical domain) and personalization (individualized preferences and possibilities), this is adding to the strain on all three dimensions of sustainability.

## 2.7 Consequences by Subsector

What do all these expected developments mean for the sustainability of health and social care? In its care expenditure prognosis for 2015–2060, the RIVM has calculated the consequences for its various subsectors (see Fig. 2.5). According to these projections, in 2060 the largest sums in absolute terms will go to hospital care; growing by an average of 2.8 per cent annually, spending in this subsector will reach €96 billion in 2060.[117] That will make it 3.5 times larger in expenditure terms than in 2015. The effects of the ageing population are most evident in the rising cost of care for the elderly, up from almost €17 billion in 2015 to just over €70 billion in 2060. That is more than a fourfold increase and corresponds with an average annual growth rate of 3.2 per cent. Together, these two subsectors will account for 57 per

[115] https://www.rtlnieuws.nl/nieuws/artikel/5138811/crowdfunding-sma-medicijn-donaties-jayme-ziek-ziekte-kind-geld

[116] See Jeurissen et al. (2018). Moreover, the treatments concerned are frequently unproven; recent studies show that a large proportion are demonstrably ineffective and some are actually dangerous (see, for example, Snyder and Caulfield (2019)).

[117] As in Fig. 2.5, all the amounts in this section are expressed in real terms (2015 euros). Vonk et al. (2020).

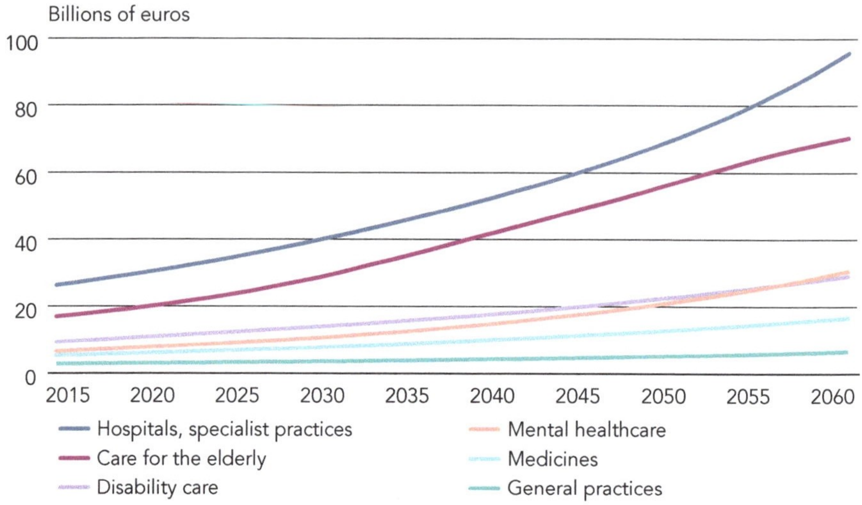


**Fig. 2.5** Care expenditure prognosis by subsector, 2015–2060 (in 2015 euros). (Source: Vonk et al., 2020)

cent of total care expenditure in 2060; in 2015 that figure was just under 51 per cent. Spending on disability care will grow only slightly more slowly, from just over €9 billion in 2015 to almost €30 billion in 2060.[118] The average age of this group is increasing as well, so it will need more care even as the amount of informal care available to it declines. As in the case of care for the elderly, moreover, this relatively labour-intensive subsector is subject to a strong Baumol effect.[119]

In relative terms, mental healthcare is set to grow the fastest. Expenditure in this subsector is predicted to increase fivefold in the period 2015–2060, due in part to the rising number of people with mental disorders. But even more so because dementia is included in this category. Some €6.5 billion was spent on mental healthcare in 2015; in 2060 that is expected to be more than €30 billion.

As well as the differences between subsectors, there are also differences in expenditure on individual conditions. Broken down to this level, spending on dementia, cancer and cardiovascular diseases will rise particularly fast. The category expected to see the biggest increase of all is mental and behavioural disorders, up from €20 billion in 2015 to nearly €83 billion in 2060—an average annual growth rate of 3.2 per cent. In part this is because care for people with dementia and learning disabilities is included in those figures. Striking, too, is the prognosis that

[118] According to Woittiez et al. (2014), the increase in expenditure on disability care between 1998 and 2014 is due primarily to a participation effect: more and more people are making use of some form of this provision. Reasons mentioned in that study are more diagnoses, the more complex society and the improving supply of care. Also, unlike other countries the Netherlands allows some access to this type of care for persons with borderline intellectual functioning (IQ 70–85) and amongst this group in particular the growth in demand is well above average (Woittiez et al., 2018).

[119] Polder (2018).

expenditure on cancer care will rise faster than that for cardiovascular diseases; cancer climbs from fifth place on the 2015 list of "most expensive" conditions to second in 2060. This is due mainly to the introduction of new medicines, which will cause the trends in the prevalence of cancer and in spending on it to diverge. The same pattern can be observed with cardiovascular diseases, although to a lesser extent, whereas in the case of dementia prevalence and expenditure look set to remain more or less in line with one another.[120] Technological developments in the form of new drugs or treatment methods thus lead to an "extra" increase in healthcare expenditure.

Indeed, the RIVM predicts what it calls an "explosion" in spending on cancer care and treatment.[121] This means that a growing share of the cost of the relevant subsectors, hospital care in particular, will be incurred treating that one disease. And there is only room for that if less is spent on other conditions. In other words, there is a risk that tackling "expensive" diseases like cancer will displace spending on "cheaper" ones, with all the repercussions that could have for the public values of quality and accessibility across the care sector as a whole. We look at these dynamics in more detail later (see Chap. 8).

**Key Points—Consequences by Subsector**

- Spending in all subsectors of health and social care is expected to rise substantially between now and 2060, with by far the most money then going into hospital care (€96 billion) and care for the elderly (€70 billion) (amounts in 2015 euros).
- In particular, spending on dementia, cancer and cardiovascular diseases is increasing significantly. The cost of cancer care and treatment is "exploding", according to the RIVM, due mainly to new technological developments.
- Mental and behavioural disorders, including care for people with dementia and learning disabilities, will be the group of conditions incurring the highest expenditure (€83 billion) in 2060.

## 2.8 The Changing Context and the Three Dimensions of Sustainability

What broad picture emerges from all these—mutually interacting—developments? First of all, in most cases it is impossible to quantify the extent to which they contribute towards the use of healthcare. Because of the way various factors interact, the effects of specific trends are hard to determine. However, we can say something

[120] Vonk et al. (2020).

[121] Vonk et al. (2020).

about their net impact upon financial sustainability. This gives us some idea of their overall magnitude, but that remains a very general picture. The OECD estimates that, in Western countries, 12 per cent of increases in expenditure on health and social care are related to demography, 42 per cent to growing prosperity and 46 per cent to a residual category that includes technology.[122] The realization that the basic picture is relatively similar in various countries with comparable levels of prosperity and demographic trends but sometimes entirely different care systems is a remarkable revelation and indicates that the developments we have outlined cannot be steered simply by redesigning the system. We look at this in more detail in Chap. 6.

Despite the fact that demographic factors—in particular increasing life expectancy—play an important role in the debate on the rising costs of care, their overall contribution towards those rises has so far been relatively limited. Technology has historically been a net driver of higher spending, although as mentioned above this can have both positive and negative effects in financial terms. Moreover, the greater possibilities opened up by technological advances influence the demand for care—especially in combination with a growing desire for freedom of choice amongst an ever more assertive public. Finally, the impact of increasing prosperity receives little attention in the public debate but is undeniably significant.

The extent of the roles played by the developments we have described varies across the different subsectors of health and social care. Better treatment possibilities facilitated by technological advances have their greatest impact in curative care, for example, whereas the repercussions of the Baumol effect and the ageing population are felt mainly in care for the elderly and the disabled. In the latter fields, demographic trends are far more influential than technological developments or growing prosperity in shaping the evolution of spending patterns—and they are also precisely the areas in which the staffing dimension of sustainability will most quickly face the most acute challenges in the coming years, in both formal and in informal care.



[122] OECD (2015a). In its own projections of total growth in the volume of care, the RIVM attributes about one-third to demographic factors and two-thirds to a residual category that includes both technology and prosperity (Vonk et al., 2020).

# Chapter 3
# Sustainability in Three Dimensions

> To safeguard the quality and accessibility of care for all, staffing and societal sustainability need to be upheld just as much as financial sustainability. This is not currently the case.

In the previous chapter we looked at current trends and developments in Dutch health and social care. We now turn our attention to their implications for the future sustainability of care. As explained in Chap. 1, in this report we take a broader than usual view of the concept of sustainability. In this chapter we explore the mechanisms of that wide-ranging interpretation and look at how the three dimensions of sustainability—financial, staffing and societal—are evolving. We do this by reviewing historical developments, the current situation and prognoses for the future. As part of our analysis we also address the finding that the three dimensions are closely interrelated, resulting in everything from mutually reinforcing effects to mutual trade-offs—more of one means less of the other.

## 3.1 Financial Sustainability

### *3.1.1 Trends in Spending*

In the political arena, the financial dimension of sustainability is generally the most visible. We are talking here about macro-level spending—what the Netherlands as a whole spends on health and social care—rather than the costs incurred by individual



G. Werner et al., *Financial, Staffing and Societal Sustainability of Dutch Health Care*, Research for Policy, https://doi.org/10.1007/978-3-031-58564-7_3

users of the system. In 2019 the Dutch spent €101 billion in all on care.[1] This amounted to rather more than €6000 per person, representing 13.1 per cent of our gross domestic product (GDP). Of that total, €70 billion was funded collectively—equal to 24 per cent of gross collective spending.[2] By comparison, €10 billion was spent on defence and €40 billion on education in the same year. Only social security saw a comparable level of expenditure (€81 billion).[3] Spending on care has been increasing across the board for decades, both per capita and as a share of GDP (see Table 3.1 and Fig. 3.1). In other words, on average outlay on care has been growing faster than our total national income since the 1970s.

Given ongoing demographic and technological developments, not to mention rising prosperity, that trend is expected to continue. In a preliminary study for this report, the National Institute for Public Health and the Environment (Rijksinstituut voor Volksgezondheid en Milieu, RIVM) predicts that real-terms spending on care will rise by an average of 2.8 per cent a year until 2060, whilst the economy as a whole will grow by no more than 1.0–1.5 per cent annually.[4] This means that—all things being equal—we are moving towards a total care spending ratio to GDP (overall expenditure on health and social care expressed as a proportion of the economy as a whole) of between 23 and 27 per cent during that period (see Table 3.1). Broken down into the subdomains governed by different legislative regimes in the Netherlands (under the various so-called "system laws"), absolute spending is set to increase most sharply in long-term care—that is, provision under the Long-Term Care Act (Wet langdurige zorg, Wlz).[5] This is a direct consequence of the ageing population and increasing life expectancy (see Table 3.1).

As a result, the proportion of care within the overall Care Expenditure Ceiling (UPZ; see Box 3.2) provided for under the Long-Term Care Act (Wet langdurige zorg, Wlz) increases from 30 to 40 per cent. In 2060, hospital care and care for the elderly are still expected to be by far the largest cost centres.[6] In absolute terms, all this adds up to a tripling of total expenditure in real terms (see Fig. 3.2). One significant contributory factor to this trend is the relatively slow growth of productivity in this labour-intensive sector (Baumol's law; see Chap. 2), but there is also the increasing scarcity of labour due to the stagnating size of the working population (see 3.2). Which means that more and more money will have to be put on the table

[1] Figure estimated in 2020 (Vonk et al., 2020). This is spending on care as defined by the National Institute for Public Health and the Environment (RIVM), which encompasses private as well as collective expenditure and includes spending on public welfare and social care, but excludes childcare. If we include that, the total was €106 billion (see online Appendix 2).

[2] This is the net Care Expenditure Ceiling (UPZ); that is, excluding all mandatory direct personal payments (when they are included, that is the "gross UPZ"). See Rijksbegroting (2019). For more details of the various definitions of care expenditure, see online Appendix 2. For the origin of the UPZ and its role in the budgeting process, see Box 3.2.

[3] Rijksjaarverslag (2019).

[4] Vonk et al. (2020). For the specifics of estimated GDP growth, see CPB (2019), Table 3.1.

[5] The various so-called "system laws" governing the health and social care sector are described in detail in Chap. 4.

[6] Vonk et al. (2020).

**Table 3.1** Trends and prognoses in health and social care spending, 1980–2060

| | Actual | | | Prognosis | | | |
|---|---|---|---|---|---|---|---|
| | 1980 | 2000 | 2019 | 2030 | 2040 | 2050 | 2060 |
| Total spending in real terms (2019 euros ×1 bn) | 40.1 | 64.2 | 106.2 | 144.0 | 192.0 | 251.0 | 327.0 |
| Idem per capita (2019 euros) | 2845 | 4044 | 6142 | 7801 | 10,066 | 13,013 | 16,747 |
| Collectively financed spending ("net UPZ" as percentage of GDP) | 4.4% | 5.6% | 9.2% | 11.8% | 14.8% | 17.2% | 19.1% |
| Curative medicine (Zvw) | | | 5.5% | 6.5% | 7.7% | 8.6% | 9.3% |
| Long-term care (Wlz) | | | 2.6% | 3.7% | 5.1% | 6.4% | 7.4% |
| Other | | | 1.1% | 1.6% | 2.0% | 2.2% | 2.4% |
| Care spending ratio to GDP (scenario 1[a]) | 10.1% | 10.0% | 13.1% | 15.7% | 18.7% | 21.1% | 23.0% |
| Care spending ratio to GDP (scenario 2[b]) | 10.1% | 10.0% | 13.1% | 16.8% | 21.0% | 24.5% | 27.2% |
| Growth in total nominal care spending[c] | | 4.8% | 4.5% | 4.6% | 4.8% | 4.3% | 4.0% |
| Spending growth in real terms[c] | | 2.4% | 2.7% | 2.8% | 2.9% | 2.7% | 2.6% |
| GDP growth in real terms[c] | | 2.8% | 1.4% | 1.0% | 1.1% | 1.1% | 1.2% |

Sources: Statistics Netherlands (Centraal Bureau voor de Statistiek, CBS), Netherlands Bureau for Economic Policy Analysis (Centraal Planbureau, CPB), RIVM. (All "actual" figures other than UPZ: Statistics Netherlands, with GDP for 1995 based upon reconciliation of the historical series for 1969–2012 with current definitions. UPZ: CPB, long-term trends in government expenditure. Population estimate: Statistics Netherlands population projection. Estimated spending growth in real terms: RIVM. Estimated care spending ratio and GDP: CPB 2019, *Zorgen om Morgen* (December 2019 estimates), with growth in GDP at 2 per cent inflation. The RIVM's estimate of the care spending ratio in 2060 (Vonk et al., 2020), discussed in Chap. 2, is somewhat lower because it is based upon different assumptions about economic growth in the intervening period)
*UPZ* Care Expenditure Ceiling (Uitgavenplafond Zorg; see Box 3.2), *Zvw* Health Insurance Act (Zorgverzekeringswet), *Wlz* Long-Term Care Act (Wet langdurige zorg)
[a]Scenario 1: estimated UPZ (CPB "plus 1 per cent" estimate) augmented with private spending on care as share of GDP in 2019
[b]Scenario 2: idem with unchanged share of private spending on care in UPZ
[c]Average annual growth rate in intervening period

just to attract the same amount of labour, relatively speaking, to the care sector—never mind to increase the proportion of the workforce it claims.

How much we spend collectively on health and social care is primarily a political choice. In the Netherlands as in all Western countries, outlay on this sector is rising faster than macroeconomic income (see Box 3.1). And this trend looks set to continue for some years to come. It will be some time, for instance, before we spend as much of our GDP on care as the United States (16.8 per cent of GDP in 2015).[7] On purely economic grounds, too, it is hardly surprising that we are ploughing more and more money into care; in this respect, the combination of growing prosperity and public preference is a key driving force (see Chap. 2).

[7]Compared with 10.4 per cent of GDP in the Netherlands in 2015, per the OECD's definition of spending on care; that is narrower than the RIVM definition mentioned earlier in this chapter (see also online Appendix 1).

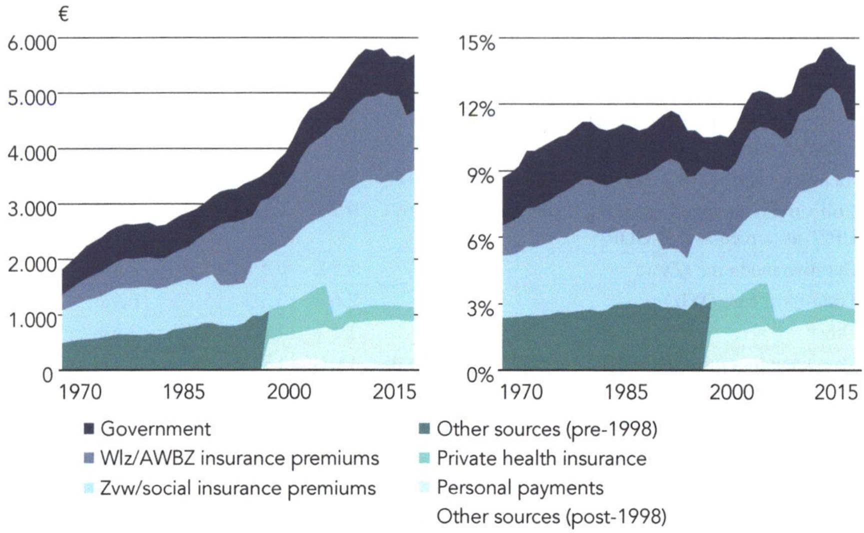


**Fig. 3.1** Sources of total health and social care spending, 1972–2016 (left: per capita; right: as a share of GDP). (In euros per capita adjusted for inflation to 2019 price levels (left) and as a percentage of GDP (right). The different colours indicate the distribution of expenditure across six different sources of funding. Prior to 1998, the "Other" category includes personal payments and private insurance; from 1998 onwards these are shown separately. Two relatively recent policy changes stand out. The introduction of the Health Insurance Act (Zvw) in 2006 unified and collectivized the national health insurance system, superseding the previous distinction between social insurance funds (ziekenfondsen) and private cover. And in 2015 responsibility for a substantial proportion of the provision up until then governed by the Exceptional Medical Expenses Act (AWBZ) was transferred to local authorities under the new Long-Term Care Act (Wlz) and Social Support Act (Wmo)). (Source: Statistics Netherlands, CBS Statline (tables 71,988, 83,039 and 82,262))

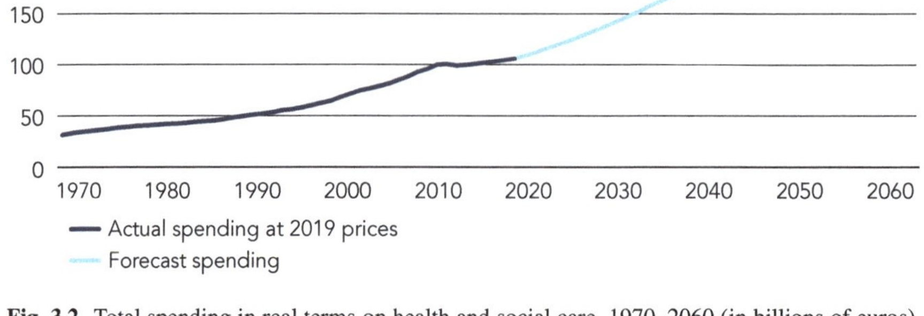


**Fig. 3.2** Total spending in real terms on health and social care, 1970–2060 (in billions of euros). (Source: Vonk et al., 2020)

**Box 3.1: Financial Sustainability from an International Perspective**

Health and social care spending as a percentage of GDP increased relatively rapidly in the Netherlands between 2000 and 2015. And according to OECD projections, this trend is likely to continue—not just in the Netherlands, but also in other Western countries (see Fig. 3.3).[8]

If we look at the various components which make up this expenditure, in every country the largest share goes to curative medicine[9]—in almost all cases between 5 and 6 per cent of GDP (5.1 per cent in the Netherlands). But the US is an outlier in this respect, at 11.9 per cent (not shown in Fig. 3.3). By contrast, spending on long-term care as a percentage of GDP is high in the Netherlands; only Japan has an even higher figure.[10] Since 2000, outlay in this field has increased everywhere.[11] Spending on drugs and medical aids is lower in the Netherlands than in many other countries, though. It is also notable that no country devotes more than a small percentage of its spending to prevention. In the Netherlands this activity, as defined by the OECD, accounts for 0.3 per cent of GDP—a figure comparable with nations like Germany (0.4 per cent), Japan (0.3 per cent) and Sweden (0.4 per cent) but slightly behind the United States and the United Kingdom (0.5 per cent).

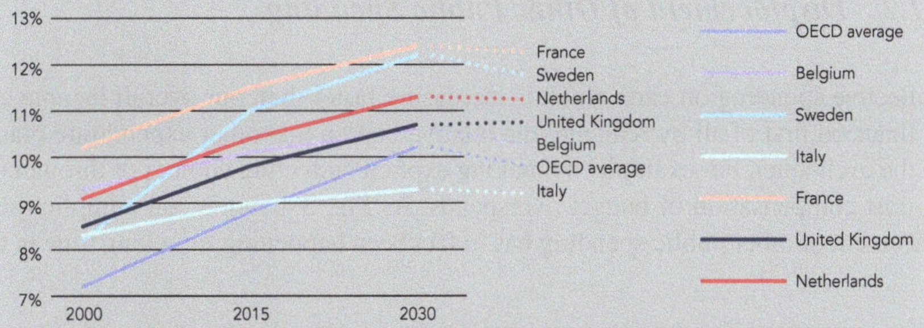


**Fig. 3.3** International spending on care as a percentage of GDP, 2000–2030 (Internationally harmonized definition of spending on care. The range of expenditure this covers is narrower than under the RIVM definition used elsewhere in the report and that covered by the UPZ. See Appendix 2 for more information). (Source: OECD, 2019a)

[8] OECD (2019a).

[9] The OECD uses the categories "curative care" and "rehabilitative care", which correspond roughly with what is usually referred to as "curative medicine" (curatieve zorg) in the Netherlands. OECD et al. (2017).

[10] Kruse et al. (2021), Appendix 3.

[11] OECD.stat, *Health expenditure and financing* (https://stats.OECD.org/Index.aspx, retrieved 21 June 2021).

Technically, the limit of financial sustainability lies at the point where the government is no longer able to finance planned expenditure through taxation or borrowing. When exactly that point is reached depends not only upon the care spending ratio discussed above, but also upon overall public expenditure, the extent of the national debt and the nation's credit rating. In practice, however, the boundary between sustainability and non-sustainability is not so unambiguous. Even before that limit is reached, a substantial increase in spending on care will put a damper on growing prosperity and thus affect the tax base (via rising collective costs), the public finances or the ability to fund other public policy domains. Like all of them, after all, care has to make its way in a world of scarce resources. This became painfully clear during the Covid-19 pandemic, but also plays out in more systematic ways. The consequences of collective spending on care growing faster than our income as a nation are determined by how that spending is financed. There are three options here: (1) reducing government expenditure in other areas; (2) increasing the sector's collective revenue (through higher taxes, social insurance premiums and/or other compulsory contributions); and (3) increasing public debt. We elaborate on these in turn below.

### 3.1.2 Displacement of Other Public Spending

Collective spending on care which is increasing faster than our overall income can be financed first of all by reducing the relative burden that other expenditure places on the exchequer. For example, by making explicit budgeting choices or through the ex-post compensation of budget overspends. As Fig. 3.4 shows, such implicit displacement of other public spending has in fact been happening for a long time in the

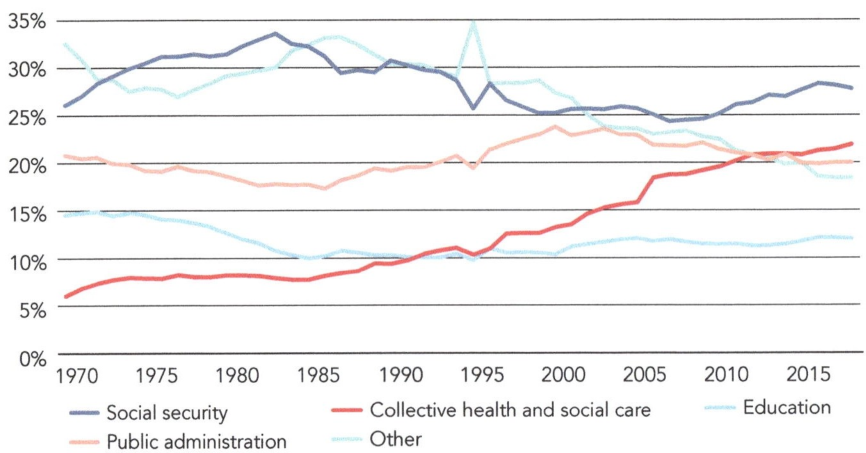


**Fig. 3.4** Spending by budget heading as a proportion of total collective expenditure, 1970–2018. (Source: CPB, long-term trends in government expenditure)

Netherlands. Education's share of the total national budget has remained constant since the mid-1980s, for instance, whereas spending on social security declined systematically until the financial crisis of 2007–2008. In relative terms, outlay on public administration has also slowed down since the turn of the millennium, reversing its previous trend. Above all, though, the category "other"– which includes defence, agriculture and economic affairs—has shrunk in size. By contrast, the share of spending devoted to collective health and social care has been rising consistently for decades. With a first marked upswing between 1966 and 1974 (from 4 to 8 per cent), but even more so since the mid-1980s—resulting in its current position, accounting for about a quarter of total collective expenditure (Fig. 3.4). Although not all of that shift is attributable to trade-offs between care and other public policy domains. In social security, for example, the fall in unemployment following the recession of the early 1980s had a significant impact. And the category "other" also includes interest payments on the national debt, which declined steadily between the early 1990s and the recent pandemic as a result of restrictive spending policies and falling interest rates—from 6 per cent of GDP in the period 1985–1993 to less than 1 per cent as of 2018. That said, it is quite apparent that the Netherlands has chosen to fill much of the "elbow room" created by these trends with increased collective spending on health and social care.

Both as a proportion of GDP (see Fig. 3.1) and as a share of government expenditure (see Fig. 3.4), spending on health and social care has been and remains on a long upward curve. When this growth is absorbed by reducing relative spending on other public policy domains, the logical consequence is that they find themselves on a steady downward curve.[12] A trend which can even end up displacing expenditure that contributes more towards overall public health than the equivalent outlay on care itself—for example, by improving education, housing or the physical environment. Moreover, such displacement effects hit less well-educated and lower-income people the hardest; increasingly expensive health and social care packages are often coupled with reduced entitlements in other areas that affect precisely those groups.[13] A study by the Dutch Health Care Institute (Zorginstituut Nederland, ZiN) has shown that displacement also occurs within care itself, or at least within curative medicine.[14] In the third part of this report we look at the phenomenon of displacement within care in more detail. Incidentally, we should point out as well that displacement by care of other public policy domains in the Netherlands now occurs not only at the national level but also, since the decentralization exercises of 2015, in the local arena. Often to a substantial extent. With limited opportunities to offset the rising costs of the provision they are responsible for (including social support and child and youth care services) by increasing municipal revenues, for example, many local authorities now face large deficits and are having to cut back on other public

---

[12] Absolute displacement occurs only when there is a fall in spending per capita in real terms.

[13] Van Ewijk et al. (2013).

[14] Adang et al. (2018). It remains difficult to identify concrete examples of displacement affecting specific forms of care.

services.[15] In this light, an arbitration board recently ruled that central government must provide local authorities with additional resources to the tune of €1.9 billion for child and youth care services.[16]

**Budgetary Policy and Overspends**

As well as making explicit budgeting choices in advance, it is also possible to offset overspends in the care sector through ex-ante deductions from other budgets. Prior to the outline agreements which capped the growth of overall expenditure on health and social care from 2012 onwards, compensatory exercises of this kind were undertaken between the so-called "budget discipline sectors". As soon as "trend-led" budgetary policy was introduced in 1994 (see Box 3.2), the Budgetary Framework for Care (Budgettair Kader Zorg, BKZ; now the Care Expenditure Ceiling, UPZ) was consistently exceeded each year.[17] Between 1995 and 2013, the cumulative BKZ and UPZ overspend totalled €26.6 billion. The amounts in question—which had reached more than 40 per cent of the UPZ by 2013—were subsequently offset from other budget discipline sectors.

**Box 3.2: Trend-Led Budgetary Policy and the Care Expenditure Ceiling**

Under the trend-led budgetary policy in force in the Netherlands since 1994, in its coalition agreement each new government sets a multi-year cap on collectively financed spending on health and social care. Known as the Care Expenditure Ceiling (Uitgavenplafond Zorg, UPZ), this is an upper limit on *net* spending—that is, excluding direct personal payments (when they are included, the ceiling is referred to as the *gross* UPZ). In addition, the financial appendix to the coalition agreement and the accompanying income and expenditure framework outline the total permissible growth in spending in each of the three so-called "budget discipline sectors". These are health and social care (per the UPZ), social security and employment and the remainder of the national budget. In the event of a subsequent financial setback, the minister concerned has to find a way to offset the loss from within their own budget so that overall expenditure remains below the preset ceiling. Windfalls may also be used for this purpose, but not in the case of new policy. The rules allow offsets *between* budget sectors only in exceptional circumstances and with explicit Cabinet approval.

At this point cost savings were implemented to prevent the deficits from increasing any further. Amongst these were incidental measures to reduce the UPZ, such as the removal from the statutory basic health insurance package of physiotherapy and dentistry for persons over the age of 18. Nevertheless, overspends offset by other

[15] AEF (2020).

[16] Van der Kaaden (2021).

[17] Jeurissen (2016) and Algemene Rekenkamer (2016). The one exception was 2006.

sectors were the main reason for the heightened growth in care expenditure up until 2012. Although it is precisely in order to eliminate this form of transfer that the budgetary rules only permit shortfalls to be reimbursed from other sectors in exceptional circumstances, the fact that this has nonetheless happened on a systematic basis shows how much politicians have struggled with allowing the budgetary process to shape what care is actually delivered.

**Consequences of Displacement**

Figure 3.4 shows that it was long possible to grow health and social care spending relative to other public expenditure. Expressed as a percentage of GDP, too, collective spending in this sector has risen systematically since the mid-1960s, at the expense of other policy domains. Circumstances have now changed, however, so that such trade-offs will not be so straightforward in the future. In the first place, this is a purely quantitative fact: as care makes up an ever larger share of the government's budget, it becomes more and more difficult for other domains to compensate for that increase in spending. An extra 1 per cent spent on care equals roughly a tenth of the total defence budget, for example, and half of all spending of culture. Secondly, staff shortages in various parts of the public sector are putting upward pressure on wages—and hence spending—across the board. Thirdly, a steady relative decline in the funding of research and education is having negative effects for fundamental research, applied technology, training and productivity growth and hence also for the nation's earning potential. And finally, the ageing population is increasing welfare spending.

In short, not only are there now new social and political desires with corresponding budgetary impacts, but our collective spending on care has reached a level at which it has real macroeconomic implications. To a certain extent, we have started feeling the backlash engendered by past care-driven spending cutbacks in other troubled public policy domains. It would thus be pretty unreasonable to expect their share of government expenditure to decline much further; yet more displacement could put even basic standards of social security, public administration, education and other essential services under strain. Not to mention the possibility that it will undermine the funding of activities which actually achieve greater health gains at lower cost than direct investment in care. It is unrealistic, then, to expect that spending on health and social care can continue to rise unabated without other domains experiencing adverse effects.

### *3.1.3 Increasing Collective Revenue*

A second option to finance collective spending on health and social care is to increase the stream of revenue into the system. In the Netherlands, the government has three main variables it can adjust directly: general taxation, the premium payable for long-term care cover under the Wlz and employers' contributions linked to the Zvw (covering primary healthcare). Since the market determines policyholders'

Zvw premiums, government has no direct control over them but can exert some influence because it defines the scope of the statutory insured package. It also controls the level of direct charges for care provision, primarily the compulsory excess under the Zvw and personal payments under the Wlz. Finally, in general terms it can introduce or increase taxes and levies to cofinance care directly from the exchequer. The burden of these imposts is ultimately borne by households and/or businesses, of course, with the question of their distribution obviously being a political issue.

Collective expenditure on care contributes towards the nation's overall earning power by increasing employment and labour productivity.[18] But because of the way the benefits are distributed—heavily weighted towards the elderly and economically inactive—in economic terms they are primarily consumptive and redistributive in nature (see Box 3.3). Consequently, only to a limited extent do those benefits generate monetized well-being that in turn helps to finance care. Meaning that care in the Netherlands largely functions as a "pay-as-you-go" system funded through a combination of taxes and (social) insurance premiums—which, being mandatory, are effectively taxes as well. Since our rising outlay on care is producing diminishing returns (see Box 3.3), it seems likely that further increasing the collective burden of these levies will slow economic growth. Which in turn will limit our capacity to expand public spending.[19]

**Box 3.3: Costs and Benefits of Collective Care**

The benefits delivered by health and social care are wide-ranging. Whilst originally, from the last quarter of the nineteenth century onwards, the primary drivers of improved life expectancy in the Netherlands were better sewerage, water supplies and built environments, since the Second World War care has been added to the list. In fact, it accounts for six of the ten extra years of life the average Dutch person has gained since 1950.[20] And it has also greatly improved our quality of life. Economically, good care helps build a labour force that is not only more employable and returns to work more quickly after illness, but also more productive. These benefits do not come free, however, and expenditure on care always has to be weighed up against the needs of other public policy domains. Calculations in a preliminary study for this report conducted by the RIVM, *Health Effects and Social Benefits of Healthcare* (*Gezondheidseffecten en maatschappelijke baten van de gezondheidszorg*), show that the quantified broad benefits of care have so far exceeded

(continued)

[18] Polder et al. (2020).

[19] Jacobs (2015). At higher rates, moreover, receipts from insurance premiums and taxes no longer increase proportionally. The exact discrepancy depends upon the type and the mobility of factors of production. This instrument is therefore eroded and the funding base for collective spending lags behind actual outlay.

[20] Pomp (2010).

**Box 3.3** (continued)

its cost.[21] But that may not necessarily remain the case in the future. This is because the returns on our ever-higher expenditure are diminishing: the more we spend on care, the smaller the marginal yield from each extra euro becomes. Or, to put it another way, it is costing more and more to achieve the same volume of additional health gains. Furthermore, as the RIVM also points out, the benefits of care accrue predominantly to groups outside the labour force, mainly the elderly. Finally, we should not only consider whether an investment yields more than it costs but also whether spending the money on something else might actually achieve greater health (or other) benefits.

In economic terms, four effects of increasing collective costs for the care sector can be identified. First of all, any rise in the cost to taxpayers and policyholders of funding care leads to displacement of other personal spending.[22] To the extent that this shift is in line with the public's preference for more care, that effect is not problematic. This may change, however, if the growth in private consumption falters, or is largely checked by higher premiums and taxes; in that situation, the benefits of providing more care might not continue to outweigh the greater costs and the ever-shrinking scope for other forms of consumption to expand.

Secondly, higher collective costs have an adverse effect for the supply of labour—and hence for increasing national prosperity. This point also touches on staffing sustainability, but we discuss it here because the actual cause is financial in nature. Estimates specific to the Netherlands of labour supply effects for various groups suggest that an increase in the *marginal* tax burden—that part of each extra euro earned that a worker has to pay in tax or other compulsory levies—primarily influences decisions on whether to work more or fewer hours, whereas the *average* burden is a determinant as to whether or not a person actually joins the labour force. In this respect, women's decisions concerning the number of hours they work seem particularly sensitive to financial incentives.[23] This is especially relevant because 82 per cent of all health and social care workers are female (see 3.3). In short, the higher collective costs required to pay for further increases in spending on care may actually be contributing indirectly to staff shortages in the sector.

Thirdly, similar behavioural effects also apply to entrepreneurship—although our empirical knowledge concerning this point is less precise. Imposing high taxes and social insurance contributions on businesses progressively shrinks the share of their gross earnings they are able to retain, which in turn reduces their

[21] Polder et al. (2020).

[22] In theory, households could also draw upon their savings or their assets to maintain their desired level of consumption. But both of these options are finite. Moreover, the Dutch situation is characterized by a capital-funded pensions system with relatively low free savings, in which employees' assets are not accessible.

[23] Mastrogiacomo et al. (2011). For an international overview of labour supply elasticities for women, see Killingsworth and Heckman (1987).

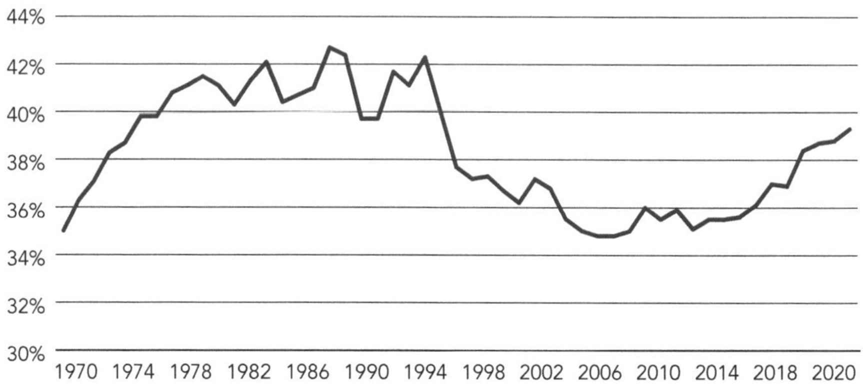


**Fig. 3.5** Collective costs in the Netherlands, 1970–2019 (as a percentage of GDP). (Source: CPB, core data table for 2021 Central Economic Plan (CEP))

entrepreneurial incentive and hence undermines economic growth in general.[24] And the expectation that this burden will rise in the future reinforces the negative effect. Whilst this phenomenon applies universally to all levies on business, there is a direct link with rising spending on care due to the system of employers' social insurance contributions.[25]

Finally, a growing collective onus to pay for care pushes up the cost of labour in particular, and hence that of production. Due to the ageing population, moreover, this financial burden is going to be borne by an ever-smaller group in relative terms. Given the openness of the Dutch economy, this will have knock-on effects for our nation's international competitiveness and so also slow down the economic growth arising out of foreign trade.[26]

The four mechanisms outlined above are relevant not just theoretically or for the long term, but have actually been making themselves felt for some time. Figure 3.5 shows the sum of taxes and social insurance premiums levied in the Netherlands since 1970, as a percentage of GDP. After a sharp decline between the mid-1990s and 2003, in the past decade this proportion has increased systematically to a level not seen since the end of the 1970s. Especially from 2009 onwards, the rise in the care spending ratio to GDP has been accompanied by a steady increase in this collective burden of taxation and other levies. At the 2019 figure of 39 per cent of GDP

[24] Cf. Alesina and Rodrik (1994), Alesina and Perotti (1995), and Alesina et al. (2002).

[25] Cf. Baicker and Chandra (2005).

[26] See also Ministerie van Financiën (2020a), Chap. 2. As mentioned earlier, it should be noted that rising care costs are a feature of all OECD economies. Consequently, the extent of this effect is limited within that particular group—but greater when it comes to emerging economies.

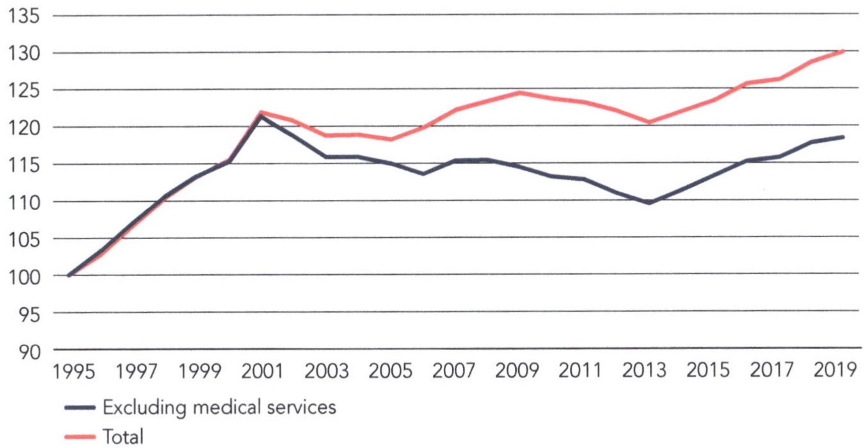


**Fig. 3.6** Index of average household real income, 1995–2019, including and excluding the use of healthcare (1995 = 100). (Source: processed from data supplied by Statistics Netherland (extracted from national accounts))

(the most recent available), we are back to the 1994 level and 60 per cent of the decline seen up until 2003 has been reversed.[27]

These dynamics have major implications for the evolution of real household incomes. Measured since 1995, health and social care has absorbed almost 40 per cent of real growth (see Fig. 3.6).[28] Since 2001, in fact, the increase in disposable income has been more than fully offset by growth in the consumption of medical and social welfare services. For its 2013 study *The Future of Health Care* (*Toekomst voor de Zorg*), the Netherlands Bureau for Economic Policy Analysis (Centraal Planbureau, CPB) calculated that even in a relatively cautious scenario—one in which collectively financed spending on care rises to 22 per cent of GDP in 2040—a two-earner family with a total income one-and-a-half times the modal average will

[27] Moreover, the actual collective burden is higher than the combined cost of taxes and statutory contributions alone. This is due to what are known as "non-tax compulsory payments". In the Dutch case, these are particularly high due to the nature of the pensions system and the mandatory health insurance premium (Zvw). Averaged across different household types with incomes between 67 and 167 per cent of the average wage, in 2019 the total "wedge" in the Netherlands was 13 per cent above the OECD average (Brys, 2011; updated data in OECD, 2021). Because pension contributions are a combination of deferred pay and investments, however, and also because the health insurance premium is independent of economic activity, the effect is not the same.

[28] Since the number of persons per household is decreasing (and so the number of households is increasing), average household income also appears to be decreasing unless we correct for this factor. That correction is made by calculating the figures based upon the average household size in 2019. The definition used is thus total real household income as per the national accounts divided by total population and then by average household size in 2019. That was 2.15 persons, down from 2.35 persons in 1995.

by then be spending 36 per cent of its gross earnings on taxes and premiums to finance care.[29] In a second—less cautious—scenario, that figure rose to 47 per cent. Even though opinion surveys consistently indicate that they want more and better care (see 3.3), it has to be highly questionable whether people will actually be willing to spend a third to half of their household income on it.

As with the option of financing the sector's growth by displacing other forms of public expenditure, the scope to increase revenue from collective sources is not only limited, then, but has actually diminished in recent decades. With the care spending ratio to GDP expected to exceed 20 per cent by the 2040s (see Table 3.1), this alternative alone looks incapable of coping with future needs without engendering the adverse effects outlined above.

### *3.1.4 Public Debt*

As a third and final route, it is possible to increase public borrowing in order to pay for the rising demand for care. Driven by the economic recovery from 2014 onwards, the Dutch national debt had declined from 68 to 49 per cent of GDP by 2019. Under unchanged external conditions and keeping to planned policy, moreover, at that point the CPB was predicting a further decline. That was before the pandemic, however, when spending on a range of support packages plus the decline in economic activity and hence in government revenues pushed the national debt-to-GDP ratio up again. As of 2020 it stood at 55 per cent and, based upon the latest available estimates by De Nederlandsche Bank (DNB, the Dutch central bank), that figure will have risen to more than 56 per cent in 2021 before falling back to 52 per cent in 2023.[30] Depending upon the rate of economic recovery, pressure on spending and choices regarding the pace of deficit reduction, further decline of the ratio is expected in subsequent years.

Despite recent events, at the current very low interest rates the Netherlands retains substantial scope to move to a broader degree of public debt financing. Whilst borrowing to cover collective expenditure need not leave the public finances unsustainable in the long run, that is true only under specific conditions.[31] First and

[29] Van Ewijk et al. (2013) and Van der Horst et al. (2011). In these studies the CPB used a broader definition of the term "collectively financed care" than that used in periodic sustainability analyses and elsewhere to calculate the Care Expenditure Ceiling (UPZ). As a result, the care spending ratio to GDP is around 1 per cent higher.

[30] DNB (2021).

[31] Influenced in part by a 2019 speech by IMF chief economist Oliver Blanchard (Blanchard, 2019), debate has arisen concerning the utility and necessity of government borrowing. The pertinent observation here is that some countries' current nominal income growth exceeds the interest rates on their debt. Given that governments are not obliged to pay off their debts (but do have to refinance them), this results in an enlarged fiscal space. But that applies only to incidental spending (the debt ratio then falls over time). An additional consideration is that financial stability risks have increased systematically since the 1980s (Taylor, 2012; WRR, 2016). As of 2022, rising inflation has also been pushing interest rates up again.

foremost, the expenditure concerned must be incidental—a criterion health and social care most certainly does not meet. Indeed, spending in this sector is almost entirely structural in nature: it is not a one-off investment but an annually recurring expense. Borrowing for this kind of expenditure means that interest has to be paid not only on the current year's deficit, but also on all previous ones. With an accelerating rise in the debt-to-GDP ratio as a result. A second key condition is that the spending must be economically productive—that is, in the form of investments that improve the economy's earning power. These do not affect the debt-to-GDP ratio because its denominator, GDP, increases proportionally. Good examples include investments in innovation or infrastructure. Although spending on care does include a component of this, most of it—as we saw earlier—does not meet the standard here. This is because a large proportion is spent on people outside the labour force. Which does not mean that there are no broad, non-financial societal benefits involved, of course, but rather that financial sustainability is maintained only if those benefits can actually be monetized.[32]

In short, then, with expenditure financed by borrowing the debt-to-GDP ratio will continue to rise. Depending upon the amount of interest payable relative to the level of debt and the credit risk involved, moreover, its cost will either displace other expenditure or increase the strain on collective funding. Deferred liabilities also pose a risk if they have to be refinanced at a higher interest rate. This is relevant in part because the risk of financial crises and debt revaluation has increased substantially in recent decades.[33] Ultimately, the nation's entire creditworthiness could be at stake. But even before that point is reached, a high level of debt and rising interest rates due to elevated credit risks constrain the economy as a whole.

**Key Points—Financial Sustainability**

- The cost of health and social care is rising faster than our macroeconomic income. We expect to be spending more than 20 per cent of GDP on this sector by the middle of the century. A similar trend is occurring in all Western countries.
- Failure to limit growing collective spending on care will lead to displacement of other expenditure, higher costs for individuals and businesses or rising public debt.
- Care has been the only major public policy domain to have seen a systematic increase in its funding as a percentage of GDP in recent decades. Given the sector's ongoing expansion, such implicit displacement of other domains cannot be sustained without damaging their public values—and possibly even overall public health.

(continued)

[32] Polder et al. (2020).

[33] Cf. Taylor (2012), Schularick and Taylor (2012), and Jordá et al. (2016).

- The marginal benefits of additional spending on care diminish with each extra euro. Moreover, the benefits accrue mainly to people outside the labour market. This has negative implications for overall economic growth and for the tax base (including social insurance premiums), and thus indirectly for the sector's own financial sustainability.
- Since 2001, the increase in disposable income has been more than fully offset by greater consumption of collectively financed care. If spending rises at the rate currently being forecast, by 2040 households will be ploughing between a third and half of their gross income into care.
- Financing structural expenditure by running up public debt is not a sustainable approach, even at the current low interest rates.

## 3.2 Staffing Sustainability

### *3.2.1 Staff Shortages and Working Conditions*

Since the economic crisis of the 1980s, debate on the sustainability of health and social care has focused upon its affordability. Yet it is not necessarily the displacement of other needs, the relatively slow growth of the tax base or the increasing strain on collective resources which are going to limit the sector's sustainability in the short run. Given its expected demand for workers, the historically unprecedented phenomenon of a stagnating workforce and the limited scope to increase labour-market participation any more than has already been achieved, we can make a plausible argument that staffing sustainability is in fact a more acute problem than affordability. As with rising spending on care, this is not a uniquely Dutch phenomenon (see Box 3.4). Demographic trends such as the ageing population are affecting both the demand for care and the supply of labour in all Western countries. Especially if the current intensive levels of staffing are maintained, personnel shortages are bound to be further exacerbated. In this section we discuss those shortages in conjunction with related problems such as working conditions and staff turnover, as well as looking at the long-term prognoses in this regard (up until 2060).

**Box 3.4: Staffing Sustainability in an International Perspective**

The existing shortages of health and social care personnel throughout Europe only look set to become even more acute in the future.[34] This applies not only to nursing and personal care workers, but also to doctors. One major contributing factor is the sector's ageing workforce, combined with increased demand for care due to the ageing general population. Relatively high staff turnover due to low pay, long hours and stressful work is also a pan-European issue,

(continued)

[34] European Commission (2010).

**Box 3.4** (continued)
according to a survey of nurses in twelve countries.[35] Likewise, there is widespread concern about current and future GP shortages.[36] Whilst the total number of doctors per capita has increased almost everywhere, in most countries the proportion of general practitioners is decreasing. This problem is particularly acute in more remote rural areas (in Finland, France, Germany and Romania, for example, as well as the Netherlands).[37] Shortages of nurses and professional carers for the elderly are also likely to become an increasing problem across the continent.[38] One factor here is part-time working. The great majority of care workers (82 per cent in the Netherlands) are female, but in many places a large proportion of women work part-time: in Belgium 41 per cent, for instance, and in Germany 47 per cent. And especially in the Netherlands, where the figure is 73 per cent. Incidentally, the Netherlands also ranks first in terms of the proportion of men working part-time (23 per cent, compared with less than 10 per cent in other European countries).[39]

**Current Staff Shortages**

As Fig. 3.7 shows, since the economy picked up with effect from 2014—at least until the outbreak of Covid-19 in March 2020—the job vacancy rate (the number of unfilled vacancies per 1000 jobs) increased across the board. The care sector was no exception, with the largest number of openings being for home-care workers but nurses, psychologists and GPs also in high demand.[40] In response, steps have been taken in recent years to eliminate barriers in the labour market for care personnel. As well as targeted recruitment and incentives, as set out in the Ministry of Health, Welfare and Sport's 2018 plan of action for work in care (*Actieprogramma Werken in de Zorg*), these also cover training. Nursing degree graduations increased from a more or less constant level of around 2400 per year up until 2013 to more than 4400 in 2018.[41] Partly as a result of this, levels of employment rose once again (in hours worked from 2016 and in people employed from 2017), as did both the take-up of jobs and admissions to care-related training courses, thus somewhat mitigating the expected shortfall in staffing in the coming years.

---

[35] RN4cast (2012).

[36] OECD (2018).

[37] See Nivel and Prismant (2019) (factsheets on 20 regions, https://www.ssfh.nl/werken-in/arbeidsmarkt-in-cijfers/regionale-cijfers/). For the international situation, see European Commission (2010).

[38] See Kruse et al. (2021).

[39] van den Brakel (2020).

[40] Van der Werff et al. (2019).

[41] Source: CBS Statline. The number of new doctors qualifying each year in the Netherlands fell from 3742 to 2717 between 2012 and 2018, due in part to restrictions on admissions to medical studies.

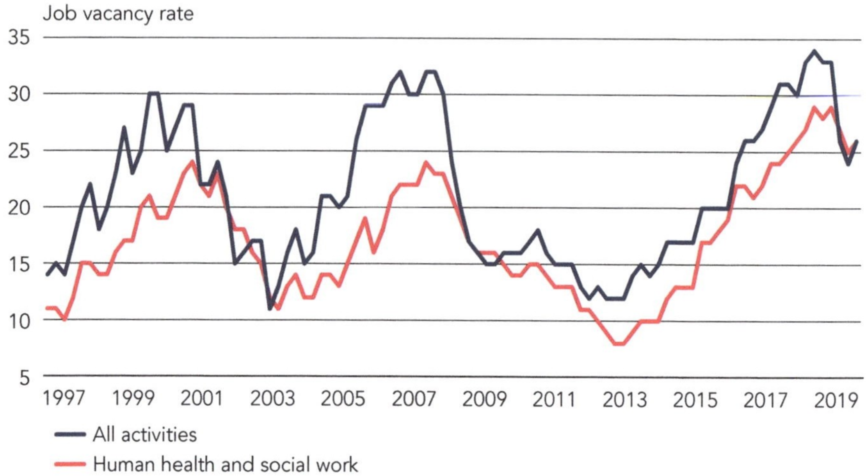


**Fig. 3.7** Job vacancy rates in the economy as a whole and in the category healthcare and welfare, 1997–2020 (seasonally adjusted quarterly data). The vacancy rate is the number of unfilled vacancies per 1000 jobs. (Source: CBS Statline)

Despite this, systematic understaffing still existed on the eve of the pandemic. A progress report on the plan of action from late 2019 found that this would not be as great as had previously been feared, but nevertheless projected a shortfall of 80,000 workers by 2022.[42] Moreover, the number of actual vacancies in the last quarter of 2020 remained at a record level: 36,700.[43] In 2019, before Covid-19 struck, a total of 169,000 job openings arose, 30 per cent more than at the previous peak in 2008. The proportion of employers in the care sector reporting that they had hard-to-fill vacancies was high, too; they included almost all hospitals (94 per cent) as well as the majority of providers in mental healthcare (84 per cent), nursing care (76 per cent) and disability care (68 per cent).[44]

In nursing and personal care, the bulk of open positions require a professional-level vocational qualification (Dutch MBO level 3 or higher). They include specialist intensive care, emergency care, mental healthcare and district nurses. Intelligence Group's (2019) *Labour Market Behavioural Survey* (*Arbeidsmarkt Gedragsonderzoek*) shows that labour market tightness (the number of vacancies per jobseeker) at this level averaged one to four; that is, each active jobseeker had four vacancies to choose from. Amongst district and specialist nurses, the ratios

[42] Commissie Werken in de Zorg (2019).

[43] Source: CBS Statline. These figures refer to the broad category "human health and social work activities" in the Statistics Netherlands Standard Industrial Classification (In Dutch: Standaard Bedrijfsindeling). The number of vacancies in 2019 was 37,400, and in 2020 it was 36,600. The average in the two previous decades (1999–2008 and 2009–2018) was 19,600.

[44] Source: AZW employer survey (https://www.azwinfo.nl/publicaties/werkgeversenquete-2019/). The collective agreement for nursing care covers nursing homes, care homes and home care.

were even higher: one to seven and one to eight respectively.[45] Staff shortages have also increased in other professions across the sector, from residential support workers in disability care to operating theatre assistants and nurse anaesthetists. This is a systemic problem because, besides the growing demand for care, large numbers of personnel will have to be replaced in the coming years since almost a quarter of current care workers are aged over 55 (see also Chap. 6). In addition, there are major regional differences in the staffing situation; the shortages are greater outside the Randstad conurbation in the west of the Netherlands, especially in areas of population decline (see Chap. 2).

**Workloads, Absenteeism and Turnover**

The physical and psychological strain of work in the care sector only exacerbates its capacity problems, and they are further compounded by the increasing pressure of work caused by the unremitting growth in demand and persistent shortage of staff. The result is above-average absenteeism due to illness, high levels of burnout and relatively high staff turnover, and hence a limited average employee retention rate.[46] The AZW Care Survey (AZW-Zorgenquête), conducted annually since 2014, shows that workloads and emotional strain in the sector have increased throughout that time; in 2019 these issues were mentioned by 50 per cent of employers, with GPs particularly badly affected (72 per cent). Of all the employees surveyed, 48 per cent stated that their workload was "too high" or "much too high". And the figures were even higher in child and youth care services and specialist medical care, at 53 and 54 per cent respectively.[47] The rate of sick leave in health and social care had consistently been some 1.5 percentage points higher than in the economy as a whole ever since Statistics Netherlands initiated its current sector-by-sector monitoring sequence in 1996, but that differential increased sharply with the economic recovery from 2014 onwards.[48] That said, it should be noted that this form of absenteeism declined systematically between the turn of the century and 2013, and in the late 1990s in particular was significantly higher than it is now. Also worthy of mention is the distinction between the slightly above-average figure for the sector as a whole and the substantially higher rate in nursing and personal care. The pandemic saw a sharp rise in absenteeism, too, and the question now is whether and to what extent that trend will continue.

---

[45] Intelligence Group (2019).

[46] For the position of health and social care in this respect, see the scatter diagram in WRR (2020b, p. 118). Together with secondary-school teachers and tutors in vocational further education, doctors and nurses score the highest of all professions on the aggregated indicator "quantitative, emotional and mental workload". At the same time they are also in the negative quadrant for professional autonomy and time pressure.

[47] AZW care surveys, 2018 and 2019. Incidentally, perception of the level of independence in terms of greater autonomy to choose one's own working hours did increase. See also www.cbs.nl/nl-nl/nieuws/2016/46/werknemers-in-zorg-ervaren-hoge-werkdruk

[48] From 4.8 to 5.7 per cent in 2018 and 2019 (Source: CBS Statline).

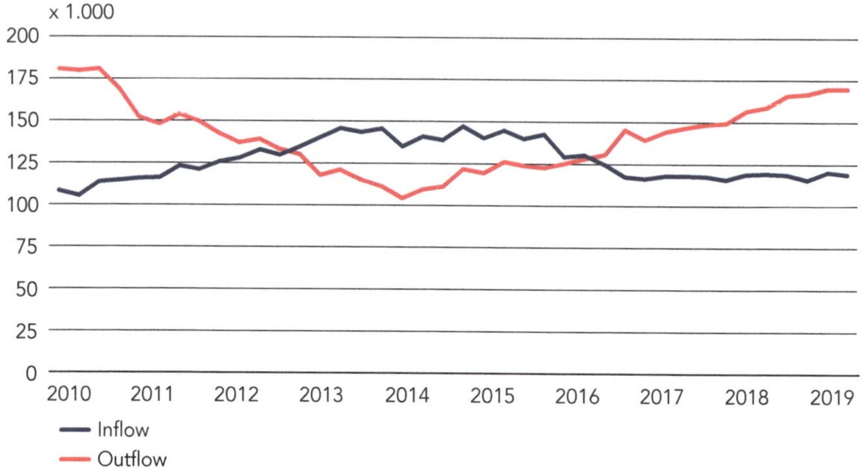


**Fig. 3.8** Staff turnover in health and social care, 2010–2019 (in thousands of people). (Source: Statistics Netherlands, AWZ Statline)

So while the staff shortages in large parts of the care sector are substantial, and workloads and turnover are certainly contributory factors, some nuance is in order here. First, given the general tension in the labour market, the sector's position was not exceptional until early 2020. Although the vacancy rate in care had been reaching record levels, it was even higher on average in the economy as a whole (see Fig. 3.7). Indeed, the difference compared with construction, hospitality and IT was quite considerable. The complicating factor here, creating a problem of staffing sustainability for care in particular, is that society regards shortages in this sector—as also in education, for instance—as more objectionable than elsewhere.

Overall staff turnover in health and social care is relatively high, with outliers of between 11 and 12 per cent per year in nursing, residential and home care and in child and youth care services.[49] The relationship between working conditions and turnover is not straightforward, though, and needs to be considered over a longer period. Underlying the resumed growth in the number of people employed in the sector since the end of 2016 is not only an influx which has been accelerating since the third quarter of 2014 but also a *fall* in outflow in 2016 and 2017, then stabilization until the end of 2019 (see Fig. 3.8). Combined, these developments led to a net intake of 67,000 people in 2010, an outflow of 31,000 in 2014 and an intake of 50,000 in 2019.[50] On balance, then, workloads and sickness have not increased the

[49] On average over the period 2014–2019, the figures were 10.8 per cent in nursing, residential and home care and 12.1 per cent in child and youth care services. The rate for care in general was 9.4 per cent, for general hospitals it was 6.7 per cent and for university hospitals 7.7 per cent. Calculations based upon AZW Statline data from Statistics Netherlands (https://azwstatline.cbs.nl/#/azw/en/dataset/24049NED/table?ts=1593595854441 and https://azwstatline.cbs.nl/#/azw/nl/dataset/24017NED/table?ts=1620042632938).

[50] This makes average intake in the past decade 10 per cent of total employment in the sector, and average outflow 9 per cent. Source: azwstatline.cbs.nl.

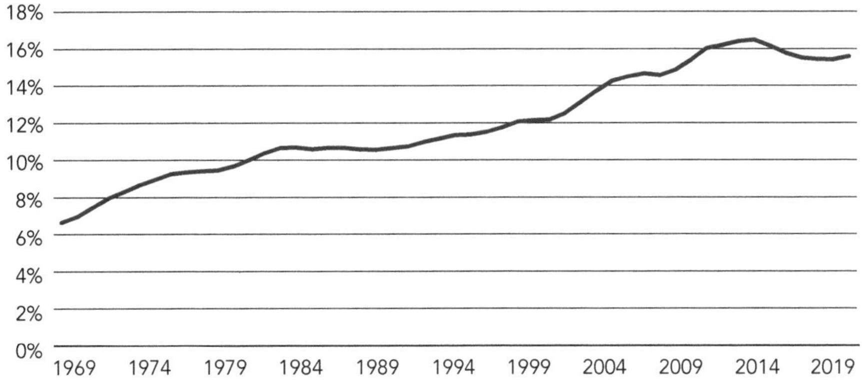


**Fig. 3.9** Jobs in health and social care, 1969–2019 (as a percentage of total employment, measured in job numbers). (Sources: CBS Statline (labour datasets))

number of people leaving the sector as a whole in recent years. Looking to the future, moreover, incoming personnel seem to be in the ascendant: just over a third of the increase in employment in care since the end of 2016 is attributable to reduced outflow, two-thirds to higher inflow.

**Shortages Due to Increasing Demand and Fiscal Policy**

Staff shortages in health and social care remained in step with the overall tightness in the labour market until early 2020. Sector-specific characteristics, however, mean that problems in this area are set to persist well into the future. As the population continues to age, demand for care is increasing across the board: at GP surgeries and health centres, in domiciliary nursing and personal care, in physiotherapy and at hospitals. Likewise, over a prolonged period the sector's demand for labour has grown faster than that in the economy as a whole and so its share of total employment in the Netherlands has risen systematically.[51] Since the early 1970s, the percentage of the Dutch workforce employed in care has grown from under 7 to more than 15 per cent (see Fig. 3.9). A good deal of this rising demand comes from care for the elderly. Demographic developments mean that this trend will continue unabated, not least because opportunities to increase labour productivity in that area—through greater use of technology, for instance—have hitherto proven limited. But we also find major staffing challenges in other parts of the sector, such as mental healthcare, child and youth care services and disability care, not to mention the supply of specialist and general nurses, GPs and some medical specialists.

But the current shortages are also due to policy effects that we should regard as harbingers of the future. In Fig. 3.9 we see an unprecedented downturn in the curve after 2013, when the care sector's share of total employment (measured in job numbers) fell from 16.5 to 15.5 per cent. In the same time period the absolute number of

[51] That share increased from 12.1 per cent in 1995 to 15.5 per cent in 2019. Measured in job numbers, it was less than 10 per cent up until 1980 (Statistics Netherlands labour data). See also Fig. 3.9.

**Table 3.2** Health and social care personnel by domain, 2010–2019

| | Absolute (persons ×1000) | | | | Share |
|---|---|---|---|---|---|
| | 2010 | 2013 | 2016 | 2019 | 2019 |
| University hospitals | 67 | 69 | 71 | 77 | 6.2% |
| General hospitals and other specialist medical care | 215 | 213 | 213 | 217 | 17.6% |
| Mental healthcare | 83 | 92 | 86 | 94 | 7.6% |
| General practitioners and health centres | 25 | 25 | 28 | 32 | 2.6% |
| Other care and welfare | 106 | 116 | 116 | 125 | 10.2% |
| Nursing, residential and home care | 412 | 427 | 386 | 425 | 34.5% |
| Disability care | 155 | 165 | 162 | 178 | 14.5% |
| Child and youth care services | 34 | 31 | 28 | 32 | 2.6% |
| Social work | 62 | 51 | 51 | 53 | 4.3% |
| Total care and welfare[a] | 1158 | 1189 | 1141 | 1233 | 100.0% |
| Growth per annum | | 0.9% | −1.4% | 2.6% | |

[a]Excluding childcare. (Source: Statistics Netherlands (AZW Statline))

jobs in the sector actually fell slightly, from 1.62 million in 2012 to 1.56 million in 2015, before rising again to 1.68 million in 2019.[52] In the six years prior to 2012, by comparison, the figure had increased by just over 200,000 jobs. Even during the recession of the 1980s, there had never before been a fall of that kind. What it reveals is that the policy of fiscal restraint imposed from 2012 onwards in response to the impact of the financial crisis upon the public finances and the previous accelerated growth in spending had profound repercussions for employment in the care sector.

Particularly prior to 2016, the main cause of staff shortages was a combination of the growing demand for care and budgetary restraint. The situation varied greatly across the sector, though. Table 3.2 shows the evolution of employment levels by care domain since 2010. In relative terms, workforce shrinkage was greatest in child and youth care services and in nursing, residential and home care (by 10 per cent). Growth was more evenly spread. The current staffing shortfalls indicate that, in the absence of a parallel slowdown of growth in the volume of care, the budget control policy implemented after 2012 resulted in a catch-up effect in the demand for labour. This is also the broader implication of the recent changes outlined above with regard to workloads and absenteeism: they foreshadow future situations in which issues of financial sustainability necessitate budgetary intervention, which itself has inevitable repercussions for staffing sustainability. On the other hand, a failure to slow down cost growth in combination with a commitment to increased recruitment—through wage competition, for instance—will only exacerbate the financial

[52]Statistics Netherlands data from 1995 onwards specifies volume of labour in terms of both persons employed and hours worked. The labour datasets for earlier years provide only numbers of jobs. The long-term graph in Fig. 3.9 is based upon those figures. The figures for numbers of people employed in the sector from 2012 onwards have been given above; calculated using them, its share of total employment fell from 16.3 per cent in 2013 to 15.3 per cent in 2017–2018. An increase to 15.5 per cent followed in 2019.

sustainability problem. Consequently, labour market policy in health and social care finds itself caught between the Scylla of staff shortages and the Charybdis of financial sustainability. The key question in this regard is what level do we expect the sector's long-term demand for labour to reach.

### 3.2.2 Projected Long-Term Labour Needs in the Care Sector

In 2013 CPB researchers projected that, by 2040, between 22 and 29 per cent of the Dutch labour force would have to be working in health and social care just to keep up with increasing demand.[53] That, however, was at the peak of the sector's growth in the wake of its 2006 reform. A decade on, is there reason to believe that the scenario needs to be adjusted? And if so, what are the implications? To answer these questions, the WRR has produced a new projection of the expected staffing situation and extended it to 2060.[54]

The starting point for this exercise was the share of the total national labour force working in the care sector. At present (2019) it employs 1.49 million people in 1.68 million jobs, delivering 1.09 million working years per annum (see Table 3.3). This amounts to 15.5 per cent of the workforce in terms of personnel numbers (one in 6.4) and 12.7 per cent in terms of hours worked—the difference being due to the high proportion of part-time care staff. Self-employment is not that common (14.5 per cent of personnel), nor is it rising systematically, although more and more nurses are working on a freelance basis or through agencies. For a proper understanding of

**Table 3.3** Employment in human health and social work, 1995–2019 (in thousands of persons)

| | 1995 | 2002 | 2008 | 2013 | 2019 |
|---|---|---|---|---|---|
| Human health | 335 | 426 | 507 | 555 | 592 |
| Social work (inc. personal care) | 541 | 679 | 798 | 872 | 893 |
| Human health and social work | 876 | 1105 | 1305 | 1427 | 1485 |
| Employees | 747 | 964 | 1115 | 1224 | 1269 |
| Self-employed | 129 | 141 | 191 | 203 | 216 |
| Percentage of total employment | 12.1 | 13.1 | 14.6 | 16.3 | 15.5 |
| Percentage self-employed | 14.7 | 12.8 | 14.6 | 14.2 | 14.5 |
| Percentage women | 78.7 | 79.1 | 79.2 | 81.6 | 81.9 |

Source: Statistics Netherlands, CBS Statline

[53] Van Ewijk et al. (2013).

[54] The Dutch Ministry of Health, Welfare and Sport has recently commissioned a forecasting model for the labour market in "human health and social work" (see footnote 46). This covers a shorter time span than our projection (to 2030 rather than 2060), but offers more detail over that period (breakdowns by region and domain, for example). We discuss these models' different assumptions, outcomes and underlying definitions in more detail in online Appendix 3.

these figures, it should be noted that we are here using a broad definition of jobs in care which includes, amongst others, administrative, process support and managerial positions.[55] Labour market trends may be different for those occupations, although given the sector's complexity it is unlikely that there will be any fundamental shift in their numbers as a proportion of its overall workforce in the future.

To gain an idea of the order of magnitude of future staffing shortfalls, we first estimated the demand for labour over the period in question. For this we drew upon the prognosis of the volume of care required between now and 2060 from the RIVM preliminary study referred to above.[56] Data on labour volume and (indexed) sectoral expenditure from Statistics Netherlands was used to estimate the volume of care delivered per working person in the period 1995–2019.[57] We then applied an extrapolation of that outcome to the RIVM prognosis, taking the actual volume of care per working person in 2019 as our starting value. This in turn enabled us to estimate the relationship between staff numbers and care spending in constant 1995 prices between then and 2019. As a counterpart to this projection of the demand for labour, we used an estimate of the evolution of its supply based upon the Statistics Netherlands population forecasts, with the overall employment rate and the care sector's share of it at the end of 2019 as starting values. We explain our method in more detail in Appendix 3.

The results are shown in Table 3.4.[58] To be clear, this is a projection intended to encapsulate the full scope of the policy challenge; no assumptions are made about future rises in labour force participation, nor about budgetary constraints. We have applied the long-term growth in volume forecast by the RIVM, which closely matches the nominal estimate from the CPB. As such, this is not a prognosis of the actual future labour shortfall but of the expected difference compared with the situation in 2019. Furthermore, we must here emphasize once again that these figures provide only an order of magnitude to be taken into account if trends in the demand for care and supply of labour supply unfold as currently foreseen. If only because of the inevitable policy response to growing scarcity, however, that is as good as certain not to happen. In addition, the volume of care delivered per working person may well be influenced by future substitution of labour with technology—although the extent to which that is actually achievable and has any labour-saving effect remains to be seen (see Chap. 5).

---

[55] Specifically, these are codes 86–88 in the Statistics Netherlands Standard Industrial Classification (Standaard Bedrijfsindeling, SBI 2008): "Human health and social work activities".

[56] Vonk et al. (2020).

[57] To make this estimate, we have used the longest possible period. The reason being that, under the influence of the budgetary policy implemented between 2012 and 2016, the effect upon employment of the growing demand for care has been systematically lower in recent years. Using a shorter period would have resulted in this factor disproportionately affecting the predicted relationship and thus distorting the long-term projection.

[58] The proportion of the labour force employed in the care sector in 2019 is higher in Table 3.4 than in Table 3.3 because the denominator is lower in the former (9267) than the latter (9576). This is a product of the different definitions used.

**Table 3.4** Long-term projection of labour supply and demand in care, with unchanged participation (in thousands of people)

| | 2019 | 2030 | 2040 | 2050 | 2060 |
|---|---|---|---|---|---|
| Total population | 17,282 | 18,354 | 19,072 | 19,482 | 19,830 |
| Potential labour force | 12,221 | 12,524 | 12,284 | 12,620 | 12,974 |
| Actual labour force | 9267 | 9440 | 9259 | 9512 | 9779 |
| Inactive labour force | 2954 | 3084 | 3025 | 3108 | 3195 |
| Unutilized potential | 402 | 414 | 406 | 417 | 429 |
| Labour demand in care | 1485 | 1873 | 2342 | 2897 | 3574 |
| Labour supply in care at current share | 1485 | 1513 | 1484 | 1524 | 1567 |
| Total shortfall at current share | | 360 | 858 | 1373 | 2007 |
| Total shortfall as percentage of labour force | | 3.8% | 9.3% | 14.4% | 20.5% |
| Share of labour force demanded by care | 16.0% | 19.8% | 25.3% | 30.5% | 36.5% |

Sources: WRR projection based upon Statistics Netherlands and RIVM data (Statistics Netherlands: population forecast (per June 2021) and labour datasets, 1995–2019. RIVM: volume of care, 1995–2019. Calculations as described in online Appendix 2. Note: care sector's share of total employment in 2019 as in Table 3.3)

Our projection shows that as early as 2030 a fifth of the entire labour force will have to be working in care to fill the demand for staff we currently expect on the basis of forecast volume growth.[59] And from the middle of this century onwards that figure will rise to around 30 per cent (see Fig. 3.10). In absolute numbers and assuming an unchanged relationship between care volume and labour input (including choice of hours and continuing the historical trend in care volume per worker), demand for labour increases by some 390,000 people up until 2030. And by 2040, when population ageing peaks, as many as 860,000 or so workers will be needed to fully satisfy the sector's needs. To meet this demand, the annual net increase in the number of people working in care will have to go from just over 23,000 in the past two decades (1999–2019) to more than 36,000 by 2030 and 48,000 in the subsequent ten years. As of 2060, the staffing shortfall in the sector compared with its current share of the labour force is projected to exceed 20 percentage points.

Recruitment, moreover, will have to draw from a pool of labour that is experiencing only limited growth. A projection based upon the latest Statistics Netherlands population forecast by age and assuming the current labour force participation rate suggests that, numerically, the active population will expand only slightly between now and 2030, after which it will shrink back to about its current level up until 2040 and then start growing again, but only very modestly (see Fig. 3.11). Just how fundamentally this stagnation represents a break from the trend hitherto becomes apparent when we contrast it with the evolution of the working population between 1980 and 2020; during that period it grew from 6.0 to 9.3 million people (up 54 per cent). Variants generated by the Netherlands Interdisciplinary Demographic Institute (Nederlands Interdisciplinair Demografisch Instituut, NIDI) using stronger assumptions regarding future births, immigration and labour force participation deviate

[59] The 26 per cent calculated for 2040 falls between the CPB's previously calculated scenario values.

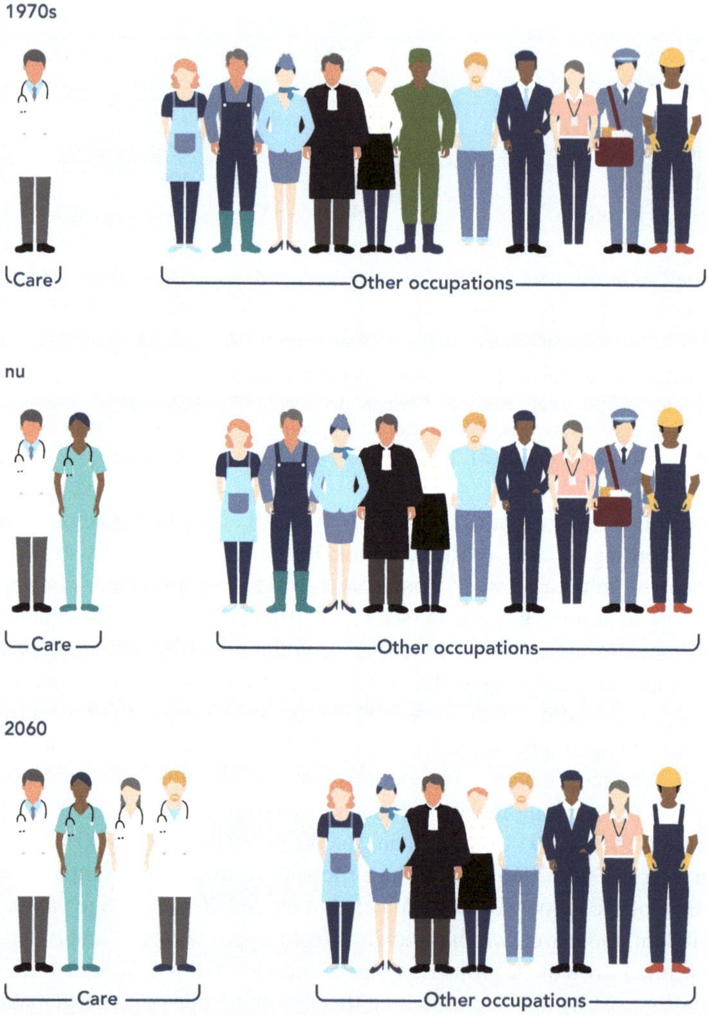


**Fig. 3.10** An increasing proportion of our population is needed to deliver care

upwards from the Statistics Netherlands forecast for 2050, moreover, although they do not substantially change the situation it paints (see Appendix 3 for more details). Even making the most extreme assumptions, the total workforce never much exceeds ten million.[60] In other words, there is only limited potential to meet greater demand for labour through higher birth rates or more immigration and so staff shortages are going to remain a permanent sustainability issue.

[60] Beer et al. (2020).

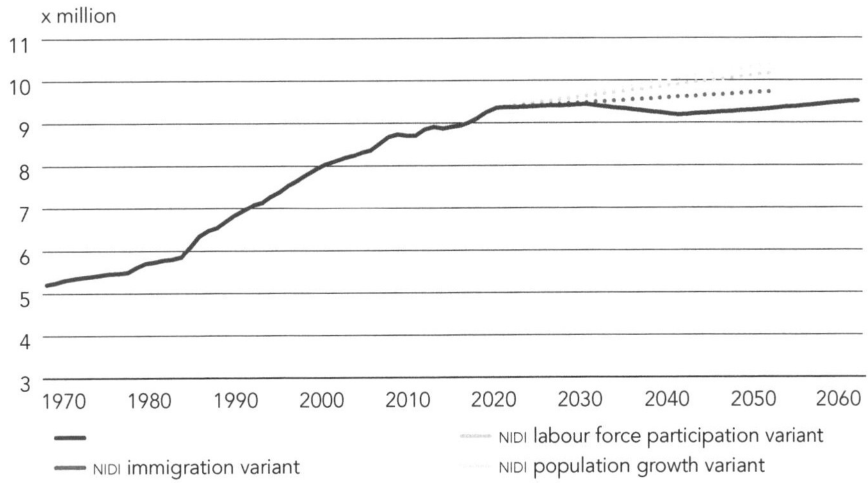


**Fig. 3.11** Actual and projected workforce trends, 1970–2060 (in millions of people). (Source: Statistics Netherlands population forecast; NIDI and CBS (2020))

**Is Staffing Unsustainability in Sight?**

As with financial sustainability, it is not easy to say where exactly the limit of staffing sustainability lies. After all, we still cannot be certain how possible it is to further extend labour force participation. But even if that can be done, the projected expansion of the workforce is never going to keep pace with the growth in demand for labour. The uncertainty here is only exacerbated by the unknown costs of the wage competition inevitably unleashed by trying to systematically secure a larger share of the available labour pool, not to mention the fact that vying for people with other sectors, private as well as public, may put an undesirable strain on their competitiveness or socially unacceptable pressure on their public values. Conversely, it is also impossible to say when the shortages caused by failing to meet the demand for labour become unacceptable. We can reasonably assume, however, that lagging ever further behind the growing demand for care will negatively affects workloads and presumably also the quality of provision. Amongst other things, this has clear implications for societal sustainability (see next section)—with less affluent and, because of their size and visibility, less influential areas such as child and youth care services, disability care, mental healthcare and care for the elderly likely to be hit hardest. As is already the case, in fact (see Chaps. 4 and 7). We look in more detail at policy options to promote the staffing sustainability of care later in this report (see Chap. 6).

**Key Points—Staffing Sustainability**

- The growing demand for health and social care and the stagnating workforce make staffing sustainability a systemic problem for the sector.

(continued)

- The current labour shortages are caused by a combination of increasing demand for care and budgetary restraint. Unless growth in the volume of care provided is curbed, a budget control policy of the kind implemented after 2012 results in a catch-up effect in the demand for labour.
- Rising demand for labour is particularly prevalent in care for the elderly, but is also evident in mental healthcare, in disability care and amongst nurses (specialist and general) and GPs.
- Without policy changes, one in three workers will have to be employed in the care sector by the middle of the century. Not only is this unrealistic, it is also undesirable for the wider economy and for other public policy domains.

## 3.3 Societal Sustainability

### *3.3.1 What Is Societal Sustainability?*

Societal sustainability, the third of the three dimensions we have identified, is harder to define and measure than the two already discussed. In this report we use the term "societal sustainability" to refer to public support for the health and social care system. To what extent do people feel that its accessibility and quality—the public values most closely associated with care—are up to scratch? How do they perceive the relationship between its cost (to them personally and to society as whole, the "collective") and its benefits? If public backing for the sector or for any part of it declines, it cannot function properly. And that will create social and political pressure for change. How that pressure manifests itself and what effects it might have is a second question, which we explore later in this section. As with the other dimensions, incidentally, societal sustainability does not have some hard and fast tipping point at which care suddenly becomes unsustainable. It is also true here, perhaps even more so than with financial or staffing sustainability, that what is or is not considered acceptable depends upon our expectations—and upon how these shift over time.

As we define it, societal sustainability is a broad phenomenon. By which we mean that it is an overarching concept encompassing a number of related perceptions. And hence impossible to measure directly, if only because people most probably do not have clear views about "care" or "the care system" as a general concept, as opposed to its specific parts. That said, by exploring those individual components and looking at how they are evolving we can still say something about the direction in which societal sustainability is moving.

To do this, we examine societal sustainability in terms of public attitudes towards four distinct factors: (1) the quality of care, (2) its accessibility, (3) solidarity with the system and (4) trust in care and approaches to prudence (see Fig. 3.12). In each case we outline the current state of the relevant research, including its limitations, before finally describing how impediments to societal sustainability may feature in the political and social debate and what their consequences might be.

**Fig. 3.12** Four aspects of societal sustainability

### 3.3.2 *What Societal Sustainability Is Not*

First, though, it is important to understand what societal sustainability is *not*. For one thing, it is not directly about specific breaches of quality or accessibility standards. Bodies like the Health and Youth Care Inspectorate (Inspectie Gezondheidszorg en Jeugd, IGJ), the Dutch Healthcare Authority (Nederlandse Zorgautoriteit, NZa) and the Netherlands Court of Audit (Algemene Rekenkamer) quite regularly publish reports showing that certain aspects of quality or accessibility are not up to scratch in a particular field or at a particular provider. However, such cases *in themselves* do not necessarily mean that societal sustainability has been compromised. After all, people may be disinterested, have other priorities or not find the identified shortcomings that problematic. And even if that is not the case, shortfalls in quality or accessibility—however tragic they may be for those directly affected—do not automatically undermine public support for the overall system. Although that can change, of course, perhaps as a result of the publicity surrounding such a report.

This brings us to the second thing that societal sustainability is *not*. For us it is about the views of the public as a whole and not specifically about the experiences of particular groups of patients or users. Measuring the "client experience" is an important factor in assuring the quality of care (see Appendix 1), but societal sustainability reflects the broad views held by society as a whole. Health and social care, after all, ultimately "belongs" to every one of us, including people who are not (or not yet) its users. Their support is essential too, if only because we demand financial solidarity with the system in the form of insurance premiums and taxes from all members of society and not just from the "consumers" of care. Sooner rather than later, moreover, the public discourse inevitably turns its attention to the allocation of human and material resources within the sector or across it and other public policy domains. These are all areas in which opinions throughout society matter.

Thirdly, societal sustainability need not always coincide with the way care professionals view the situation. Public concerns about accessibility or quality might not be widely shared within the field in question, for instance. As an example, take the fact ambulance services do not always meet their 45-min target for emergency patients to reach hospital. This has caused considerable disquiet in the community, but not so much amongst many of the experts on this topic.[61] In the reality of politics and government, however, public concerns remain relevant because they can strain the societal sustainability of care.

### *3.3.3 Where Does Societal Sustainability Stand?*

**Views on Quality of Care**

Society's views concerning the quality of care are a first key pillar of societal sustainability. One important source of information on this subject is the Continuous Public Perspectives Survey (Continu Onderzoek Burgerperspectieven, COB), a poll of views on various topics conducted quarterly via focus groups and questionnaires by the Netherlands Institute for Social Research (Sociaal en Cultureel Planbureau, SCP) since 2008. In the final quarter of 2018, the Dutch public cited health and social care as the most pressing issue facing the country; they were concerned in particular about staffing (not enough personnel, high workloads, low pay), high costs, waiting lists, bureaucracy and the power of insurers in this sector. Only a minority of respondents (30 per cent) were satisfied with the quality of care as a whole, whilst 39 per cent believed that that had deteriorated over the previous five years.[62] When it came to care for the elderly, the figure was even higher: 54 per cent. And 30 per cent of those surveyed expected care in general to deteriorate in quality over the next five years, rising to 40 per cent in the case of care for the elderly.

Public views on the quality of care in different domains vary considerably (see Fig. 3.13). People are most satisfied with GP services, immediately followed by specialist medical care. In both of these areas, more than 80 per cent of respondents rated the quality of provision as 7 out of 10 or higher. The greatest concerns are about care for the elderly in nursing homes (marked 5 or lower by almost 50 per cent of respondents), about child and youth care services and about mental healthcare (marked 5 or lower by more than 40 per cent); see Fig. 3.13. Incidentally, the separate Local Voters Survey (Lokaal Kiezersonderzoek) shows that the Dutch hold their national government responsible for the quality of health and social care, even in those domains where responsibility has been decentralized.[63]

[61] Gezondheidsraad (2020).

[62] Den Ridder et al. (2019); see also Dekker et al. (2016).

[63] De Blok and Van der Brug (2016).

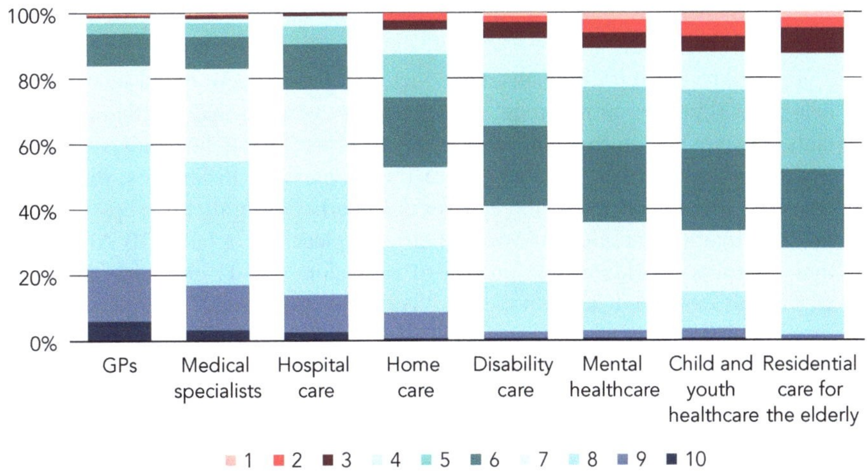


**Fig. 3.13** Public satisfaction with quality in various domains of health and social care, 2019 (in per cent). Respondents (general population, age 18+) were asked to indicate their satisfaction with the quality of care in various domains on a ten-point scale from "very dissatisfied" (1) to "very satisfied" (10). (Source: Den Ridder et al., 2019)

So the Dutch clearly have concerns about the quality of care, now and for the future. But where do these concerns come from? It is apparent from the COB focus groups that people believe that the perceived decline in quality is due mainly to lack of staff and time—their implicit assessment thus being that pressures on staffing sustainability (not enough personnel, excessive workloads) undermine quality. This is a good example of an interaction between the different dimensions of sustainability: pressure on staffing sustainability gives rise to pressure on societal sustainability.

Public concerns regarding the quality of care may overlap with those within the sector, which can put support for the system under further strain. Clear parallels can be drawn here between the views of ordinary citizens and those of care providers (see Box 3.6).

**Box 3.6: Views Amongst Care Professionals**
As in the public arena, within the sector itself we find plenty of strongly held opinions about the Dutch health and social care system, its quality and its accessibility. These are impossible to distil into one single comprehensive picture, however, because of the many different professional groups, roles, types of institution, interest groups and domains involved (see Chap. 4 for a general overview of the Dutch healthcare system). Instead, by way of an example we confine ourselves here to the opinions of nursing and personal care workers across the sector.

(continued)

**Box 3.6** (continued)

In 2019 research institute Nivel conducted a questionnaire-based survey of nearly 1200 nurses, professional carers, support workers and practice assistants active in first-line patient care.[64] They were working in hospitals, mental healthcare (not further specified), care for people with disabilities, district nursing, GP care and residential care for the elderly.[65] Overall, these providers rated the quality and safety of care in their workplaces as 7+ out of 10. Almost three-quarters considered the quality of provision "good" or "very good", whilst half described safety policy as "good" or "very good". There is also room for improvement, though: 15 per cent indicated that quality was regularly to frequently "not good" and 9 per cent that safety was regularly or frequently compromised. Finally, almost a quarter of respondents stated that they were working in a "crisis situation" and trying to do too much too fast. They also reported spending a lot of time on record-keeping and reporting, leading to perceptions of increased workloads and reduced professional autonomy.[66] And the lower they rated the quality of care, the more likely they were to report a shortage of qualified staff in their workplace: of those describing quality of care as "good" or "very good", only about three out of ten indicated a lack of qualified staff, but that figure rose to nine or more out of ten when perceived quality was "moderate" or "poor". Looking at individual domains, it is noticeable that staff in GP care were most positive about quality and safety and also most proud of their work. They were followed by disability care professionals. By contrast, mental healthcare stands out in a negative sense (see also Chap. 4); workers in this domain still rated its quality and safety as satisfactory overall, but a far higher proportion noted that these factors—safety in particular—regularly fell short of acceptable standards. Moreover, a much lower share stated that they were proud of their work: 66 per cent, compared with 82–84 per cent in hospitals, disability care and district nursing and 91 per cent in general practice.

**Views on Accessibility of Care**

When it comes to the accessibility of care, we again focus upon public perspectives. Accessibility can be subdivided into three components: time (waiting lists), distance (travel time to provider, for instance) and personal cost (individual affordability) (see also Appendix 1). The 2019 COB survey reveals that only 19 per cent of respondents were not at all concerned about whether they would be able to access the

---

[64] Nivel, the Netherlands Institute for Health Services Research, is an independent non-profit body with close staffing links to a number of universities. See https://www.nivel.nl

[65] Verest et al. (2019).

[66] As demonstrated, for example, at a dialogue with nursing personnel organized by the SER. See https://www.ser.nl/-/media/ser/downloads/overige-publicaties/2019/ruimte-voor-de-zorgprofessional.pdf

medical care they may need in the future. And in the case of care for the elderly, the figure was just 13 per cent. An overwhelming majority of those surveyed were thus worried to a greater or lesser extent about the accessibility of care, now and looking ahead. Whilst such concerns are widespread, though, they are not necessarily increasing. For medical care, in fact, the percentage was more or less the same as in 2012 (at that time this was not measured separately from care for the elderly).[67] The focus group results showed that here too concerns about accessibility were driven mainly by a fear of long waiting lists for treatment. In addition, high perceived personal costs—the mandatory health-insurance excess, direct charges and so on—played an important role. But in general the geographical component of accessibility (distance from care providers) seemed to generate fewer concerns.

The Dutch are thus genuinely concerned about the quality and accessibility of care. Strikingly, however, their perspectives are not much different from those found in other European countries (see Box 3.7). We should point out, though, that these findings only paint a broad picture and in particular teach us little about "smaller" domains such as child and youth care services and disability care.

**Box 3.7: International Views on Quality and Accessibility**
The European Quality of Life Survey (EQLS) uses a standardized method to examine the *perceived quality* of public services such as health and social care in various European countries.[68] With regard to curative medicine, in 2016 (the date of the last survey) the Netherlands was in the second rank with an overall score of 7.3 out of 10 (joint eighth place with Germany and Denmark; the European average was 6.7). The lower scorers, however, were mainly less prosperous countries in eastern and southern Europe. In terms of satisfaction with the quality of curative medicine, therefore, our nation was languishing at the bottom of the group of affluent northwestern European countries. Views regarding long-term care were rather less positive, not only in the Netherlands but also in other countries; here we scored 6.4 overall, compared with a broad European mean of 6.2. This is particularly striking because the Netherlands invests more than average in formal long-term care.[69]

The EQLS also looks at *views on the accessibility of care*. In the case of primary care (GPs), for instance, this factor is assessed using a number of variables (distance, cost, waiting time, etc.). Here the Netherlands—together with Denmark, Finland, Spain and Sweden—was one of the countries in the top ten in all respects in 2016. The accessibility of formal long-term care was relatively good here, too, with just over 63 per cent of those surveyed

(continued)

[67] Den Ridder et al. (2019) and Kooiker et al. (2012).

[68] Eurofound (2019).

[69] Kruse et al. (2021).

**Box 3.7** (continued)

reporting that it is relatively easy to pay for (compared with the European average of 47 per cent). This is in line with the observation that personal contributions are relatively low in our system (see also Chap. 7). Consequently, this form of care is fairly widely used by the Dutch: 12 per cent of respondents here reported that they or someone close to them use long-term care in an institution (European average 5 per cent), rising to 23 per cent in the case of long-term care at home (European average 12 per cent).

**Views on Solidarity in Care**

In a collective system, solidarity is crucial to ensure high-quality, widely accessible health and social care. When we look at this factor, though, our perspective shifts. In the case of quality and accessibility, we primarily consider perceptions of the "outcome" of care—in other words, its benefits and whether society regards these as sufficient. With solidarity, by contrast, our focus is not only the benefits of care but also its cost. Although there are different interpretations of the concept of solidarity, one essential feature they all share is the issue of who must contribute financially in order to generate those benefits. Solidarity therefore inevitably involves net beneficiaries on one side of the coin and net contributors on the other, although they cannot always be identified specifically. In care as in other sectors, in this respect solidarity is a broad concept. And it can mean different things in different situations. For example, it may refer to a feeling we experience with regard to other individuals or groups. Or to a particular action, such as donating money to a charity or paying premiums for collective health insurance. Another important distinction is between compulsory solidarity, as with legally mandated insurance premiums, and voluntary solidarity in the form of, say, volunteering, charitable giving or organ donation. In health and social care, all of these forms and versions of solidarity play some role. Ultimately, what the whole concept comes down to is a willingness to contribute towards the well-being of others.

We regard solidarity as a component of the societal sustainability of health and social care because the demand for such provision—and hence outlay on it—is distributed unevenly across the population.[70] Most of us require little or no care in an average year, but some people need significantly more. In the Netherlands in 2013, for instance, 48 per cent of spending on healthcare went to the "most expensive" 5 per cent of patients and 52 per cent to the remaining 95 per cent of patients.[71] This unequal distribution means that without the solidarity of healthier and wealthier people, good healthcare would be largely inaccessible to the sick and those on

[70] Vonk et al. (2020).

[71] Wammes et al. (2017); this refers to spending on healthcare under the Health Insurance Act (Zvw).

low incomes. Our goal as a society that access to healthcare should be based primarily—or even solely—upon medical necessity thus requires net financial (and other) input from relatively healthy and relatively affluent people.

There are all kinds of characteristics we can use to classify solidarity. The main relevant distinction in care is between risk and income solidarity. By risk solidarity we mean that between people who differ in the risk they run of becoming ill. In financial terms, this entails those at low risk contributing more on average in order to care for those at high risk.[72] Examples of high-risk groups include the elderly, people with chronic medical conditions and those with a genetic predisposition to disease. In the Netherlands, we find risk solidarity at work at a practical level in the ban on premium differentiation for the statutory health insurance package; in other words, insurers are not allowed to charge high-risk policyholders more for their standard cover. Income solidarity, meanwhile, refers to that between people on high and low incomes, with higher earners paying towards the care of those of more modest means. In Dutch health and social care, this is done through the redistribution of wealth built into the tax system (specifically progressive taxation, the means-tested Healthcare Benefit and employers' social insurance contributions). Income solidarity is necessary because per-capita spending on care (more than €6000 in 2019) is so high that good provision would otherwise be inaccessible to a substantial section of the population.

Risk and income solidarity together are indispensable if everyone is to enjoy easy access to high-quality care. But although they work in quite different ways (the former from the healthy to the unhealthy, the latter from the rich to the poor), this distinction is not always drawn in the public debate. Which is probably related to the fact that it is not so clear-cut in practice. This is because there is a strong relationship between income and both demand for care and spending on it: on average, people on higher incomes make considerably less use of the system.[73] Although this correlation is anything but absolute, of course: there are both sick high earners and healthy low earners. Nevertheless, the strong correlation at group level means that the practical effect of the two forms of solidarity coincides to a large extent. It still makes good sense to distinguish between them, though, as one may well be more sustainable than the other (see below). At the same time, it is also possible that pressure on one form also ups the pressure on the other. In this report, unless otherwise specified we use the term "solidarity" to refer to the broad concept—that is, risk and income solidarity combined. Where distinctions do need to be drawn, we say so explicitly.

---

[72] This is true on average at the group level, but not necessarily at the individual level. It is of course quite possible for an individual member of a low-risk group to use more care, sometimes much more, than individuals in the high-risk group. Moreover, we are here referring explicitly to net effects: it is certainly not a matter of people in the low-risk group not contributing—they pay their premiums and taxes too, after all—but of the net direction of monetary flows at the group level.

[73] Vonk et al. (2020).

**Solidarity in the Care System—What Do the Dutch Think?**

The biennial Solidarity Monitor (Solidariteitsmonitor) survey conducted by Nivel shows that willingness to help fund treatments that respondents themselves do not need is high in the Netherlands.[74] Just over 70 per cent of those polled in 2019 were positive on this point, and there has been no clear trend up or down since the first survey in 2013. Interestingly, though, *expected* solidarity—the extent to which people expect others to share that willingness—is substantially lower, at about 60 per cent. But here too, no particular trend can be observed; it is just that respondents are consistently more pessimistic about how much solidarity they think they can expect from others than about the amount they themselves are prepared to display. Potentially, this might reflect concerns about the extent to which "the system" will provide people with the care they think they are going to need in the future.

The Solidarity Monitor also reveals that the lower a person's income and level of education, and the worse their health, the less solidarity they expect from others. This suggests that groups lower down the socio-economic ladder have greater doubts about whether the system can provide them with the care they expect to need. Moreover, the monitor indicates that groups in a worse position are less willing to show solidarity with others. For those on lower incomes, this may be explained by the fact that they perceive their own spending on care as a major financial burden—an effect we observe despite the fact that personal payments for care in the Netherlands are relatively low by international standards and the fact that Healthcare Benefit (Zorgtoeslag) covers a very substantial portion of the statutory health insurance premiums of those on low incomes.

Results from other exercises in this field, such as the SCP's COB and Radboud University's citizen's forum on choices in healthcare (Burgerforum "Keuzes in de zorg"), confirm the overall picture.[75] In questionnaires and focus groups alike, the Dutch generally express a considerable readiness to help pay for the treatment of others. Solidarity as a universal value is thus highly prized. But can anything more be said about its specific forms, such as risk and income solidarity?

**Dutch Support for Risk Solidarity**

According to the Solidarity Monitor, less than 10 per cent of respondents believe that people in poor health should pay higher insurance premiums. And the same goes for those with a genetic predisposition to disease: only 3 per cent think they should pay more for their statutory cover. This can be interpreted as solid support for the notion of risk solidarity. In a deregulated insurance market, after all, both groups would face significantly higher premiums. But risk solidarity applies to a lesser extent when it comes to age. In fact, there is quite substantial backing for the idea of making older people pay more. This notion is especially popular with the young (30 per cent), and understandably less so amongst older people themselves (8 per cent),[76] although clear majorities across the board still oppose any such

[74] Kooijman et al. (2018) and Holst et al. (2020).

[75] Den Ridder et al. (2019) and Baltussen et al. (2018).

[76] Kooijman et al. (2018).

restriction to (compulsory) risk solidarity. Nevertheless, these figures show that risk solidarity along the age axis is under greater pressure than in the case of disease in general and hereditary conditions in particular.

This form of solidarity comes under even more strain when we look at lifestyle factors. Substantial proportions of those surveyed think that smokers (54 per cent), excessive (or even moderate) alcohol users (44 per cent) and "people with an unhealthy lifestyle" (38 per cent) should pay higher premiums.[77] Non-smokers, non-drinkers and active participants in sport are even more strongly of this opinion. However, the results here again show no clear trend: since 2013 neither substantially more nor fewer people have started to feel this way. Recent Statistics Netherlands findings confirm these results: about half of those surveyed broadly supported the idea of higher premiums for people who smoke or who drink heavily, whilst the same applied to a lesser extent (around 25 per cent) to those who exercise little or are overweight.[78]

These results indicate that people display significantly less solidarity when it comes to risks they feel are—at least partly—due to someone's own behaviour.[79] Risk solidarity for "bad luck" (inherited disorders) is high, but that for avoidable risks—sometimes called lifestyle solidarity—is considerably lower.[80] This is consistent with the more general observation that personal responsibility is often an important consideration when judging solidarity; other research identifies it as one of the five factors that determine who people display solidarity with.[81]

**Dutch Support for Income Solidarity**

We can take a similar approach to gauge public support for various forms of income solidarity. Again, the Solidarity Monitor reveals broad backing for the general idea that high earners should contribute more (43 per cent)—although by no means to the same extent as with many forms of risk solidarity. Moreover, support for this concept appears to be waning amongst high earners themselves (down from 48 per cent in 2013 to 33 per cent in 2017). Conversations in focus groups seem to corroborate this: even amongst members of high-income groups we find a relatively positive attitude towards the principle that "the broadest shoulders should bear the heaviest burden", but at the same time they are also more likely to point out its limits.[82] Likewise, SCP research from 2012 found that most people expect desirable additional investments in health and social care to be funded primarily by those earning

---

[77] Kooijman et al. (2018).

[78] De Witt (2019).

[79] We do not elaborate here on whether that perception is justified.

[80] Some authors use the term "lifestyle solidarity" to refer to risk solidarity associated with lifestyle-related health problems. See Groot and Van Sloten (2012).

[81] The other four are: (1) the extent of need for help; (2) identification with the beneficiary; (3) reciprocity; and (4) the beneficiary gratefulness and compliance; Van Oorschot (1998, 2000). See also Jeurissen (2005) for further analysis around the theme of personal responsibility, lifestyle and solidarity in care.

[82] Den Ridder et al. (2019).

more than they do. And in its turn the uppermost income group wants to see more efficiency.[83] These findings indicate that income solidarity is under greater strain than risk solidarity, and may be declining. Which suggests that the societal sustainability of the current system is more likely to come under pressure along the income solidarity route than through risk solidarity, except in the case of lifestyle solidarity.

**Views on Trust and Prudence**

Finally, we look at a category of views that we summarize under the heading "trust and prudence". This is all about whether we as a society have confidence in the Dutch health and social care system and whether we think that the human and material resources we all invest in it are being used prudently, as well as whether they are being allocated for what are viewed as a legitimate care purposes. This latter aspect, in particular, has not yet been the subject of much systematic academic scrutiny, but we can discern something about it when, for example, we look in detail at the outcomes of the SCP focus groups.

Nivel's Trust in Healthcare Barometer (Barometer Vertrouwen in de Gezondheidszorg) reveals that overall confidence in the Dutch system is high. Especially when it comes to GPs, medical specialists and nurses: around 90 per cent of respondents between 2006 and 2018 express "trust" or "high trust" in these professionals.[84] The equivalent figure for hospitals hovers consistently around 70 per cent. In stark contrast, public trust in nursing homes is much lower: only about 35 per cent. And health insurers perform even worse, at just 25 per cent—one key reason being that people do not believe that they have the interests of their policyholders sufficiently at heart.[85] Overall, these figures indicate that the Dutch trust individual providers of care more than the institutions behind them.

SCP research shows that three-quarters (75 per cent) of people in the Netherlands think that more money should be allocated to health and social care—even if that is done to the detriment of other public policy domains (71 per cent).[86] And that extra funding, they say, should go to things like more and better-paid staff, care for the elderly and lower personal costs (a reduced insurance excess, for instance). Despite this strong support for greater investment in care, however, only 36 per cent of respondents want premiums and taxes to be raised to pay for it and just 28 per cent are willing to pay more in premiums or taxes themselves. Other "solutions", such as increasing the mandatory excess or slimming down the statutory basic package, are also far from popular (9 and 25 per cent in favour, respectively), mainly because people are concerned about their effects upon the accessibility of care and about creating a divide between those who can and cannot afford it. Consequently, about 30 per cent of respondents are unwilling to choose any of these three strategies (higher premiums and taxes, a more limited basic package, a higher excess).

[83] Kooiker et al. (2012).

[84] Kooijman et al. (2018).

[85] Maarse and Jeurissen (2019). Less is known about this factor in the case of other purchasers of care, such as care administration bureaus.

[86] Den Ridder et al. (2019).

However, a previous SCP study found that people hope—and indeed expect—that more resources can be freed up to stem the feared decline in the quality and accessibility of care more or less solely by increasing efficiency, countering waste and bureaucracy, reducing the influence of market forces and cutting back on management.[87]

Incidentally, international research indicates that costs not related to the primary process are slightly higher than average in the Netherlands but still comprise only a small part of total expenditure on care.[88] This, though, does not alter the fact that red tape and administrative pressures are important negative factors affecting the way workers in the sector perceive their jobs and workloads (see Box 3.6). Even if savings in these areas have little impact upon overall spending, then, they could well influence staffing sustainability (by reducing absenteeism and staff turnover, for instance) and hence also societal sustainability, specifically by bolstering trust in the system.

### *3.3.4 Limits to Our Understanding of Societal Sustainability*

Our knowledge of the factors underlying societal sustainability remains incomplete. For instance, we only partially know how and on what basis people form their views concerning quality, accessibility, solidarity and prudence. Indeed, it is not at all self-evident that ordinary citizens really understand the health and social care system with its numerous governing statutes, institutions, regulations and monetary flows. Opinions in many cases seem to be formed mainly by a mixture of personal and anecdotal experience, combined with media-driven perceptions. For example, research confirms that few people really understand how much they actually pay into the system through less visible routes such as the income-related contribution for curative medicine (the "employer's contribution" under the Zvw). Never mind the reality that the total contribution per person averages €6000 a year.[89] As a result, statements of support for investment in care or for solidarity may not always translate into concrete willingness to pay; the fact that people greatly underestimate how much they already spend on the care sector suggests that that willingness might decline if this were to become clear.

A related limitation lies in the difference between what economists call "stated preferences" and "revealed preferences". In surveys, people are inclined to give socially desirable answers. Consequently, what they claim to favour (their *stated* preference) does not always correspond with their actual behaviour (their *revealed* preference). This is particularly troubling in a case like that of the Dutch care

---

87 Kooiker et al. (2012).

88 On average across the OECD as a whole, these represent 3 per cent of total spending on care. The figure for the Netherlands is just over 4 per cent (Mueller et al., 2017).

89 Kooiker et al. (2012) and Baltussen et al. (2018).

system, where statutory contributions make it only marginally possible to measure people's revealed preferences through their consumption behaviour. A hypothetical health insurer charging higher premiums for elderly people or smokers might be very popular with paying policyholders—or it might not, but we do not know for sure.

Nevertheless, there have been some attempts to sidestep such limitations. In one study, for instance, respondents were asked to put together their ideal basic health insurance package.[90] Along with each choice they made to include or exclude a particular treatment, they were shown its direct financial impact: how much it would raise or lower their premium. In this way the researchers were able to assess the extent to which people are still willing to show solidarity with others if that has clear financial consequences for them personally. What they found is that participants were indeed more reluctant to favour the reimbursement of treatments they consider lifestyle-related. On the other hand, there was a high degree of solidarity with people with genetic conditions. Unlike the opinion studies by Nivel and SCP, however, this research exercise did not reveal any age-related effect on solidarity; respondents were not less inclined to reimburse care for older patients. One possible explanation is that participants in this particular study were presented with a very concrete age limit (specifically, reimbursing treatments "only for persons younger than 75"), whereas the Solidarity Barometer asks whether "elderly people should pay more for basic health insurance". So the exact phrasing of the question matters: whilst a section of the population is less willing to display financial solidarity with the elderly, by favouring premium differentiation (higher premiums for older people), there is no widespread desire to exclude them completely from collective insurance cover, either for certain conditions or by imposing a strict age limit.

A similar study shows that the conditions people include in their hypothetical ideal package vary quite considerably.[91] Only about 20 per cent would want it to cover transgender epilation, for instance, but some 90 per cent would include kidney dialysis and treatments for prostate cancer.[92] Although this research did not examine the extent to which respondents would make reimbursement dependent upon such factors as income, medical history, lifestyle or age, what it did reveal is that outcomes were not substantially different according to whether or not the direct financial consequences of their choices were revealed to participants. This suggests that, at least in some cases, stated preferences are not that different from revealed ones.

One final way to study people's actual solidarity behaviour is to look at the limited choices available within the Dutch health insurance system. Essentially, these come down to the option to increase one's excess beyond the statutory minimum (currently €385 per annum) and the voluntary take-up of supplementary cover,

[90] Hansen et al. (2005).

[91] Victoor et al. (2011, 2014).

[92] Looking at the full list of results suggests that the Dutch have a preference for medical necessity or urgency as the primary determining criterion. This may well reflect a predisposition towards the so-called "rule of rescue"—the idea that the most urgent conditions deserve priority (see Chap. 7).

which insurers offer as an add-on to the basic statutory package. When people at low risk of falling ill opt to raise their excess and so pay lower premiums, that potentially weakens risk solidarity within the system. Another way this can happen is when health insurers apply implicit forms of risk selection despite their obligation to accept all applicants for the basic package and the ban on premium differentiation. In a 2016 study the NZa found indications that such practices are straining risk solidarity within the Dutch system.[93] Whilst this does not imply that people are deliberately trying to undermine the principle of solidarity, it does reveal that it can be weakened even by the limited choices consumers are allowed to make.

### 3.3.5 Societal Sustainability Under Pressure

Societal sustainability, as mentioned previously, is all about maintaining broad public support for the health and social care system. We have found that the Dutch consider the quality and accessibility of care in some areas inadequate. They are concerned in particular about quality being compromised by staff shortages and high workloads, especially in care for the elderly, child and youth care services and mental healthcare. But note that this does not necessarily mean that these aspects are *actually* below acceptable standards—what we are talking about here is people's perceptions.

Given these widely held concerns and the importance people attach to good care, it is not surprising that there seems to be widespread support for increased funding. That is a logical response to the belief that quality and accessibility are not up to scratch, and at first glance suggests a clear orientation in favour of the political and policy response needed to achieve the desired improvement in societal sustainability. In reality, however, that solution—pumping more resources into care—just draws us away from the benefit side of societal sustainability to its cost side. And there we soon run into limits. After all, only a relatively small proportion of the population (barely more than a quarter) is willing to pay additional insurance premiums or taxes to finance the investments that would be required.

Which brings us to the notion of solidarity. As an abstract principle, this remains highly and enduringly popular. Certainly when it comes to income solidarity: there is still broad support for the principle that higher earners should contribute more than those of modest means. Much the same also applies to risk solidarity, although here we have to add some riders. As outlined above, there is a strong willingness to stand with people affected by "bad luck" (such as a genetic condition), but considerably less so in the case of the elderly and especially those afflicted by lifestyle-related diseases. All of which implies that there is a definite limit to the Dutch public's readiness to absorb the rising cost of the care system through greater income and risk solidarity. Maintaining the principle of equal access to care for all,

[93] NZa (2016).

regardless of income, will place an ever larger burden upon higher earners in particular. And the strain that puts on income solidarity is sure to restrict the room for manoeuvre in future public policy, although at this stage it is not easy to specify exactly where the boundaries will lie.

Based upon these observations, we can identify a number of impediments likely to be encountered in the future. Firstly, given the financial and staffing challenges facing the sector, it seems very probable that aspects of its quality and accessibility will come under further strain. This could dent public faith in the system and redouble calls for more investment. Secondly, the forms of solidarity already under pressure now—especially those linked to age and lifestyle—are the exact ones set to be called upon even more in the future as a result of ongoing trends in the composition and health status of the Dutch population (see Chap. 2). This means that there will be additional pressures at precisely the points where solidarity is already vulnerable. Thirdly, there are tensions around the scope of the statutory collective benefits package. People already consider care expensive, but at the same time are concerned that a more limited package would contribute towards a two-tier society.

On the one hand we hear persistent calls to improve the benefits side of the health and social care system, but on the other public attitudes towards its cost side seem to preclude the financial input that would require. Which leaves public policymakers with little room for manoeuvre. From our analysis, however, it is impossible to predict when this situation might tip over into societal unsustainability. As with the other dimensions of sustainability, there will be no single watershed moment. But we can reasonably expect the first cracks to appear in lifestyle-related healthcare, in care for the elderly and in the role played by income solidarity within our system.

How would a breakdown of societal sustainability manifest itself? In his classic work *Exit, Voice and Loyalty,* the American political economist Albert Hirschman sees two options: when a service or product is deemed to have deteriorated in quality, people can choose either "exit"—that is, switch to another organization or supplier—or "voice", meaning that they try to rectify the situation through actions or complaints that result in an improvement in quality. And the degree of loyalty they feel to the supplying organization helps determine which of the two options they choose, or in what combination. This latter factor is important in light of our earlier conclusion that whilst the Dutch very much trust their health and social care providers, that is far less the case when it comes to the institutions in this sector—and health insurers in particular. In our system, moreover, the "exit" option is very limited. Basic health insurance cover and taxes are mandatory, after all, and the private care sector is relatively small and confined in scope (provision covered by optional supplementary insurance, for instance).[94] By contrast, there is great potential for "voice" in the Dutch system. By airing discontent in the political arena or through public campaigns, for example. At the same time, this option also has limitations: in the most formal medium for expressing *voice*—elections—care is very rarely, if

[94] Nevertheless, parts of the care sector have seen an increase in parallel private provision—private nursing homes, for instance. See Bos et al. (2020).

ever, the sole issue at stake, which can make it difficult to address specific concerns properly.[95] And because "exit" is only a very limited option in care, unlike in other markets, there is a risk that warning signs of impending social unsustainability due, say, to inadequate quality or accessibility might be overlooked. A further complicating factor here is the fact that the most vulnerable groups have the fewest opportunities to express "voice" within the broad landscape of health and social care (see Chaps. 4 and 8).

Something similar applies on the cost side. Legislation and regulations can be used to enforce solidarity within the care system in the short term, but without broad public backing this approach is not sustainable for any length of time. People cannot evade compulsory contributions such as health insurance premiums, but in the long run they can weaken solidarity by political means, such as voting for a higher excess, for higher personal contributions or for greater scope for risk selection.[96] We can impose solidarity in the short term, then, but to survive in the long term that obligation must be regarded as socially acceptable and legitimate.

Perhaps the greatest risk lies in a scenario where perceptions of declining quality and accessibility are accompanied by diminishing support for the principle of solidarity. This is especially true if there is also distrust of the care system on the grounds that it is not prudent and fair, and if it is felt in parallel with that the collective benefits package is being stripped down. In that combination of circumstances, public backing for the system could well be seriously undermined. People might then come to consider the obligation to pay into it unjustified, since they feel that they are receiving little in return in terms of quality and accessibility. This could create a negative spiral in which part of the population seeks private alternatives and so support for compulsory premiums and contributions declines even further. This scenario may not be very likely, but government should nevertheless ensure that the risk of it arising is kept to an absolute minimum.

**Key Points—Societal Sustainability**

- There are clear impediments to broad public support for the health and social care system in the Netherlands.
- The Dutch feel in particular that the quality of care for the elderly, of child and youth care services and of mental healthcare is inadequate. Their main concerns are about the impact of staff shortages and excessive workloads.
- Concerns about the accessibility of care centre on waiting times and on personal costs such as the mandatory health insurance excess and direct charges, which are perceived as high even though they are actually relatively low by international standards.

(continued)

[95] Care is not unique in this, of course. The same applies to all social issues to a greater or lesser extent.

[96] Hirschman (1970).

- Solidarity by lifestyle (avoidable risks) and age (older people) is under pressure. Overall, however, the Dutch are willing to accept a high degree of income and risk solidarity.
- Trust in care providers is high, but far less so when it comes to institutions such as hospitals—and especially nursing homes and health insurers.

## 3.4 Increasing Pressure on Intertwined Sustainabilities

In the public and political debate on the sustainability of care, financial considerations have attracted the most attention. But this issue should really be viewed from a broader perspective. Safeguarding quality and accessibility, the core public values of health and social care, it is not just about financial sustainability but also about the staffing and societal dimensions. Moreover, this whole topic is more urgent than is often thought. Although a strict interpretation of financial sustainability—"Do we have the resources we need?"—could limit overall sustainability in the future, the core problem in fact lies in the increasingly tough trade-offs we are having to make. Or, in other words, in the undesirable effects of unsustainable growth both within the care sector and elsewhere. Long before the affordability of an ever-growing care system reaches a critical point, we are going to experience more and more serious adverse effects—driven especially by staffing issues—for the quality and accessibility of care, for other areas of public spending and perhaps even for our general prosperity as a nation.

Whilst financial sustainability certainly presents a challenge in the long term, staffing is the most acute and pressing dimension right now. Over time it is expected that more than a third of the national workforce will have to be employed in care in order to meet demand. The question is whether such a shift in employment in favour of the public sector—which would comprise the bulk of the economy in that situation—is feasible, never mind desirable. Our total labour force is not likely to increase much in size, whilst demand for care is growing strongly. This will make it more and more difficult to deliver the quality and accessibility the Dutch people expect from their health and social care system.

Societal sustainability is also under pressure. People have increasing concerns about the quality and accessibility of care, whilst at the same time attaching very great importance to good provision.

Solidarity is being strained too, and precisely when it comes to those areas where demand is going to be highest in the future—care for the elderly and the treatment of avoidable lifestyle-related conditions, such as the effects of smoking and obesity. Some people, moreover, want to see more investment in care but believe that its personal cost to them is already too high and so the extra resources should be generated primarily by improving efficiency. But as we show later in this report, that scenario is not really feasible. Bearing all this in mind, the greatest risk therefore seems to be a situation in which perceptions of declining quality and accessibility are accompanied by diminishing support for the principle of solidarity and confidence in the system in general. Societal sustainability thus imposes political constraints even before the limits of financial sustainability heave into view.

The three dimensions of sustainability are closely intertwined. If one worker in three in 2060 is needed by health and social care to meet demand for its services, that will inevitable engender wage competition with other sectors. This shows that financial and staffing sustainability can have opposite effects: more of one is less of the other. In addition, financial sustainability is linked in complex ways to public support for the sector. On the one hand it can be expected that as expenditure on care rises, quality will improve and its perceived benefits increase. On the other, society also has ever-higher expectations of the sector and rising spending on it only intensifies appeals for solidarity. Finally, staffing and societal sustainability are inextricably linked as well. Indeed, a lack of staff perhaps puts the greatest pressure of all on societal sustainability because it not only comes at the expense of attention for individual patients or users but can also jeopardize access to care—as we saw during the pandemic with the shortage of intensive-care nurses.

All this makes assuring sustainable care a political balancing act. Sustainability is not a matter of optimization, but rather is all about finding the equilibrium between its three dimensions which is essential to safeguard the underlying core public values of health and social care: quality and accessibility. In practice, the sustainability challenge is in fact a distributional issue: a clash between rising demand for care and constraints on the human and material resources available to provide it, compounded by people's natural reluctance to spend an increasing share of their income on that provision. The balancing act is never-ending; the trick is to perform it in such a way that the public interest continues to be upheld as effectively as possible, both within the care sector and outside it.

# Chapter 4
# Organization and Performance of Dutch Health and Social Care

> The public values of health and social care—quality and accessibility—are not adequately safeguarded in all parts of the sector.

As shown in the previous chapter, staffing, financial and societal sustainability are important to safeguard the key public values of health and social care: quality and accessibility. We described there how all three dimensions are under ongoing pressure and how the issue of sustainability in care is in practice a distributional one. This makes it important to examine the state of the public values in different parts of the system.

We now thus shift our focus from sustainability to the "outcome" of care in terms of quality and accessibility, basing our approach upon the five so-called "system laws" which underlie the sector's current structure and organization in the Netherlands. In particular, we highlight a number of impediments to quality and accessibility affecting different aspects of care. In so doing we take both a sectoral and a life-course perspective: what are the obstacles facing the sector's various component domains and its users in the various phases of their lives?

## 4.1 Current Organization of the Care Landscape

**The Five System Laws**

Since 2015, five so-called "system laws" have governed the basic organization of health and social care in the Netherlands, each regulating a different part of the system. They are the Health Insurance Act (Zorgverzekeringswet, Zvw), the Long-Term Care Act (Wet Langdurige Zorg, Wlz), the Social Support Act (Wet Maatschappelijke Ondersteuning, Wmo), the Public Health Act (Wet Publieke Gezondheidszorg, Wpg) and the Youth Act (Jeugdwet).



G. Werner et al., *Financial, Staffing and Societal Sustainability of Dutch Health Care*, Research for Policy, https://doi.org/10.1007/978-3-031-58564-7_4

The *Health Insurance Act (Zvw)* is probably the best known and, to the general public at least, the most visible of these statutes. It also accounts for the lion's share of expenditure: of the total of more than €101 billion spent on health and social care in 2019, both publicly and privately, €46.5 billion was in fields covered by the Zvw.[1] GP care, specialist medical care and some mental healthcare (see Box 4.2), as well as medicines, oral care, paramedical care, district nursing and obstetric care, are all examples of provision it regulates and finances, at least in part.

The *Long-Term Care Act (Wlz)* is probably the second best-known of the system laws, and also second in terms of its scope. It accounts for €21.3 billion of the sector's spending in 2019[2]—as the name suggests, mainly for long-term provision such as disability care and institutions, nursing homes and some mental healthcare. The Wlz focuses upon vulnerable people requiring permanent (round the clock)—and often intensive—supervision or care. In most cases this occurs in a residential setting—a nursing or care home—but support can also be provided at home, particularly in the case of elderly people and children with disabilities; in many cases they are allocated a personal budget (persoonsgebonden budget, PGB). In 2018, some 278,000 people used care governed by the Wlz and 80,000 of them received that in their own home.[3]

The *Social Support Act (Wmo)* entered into force in 2015 and devolved responsibility for a wide range of social care from central to local government. That included domestic help and support for informal carers, as well as day centres, some forms of sheltered housing, help for the homeless and parenting support—all activities with a more "social" dimension than the primarily clinical forms of care covered by the Wlz. Total spending on this provision across all Dutch local authorities amounted to €5.3 billion in 2019.[4] Unlike the Zvw and Wlz, which guarantee access to healthcare financed through the national collective insurance scheme, the social care governed by the Wmo is not an automatic entitlement. In the Netherlands it is assumed that citizens themselves are primarily responsible for the way they participate in society; but if their own network (family, friends and so on) is unable to provide any support they need in order to do so, they can turn to their local authority for assistance and it is required to respond with either generic or customized provision.

---

[1] Source: CBS Statline, table "Care expenditure and financing from 1972 onwards": https://opendata.cbs.nl/statline/#/cbs/nl/dataset/83075NED/table?ts=1624284109940. This amount includes mandatory payments only (insurance premiums and the employer's contribution), not personal ones (the insurance excess, supplementary cover and so on). Total expenditure is therefore higher.

[2] Source: CBS Statline, table "Care expenditure and financing from 1972 onwards": https://opendata.cbs.nl/statline/#/cbs/nl/dataset/83075NED/table?ts=1624284109940. Again, personal payments are not included.

[3] CBS (2018b).

[4] Source: Statistics Netherlands (CBS), "Spending under the Wmo": https://www.cbs.nl/nl-nl/onze-diensten/methoden/onderzoeksomschrijvingen/korte-onderzoeksbeschrijvingen/uitgaven-wet-maatschappelijke-ondersteuning

The *Youth Act* is the only system law which is age-led rather than covering specific forms of care. The actual provision concerned is often governed by the other system laws (usually the Zvw or Wlz), but under the Youth Act the beneficiary's local authority is responsible for its co-ordination. Spending linked to this statute amounted to €5.4–5.6 billion in 2019.[5] In that year almost half a million children and young people up to the age of 18 made use of child and youth care services in some form (see also Chap. 2).[6] These are subdivided into three categories: child and youth support (jeugdhulp), child protection (jeugdbescherming) and juvenile rehabilitation (jeugdreclassering). The first of these, child and youth support, refers to assistance offered by the local authority with parenting and upbringing problems, as well as for young people with mental disorders, intellectual disabilities or physical illnesses. Take-up of these services is voluntary, but if the situation merits it—usually meaning that the child is unsafe or at risk—and their parents or legal guardians refuse to co-operate, it is possible to enforce safeguarding interventions by means of a child protection order. Finally, juvenile rehabilitation refers to the supervision of young people who have committed a criminal offence and received a judicial referral order. In 2020 a national Youth Authority (Jeugdautoriteit) was established to oversee child and youth care services and to ensure the continuity of their crucial forms by, for example, mediating in the procurement of provision.

Through the *Public Health Act (Wpg)*, the Dutch government organizes and funds a wide variety of preventive healthcare activities. This system law is different in nature from the other four in that it focuses upon disease prevention, health promotion and health protection, and thus upon precluding the need for care rather than facilitating its delivery. But whilst the Wpg is all about prevention, not all prevention is covered by it. Not only do the other system laws also provide for activities of this kind, so too do other schemes, initiatives and measures not directly related to health and social care (see Box 4.1).

**Box 4.1: Forms of Prevention and Their Cost**

In broad terms, three forms of preventive healthcare are covered by the Wpg and other measures. *Disease prevention* is about staving off illness before it occurs or diagnosing it at an early, easier-to-treat stage—through vaccinations, for instance, or mass screening programmes like the blood spot test for newborn babies and various forms of cancer screening. *Health promotion* tries to encourage people to live healthier lives. Besides interventions in the medical domain such as public information campaigns, anti-smoking programmes and the so-called "combined lifestyle intervention" (a comprehensive behavioural change

(continued)

[5] AEF (2020).

[6] The upper age limit can be extended to 23 in certain cases, but only with the explicit approval of the local authority or a court.

**Box 4.1** (continued)

programme for obese and overweight people), connecting with the social domain and the living environment is also important here. By, for example, addressing debt problems, creating play areas (especially in deprived areas) and setting up information and training programmes.[7] Finally, *health protection* is about shielding the population from health risks. Monitoring the quality of drinking and swimming water, sewage treatment, waste disposal and road safety are just a few of its numerous aspects.

Many of the activities making up all three forms of prevention are facilitated not by the Wpg but by the other system laws governing the care sector, or even by other means altogether. Of all the system laws, the Wpg is by far the least well-funded. In 2019, according to the national budget, its allocation was just over €0.7 billion. The majority of that went to disease prevention (€521 million), followed by health protection (€125 million) and health promotion (€65 million).[8] However, total expenditure on preventive healthcare is significantly higher. In all, almost €2.2 billion was spent on forms of prevention delivered by health and social care providers in 2019.[9] And even more goes to prevention in its broadest sense: €12.5 billion (1.8 per cent of GDP) in 2015. The bulk of this money does not pass through the care budget—spending on sewerage and drinking water, for instance—and so is not considered "care expenditure".

Finally, some forms of care fall under more than one system law. Mental healthcare is a case in point: in its various forms this can be provided, financed and organized within the scope of all laws described above (see Box 4.2).

**Box 4.2: Mental Healthcare in the Netherlands**

Mental healthcare encompasses a wide range of conditions including depression, psychosis and anxiety disorders, as well as addiction care and some aspects of forensic care. Not to mention preventive activities across this broad spectrum. Since 2014, mental healthcare services in the Netherlands have been divided into three clusters: (1) mental healthcare support for GP services (specialist practice support workers); (2) basic mental healthcare; and (3) specialist mental healthcare. GPs with mental healthcare support only treat minor problems and make referrals to the other two forms. Basic mental healthcare

(continued)

[7] Broeders et al. (2018).

[8] Rijksbegroting (2019).

[9] CBS Statline, table "Care spending: care providers and financing": https://opendata.cbs.nl/statline/#/cbs/nl/dataset/84053NED/table?ts=1624286180119

**Box 4.2** (continued)

treats mild to moderate short-term conditions, whilst the specialist cluster deals with more complex and often long-term conditions. All in all, these services are delivered by a multitude of different types of institution and by all kinds of provider—not just dedicated mental healthcare institutions, but also at various other points in primary, secondary and tertiary care. They include general and university hospitals (secondary and tertiary care), where psychiatrists and other professionals (psychiatric nurses, psychologists and so on) are available. By its nature, mental healthcare falls principally under the heading "curative healthcare" (governed by the Zvw), but to an extent also within long-term care (Wlz). And other aspects count as social care (Wmo)—for instance, when patients remain living at home or return after inpatient treatment and receive support there.

**Users, Providers and Buyers and Their Roles Under the Five System Laws**

Three distinct "roles" can be distinguished within the framework created by the system laws: care user, care provider and care buyer. In other words, those who need care, those who deliver it and those who pay for it. Within the various subsectors of Dutch health and social care, these roles are played by different actors. Only the Zvw provides for a system in which market forces play a part, albeit subject to strict limitations. As Fig. 4.1 shows, this in fact consists of three separate markets. Providers of care under the Zvw are usually paid for it by health insurers, who in this case therefore play the role of care buyer. Everyone living in the Netherlands is obliged to take out a policy covering the basic statutory health benefits package with one of those insurers. They thus compete for consumers' business, creating a (regulated) market for health insurance. When a person needs some form of care, its providers then compete to supply it. In this "care delivery" market, the consumer (the "care user") is expected to base their choice of provider upon information about the quality and price of the care on offer. The third market is in care procurement, with the health insurers contracting providers to treat their policyholders at the best possible rates.

The situation created by the Zvw differs substantially from that under the other system laws, where there is usually just one care buyer—typically a local authority or an executive agency. In the academic literature, this is also referred to as a "single payer" system. The Wlz, for example, provides for regional single payers: each region has just one care buyer and so there is no health insurance market.[10] But there are still competing providers, so a care procurement market does exist. The Wmo system is similar, also with competing providers and a single buyer—in this case the

[10] There are some strong regional patterns in the relative dominance of health insurers, however; in certain parts of the country one particular insurer has a high market share.

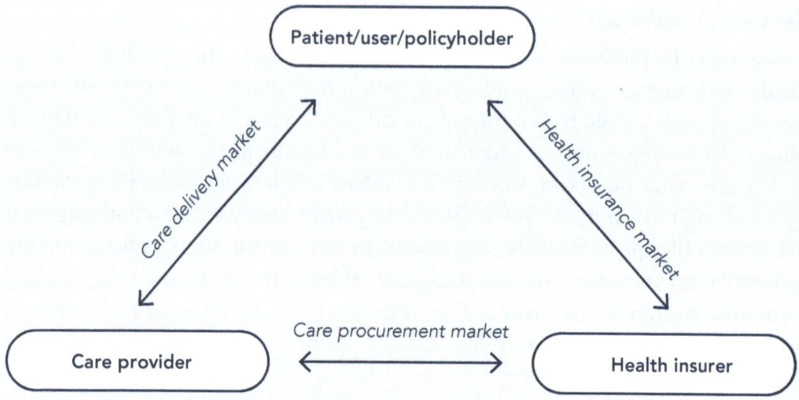


**Fig. 4.1** The regulated markets under the Zvw

local authority. Moreover, many individual beneficiaries are granted a personal budget (PGB) with which they can purchase care themselves. Users of this form of provision pay a personal contribution; since 2020 that has been a fixed "subscription fee" of €19 per month. Funding for care under the Wmo ultimately comes from municipal budgets, and in turn local authorities receive the majority of their resources from the state through the Local Government Fund (Gemeentefonds). A portion of that funding is earmarked for Wmo-based services, but that can also be supplemented with revenue from municipal taxes. Like the Wmo and Wlz, the Youth Act provides for a single local buyer of care (the local authority) and competing providers. And the funding regime is the same as under the Wmo: here again, the local authority decides how to allocate its child and youth care services grant from the Local Government Fund and whether to top that up from local resources. Activities governed by the Wpg are financed from the municipal budget too, and thus yet again ultimately from the Local Government Fund and municipal taxes. Consequently, the extent of investment in preventive healthcare varies from one local authority to another.[11]

**Actors and Responsibilities**

The framework created by the five system laws governing health and social care in the Netherlands involves a multitude of actors, numerous distinct monetary flows and a host of supervisory and regulatory bodies. Dozens of governmental, public, hybrid and private parties at the local, regional and national levels are responsible for executive and managerial tasks, and a huge number of diverse private providers deliver actual care in all its forms—most on a non-profit basis.[12] They range in size

[11] Soeters and Verhoeks (2015).

[12] Regular Dutch hospitals are non-profit foundations, for instance. Specialist clinics are allowed to operate on commercial basis, however.

from individual practitioners working alone to large, complex organizations such as hospitals and mental healthcare institutions. At national level, ultimate responsibility for the system as a whole lies with the state, and specifically with the Minister of Health, Welfare and Sport (Volksgezondheid, Welzijn en Sport, VWS).[13] For the most part, however, neither the minister nor their department is involved directly in the day-to-day governance or management of health and social care; in different parts of the system, those responsibilities are devolved to different executive and regulatory organizations or to lower levels of government. And whilst the ministry's steering role in some domains was intensified or strengthened on a temporary basis during the Covid-19 pandemic, even then primacy generally remained with care providers, community health services and other actors.

A number of institutions exercise responsibilities across the entire system, not just in one part of it. The Health and Youth Care Inspectorate (Inspectie voor de Gezondheidszorg en Jeugd, IGJ), for instance, oversees the quality, safety and accessibility of healthcare and child and youth care services, of providers in these domains and of medicines and medical devices. The National Health Care Institute (Zorginstituut Nederland, ZiN) advises on the composition of the basic statutory health benefits package, and is also tasked with quality control.[14] As part of the latter remit, for example, in 2017 it compiled a quality framework for nursing homes that set requirements for the standard of their staffing. Working with all relevant parties, the ZiN also facilitates and monitors a programme to encourage "appropriate use"—provision that adds value—in specialist medical care through more systematic evaluation.[15] The Dutch Healthcare Authority (Nederlandse Zorgautoriteit, NZa), meanwhile, monitors the implementation of and compliance with the system laws, amongst other things by ensuring efficient spending of care funds. Another of its tasks in this respect, in conjunction with the Netherlands Authority for Consumers and Markets (Autoriteit Consument en Markt, ACM), is to prevent providers and insurers accruing excessive market power. In addition, the NZa oversees the accessibility of care (by, for example, monitoring emergency response and waiting times). In addition, a whole range of other actors are active outside the scope of the system laws and the other statutes regulating health and social care (see Box 4.3).

---

[13] In prime minister Mark Rutte's third government ("Rutte III", 2017–2022), responsibility for the Dutch health and social care system was divided between two cabinet ministers and one junior minister (staatssecretaris)—all in the Ministry of Health, Welfare and Sport—for the first time. For the sake of convenience, we refer here to "the Minister of Health, Welfare and Sport" because this has traditionally been a unified portfolio and the department continues to work with one budget. Nor will we discuss here either the exact division of responsibilities in Rutte III or the situation in its successor administration, "Rutte IV" (since January 2022), which was in power when this report was completed.

[14] The ZiN originally had a separate Quality Institute (Kwaliteitsinstituut) as a satellite organization. That has since been disbanded and subsumed into the ZiN itself.

[15] https://www.zorgevaluatiegepastgebruik.nl/de-zegg-partijen/

**Box 4.3: Actors and Responsibilities Outside the Scope of the System Laws**

Beyond the scope of the system laws, many other actors are active within the broader Dutch health and social care system. These include interest groups and professional bodies such as the Federation of Medical Specialists (Federatie Medisch Specialisten, FMS) and Nurses & Carers Netherlands (Verpleegkundigen & Verzorgenden Nederland, V&VN), scientific associations like the Dutch College of General Practitioners (Nederlandse Huisartsen Genootschap, NHG), trade unions including FNV Healthcare (FNV Zorg) and patient organizations such as the Netherlands Patients' Federation (Patiëntenfederatie Nederland). There are also numerous other laws governing care or aspects of it. These range from general legislation applicable more widely than in care alone, such as privacy, competition and administrative laws, to specific statutes covering a particular part of the sector or particular institutions. Examples are the Medicines Act (Geneesmiddelenwet), the Licensing of Healthcare Institutions Act (Wet toelating zorginstellingen, WTZi) and the Individual Healthcare Professions Act (Wet op de beroepen in de individuele gezondheidszorg, BIG-wet), which regulates professional qualifications.

Some aspects of care itself fall outside the scope of the five system laws, too. Take occupational medicine (financed and practised by or on behalf of employers) and insurance medicine (financed and practised by or on behalf of non-health insurers), for instance. It is also possible to develop policy with a health focus—or with implications for it—in other public policy domains. Examples include measures to improve road safety, occupational health and safety, environmental quality and so on.

What is clear from all this is that the matrix of laws, actors, institutions and regulatory mechanisms making up the Dutch care sector is highly complex. The system laws cover a very broad spectrum of health provision, encompassing the full range of health and social care, and each imposes different forms of organization, responsibilities and sources of funding within its particular ambit. A certain degree of delineation is unavoidable if the sector is to be organized effectively. But ordinary people ultimately have little time for relatively abstract concepts like "system laws". They have a need for care, and they want it satisfied. Nevertheless, they do sometimes find themselves caught up in the complexity of the system. Transitions between the jurisdiction of the different system laws, in particular, do not always run smoothly. When a patient's condition deteriorates and so they no longer fall under the Wmo, for example, but under the Wlz. Or when it improves and they need care at home (under the Wmo) rather than in hospital (Zvw). People can and do experience problems at these "boundaries" (or "partitions" as they are known in the jargon), and that can affect the quality of their care. Or even the very sustainability of our system—as, for instance, when someone occupies an expensive hospital bed for longer than necessary because home care has not yet been arranged. Patients with multiple conditions (multimorbidity) also frequently encounter partition issues. What if the different forms of care they receive under the Wlz, the Zvw and the Wmo are not properly harmonized? That can cause major logistical problems for patients and providers alike and lead to high reconciliation costs. In many cases it also has financial repercussions for the person concerned, the so-called "care trap". And it is not only users who run into these partitions, but care providers as well (see Box 4.4).

**Box 4.4: Departitioning and Integrated Care**

"Partitions" can make it difficult for someone to receive the care they need, or for providers to deliver it. And overcoming such barriers often involves high transaction costs. In response, there have been frequent calls for "departitioning". Which in many cases in fact ultimately means "repartitioning", in the sense that barriers perceived as inconvenient are simply repositioned or replaced by new ones elsewhere. Creating a real risk that the patient will eventually run into the same problems again, just at a different point in the system.

One important concept in the context of departitioning is "integrated care". The National Institute for Public Health and the Environment (Rijksinstituut voor Volksgezondheid en Milieu, RIVM) defines this as "the coherent design of prevention, care and welfare so as to improve health and the quality of care and to temper the growth of care costs".[16] Care chains for diabetes are one relatively well-known form of integrated care. The concept can also be extended beyond the care system into other domains. In many cases this means involving social services as well, in the form of preventive activities, local amenities and welfare provision. So a patient with diabetes, for example, not only receives the medical care they need for their condition but also support if they are lonely or not socially adept.

Departitioning—which often involves close collaboration between different professional disciplines—does appear to make a positive contribution when it comes to factors like patient satisfaction and the quality of care, but there is little evidence of its effectiveness in reducing the use of care or its cost.[17,18,19,20,21]

---

[16] RIVM (2015).

[17] Baxter et al. (2018).

[18] Wolfe et al. (2020).

[19] Rocks et al. (2020).

[20] Damery et al. (2016).

[21] Looman et al. (2019).

**Key Points—Current Organization of the Care Landscape**

- The five so-called "system laws" regulate health and social care in the Netherlands for different user groups. Some forms of care are covered by more than one of these laws (mental healthcare, for example).
- Not only within the framework created by the system laws, but also outside it, a multitude of actors, numerous distinct monetary flows and a host of supervisory and regulatory bodies are active.
- The system of limited market forces allowed to operate under the Health Insurance Act (Zvw) in fact creates three strictly regulated markets: for health insurance (competition between insurers for policyholders), for care delivery (competition between providers for patients) and for care procurement (negotiated contracts between insurers and providers).
- Under the other system laws there is only one care buyer per geographical area or region, so no market forces are at work.

## 4.2 Quality and Accessibility of Care from a Life-Course Perspective

Following our discussion of the formal structure of the Dutch health and social system, we now turn our attention to its overall performance. To do this we look at outcomes in terms of quality and accessibility across the various fields of care. Criteria widely used internationally to assess these factors are life expectancy, preventable mortality from treatable diseases and perceived health (see Box 4.5).[22] From that perspective the Netherlands appears to be one of the best-performing countries in the world, along with Switzerland, Japan and Spain. This picture applies particularly to curative healthcare, but our GP care, acute care and disability care are also high in quality and, from a comparative perspective, generally well-accessible. Table 4.1 summarizes findings for the Netherlands from various sources with regard to the quality and accessibility of care in these fields across all stages of life.

**Box 4.5: Care Outcomes Compared Internationally**

Viewed from an international perspective, there appears to be relatively little cause for concern about Dutch health and social care in terms of either its quality or its accessibility. OECD figures, for example, reveal that the Netherlands has a relatively low rate of avoidable deaths (101 per

(continued)

[22] OECD (2019b).

**Box 4.5** (continued)

100,000 people, versus 133 for the OECD as a whole) and a very modest proportion of the population reporting poor health (4.5 versus 8.7 per cent). Accessibility also seems to be in order, with only 12.4 per cent of the population reporting an unmet desire for care, compared with an OECD average of 20.6 per cent. As for the financial dimension of accessibility, the Netherlands actually comes out top: just 5.7 per cent of people report that they have foregone care for financial reasons, well below the OECD average of 17.2 per cent. The OECD therefore regards Dutch health and social care as generally effective and accessible.

**Table 4.1** Quality and accessibility of care in all life stages

| Field | Quality | Accessibility |
|---|---|---|
| Acute care[a] | Providers manage quality of care adequately[b,c] | Under pressure due to rising demand for care (ageing population) and impending shortage of care professionals. |
| GP care | High quality, as demonstrated in several international studies[d] | Ninety per cent patients satisfied with opening hours and accessibility of their GP surgery[e] |
| Curative healthcare | The Netherlands is amongst the best performers[f] | Within Europe, the Netherlands is one of the countries with the best access to care. But there are long waiting lists in mental healthcare for children and young people. |
| Disability care[g] | Quality adequate to good[h] But clients too often experience unequal and dependent position with regard to caregiver and provider[i] | Three out of five people (58 per cent) with intellectual disabilities fail to arrange the care they need from local authorities[j] |

[a]"Acute care" encompasses acute hospital, obstetric, ambulance and GP care
[b]https://www.zorginstituutnederland.nl/publicaties/publicatie/2020/02/19/kwaliteitskader-spoedzorgketen
[c]https://puc.overheid.nl/nza/doc/PUC_529500_22/1/
[d]OECD (2019b)
[e]Brabers and De Jong (2019)
[f]OECD (2019b)
[g]About 113,800 people with intellectual, physical or sensory disabilities made use of long-term care in 2018. More than 85 per cent (96,000) of them had an intellectual disability
[h]https://www.igj.nl/actueel/nieuws/2020/01/13/steekproef-inspectie-onder-26-kleine-instellingen-gehandicaptenzorg-de-meeste-scoren-voldoende-tot-goed. Quality framework, developed in the field, since 2017
[i]Schuurman (2018)
[j]Nieuwenhuis (2018)

That said, there are still problems in all of these sectors. The waiting lists at Dutch hospitals, for instance, were lengthening even before the Covid-19 pandemic.[23] And issues in other parts of the sector are even more serious, sometimes even urgent. Moreover, these are fields for the most part not included in international statistics. In particular, care for elderly people dependent upon support, for young people—especially those in need of mental healthcare, child protection or juvenile rehabilitation—and for patients with severe mental disorders (specialist mental healthcare). The previous chapter showed that it is precisely these areas which the Dutch public is increasingly concerned about.[24]

Below we examine the impediments to good and accessible care at different stages of life: the "first thousand days" from pre-conception to the first years of life; childhood and adolescence; adulthood, with a focus upon people with mental disorders; and old age.

### *4.2.1 Care During the "First Thousand Days"*

The period from pre-conception through pregnancy, birth and the first years of life—the "first thousand days"—are crucial in every child's development.[25] The majority of children make a good start in life and grow up healthy, but for a substantial number[26] this is not the case due to unfavourable pregnancy outcomes (premature birth, low birth weight or a combination of the two). In the Netherlands these are more common in areas of low socioeconomic status where poverty, unemployment and debt problems are commonplace.[27] Children born into single-parent families or into families where both parents are using mental health services are at an increased risk of suffering problems in their own mental (or physical) development. Premature birth and retarded foetal growth may be associated with a higher risk of various diseases.[28]

There was great shock and disbelief when, in 2004, European figures revealed that the rate of perinatal mortality (death from the 20-second week of pregnancy onwards or in the first 28 days after birth) in the Netherlands was comparable with that in eastern European countries, and certainly well above the average for western Europe as a whole. The causes were sought in a lack of standardized care (guidelines, co-operation), the incidence of twin pregnancies following in vitro fertilization and of teenage pregnancies, insufficient anticipation of premature births and the

---

[23] See https://www.volksgezondheidenzorg.info/prestatie-indicatoren-voor-gezondheidszorg/toegankelijkheid#node-wachttijd-ziekenhuiszorg-polikliniek

[24] Dekker and Den Ridder (2019).

[25] Roseboom (2018).

[26] About 25,000 (14 per cent of the total) each year; see Waelput et al. (2017).

[27] Steegers (2017).

[28] Raju et al. (2017).

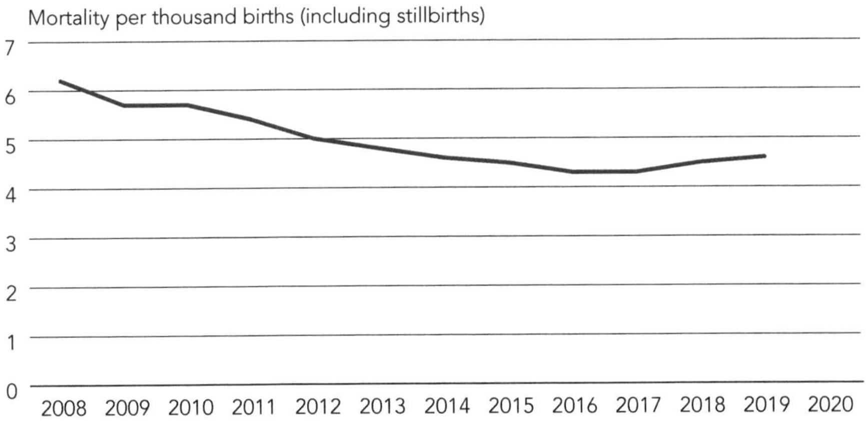


**Fig. 4.2** Evolution of perinatal mortality, 2008–2018. (Source: Perinned 2020)

prevalence of risk factors in pregnant women (smoking,[29] alcohol consumption, obesity and low socioeconomic status). Measures addressing these and other factors likely to increase the vulnerability of pregnant women[30] resulted in a decline in perinatal mortality in the period 2010–2015. The Netherlands is now close to the European average on this indicator (see Fig. 4.2).

How have the quality and accessibility of maternity care fared since then? Perinatal mortality stagnated from 2015 onwards, and in recent years it has even risen slightly again. Perhaps implementation of the Integrated Maternity-Care Standard (Zorgstandaard Integrale Geboortezorg)[31] registered with the ZiN's Quality Institute (Kwaliteitsinstituut; see note 14) in 2016 will eventually reverse this, but a three-year evaluation by the RIVM of an integrated maternity-care pilot has shown no significant impact upon care outcomes as yet.[32] Whether that is related to the faltering implementation of integrated maternity care is unclear.[33] Whatever the case, a comparison of the Dutch figures with those from Scandinavian countries shows that there is still room for improvement.[34] The quality and accessibility of

[29] The number of women who smoke during pregnancy remains substantial: 16 per cent of those with lower education, 11.5 per cent of those with secondary education and 2.7 per cent of those with higher education (https://www.staatvenz.nl/kerncijfers/roken-vrouwen-tijdens-zwangersc-hap). Trimbos and WODC (2020).

[30] Steegers et al. (2020).

[31] "Integrated maternity care" refers to the entire course of care from the pre-conception phase to the first six weeks after birth, including co-operation between the providers involved (maternity services, midwives and gynaecologists). In its integrated form, this is demand-driven and mother-centred.

[32] RIVM (2020c).

[33] Ministerie van Volksgezondheid, Welzijn en Sport (2020).

[34] See Euro-Peristat Project (2018). In 2017 a "maternity care agenda" for 2018–2022 was drawn up by the Dutch College for Perinatal Care (College Perinatale Zorg, CPZ). This sets out plans to further strengthen maternity care services in the Netherlands in the coming years.

maternity care are under pressure in some regions due to a scarcity of care professionals there. And Covid-19 has only further increased that pressure.[35]

Unfortunately, little progress appears to have been made in respect of preventive interventions in the pre-conception period. Pre-conception care refers to the package of measures taken before conception to promote the health of the future mother and her child, and to help her make informed reproductive choices. This topic has been on the agenda for 30 years, during which numerous projects have been conducted and a raft of scientific publications, reports and evaluations have been published showing the opportunities offered by pre-conception care. Not only do these interventions positively influence pregnancy outcomes, they are also cost-effective and even cost-saving.[36] So why are they still not being implemented widely and successfully? The problem, it seems, is a persistent lack of knowledge on the part of care providers about the meaning and substance of pre-conception care, in both its general of specialist forms. Time constraints also appear to play a role here.[37] Moreover, the target group—people with a desire to have children—can be difficult to reach; whilst they are open to information about pre-conception care and recognize its importance, few take the next step and actually arrange a consultation.

**Key Points—Care During the "First Thousand Days"**

- The "first thousand days" are crucial in every child's development. But a proportion of children do not make a good start due to premature birth, low birth weight or a combination of the two. This can lead to serious health problems.
- In the Netherlands, unfavourable pregnancy outcomes are more common in areas of low socioeconomic status.
- The Netherlands scored well above the western European average for perinatal mortality in 2004. Changes to the organization of maternity care improved the situation from 2010 onwards.
- A shortage of care professionals is putting pressure on the quality and accessibility of maternity care.

### 4.2.2 *Care Services for Children, Adolescents and Young Adults*

Most young people in the Netherlands are doing well. Some, however, need support in the form of child and youth care services. These include children with disabilities, with mental health problems and from families for whom parenting and

[35] van der Erf and Strijbosch (2020).

[36] Gezondheidsraad (2007) and Doyle et al. (2009).

[37] Schonewille-Rosman et al. (2019).

upbringing are problematic. In Chap. 2 we noted that the demand for child and youth care services has increased significantly over the years. This presents local authorities with a serious financial challenge. Total expenditure on child and youth care services in 2019 was in the range €5.4–5.6 billion, well exceeding the allocated budget for that year of €3.8 billion. That makes the deficit between €1.6 billion and €1.8 billion.[38]

In what state are the quality and accessibility of child and youth care services since their decentralization to local authorities in 2015? Inspectorate reports have been very vocal about these aspects in a number of specific fields. One, for example, described the failure to provide immediate and appropriate care to vulnerable young people subject to child protection and juvenile rehabilitation orders as "not acceptable".[39] It found that the certified institutions to which responsibility for these tasks is delegated by the public authorities are unable to fulfil their statutory mandate adequately due to the severe problems affecting the youngsters concerned combined with staff shortages, turnover and absenteeism, a lack of appropriate provision available for immediate deployment and insufficient financial security. In response, the ministers responsible (Health, Welfare and Sport; Justice and Security) acknowledged that the transformation of child and youth care services is a wide-ranging process and that their quality and accessibility still leave much to be desired.[40] As well as taking a series of measures to enable these services to be delivered regionally or supraregionally, the ministers also pledged greater financial assistance for local authorities.[41] They further indicated that they would take specific action in response to the concerns identified with regard to staffing capacity and reach clear agreements with the 42 child and youth care regions on issues including progress in tackling waiting lists. And in spring 2021 the Social and Economic Council (Sociaal-Economische Raad, SER) released a ten-point plan to improving these services in the short term.[42]

Inspectors have also pulled no punches about the state of mental healthcare for young people since the introduction of Youth Act.[43] Points they criticize include the lack of expertise to be found in local teams, the excessive focus during triage upon

---

[38] AEF (2020).

[39] IGJ and IJV (2019).

[40] *Kamerstukken* ii 2019/2020, 31839, no. 730.

[41] As of 2021, a total of €1 billion had been made available to local authorities. After the Association of Dutch Local Authorities (VNG) filed a case against the state to force arbitration on the grounds that the current budgets were grossly inadequate, a "committee of sages" was formed and—accepting its conclusion—the Ministry of Health, Welfare and Sport pledged an additional €1,31 billion for 2022 (https://www.rijksoverheid.nl/actueel/nieuws/2021/06/03/ruim-%E2%82%AC13-miljard-extra-naar-gemeenten-voor-tekorten-jeugdzorg-in-2022).

[42] SER (2021b).

[43] Friele et al. (2019).

diagnosis rather "the whole child", insufficient co-operation with specialist mental healthcare providers and the huge differences between local authorities in how they organize provision and in their supervisory arrangements. They also point out that a lack of measurable indicators hinders the ability to evaluate and manage the care provided based upon substantiated data. Moreover, the IGJ notes that Covid-19 has significantly exacerbated the above issues. As a result of the restrictive measures imposed to fight the pandemic, both the number of young people with mental health problems and the severity of their conditions have increased, and existing waiting lists have lengthened further.[44] In a number of regions the providers of appropriate specialist care, in particular, have become unable to meet demand and are also coming under severe budgetary pressure.[45]

**Key Points—Care Services for Children, Adolescents and Young Adults**

- Child and youth care services face major challenges with regard to quality and accessibility. In particular when it comes to providing immediate and appropriate care to vulnerable young people subject to child protection and juvenile rehabilitation orders.
- The decentralization of child and youth care services in 2015 has further magnified these issues.
- The accessibility and quality of mental healthcare for young people, especially specialist provision, are inadequate. The pandemic has only worsened the situation in some regions, leading to a lack of prompt and appropriate help for children with severe mental disorders.

### 4.2.3 *Care for Adults with Mental Disorders*

Measured on an annual basis, nearly a fifth of Dutch adults experienced a mental disorder in the period 2007–2009.[46] Often these are transient and pass with appropriate treatment, and sometimes even of their own accord. The number of people suffering from severe mental disorders (SMDs) has remained fairly stable for many years.[47] The Netherlands has traditionally had a relatively large capacity at inpatient mental healthcare facilities for people with these conditions, but since 2013 the national government, care providers, health insurers and patient organizations have agreed to scale that back in favour of greater capacity and better quality in outpatient care.

---

[44] Although there is in fact no comprehensive system for the reporting of waiting lists in this field; see Van den Berg et al. (2014).

[45] IGJ (2021).

[46] Veerbeek et al. (2012).

[47] At about 210,000, most of whom are not treated in hospital; some 180,000 receive outpatient care only. See https://www.vektis.nl/intelligence/publicaties/factsheet-ernstige-psychiatrische-aandoeningen

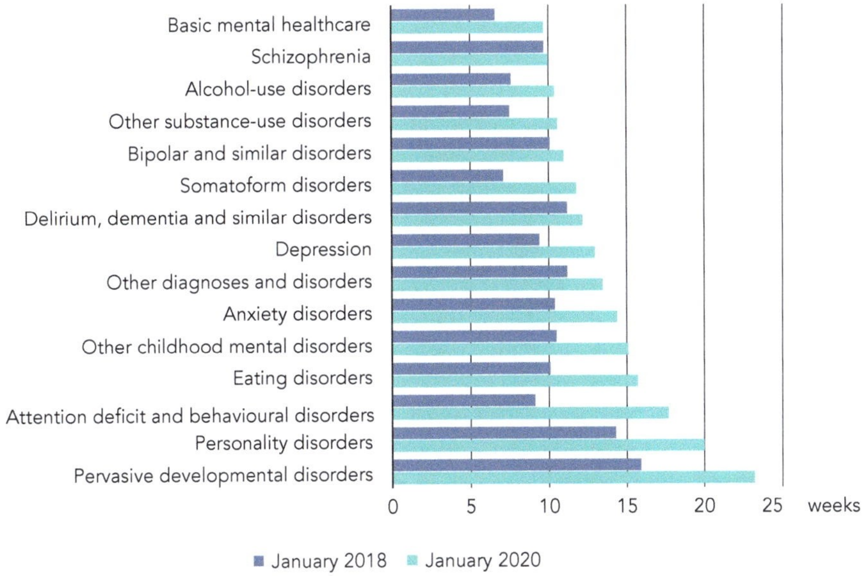


**Fig. 4.3** Waiting times in mental healthcare by diagnosis, January 2018–January 2020 (in weeks). (Source: vektis 2020)

Inspectorate IGJ has been critical of the quality of mental healthcare, and even more so of its accessibility. An alarming report on this topic was published in 2018,[48] whilst a follow-up report from 2020[49] showed that outpatient care in regions inspected by the IGJ had been lacking in capacity and consistency of care for many years. The inspectors further noted that the number of residential mental health facilities has been declining rapidly (the number of days spent in specialist mental healthcare fell by 24 per cent in the period 2013–2017), but the increase in outpatient capacity has failed to keep up with this trend. The following problems were encountered: waiting lists, insufficient co-operation between mental healthcare and GPs, barriers to discharge from care facilities due to a lack of co-ordination between them and local authorities and varying experiences with health insurers. The scale of these issues varied widely across the country.

The waiting lists, according to the IGJ, are the result of reduced throughput and lack of co-operation, and they remain stubborn in their prevalence. Figure 4.3 shows that waiting times in mental healthcare have increased across the board over the past two years. And that they are shortest in basic mental healthcare. Waiting time is divided into two components: an application period and a wait for actual treatment. The former exceeds the maximum deemed acceptable—known in the Netherlands as the "Treek norm"—in all diagnosis categories.[50] The wait for treatment is

[48] IGJ (2018).

[49] IGJ (2020a).

[50] IGJ and NZA (2020).

shortest in basic mental healthcare, but much longer in the more severe categories. With regard to waiting lists, the IGJ noted a striking lack of data from which it is possible to manage them effectively (such as epidemiological care-demand data at the regional level). In a joint statement, the IGJ and NZa recently declared that waiting times have to be reduced. To achieve this, GPs, psychiatrists, psychologists and institutions at the regional level need to co-operate far better when referring patients with mental health problems.[51] The authors also point out the roles that health insurers and local authorities should be playing.

Another area of concern is staff shortages. Mental health nurses and professional carers also increasingly consider this a problem; in 2013 some 25 per cent of them felt there were not enough staff to provide good care, a proportion which had risen to 43 per cent by 2019.[52] Mental healthcare providers appear to be struggling to attract new practitioners. A shortage of training places is partly to blame, but so too is the fact that more and more psychiatrists are opting for self-employment. The Netherlands Court of Audit (Algemene Rekenkamer) has come to the same conclusions as the IGJ, putting the number of people requiring specialist mental healthcare—most with severe psychiatric disorders—at 11,000. To the causes cited by the IGJ, the court adds problems discharging inpatients as well as insufficient inpatient treatment capacity and perverse financial incentives. Apparently, it is more advantageous for providers to help patients with relatively mild care needs before those with more serious requirements.[53] According its 2017 coalition agreement, the previous Dutch government (2017–2022) believed that the solution to the problem of waiting lists lay in "the regions", but the Court of Audit considers them a product of imbalances in the system and argues that the responsibility rests with national government.

**Key Points—Care for Adults with Mental Disorders**

- The quality and accessibility of mental healthcare, especially the accessibility of specialist care, are cause for concern. To a large extent, financial and staffing problems are to blame for this.
- The number of inpatient facilities has been decreasing rapidly, whilst outpatient capacity has not increased accordingly. This is putting huge pressure on quality and accessibility.
- Problems include waiting lists, insufficient co-operation between mental healthcare and GPs, barriers to discharge from care facilities due to a lack of co-ordination between them and local authorities, a lack of management data and perverse financial incentives.

[51] The official "acceptable waiting time" between registration and treatment is 14 weeks.

[52] Incidentally, the percentages are higher—in equal measure—in hospital care and long-term care. See https://www.volksgezondheidenzorg.info

[53] Algemene Rekenkamer (2020a).

### 4.2.4 Care for the Elderly

In reforming long-term care in 2015, one of the government's declared aims was to systematically reduce rising expenditure on provision up until then governed by the Exceptional Medical Expenses Act (Algemene Wet Bijzondere Ziektekosten, AWBZ). This involved cuts: residential facilities providing only basic care were no longer funded and responsibility for supervised care of the elderly, day centres and the like was transferred to local authorities under the new Wmo—but with substantially reduced financing. Local authorities are currently facing large overspends of their social support budgets and the national government has had to pump large sums of money into long-term residential care after its quality was found to be substandard.[54]

As for the accessibility of long-term care, waiting lists for nursing and care homes have increased systematically since 2018. Figure 4.4 shows the month-by-month data from 2015 onwards.

As the diagram reveals, the number of people with disabilities on the waiting lists has remained roughly constant in recent years (420 on average).[55] In the nursing and care homes (for the elderly) category, however, the number increased systematically

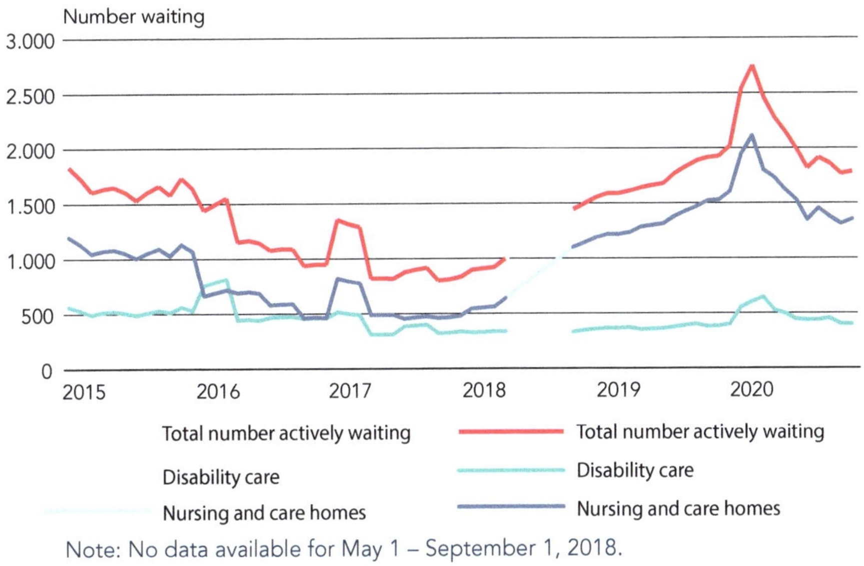


**Fig. 4.4** Number of people waiting for long-term care under the Wlz, 2015–2020 (monthly figures). NB. No data available for 1 May-1 September 2018. Sources: Statistics Netherlands and IStandaarden (https://mlzopendata.cbs.co.uk/#/MLZ/en/dataset/40046NED/table?dl=45D41; https://www.istandaarden.nl/wachtlijsten/archief-wachtlijsten/archief-2014 (multiple years))

[54] Kruse et al. (2021).

[55] The Treek norm for long-term care covered by the Wlz is six weeks.

from around 1000 in 2017 to a peak of more than 2700 in February 2020. These may not seem that many, but with a population of approximately 110,000 nursing home residents it represents some 2 per cent of the total. The curve has only turned downward more recently due to deaths in nursing homes during the Covid-19 pandemic.

Decentralization was largely intended to save costs, but in part also driven by a desire to bring the delivery of care closer to the community and so better match it with individual needs. But we still see local authorities struggling with their new tasks. In short, there are important questions surrounding the sustainable organization of this form of provision.[56] An international comparison of long-term and social care for the elderly produced for this report[57] has found that Japan, Denmark, Germany and the United Kingdom, like the Netherlands, appear to be struggling with the problem of ever-increasing demand combined with calls for better quality. All the countries mentioned are trying to reduce reliance upon nursing homes and instead encouraging older people to keep living at home. The Danes have been the most successful in this effort. Japan initially opted for more residential care to improve both its quality and the quality of life for the elderly, but soon ran into financial barriers. In any case, enabling people to remain longer in their own homes does not necessarily mean that they consume less care. Moreover, the working-age population is declining everywhere and informal care alone is never adequate. In face of these challenges, the countries listed are all making different choices. And in their endeavours to manage the situation with quality in mind, all to some extent have been oscillating between more centralized and more decentralized approaches.[58]

In recent years, staff shortages in long-term care have become more and more acute in the Netherlands. Figure 4.5 shows that nurses and professional carers in this field themselves feel that the personnel at their own workplaces are increasingly underqualified. And we have already seen, in Box 3.6, that there is a clear relationship between a lack of qualified staff on the one hand and perceived lower quality and sustainability of care on the other.

The state of Dutch residential nursing care hit the headlines in mid-2016 when the IGJ published a "blacklist" of homes it claimed were delivering substandard care. But an improvement programme launched in 2015 under the title "Dignity and Pride, Loving Care for Our Elderly People" (Waardigheid en Trots, liefdevolle zorg voor onze ouderen) and the quality framework for nursing homes adopted by the ZiN in 2017 have since boosted quality quite substantially. The quality framework, for example, sets out what clients and their loved ones should expect from nursing homes. Following visits to a large number of providers, in 2020 the IGJ found that the delivery of person-centred care—one of the major shortcomings identified in 2016—had greatly improved. Nevertheless, the inspectors did still find areas where things needed to be done better; in particular when it came to employing enough staff with appropriate skills and to the systematic monitoring and enhancement of

[56] Kruse et al. (2021).

[57] Kruse et al. (2021).

[58] Kruse et al. (2021).

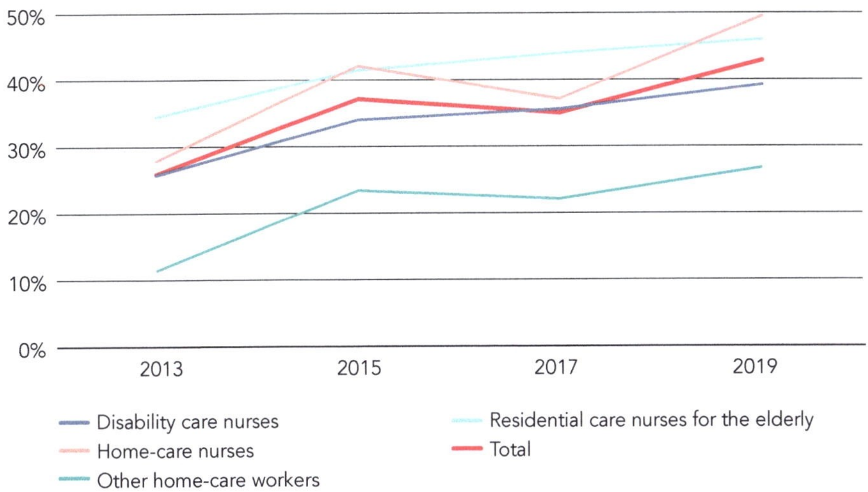


**Fig. 4.5** Insufficiently qualified staff in long-term care, 2013–2019, according to nurses and professional carers. (Source: The State of Public Health and Care, Nivel Nursing and Care Panel, 2020)

quality and safety. Concerning the latter point, however, it has also been argued that the standardized safety norms applicable throughout the care sector may be too rigid for nursing and care homes. An example showing how residents' own wishes and desires can instead be prioritized is described in Box 4.6.

**Box 4.6: Enjoying Life in Nursing Care**

Safety is a priority at Dutch nursing homes, and as such is often strictly regulated. But well-being is at least as important for vulnerable residents in the final phase of their lives. In a pilot project supported by the Ministry of Health, Welfare and Sport, the "Life Enjoyment Plan for Nursing Care" (Leefplezierplan voor de zorg), between April 2017 and April 2019 eleven residential care organizations investigated what happens when residents' own wishes and desires are taken as the benchmark of quality. The results were promising. Residents, their families, friends and informal carers were very enthusiastic, as were team members. Focusing upon positive experiences enhanced nurses' and professional carers' job satisfaction; they really enjoyed being able to make a difference to their residents' quality of life. Given this successful outcome, the pilot has since been followed up with a two-year project scaling up use of the Life Enjoyment Plan from team level to cover two entire homes.[59]

[59] https://www.leydenacademy.nl/leefplezierplan-op-locatie/

That the commitment to safety was lopsided, without at the same time properly anticipating potential risks, became painfully clear during the first wave of Covid-19. Not only were nursing homes omitted entirely from the emergency preparedness plans drawn up by the Ministry of Health, Welfare and Sport and the RIVM, but personal protective equipment (PPE) and tests were also in short supply, resulting in a huge number of infections and deaths in these facilities.[60] Lockdown measures, including a ban on visits, were strictly enforced, leaving many elderly people desperately lonely and their quality of life also compromised in other ways. In mid-2020 the IGJ conducted interviews on a large scale to gather information about quality and safety in nursing, residential and home care. Its conclusion was these services had shown resilience and demonstrated their ability to innovate quickly and act in concert when necessary.[61] The quality of home care appeared to have suffered during the pandemic, however, not least because many clients themselves refused to be visited for fear of infection during the period when PPE was largely unavailable. As a result of their experiences during the first wave, providers expressed the importance of allowing scope for personal customization in order to put the well-being of individual clients first. In addition, day centres should be allowed to continue operating on a wider scale so as to provide respite for informal carers.

Over a quarter of over-75 s in the Netherlands use community-based care services such as district nursing. To improve this provision, a quality framework for district nursing was adopted in 2018 and additional funding made available for the period 2019–2022. That financial injection (€455 million), enshrined in the framework agreement for district nursing, was intended to enhance quality, to ensure the delivery of the right care in the right place and to prevent subsequent demand for more expensive provision. A questionnaire-based survey of nurses and professional carers in 2019 (the Nivel Nursing and Care Panel) found that awareness of the quality framework itself remains patchy, although the vast majority of respondents did feel that care was being delivered in line with its criteria as described to them.[62] Areas in need of improvement include team composition and co-ordination with clients on the timing of care. Although this sounds positive, there are still stumbling blocks. Those senior citizens most in need of district nursing services also tend to be those with a limited income, education, support network and life, digital and self-management skills. The longer they live at home, the more likely elderly people are to suffer falls, dehydration or malnourishment and so require emergency hospitalization. But hospitals strive to discharge their patients as quickly as possible, which often results in these people returning to a precarious home situation where little or

[60] https://www.vilans.nl/artikelen/analyse-waarom-de-ouderenzorg-achterbleef-tijdens-de-coronacrisis

[61] IGJ (2020b).

[62] Ninety per cent of those surveyed indicated that their "clients" often or always have access to their own patient records, 88 per cent felt that they provide safe care and 85 per cent believed that this care is provided by good and qualified professionals (https://www.nivel.nl/nl/nieuws/wijkverpleegkundigen-kwaliteit-van-ons-werk-goed-maar-kwaliteitskader-wijkverpleging-slecht).

nothing has changed. In fact, one in three who do so die within six months. It is to improve this prognosis that initiatives like the "transmural care bridge" have been developed (see Box 4.7).

**Box 4.7: Transmural Care Bridge Cuts Deaths by More than a Third**
The aim of the so-called "transmural care bridge" is to prevent mortality, loss of function and rehospitalization in frail elderly people. This is done by identifying those at risk whilst they are in hospital, drawing up a personal care and treatment plan for them (jointly by the geriatric and nursing teams) and ensuring what is known as a "warm transfer" to home-based care. A district nurse then monitors the subject more closely than usual, visiting them at home up to five times in the first few months after discharge when they are at their most vulnerable. The effect of this integrated care trajectory has been tested in a randomized clinical trial involving 674 elderly people; half received the transmural care bridge intervention, the other half were discharged from hospital in the usual way. Thirty days after discharge, 37 per cent fewer members of the intervention group had died by comparison with the control group.[63]

**Key Points—Care for the Elderly**
- Shortages of professional staff and informal carers are undermining care for the elderly.
- A single-minded focus upon safety does not improve the quality of life of older people. This became painfully clear during the first wave of Covid-19.

## 4.3 Conclusion: Quality of Care in Certain Fields Requires Urgent Attention

The limited extent to which the public values quality and accessibility are safeguarded in some specific parts of the Dutch health and social care sector stands in sharp contrast with the situation in curative healthcare. Where that is concerned, for years the Netherlands has been scoring well compared with other European countries. Consequently, curative healthcare is often regarded as the showpiece of the Dutch system. Which is understandable given that this form of care is all about treating, and if possible curing, disease. And that appeals.

[63] Buurman et al. (2016).

| Life stage | Quality | Accessibility |
|---|---|---|
| The "first thousand days" | Perinatal mortality remains a concern; the shortage of care professionals is impacting quality. | Capacity issues are straining accessibility. |
| Children and young people | Serious pressures in mental healthcare for young people, child protection and juvenile rehabilitation. | Lack of immediate and appropriate mental health, child protection and juvenile rehabilitation care. |
| Adults with mental disorders | The IGJ describes the quality of specialist mental healthcare as "worrying". | Persistent waiting lists for adults with severe mental disorders. |
| Elderly people | The quality of residential care has greatly improved; that of home care is highly dependent upon the quality of professional and informal carers. | Care for older people living at home highly dependent upon social network; pressures due to shortages of professional and informal carers. |

**Fig. 4.6** Quality and accessibility of care by life stage

If we look at care through the lens of vulnerable groups in the various stages of life, however, its public values are not always upheld quite so effectively. For some the main issue is accessibility, for some quality and for some both. For example, we find major problems with quality and accessibility across the board in child and youth care services, and even more so in certain areas: child protection and juvenile rehabilitation. Waiting times in mental healthcare—and especially for the specialist treatment required by the most complex and vulnerable patients—are also discouragingly long, for adults and young people alike. Finally, there are evident shortcomings in care services for vulnerable elderly people, a group already heavily reliant upon the efforts of their own social network. If that falls away, appropriate care can be hard to come by. Figure 4.6 summarizes the current state of affairs by stage of life.

Not surprisingly, it is in child and youth care services, mental healthcare and care for the elderly that the biggest impediments to quality and accessibility have appeared, as around 2015, major transformations in all three of these domains required huge adjustments on the part of all involved—users, professionals and providers. In child and youth care services, in fact, ever since 1974 there have been repeated system reforms and other interventions because goals were not being met or because society had been rocked by an incident that made the government feel compelled to make adjustments—even though this was frequently at odds with the basic democratic principle that lower levels of government should be free to pursue their own policies in matters devolved to them.[64] The fact that the decentralization of 2015 was accompanied by a 15 per cent reduction in the budget for child and youth care services has presented local authorities with a well-nigh impossible task. All the more so because care for the elderly was also radically reformed at the same time: care homes were closed en masse, access to nursing homes was restricted to those older people with the greatest care needs and the AWBZ was superseded by the Wmo. The latter transition, in particular, shifted another major burden onto the shoulders of local authorities and again drained them financially, since this reform too was accompanied by a substantial budget cut.

The underlying reasons for the inadequate quality and/or accessibility of care experienced by the Dutch public thus pertain primarily to financial and staffing issues. On top of which there is a definite relationship with the new pattern of roles and responsibilities brought about by the decentralization of child and youth care services and of social support.[65] The shift in mental healthcare away from institutional provision towards care in the community began in 2013, but development of the necessary outpatient facilities has never caught up. As a result, many people with severe psychiatric disorders are not receiving the care they need and long waiting lists have become a persistent problem. A situation exacerbated by inadequate co-operation between mental healthcare on the one hand and both GPs and local authorities on the other, as well as by the different approaches adopted by different health insurers.

Finally, the WRR agrees with the Netherlands Youth Institute (Nederlands Jeugdinstituut, NJi), the IGJ and the Association of Dutch Local Authorities (Vereniging van Nederlandse Gemeenten, VNG) that the ever-expanding demand for child and youth support and for the most basic forms of mental healthcare is chronically overstretching the supply side of the system.[66] And expecting financial and staffing resources alone to resolve the situation is not enough. Thought also needs to be given to the values we as a society consider most important (with regard to parenting and care for the elderly, for example), to the role prevention has to play and to the whole question of what parts of the system should be financed with public money. We discuss this in more detail in Chap. 9.

---

[64] ROB (2020).

[65] Kromhout et al. (2020).

[66] van Yperen et al. (2019), VNG (2020), and Kruse et al. (2021).

# Chapter 5
# Sustainability Through Efficiency

Pursuing efficiency in health and social care remains important, but in itself will not solve the sustainability issue.

An activity is considered efficient when relatively little input is needed to achieve its intended results. In health and social care, this means using the minimum possible human, material and financial resources to bring about a certain health benefit or a certain improvement to quality of life. Economists also refer to this approach specifically as *productive efficiency*: how do we "produce" better health at the lowest cost, in the broad sense of the word? Or in other words, how do we avoid "wastage" in the delivery of care? This contrasts with *allocative efficiency*, which is about whether people and other resources are deployed in the right place in the light of our society's wishes and goals.[1] That is the core theme of the third part of this report (Chaps. 7, 8, and 9), where we look at choices and prioritization in the Dutch health and social care system. Our focus in this chapter is productive efficiency, and in particular the potential for its improvement in terms of resource allocation or cost-effectiveness. In the next chapter we turn our attention to the human dimension of efficiency and home in on the issue of staffing sustainability.

What is the relationship between efficiency and the sustainability challenge? By organizing the provision of care more efficiently, in principle fewer people and resources are needed to meet the same demand. And so, in theory at least, our society's growing care needs can continue to be met within the restrictive (and interrelated) parameters of financial, staffing and societal sustainability identified earlier in this report—for example, by not overstretching the system's reliance upon collective solidarity. In practice, moreover, this approach has been at the heart of Dutch

[1] Baicker et al. (2012); Tanke (2018).



G. Werner et al., *Financial, Staffing and Societal Sustainability of Dutch Health Care*, Research for Policy, https://doi.org/10.1007/978-3-031-58564-7_5

health and social care policy in recent decades, manifesting itself through both comprehensive system reforms and more modest adjustments. The question is whether this strategy of "sustainability through efficiency" is a futureproof one given the scale of the challenge we now face.

To find the answer, we need to look first at the overall potential for greater efficiency in health and social care. We begin by exploring how government is trying to improve efficiency through policy interventions, and how the complexity of the system is complicating that effort (Sect. 5.1). From an academic perspective, it is often difficult to predict how effective policy initiatives are likely to be in this regard. For instance, the complexity of care and the multitude of actors involved in its delivery can produce unexpected side-effects. Even looking back, the effects of previous policies are often difficult to evaluate in controlled studies.[2] The second step is to explore whether the different systems found in other countries perform any better than ours, and might perhaps provide a solution to our sustainability problems (Sect. 5.2). Finally, in Sect. 5.3 we analyse which pathways have the greatest potential to improve efficiency within our current system.

## 5.1 Efficiency Policy and Complexity as Constraints

**Focus Upon Efficiency**

The Dutch government has made repeated efforts over the past three decades to improve the efficiency of our health and social care system. Measures implemented over that period have ranged from a complete overhaul of curative healthcare culminating in the introduction of the Health Insurance Act (Zorgverzekeringswet, Zvw) in 2006 to a drive to cut costs by decentralizing responsibility for large swathes of social care under the 2015 Social Support Act (Wet maatschappelijke ondersteuning, Wmo) and Youth Act (Jeugdwet; see also Chap. 4), and in parallel with that the implementation of framework agreements incorporating efficiency rebates as a budgetary instrument. Other more specific initiatives have sought to adjust the supply of various forms of care and to encourage more efficient behaviour on the part of all the actors involved, from care providers to buyers, and even patients themselves.

One example of such a measure is the so-called "preferential policy", under which health insurers are only permitted to reimburse the cheapest version of a group of medicines with the same active ingredient. This creates a clear incentive for patients and practitioners to choose that product, thus achieving the same health

[2] The "gold standard" is the randomized controlled trial, in which an intervention is applied or not applied at random within a test population. By comparing the "untreated" control group and the "treated" group, effects can be determined over time. This methodology is widely used in medicine to determine the effectiveness of treatments (a form of evidence-based medicine), and also increasingly to analyse the effectiveness of public policy (evidence-based policy). But it is still only rarely applied to policy interventions in care, particularly those on a large scale—and often that is simply not possible.

gains at lower cost and so making the treatment in question more efficient. A second example is the policy effort to shift the delivery of care to different institutions or providers (from hospitals to primary care, for example, or from medical specialists and GPs to nurse specialists), an exercise dubbed "The Right Care in the Right Place" (Juiste Zorg op de Juiste Plek, JZoJP) in its most recent incarnation, the idea being that the alternative provider can offer the same quality at lower cost, which increases efficiency.[3] To this end, the JZoJP programme uses a combination of financial incentives (known as "transformation funds"[4]), information sharing (regional overviews, knowledge-sharing platforms) and other means to support care providers.[5] Initiatives of this kind—specific measures aimed at improving efficiency within the current system—have come to dominate the budgetary and policy process in recent years. Before addressing their effectiveness in a general sense, below we first analyse how the sheer complexity of health and social care limits the ability to manage its efficiency in a predictable fashion.

**Complexity as a Constraint**

The Dutch care sector is a behemoth made up of almost countless different institutions and actors. It employs more than 60,000 doctors, about half of whom are active in at least 245 hospitals and other specialist medical institutions. The number of other professional practitioners—working in everything from physiotherapy to general practice, mental healthcare to disability care—also runs into many tens of thousands.[6] In emergency care alone, more than six million treatments are performed each year. And about 300,000 people are currently in long-term care. All of these services are governed by the five system laws described in Chap. 4, which together are intended to create an accessible, high-quality—yet also efficient—system (see online Appendix 4 for a detailed description).

This sector clearly has all the characteristics of a complex system.[7] Not only does it involve a large number of actors—providers, patients, buyers and regulators—but it is organized in such a way that none has a complete overview of the situation or

---

[3] This aspiration is far from new and existed long before the JZoJP programme was established. Historically, the term "substitution" was generally used to denote ideas of this kind.

[4] The idea is that transformation funds help providers finance the transition to alternative ways of delivering care. For example, if they have to divest themselves of current provision—and hence turnover—as part of the JZoJP. But an evaluation by the NZa reveals that take-up has been limited. In 2019, for instance, only just over €29 million of the available €70 million was used (NZA, 2019a).

[5] Taskforce Juiste Zorg op de Juiste Plek (2018).

[6] Volksgezondheidenzorg.info. Statistics Netherlands' self-employment figures report a total of 37,090 self-employed persons in health and social care in 2018, of whom 10,940 were general practitioners and 10,260 were physiotherapists. Company statistics show a total of 1781 large and medium-sized care-related businesses and 21,550 small ones, 19,150 of them in nursing and home care. See https://opendata.cbs.nl/statline/#/CBS/nl/dataset/84602NED/table?dl=4AF8E, https://opendata.cbs.co.uk/statline/#/cbs/en/dataset/83626NED/table?dl=4AF8C

[7] For general introductions to complexity theory, see: Waldrop (1992) and Anderson (1999). For introductions to its application in the organization and governance of care, see: Martínez-García and Hernández-Lemus (2013), Anderson and Mcdaniel Jr. (2000), Begun et al. (2003), Kannampallil et al. (2011), and Sturmberg et al. (2012).

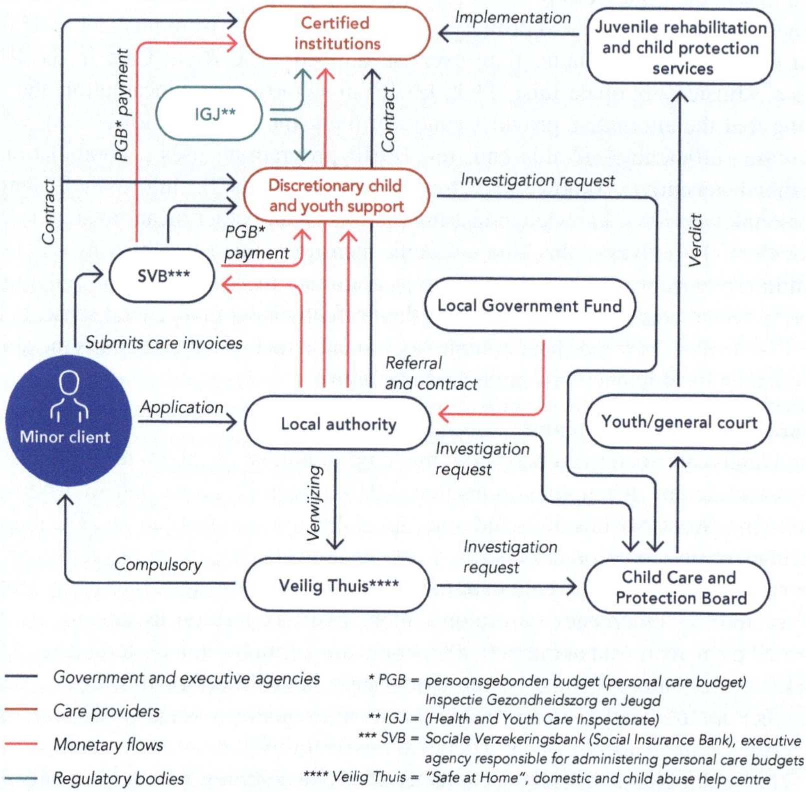


**Fig. 5.1** Monetary flows, responsibilities and roles under the Youth Act

is able to exert influence much beyond its own sphere (for an illustration of this complexity, see Fig. 5.1 for the network of actors and relationships governed by the Youth Act—just one relatively small part of the entire system). Furthermore, it features multilevel governance and the actors involved also influence each other.[8] Its legal framework is complex, too, and includes a multitude of policy incentives. The term "complexity" here reflects the fact that only to a limited extent can outcomes at the system-wide level be traced back to individual actions. From which it follows that it would be an illusion to think that it is possible to manage specific outcomes in detail. Indeed, in a complex system the actions and reactions of the various actors and the resulting net effects are never easy to predict; unexpected repercussions and side-effects always occur. A good example is the way the preferential policy for drugs mentioned above has affected security of supply (see Box 5.1).

[8] Cf. Chambers et al. (2012), Masic et al. (2012), and Ferlie et al. (2011).

**Box 5.1: Preferential Policy: An Unexpected Side-Effect**
In terms of financial efficiency, the so-called preferential policy under which health insurers are only allowed to reimburse the cheapest variant of a drug (the "preferred medicine") has proven a great success. Between 2009 and 2015, the period in which it first took effect, per-capita spending on medicines in the Netherlands fell by 2.8 per cent. That compared with a 2.3 per cent increase across a group of 31 OECD countries.[9] But there was also an unexpected downside: because pharmaceutical companies would rather sell to countries where they can command higher prices, the Netherlands began to experience supply problems. In the period 2008–2016, the number of preferred medicines affected by shortages increased from zero to 115. Although drugs not covered by the preferential policy were also affected, with the number in short supply rising from 156 to 647, relatively speaking that was a much smaller increase.[10] For patients such an effect can cause uncertainty and mean that they are frequently forced to take an alternative medication, which may not have the same efficacy as the one they used before.

**Realism in Efficiency Policy**
In a complex system, it is hard to predict the full impact of policy interventions. But what can we say in general terms about the effectiveness of the efficiency-driven policies implemented in the Netherlands in recent decades? Looking at their costs and benefits across the board, our first conclusion has to be that the actual returns often fall short of expectations. The Netherlands Court of Audit (Algemene Rekenkamer) has specifically highlighted this point with regard to the shift towards "cheaper" providers,[11] with phenomena such as "infill" effects (the capacity released is simply used for other things) and "waterbed" effects (the point of delivery changes, but the amount of care provided does not decrease) being responsible.[12]

From the perspective of complexity theory, this comes as no surprise. Providers who previously offered care that has now been displaced or deemed not appropriate inevitably respond to the changing situation. Sometimes this happens subconsciously: because there is now less pressure on capacity, practitioners become less strict when indicating other forms of care. And sometimes, at least in the short term, it is a more structural issue. Moving care out of a hospital does not immediately generate savings, after all, because it takes time to adjust spending on buildings, people and ancillary services in line with the reduced use of the facility.

---

[9] OECD (2017).

[10] KNMP Farmanco (2017). For the impact of preferential policies in the market for medications, see also Berenschot's analysis (Carp et al., 2018). This argues for stricter conditions in preferential procurement, the monitoring of shortages, relaxation of the policies in the event of recurrent shortages, their curtailment in cases of proven poor deliverability and general simplification.

[11] Algemene Rekenkamer (2016).

[12] Vlaanderen and Klink (2018), Stadhouders and Kruse (2018), and Stadhouders et al. (2016).

Incentives can also play a part. Take the case of the small town of Afferden in the Dutch province of Limburg, for instance, where the transfer of care services to GPs was so "successful" that it undermined the funding base of the local hospital, putting it at risk of closure.[13] This shows how, in some cases, care that could in principle be offered more efficiently elsewhere should actually be kept where it is so that the institution concerned can use the revenue it generates to cross-subsidize other, less lucrative provision.

A second observation is that the intended effects of efficiency measures often take a long time to materialize. This is because the various actors involved have to adapt, and organizations have to be restructured. An example of this is the programme of reforms implemented at two regional hospitals in the south of the Netherlands, the Beatrixziekenhuis in Gorinchem and Bernhoven in Uden. An independent evaluation found that whilst a combination of long-term contracts with health insurers to reduce so-called "production incentives" (which encourage providers to deliver more care than is strictly necessary) and greater co-operation with local GPs would eventually improve efficiency, that effect could take years to materialize.[14] Whilst the permanent pressure to cut spending makes it tempting to introduce one cost-saving initiative after another, the administrative burden created by these constant changes can easily prove counterproductive when it comes to effectiveness. For example, the Court of Audit found that they may undermine efforts to promote appropriate use of care: the large number of programmes and policy initiatives can potentially ask too much of the workforce.[15] Since actors within the care system adjust their behaviour accordingly, moreover, over time efficiency measures may lose their edge or even start to have adverse repercussions. This effect is reinforced because, in practice, the purpose of and analytical justification for such measures are driven strongly by financial accountability[16]—possibly to the detriment of public values like the quality and accessibility of care. Once again, the preferential policy for drugs exemplifies this phenomenon (see Box 5.1). And its consequences also illustrate a broader point: in a complex system with many independent actors who all have their own interests and preferences, side-effects always occur and these can never be fully anticipated at the moment of first implementation.

**Realism About Complexity**

Despite all this, complex systems are not inherently problematic; rather, they reflect a high degree of system development. The complexity of Dutch health and social care is largely a product of the need for high-quality and increasingly specialized provision, fuelled by greater knowledge, better technology and growing prosperity. However, complexity does limit the extent to which policy can manage outcomes and—importantly for sustainability—the efficiency of care in a predictable, linear fashion.

---

[13] Jung et al. (2019).

[14] Douven et al. (2020).

[15] Algemene Rekenkamer (2020b).

[16] Lipsitz (2012).

But the observation that complexity is to some extent inevitable does not mean that *all* added complexity is valuable. Care policy should avoid unwittingly or unthinkingly creating superfluous additional institutions and management or control mechanisms, if only to counter the increasing administrative burden being experienced on the shop floor (see also Chap. 3) and hence the growing pressure on staffing sustainability (see also Chap. 6). One way to keep this dynamic in check is to price additional requests: if someone asking for more information has to pay for it, that creates an incentive to think more critically about whether they really need it. There is also a political responsibility to prevent excessive complexity: it is all too tempting to respond to every new incident in the care sector with yet more policy incentives, initiatives or institutions. That tendency can be tempered by assessing in advance whether the resulting extra complexity is proportionate to the policy objective, and by evaluating any side-effects and behavioural responses it might cause. All in all, then, the complexity aspect of efficiency policy demands modesty regarding the role that policy is assigned in meeting the sustainability challenge. Not just because its focus is often purely financial and the returns likely to be limited, but above all because the resulting side-effects and behavioural responses often fail to conform to expectations.

**Fragmented Policy Data as a Complexity Problem**

All of this suggests that we should be cautious both in instituting efficiency measures and in "chalking up" their effects. With that in mind, the continuous, prompt and broad monitoring and evaluation of health and social care policies are a must. Which in turn requires access to good data that measures outcomes effectively in terms of efficiency and the public values of quality and accessibility. This is important firstly because the collective nature of the sector's financing means that data has a key role to play in the public debate and must therefore not only be accessible, but also be up to date, insightful, consistent and comprehensive. And secondly because we need to gauge results not only in terms of economic indicators such as expenditure but also as they relate to broader normative goals, in particular the accessibility and quality of care.

The sector's complexity, however—from the specialist nature of the product to the multiplicity of institutions supplying it—means that the relevant information is generated in a diffuse and disparate manner. As outlined in Box 5.2, responsibility for the collection, collation and publication of data concerning expenditure, employment and performance indicators in care is currently spread across a variety of institutions, including Statistics Netherlands (Centraal Bureau voor de Statistiek, CBS), the National Health Care Institute (Zorginstituut Nederland, ZiN), the Dutch Healthcare Authority (Nederlandse Zorgautoriteit, Nza) and the National Institute for Public Health and the Environment (Rijksinstituut voor Volksgezondheid en Milieu, RIVM). The way these bodies divide up tasks between themselves is only in part a product of their formal statistical responsibilities. As a result, it is often difficult to obtain detailed, up-to-date information concerning the quality and accessibility of different aspects of care in a structured manner. Moreover, the policy horizon is sometimes short because the definitions and parameters used when recording data change over time. This in turn is linked to the ad-hoc nature of many initiatives to track and evaluate outcome data in care; new monitoring systems with their own sources, definitions and infrastructure are often set up in line with a particular government's policy priorities, for instance, but are not maintained over the longer periods—multiple government terms—needed for their results to inform future health and social care policy effectively.

**Box 5.2: Complexity and Fragmentation in Policy Data**

Under the heading "health accounts", Statistics Netherlands compiles time series of total and collective expenditure on healthcare and on employment in the sector. These are published on its Statline website. This data is then used to compile the Care Figures Monitor (ZorgCijfers Monitor), managed by the ZiN, which has been tracking the cost evolution of specific forms of care on a quarterly basis since 2018. Meanwhile, the Cost of Disease (Kosten van Ziekten) section of Statline, managed jointly with the RIVM, breaks down the same expenditure by disease type. A core set of performance indicators can be found on the RIVM-operated "public healthcare information" website, volksgezondheidenzorg.info; these cover quality, accessibility, affordability and efficiency. The "quality" section lists 44 indicators divided into six clusters,[17] "accessibility" has 13 indicators and "affordability" eight. Whilst the data for most indicators stretches back to 2010, a methodological break means that the figures for waiting times in curative healthcare from 2019 onwards are incompatible with those from previous years.[18] Finally, much of this data is brought together on the "state of public health and healthcare" website, www.staatvenz.nl, which claims to provide "the most up-to-date key figures for the policy of the Ministry of Health, Welfare and Sport".

As well as these sources of primary data, there is also the overview of performance indicators in the Dutch Healthcare Performance Report (DHCPR). This has been published regularly since 2006, making the Netherlands one of the first countries in the world to provide such comprehensive reporting.[19] Generating a clear picture that enables the effective identification of problems is hampered, however, by fragmentation and by the desire to meet the needs of patients, professionals and policymakers alike. As a result, no fewer than 125 indicators are listed. Nevertheless, such statistics are receiving increasing coverage in the international literature—through studies of "value-based healthcare", for instance.[20]

---

[17] Those clusters are "birth and pregnancy", "staying healthy", "recovery", "recovery (acute care)", "living with an illness or disability" and "end-of-life care". Reflecting the "state of public health and healthcare" data, they cover various key life stages.

[18] Until July 2018, waiting-time data was collected and processed by Mediquest.

[19] van den Berg et al. (2014).

[20] Porter and Teisberg (2006).

**Table 5.1** Parties responsible for managing national healthcare datasets

| | |
|---|---|
| 1–2 responsible parties | Czech Republic, Iceland, Italy, Japan, Switzerland, Turkey, England, Scotland. |
| 3–4 responsible parties | Canada, Denmark, Finland, Israel, New Zealand, Singapore, Spain, Sweden, United States. |
| 5–6 responsible parties | Korea, Wales. |
| 7 or more responsible parties | Ireland, Netherlands, Norway. |

Source: OECD (2015a); available online at https://read.oecd-ilibrary.org/social-issues-migration-health/health-data-governance_9789264244566-en#page5

That there is also room for improvement here when it comes to international comparisons, a 2015 OECD study makes clear in a number of ways.[21] This reported on an analysis of the share of national healthcare datasets that met common criteria concerning availability and use.[22] Of the 22 nations studied, we find the Netherlands in seventeenth place. Our country scored relatively poorly, for example, on availability, extent of data coverage and the proportion of available datasets that are linked periodically for research and monitoring purposes.[23] When it came to the disclosure and accessibility of outcome data, too, the Netherlands languished in the lower regions.[24] Finally, a ranking of the same 22 countries by the number of parties responsible for managing national datasets highlights another point mentioned above: the fragmentation in data collection, collation and publication. Besides the Netherlands, only Norway and Ireland have seven or more responsible parties (see Table 5.1).

The upshot of all this is not so much a lack of data as an overabundance, plus a failure to disclose it systematically—especially on the output indicators side. And amidst all this fragmentary information, vulnerable groups are especially likely to be overlooked. Take the growing waiting lists in mental healthcare, for instance, which only really came to public attention when a patient took a seat in the entrance hall of the Ministry of Health, Welfare and Sport (VWS) in January 2020 in protest after multiple suicide attempts and hundreds of days waiting for a treatment place.[25] Similarly, users of child and youth care services only found their plight being highlighted once the juvenile courts started sounding alarm bells.[26] Better data certainly does not guarantee the early detection of such problems at every level, but it does improve the likelihood that they will be spotted. The multitude of indicators is

[21] OECD (2015b). Figure available at https://read.oecd-ilibrary.org/social-issues-migration-health/health-data-governance_9789264244566-en#page33

[22] Seven such criteria were formulated (in the domains "availability", "maturity" and "use") and the shares for each added up.

[23] OECD (2015b), figure and table 2.1.

[24] OECD (2015b, 67).

[25] NOS (2020). After waiting 1047 days, this patient was finally assigned a treatment place.

[26] RTL NIEUWS (2019).

inherent in the nature of care and a result of the differentiated measures used in assessment. These observations therefore do not constitute a plea to further increase administrative burdens, but rather a call to make better use of the potential tied up within existing data.[27] More systematic collection and collation of performance data, co-ordinated by a single actor, could in principle even mitigate the problem of the same information being requested multiple times. This solution requires not only guaranteed long-term funding, however, but above all political commitment to creating systematic, sector-wide and always consistent statistical output derived from primary data that is supplied on a structural basis.

**Key Points—Efficiency Policy and Complexity as Constraints**

- Health and social care is considered more efficient if it "produces" better health using fewer people and other resources. In recent decades, "sustainability through efficiency" has become a cornerstone of Dutch policy efforts in this sector.
- Efficiency's true potential is often difficult to estimate. Even looking back, the effectiveness of past initiatives in this field can only be established to a limited extent.
- Complexity is inevitable in the care system and need not be inherently problematic, but rather reflects a high degree of development.
- However, complexity does limit the potential to manage efficiency effectively. Specifically, we see that: (1) measures taken often fail to live up to expectations, financially or otherwise; (2) it can take a long time for effects to appear; and (3) unexpected side-effects are commonplace.
- Any changes to the system should therefore always go hand in hand with permanent, up-to-date and comprehensive monitoring and evaluation. Currently, these processes are inadequate.
- It is important that outcome and performance data be disclosed in a systematic and timely manner, and that its collection be safeguarded and funded in the long term.
- We must beware of "administrative overload", whereby large numbers of programmes and initiatives are implemented without allowing earlier policies to reach maturity. Changes to a complex field like health and social care need time to bed in.

---

[27] There are already many complaints from the shop floor about the administrative burden. See, for example, initiatives like "'Het roer moet om" ("We have to change course") by Dutch GPs.

## 5.2 System Reform and Sustainability

From time to time in the public and political debate on the organization of health and social care, the case is made—either implicitly or explicitly—for a complete reform of the system.[28] In other words, a fundamental redefinition of the roles and responsibilities of the actors involved. This would go much further than the measures discussed in the previous section, which would merely recalibrate the existing system. Since care is structured and organized differently in different countries, an obvious starting point is to look elsewhere to see if any of those alternatives offer better solutions when it comes to sustainability issues. Could systemic change lead to greater efficiency? With that question in mind, in this section we look in particular at various curative and long-term care systems in other developed countries. The reasons for focusing upon these two areas are threefold. First, debates around system design in the Netherlands focus primarily upon curative healthcare, and especially upon the merits of allowing market forces to operate in this domain.[29] Secondly, outcomes in terms of quality and accessibility are relatively easy to compare internationally in these areas (and in curative healthcare in particular). And thirdly, they are far by the largest parts of the system in expenditure terms. Since they are also the domains in which the greatest growth is expected in the coming decades,[30] any strategy of sustainability through efficiency must inevitably centre on them.

**Curative Medicine in the International Context**

We first look broadly at the different ways in which curative healthcare systems can be organized. Various typologies can be used to do this, but one of the most common distinguishes three roles that any system of this kind must fulfil: (1) supplying care (who provides the service?), (2) financing it (who pays?) and (3) regulation (who oversees the system?).[31] Each of these questions has three possible answers: private actors (commercial or not-for-profit private institutions), state actors (national, regional or local government) or a combination of the two ("civil society", as it were). In practice, this typology identifies five different types of curative healthcare system actually in place in various countries (see Table 5.2). In a national health service of the kind found in the UK, the Scandinavian countries, Portugal, Spain and Iceland, for example, the provision, financing and regulation of care are all government duties. The Netherlands, along with Belgium, Poland, France, Israel, Japan and others, has an "etatist" social health insurance system—meaning that healthcare

---

[28] It can be difficult to determine when a set of measures is radical enough to count as "system reform". The term is therefore used in very different ways in the public debate.

[29] The other system laws to be the subject of some debate concerning their underlying principles are the Wmo and Youth Act. This seems to be less the case with the Wlz.

[30] Vonk et al. (2020).

[31] Böhm et al. (2013).

**Table 5.2** Types of healthcare system

| Type of system | Regulation | Financing | Service provision | Countries |
|---|---|---|---|---|
| National health service | State | State | State | Scandinavian countries, Iceland, Portugal, Spain, United Kingdom. |
| National health insurance | State | State | Private | Australia, Canada, Ireland, New Zealand, Italy. |
| Social health Insurance | Societal | Societal | Private | Austria, Germany, Switzerland. |
| Private health system | Private | Private | Private | United States. |
| Etatist social health insurance | State | Societal | Private | Belgium, France, Czech Republic, Netherlands, Poland, Israel, Japan. |

Classification based upon allocation of responsibilities for the regulation, financing and provision of curative healthcare. Countries named are examples only; the list is not exhaustive. "Private" here includes both commercial and not-for-profit private institutions (most Dutch hospitals fall into the latter category)

itself is delivered by private actors whilst its regulation is a state responsibility and its financing a societal task (in the Dutch case through regulated semi-public health insurers).

It is important to remember that the categories described here are broad ones and there is also considerable variety within each of them. So whilst etatist social health insurance systems like the Dutch one have more in common with each other than with the other types, they still differ substantially between themselves. For example, not all countries in this group have multiple competing health insurers as the Netherlands does. Likewise, the primacy in national health services lies with government—but not always at the same level. In the UK central government is very much in charge, whereas in Scandinavia regional and local authorities play a much greater role. Moreover, no national system is a pure exemplar of its category—there are always deviations from the archetype. This is mostly due to its historical background. Even in the United States, usually regarded as the very embodiment of a private health system, curative healthcare for large sections of the population is delivered through government-funded or controlled programmes more reminiscent of a national health service and national health insurance system.[32]

Some time ago the OECD conducted a comparative study into the efficiency of different healthcare systems.[33] The main finding was that no one type is superior. In fact, the differences *within* groups sharing the same type characteristics were found to be greater than the differences *between* groups. The one exception—in a negative

[32] This applies, for example, to care for the elderly (through the Medicare programme), for people on low incomes (Medicaid) and for military veterans (Veterans Health Administration).

[33] Joumard et al. (2010). In this study the OECD classifies healthcare systems using slightly different variables than in Bohm et al. 2013, and a total of six groups.

sense—was the United States, where spending is exceptionally high whilst outcomes in terms of quality and accessibility are certainly not in the top tier in all respects. A more recent study has broadly confirmed these results.[34] In that analysis, the researchers calculated average efficiency scores for four of the five system types.[35] The differences between them were found to be limited and not statistically significant, except that systems based upon social health insurance (such as Germany) scored substantially lower than the other types. Of course, this does not mean that there are no efficiency gains to be made anywhere; inefficiencies can always be found in any system. Nor does it mean that there is no difference between systems (or types of system) when it comes to other outcomes (see Box 5.3, for example). But the bottom line is that, efficiency-wise, no *type* of curative healthcare system *as a whole* performs substantially better than the rest.

**Box 5.3: Organizing Healthcare in Response to Covid-19**

The recent pandemic sparked heated debate about the organization of healthcare in the Netherlands. Was the severe pressure on intensive care units (ICUs) at the height of the crisis not the ultimate proof that market forces had been allowed too much influence? Or did it instead highlight the limitations of centralized control? It is still too early to fully analyse the performance of different healthcare systems in the face of Covid-19. But we can nevertheless gain a first impression by looking at the vaccine rollout as a case study.

It is probably no coincidence that, initially at least, the UK saw by far the fastest increase in vaccination coverage in Europe.[36] Vaccine availability was an important factor in this. But so was the country's highly centralized healthcare system, the National Health Service (NHS), which allowed top-down action to be taken relatively quickly with clear responsibilities and short lines of communication. In Denmark too—also an NHS system, albeit a more regionalized one—the rollout was relatively quick once vaccines had been authorized.[37] The ability to act relatively fast in emergencies and to scale up the necessary services therefore seems to be a particular positive feature of a system under central control. In both countries, moreover, the delivery of care has historically been seen much more as a task for government than it is in the Netherlands.

(continued)

[34] Lee and Kim (2018).

[35] Private health systems were excluded because the United States is the only example of one within the OECD.

[36] Gallardo (2021).

[37] Verhelst (2021).

**Box 5.3** (continued)

From the sustainability point of view, however, we need to assess system performance more broadly. Every type of healthcare system has its strengths and its weaknesses. And when it comes to the organization of care in response to Covid-19, details matter as well. One of key themes in the Dutch debate, for example, was ICU capacity: some commentators argued that the relatively low number of critical care beds in the Netherlands (6.4 per 100,000 inhabitants) was a consequence of the stringent focus upon efficiency in recent decades, whether through market forces or not.[38] But this figure is actually about the same as in the UK's centralized, government-controlled NHS (6.6). In Germany, by contrast—a system much more like the Dutch one when it comes to curative healthcare—the number is considerably higher (29.2). Once again, we have to conclude that very different system-design models can lead to very similar outcomes and that very different outcomes can occur even when systems' designs are similar.

**Long-Term Care for the Elderly in the International Context**

In expenditure terms, long-term care for the elderly is already second only to curative healthcare. And it too is set to grow substantially in the coming decades, in the Netherlands and elsewhere. A background study for this report compared this form of provision in Japan, England, Denmark and Germany.[39] These countries were selected because, in terms of the rate at which their populations are ageing, they are either similar to the Netherlands (England, Denmark) or somewhat ahead of us (Germany, Japan) and because they represent different types of long-term care system. The authors adopted a typology featuring four categories and based upon the broad classification of welfare states originally proposed by Esping-Andersen (see Table 5.3).[40] Dutch long-term care for the elderly is best classified as "corporatist" in nature, although government plays a rather larger role here than in other countries in this category, and the family a more limited one. In other words, the Netherlands broadly conforms to the corporatist model but with strong influences from the social democratic one, and to a lesser extent from the liberal one.

From this comparison we are able to draw lessons with regard to the efficiency of long-term care for the elderly. And here once again, the key conclusion has to be that there is no best solution; that none of the systems studied really manages to solve the dilemmas surrounding the quality, accessibility and sustainability of long-term care for the elderly. Incidentally, it is more difficult to make international comparisons in this domain than in curative healthcare. "Good" care for the elderly, after all, is very much about quality of life, which is harder to measure objectively and more culturally and socially determined than clinical outcomes.

[38] Rhodes et al. (2012).

[39] Kruse et al. (2021).

[40] Esping-Andersen (1990).

**Table 5.3** Characteristics of the welfare state in Germany, Denmark, England and Japan

| | Germany | Denmark | England | Japan |
|---|---|---|---|---|
| Type of welfare state | Corporatist | Social democratic | Liberal | Corporatist/conservative |
| Role of the individual | Latent | Dominant | Dominant | Latent |
| Role of the family | Dominant | Latent | Latent | Dominant |
| Role of the state | Dominant | Dominant | Latent | Latent |
| Role of the market | Latent | Latent | Dominant | Dominant |

Source: Esping-Andersen (1990)

**System Reform Will not Resolve the Sustainability Challenges**

What conclusions for the Dutch situation can we draw from these results? In neither curative healthcare nor long-term care for the elderly do we find any alternative system abroad that is likely to be substantially more efficient than our own. So there is no reason to believe that overhauling the system, however fundamentally, would lead to substantially more efficient care and thus help solve sustainability issues. Moreover, it would incur considerable transition costs.[41] To introduce a fully public healthcare system (a "Dutch NHS", as it were), for instance, the Netherlands Bureau for Economic Policy Analysis (Centraal Planbureau, CPB) estimates the direct transition costs alone at more than €6 billion (€750 million per annum over a transition period of eight years).[42] Perhaps weighing even more heavily, though, is the long preparation time needed for any system reform—not just for the administrative work, but also to "prime" the public for the changes. As described in the previous chapter, the introduction of the Zvw took two decades. By way of an alternative, then, in the next section we look at possibilities to achieve efficiency gains within the current system.

**Key Issues—System Reform and Sustainability**

- There are big differences between the health and social care systems in different countries. One key defining factor here is the allocation of public and private responsibilities.
- All systems can be improved, but no alternative type delivers care in a substantially more efficient way. This applies to both curative healthcare and long-term care for the elderly.
- The transition costs and preparation time involved in system reforms are considerable.
- Given the lack of evidence from international comparative research of substantially better outcomes, a system reform cannot be expected to solve the sustainability challenge.

[41] Goudriaan and Heida (2015).

[42] CPB (2020a).

## 5.3 Improving Efficiency Within the Current System

In this section we look at a number of ways in which efficiency could be improved *within* our existing health and social care system. Given the huge number of initiatives, plans, strategies, manifestos, programmes and policy proposals devised to this very end over the years—with a scope ranging from the entire system to very specific subdomains—we cannot and do not pretend that we are here able to offer a comprehensive insight into where concrete gains could be made. The most systematic recent analyses of likely effects, predominantly along the axis of financial sustainability, are provided by the report *Zorgkeuzes in Kaart* ("Choices in Care Charted")[43]—in which various Dutch political parties put forward a total of 147 ideas[44] to improve the system—and the government's "broad social review" ("Brede maatschappelijke heroverwegingen", BMH) of healthcare.[45] In this section we look with a higher level of abstraction at the general directions in which the greatest potential for efficiency improvements within the system are likely to be found. As a reminder, efficiency can be enhanced by improving the outcomes of care—its quality and accessibility—as well as by reducing the use of people or resources.

**A More Efficient System in the International Context**

Although the international comparative research described in the previous section suggests that there are no substantial differences between the various types of healthcare system, considerable variation can be found within each type. Lee and Kim, for instance, have shown that within the etatist social health insurance category, the Netherlands scores relatively poorly in terms of efficiency.[46] From this we can conclude that whilst it may not be desirable to transform the system completely, it does not necessarily follow that no improvement is possible.

What might those improvements be? That question is not easy to answer based upon Lee and Kim's research. National systems differ in dozens of respects, after all, and these cannot be compared one-to-one to gauge their relative efficiencies. Nevertheless, the authors examine their entire sample of 35 countries in search of explanatory factors and do find three aspects which have a significant effect upon the efficiency of healthcare systems[47]: those with freedom to choose one's health insurer, with greater decentralization and with more accessible quality and price data concerning the supply of care are found to be less efficient on average. On the latter point, though, the authors concede that the reason for the relationship is not

---

[43] CPB (2020b).

[44] With multiple variants in many cases—the total number exceeds 200.

[45] *Kamerstukken* ii 2019/2020, 32359, no. 4. Both *Zorgkeuzes in Kaart* and the BMH consider not just small and medium-sized changes to the system, but also comprehensive reforms.

[46] Lee and Kim (2018).

[47] Factors that were investigated but found to have no significant effect were private care providers (as in the Netherlands) versus public ones, price regulation, labour-market and equipment regulation, free choice of provider, gatekeepers and budgetary constraints.

well understood and that this result conflicts with findings from other studies. As we have already seen, moreover, public availability of the data in question is relatively low in the Netherlands, suggesting that this factor plays only a limited role here. In the other two respects, however, the effect described may well be present: citizens are free to choose their health insurer and the system is relatively decentralized, especially in long-term care (procurement through 36 regional care administration bureaus) and social support (procurement at the municipal level). One reason why this might reduce efficiency is the higher implementation and administration costs of those arrangements.

**Integrated Care, Care Procurement and Decentralization**

This brings us to the themes of decentralization and procurement, and by extension the notion of market forces in health and social care. We can link these themes to a significant epidemiological development (see Chap. 2), namely the rising number of chronic patients with multiple conditions (multimorbidity). The increasing complexity of their medical needs means that more and more people are having to deal more and more frequently with different care providers, suppliers and buyers, mostly over many years. Things become even more complicated when this situation crosses the jurisdictional boundaries of the various system laws, with their different responsibilities, entitlement criteria and sources of funding. Take a mental health patient, for example, whose treatment is primarily curative (and hence largely funded under the Zvw) but who also needs varying degrees of long-term care (Wlz) and social support (Wmo). Patients and care providers alike often experience delineation problems at those boundaries—also known as "partitions". And they can affect both the quality of that person's care and the sustainability of the system more generally. As when someone occupies an expensive hospital bed for an unnecessarily long time because, say, home care has not yet been arranged.

Such issues have led to public calls for "departitioning", otherwise known as "integrated care". In other words, for better co-operation and co-ordination between various types of care provider. Appendix 4 provides an overview of the scientific evidence regarding the effectiveness of this approach, revealing that integrated care not only increases patient satisfaction but possibly also leads to better clinical outcomes. The satisfaction aspect probably bolsters the societal dimension of sustainability, an important part of the overall equation, but the implications of departitioning for the financial and staffing dimensions are either unknown or ambiguous. Without harder evidence in that regard, we should remain cautious about attributing major efficiency effects to proposals of this kind.

How does this relate to decentralization and procurement? We look first at the procurement aspect and—by association—at market forces in care (see Box 5.4 for a brief dissection of the links between them). Lack of co-operation between care buyers is often seen as a barrier to integrated care[48]: their failure to align their

[48] Menzis (2020).

procurement criteria supposedly prevents providers organizing their processes in an holistic, patient-centred fashion. This is a particular problem when they are caring for "complex" patients. They may, for example, have to deal with multiple health insurers with mutually conflicting wishes or purchasing criteria, which can hinder a transformation process within a hospital. But they face an even bigger challenge when it comes to harmonizing procurement practices under the various system laws. Each of them, after all, assigns responsibility for buying care to different bodies with different powers: local authorities under the Youth Act and Wmo, care administration bureaus under the Wlz and health insurers under the Zvw. Moreover, the regional boundaries of these procurement regimes do not always coincide.

**Box 5.4: Procurement and the Three Markets in Care**

The role played by market forces in health and social care is a hot topic in the Dutch public debate. But it is not always clear what exactly is at issue. In Chap. 4 we saw that there are actually three distinct markets in this sector. In the *health insurance* market, insurers compete for consumers' business. In the *health delivery* market, providers vie to attract patients. And in the *care procurement* market, buyers seek to secure good and efficient care. Criticism of market forces and their role can relate to any of these markets, or to all three at once. But only in curative healthcare (governed by the Zvw) do all three operate, so only there can we say that there is a full—albeit tightly regulated—market system in place. When it comes to other forms of provision—social support (under the Wmo), long-term care (under the Wlz) and child and youth care services (under the Youth Act)—a patient or user only has to deal with their local authority or regional care administration bureau; they cannot choose an alternative care buyer (unless they physically move to another district or region). In the international comparative literature this is called a "single-payer" system, because there is only one care buyer per geographical area.

The Netherlands thus has a multiple-payer system for curative healthcare and a single-payer one for the rest of health and social care. Since consumers have no choice over who buys care on their behalf, the single-payer regimes do not have health insurance markets.[49] But the other two markets described above do exist to a greater or lesser extent (depending upon the exact regulations in place[50]), because both patients (care delivery) and the sole buyer (care procurement) can in principle choose between multiple providers.

(continued)

[49] This largely coincides with the distinction drawn in Lee & Kim's (2018) study between systems with and without a choice of health insurer (multiple-payer versus single-payer).

[50] In some systems, patients' and/or buyers' choice of provider may be limited or eliminated.

**Box 5.4** (continued)

In practice, though, even in curative healthcare the importance of regulated market forces as a mechanism to achieve greater efficiency has declined over the past decade. This is due to the impact of instruments like framework agreements and the macromanagement tool, which were introduced because the Zvw as originally enacted did not appear to be achieving the degree of improvement it was supposed to bring about, especially with regard to financial sustainability. On the one hand these additional instruments serve as mechanisms to safeguard efficiency incentives in procurement processes, but to some extent they also conflict with that aim and can undermine the intended price competition.[51]

This brings us to decentralization. It seems quite plausible that organizing procurement and funding at different regional levels limits the potential for co-operation between different parts of the sector.[52] In the Netherlands, such issues are encountered when patients face problems transitioning between forms of care governed by different system laws. Incidentally, this point also touches upon the policy debate surrounding regionalization in the Netherlands. In Box 5.5 we provide a brief analysis of the meaning and interpretations of this concept. In the current Dutch discourse, regionalization seems to be closely associated—and sometimes to coincide—with pleas for closer and more intensive co-operation between different (and different types of) care providers. For example, for "complex" patients with multiple conditions, in child and youth care services or in care for the elderly.[53] The notion that more integrated care is needed is here linked to the idea that the required co-operation is best achieved at regional level.

**Box 5.5: The Regionalization of Care: An Analysis of a Diverse Concept**

The term "regionalization" has played an increasing role in Dutch policy discussions around health and social care in recent years.[54] In a general sense, the idea is that care (or particular aspects of it) should be organized and possibly also financed and purchased at the regional level. This can be argued for reasons of quality, accessibility or efficiency. Such regionalization can be either centralizing in nature (a shift from local to regional organization) or decentralizing (from national to local organization).

(continued)

[51] Schut et al. (2010).

[52] For example, in principle curative healthcare insurers (governed by the Zvw) have national coverage. Social support (Wmo) is supposedly organized at the municipal level, but in practice most procurement is undertaken through regional partnerships. And long-term care (Wlz) is divided into 31 care administration bureau regions.

[53] See, for example, Bal et al. (2019).

[54] Examples include a recent paper from health insurer Menzis on "co-operation to create healthy regions" (Samenwerking aan gezonde regio's), as well as a discussion paper issued by the Ministry of Health, Welfare and Sport on the organization of "the care of the future" (Menzis, 2020; Ministerie van Volksgezondheid Welzijn en Sport, 2021).

**Box 5.5** (continued)

A second dimension of regionalization concerns the type of provider it creates at the new regional level of organization. Are these similar to their predecessors, just covering geographically different areas, or does regionalization also involve the integration of different types of provider that previously operated separately? One historical example of the latter is the formation in the 1960s of Regional Institutes for Outpatient Mental Healthcare (Regionale Instellingen voor Ambulante Geestelijke Gezondheidszorg, RIAGGs) out of a previously disparate constellation of local providers active in social psychiatry, psychotherapy, child guidance and so on.[55]

A third dimension is the question of whether regionalization concerns only the delivery of care or also its funding and procurement. Under the current Wmo and Youth Act, for example, procurement is officially entrusted to local authorities but in practice is often undertaken in part by regional partnerships.

Finally, there is the geographical dimension. In other words, what actually constitutes a "region"? In the current Dutch policy debate, this one term can refer—amongst other classifications—to the seven medical education and training regions (Onderwijs- en Opleidings *Regio's, OOR), the eleven acute care chain regions (Regionaal Overleg Acute Zorgketen, ROAZ-regio's), the twelve provinces, the 25 community healthcare and public safety regions* (GGD–/veiligheidsregio's), the 31 care administration bureau regions (zorgkantoorregio's) or the 42 child and youth care regions (jeugdzorgregio's).

In short, the notion of "regionalization" in health and social care usually suggests an alternative to an existing geographical organizing principle. But this broad concept can be interpreted in many different ways, making it difficult to evaluate as a general phenomenon.

As stated earlier, there is some international comparative evidence to suggest that multiple care buyers and the decentralized organization of a care system are associated with lower efficiency. This seems to correlate with the idea that—in the interests of "complex" patients in particular—greater co-operation between providers is desirable but is currently not being properly achieved due to insufficient synchronization of their incentives under the different system laws, and especially at their mutual boundaries. A phenomenon only compounded by the lack of congruence in the geographical scope of those laws in a decentralized system.

**A More Efficient Procurement and Care Landscape**

What does this mean for care procurement? In our analysis, there are five dimensions to this question. The first of these concerns the form and scope of procurement: what actors should buy care, how should they interact and how should they be defined geographically?

[55] The RIAGGs no longer exist, most of their activities having subsequently been subsumed by today's mental health institutions or their precursors.

The findings outlined above argue in favour of greater commitment to co-ordination between care buyers and greater congruence in their geographical scope. In other words, for fewer different types of region. In terms of the three markets in health and social care, this would effectively mean reducing the number of buyers and hence a contraction of the health insurance market. Practically speaking, though, a commitment to greater co-ordination can mean many different things. At one extreme, for example, it could entail the creation of a universal "single payer" in all (or almost all) care domains. That is, merging all the current health insurers and other buyers into one new insurance and procurement organization. For the Dutch system, this would represent a fundamental overhaul. Indeed, referring back to the typology summarized in Table 5.3, it would transform our underlying model from etatist social health insurance to national health insurance—or, if the delivery of care were also to become a government responsibility, even a national health service.

A much more limited interpretation of the commitment to greater co-ordination is to encourage health insurers to be more congruent in their procurement of the curative healthcare covered by the Zvw.[56] One possibility here is to establish a legally binding system of "preferred health insurers" on a regional basis, with the other insurers in a given region being required to follow the procurement practices of its designated "preferred" insurer. Other options include measures to better align the procurement of care by the buyers operating under the different system laws, as recently proposed by health insurer Menzis.[57] These, too, could be made legally binding to a greater or lesser extent.

Our second dimension concerns the forms of care covered by this greater degree of co-ordination in procurement. One idea might be to exclude plannable routine interventions such as cataract, hip and knee operations—broadly speaking, forms of care that can be delivered more efficiently at specialist clinics and independent treatment centres (ITCs)[58]—from congruent care procurement. It is precisely with interventions of this kind that competition between buyers is most effective as a driver of greater efficiency. The mirror image of this model is to define only those forms of care that we explicitly wish to exclude from such competition. In a recent advisory report, the Council of Public Health and Society (Raad voor Volksgezondheid en Samenleving, RVS) suggests exactly this approach, with an exclusion for acute care.[59] Whatever exact form the model takes, the underlying principle is that market forces be allowed to operate differentially in care procurement. Public and political debate would then focus more upon the relevant trade-offs in that respect rather than upon "market forces" themselves as an abstract phenomenon.

A third dimension is the overall structure of the care landscape: the whole set of institutions which constitute the sector and the way the delivery of care is distributed between them. A more efficient landscape—one better adapted to the epidemiological and demographic developments outlined above and to ongoing advances

[56] See, for example, Kiers (2019).

[57] Menzis (2020).

[58] Kruse (2018).

[59] RVS (2020a).

in healthcare technology—may well have a structure quite different from the existing one, which is largely the product of historical evolution.[60] In this regard, it is important to ensure that the incentives built into the system do not "freeze" the care landscape in its current form; structural change must always remain possible. If organizational improvements—such as the reforms mentioned earlier at the Beatrixziekenhuis and Bernhoven hospitals—are hindered by perverse incentives rooted in regulation or funding, it is up to government to review those encumbrances. Given the sector's complexity and the constraints that imposes, in many cases the most effective way to change the care landscape for the better is through experiments with new ways of organizing provision rather than by means of large-scale programmes applied from the top down.[61] And often specifically through alliances formed by multiple providers and buyers to address concrete problems. One example is the care networks set up to deal with complex chronic conditions such as the lung disorder COPD[62] and Parkinson's disease.[63] Another is the oncology care network.[64] Structures of this kind tend to be more efficient because they create economies of scale, especially when treating patients with chronic care needs.[65] As much as possible, then, government and regulators should create the right conditions to facilitate such experiments. It is crucial, moreover, that they be evaluated quickly and comprehensively to confirm that they are achieving their intended effects and to check for the unexpected side-effects which can easily occur in a complex care system (see the beginning of this chapter). A good example of this is the thorough and broad evaluation of the Bernhoven and Beatrixziekenhuis experiments.[66] Note, too, that the wider implementation of a promising evidence-based intervention does not necessarily continue to produce the same positive results[67] and so further evaluation is always needed to enable timely adjustments at the policy level.

Our fourth dimension involves strengthening the learning ability of care providers. If experiments are found to generate greater efficiency, it is a task for government to remove any barriers preventing their further rollout. Take the Afferden case discussed earlier, for instance, where giving GPs greater care responsibilities proved so "successful" that it put the financial continuity of the local hospital at risk. In other words, an adjustment to the care landscape that was desirable from the sustainability and quality point of view was thwarted by the historical structure of that landscape. In cases of this kind, government may need to facilitate the required structural change through funding-based incentives. The NZa and the ZiN have recently made suggestions about how this can be done.[68]

---

[60] Tanke (2018).

[61] Tanke (2018).

[62] ZiN (2019).

[63] For example, the well-known ParkinsonNet initiative (https://www.parkinsonnet.nl/).

[64] NFK (2018).

[65] Vlaanderen et al. (2021).

[66] Douven et al. (2020).

[67] Al-Ubaydli et al. (2017).

[68] See, for example, the recent plan "Working together on appropriate care" (Samenwerken aan passende zorg, ZiN & NZA, 2020).

The final dimension whereby experimentation can improve the efficiency of care centres on patience. Positive effects often take a long time—sometimes many years—to materialize. This is because various actors have to adapt to new ways of organizing and designing care. It is therefore important to give consistent policies and initiatives a chance. In many cases it is better to adjust existing programmes following well-timed evaluations than to launch new initiatives—an approach which also avoids unnecessary red tape and pressure on the people involved.

**Budgetary Effects of Efficiency Measures**

Finally, we address the key question of how great a financial benefit we can actually expect a more efficient health and social care system to achieve. A general estimate of the likely impact of proposals in this domain can be found in the Ministry of Finance's "broad social review" (BMH) mentioned at the beginning of this section. The BMH divides possible measures into two main categories, according to their intent: (1) strengthening regulated competition and (2) strengthening regulated co-operation (see Table 5.4). The first of these includes suggestions like abolishing the so-called "impediment criterion" so as to allow health insurers to reimburse a significantly lower proportion of the cost of treatment not covered by a contract with a care provider, as well as strengthening the regulatory supervision of competition in the market and ensuring a greater focus upon the appropriate use of care. Amongst the possible measures in the second category are so-called "allocative standardization" (that is, reimbursement by insurers on the basis of best practices), the salaried employment of medical specialists (at present many are self-employed as individuals or members of a partnership) and extending the duty of care incumbent upon insurers and care providers.

Looking at the overall picture, we see that the estimated efficiency gains are greatest in the "strengthening regulated co-operation" category. In all, these could amount to between €2.4 and €3 billion. When it comes to "strengthening regulated competition", the BMH puts the figure at between €1.4 and €1.7 billion. The WRR does not argue here for or against implementation of any of the measures listed, in either category: that is ultimately a political matter, in which ideological and normative considerations inevitably play an important role. Our only concern is their potential impact (individually or as a whole) with regard to the topic of this report, the sustainability of the Dutch health and social care sector. From that perspective,

**Table 5.4** Estimated budgetary effects of efficiency-driven policy options from BMH 2020

| | Strengthening regulated competition (billions of euros) | Strengthening regulated co-operation (billions of euros) |
|---|---|---|
| Package management | 0.81–0.96 | 0.81–0.96 |
| Curative healthcare | 0.27 | 0.73–0.83 |
| Long-term care | 0.32–0.46 | 0.83–1.16 |
| Total | 1.40–1.69 | 2.37–2.95 |

Source: compiled from data in Inspectie der Rijksfinanciën (2020)

however, we note that—quite apart from the transition costs involved (the BMH's "co-operation" category, for example, includes taking all medical specialists into salaried employment, at a projected one-off cost of €2 billion[69])—strategies of this kind to make our system more efficient only address the issue of financial sustainability to a very limited extent. This does not mean that they have nothing to contribute, but rather that that contribution will only ever be relatively minor and so it is undesirable for these factors to monopolize the political debate. On top of that, such estimates are always shrouded in uncertainty and in the past have by no means consistently proven realistic (see also the discussion earlier in this chapter).

**Is Improving Efficiency Enough?**

A commitment to efficiency is important for the sustainability of our health and social care system, and will remain so. But even in an optimistic scenario, the yields to be gained from measures in this domain are almost always disappointing. Quite apart from triggering side-effects that are sure to affect staffing and societal sustainability, the bottom line is that the sustainability potential of efficiency-promoting policies is simply not sufficient to meet the challenge we face. After all, their total combined financial effect corresponds to no more than a year's worth of growth in the sector.[70] Of course, their yields can be supplemented through measures in other areas—updated framework agreements as a basis for stricter budgetary control, for instance, or measures from the "greater personal control" scenario, in which more limited collective entitlements (to residential and long-term care, for example) and health insurance cover are accompanied by higher or means-tested direct charges. These, however, are more matters of allocative choice (what do we offer collectively and what not?) than efficiency—a topic we consider in more detail in Part 3 of this report.

**Key Points—Improving Efficiency Within the Current System**

- International comparative evidence suggests that multiple care buyers and more decentralized organization of the healthcare system are associated with lower efficiency.
- Efficiency within the system can be improved through greater differentiation in care procurement, through better design of the care landscape where relevant and by giving care providers the space, trust and time they need to experiment.
- A commitment to efficiency is important, but on its own is not enough to resolve the sustainability challenge facing health and social care.

[69] A recent study commissioned by the Dutch House of Representatives questions the legal necessity to pay for goodwill. This could reduce the amount considerably (Meersma et al., 2021).

[70] Despite post-2012 budgetary restraint, the average annual increase in spending on health and social care over the past decade has been €2.4 billion. Over the past 20 years it has been €3.2 billion (in constant prices, €1.0 billion and €2.2 billion respectively).

## 5.4 Conclusion: A Commitment to Efficiency Is Essential But Not Enough

In this chapter we have looked at "sustainability through efficiency" in health and social care. And we have concluded that improving efficiency alone is highly unlikely to adequately address the threefold sustainability challenge we face in this domain. Figure 5.2 illustrates this point: we can make the sector more efficient and thus deliver more care with the same people and resources (topping up the dark blue "fluid" with the light blue), but not enough to meet future demand (the fluid still does not fill the jar).

So a commitment to greater *productive efficiency* on its own is insufficient to tackle the huge task ahead. Its potential yields are simply not enough. This by no means implies that we should abandon our efforts to improve efficiency—that remains a key part of the solution, not only because it helps to mitigate the scale of the challenge in the financial and staffing dimensions but also because it is crucial for societal sustainability. As shown in Chap. 3, public opinion is very much opposed to waste in health and social care and the prevailing thinking is that far too much money already goes to the "wrong" things. It is up to government and the sector itself to visibly fight wastage to the best of their ability in order to maintain broad support for our system. For both politicians and the public, however, it is highly tempting to regard a greater efficiency alone as the answer to all the sector's problems. Cutting down waste is always desirable, after all, and nobody is against it. That is also why the focus of this report is not ways to make care more efficient. Instead, we shall argue later on—after first addressing the issue of staffing sustainability in more detail—that a commitment to *allocative efficiency,* to making choices and setting priorities, is what is really needed to safeguard the future quality and accessibility of health and social care in the Netherlands.

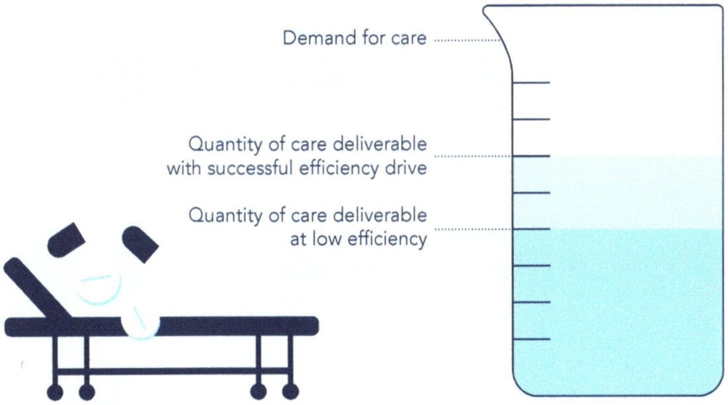


**Fig. 5.2** A commitment to efficiency is important but not enough

# Chapter 6
# Staffing Sustainability

Given the scale of the staffing sustainability problem, multiple policy approaches are required—although even they will not be enough on their own to cope with the growing demand for health and social care.

Given the expected demand for labour, the stagnating size of the workforce and the limited elasticity of labour-force participation, it is quite plausible that staffing sustainability will be a more pressing issue for the Dutch health and social care sector in the short and medium term than the financial dimension. In Chap. 3 we discussed staffing shortages in care and related problems such as workloads and retention, and looked ahead to the expected shortfalls in the long term. If nothing changes and yet the demand for care still has to be met in full, from 2040 onwards a quarter of our entire national workforce would have to be working in this sector. And a third of it between 2050 and 2060. Not only is this unrealistic, it would also have major repercussions for other sectors—public and private alike—that are already experiencing staff shortages or face them imminently due to the same scarcity of human resources. Such shortages are now becoming apparent within care, too, in some areas more than others (see Chap. 3). In this final chapter of the second part of our report, we look at ways to improve staffing sustainability. As in the rest of the report, we take a broad view and do not discuss potentially different approaches in specific subsectors.

We look first at the potential for increased efficiency. In the previous chapter we focused mainly upon efficiency in relation to financial resources—how much money we need to invest in order to achieve certain health gains. That is all about cost-effectiveness. Now we turn our attention to efficiency as it relates to the staffing of health and social care: how many people do we need to employ to provide a certain "volume" of care? In other words, what can we do about labour productivity? If that can be improved, fewer people will be needed to provide the same amount of care. Which in turn directly benefits staffing sustainability. This is all about how best to



G. Werner et al., *Financial, Staffing and Societal Sustainability of Dutch Health Care*, Research for Policy, https://doi.org/10.1007/978-3-031-58564-7_6

deploy the people—or rather the working hours—we have available (all other things being equal). The goal being to do more with the same number of hours.

Besides labour productivity, a number of other factors can help bolster staffing sustainability. These centre on the number of people—or again, to be exact, the number of hours—at our disposal. The basic goal here is to glean more hours worked in care from a more or less constant potential workforce. In broad terms, this effort falls under the heading "labour-market policy". And within it we can distinguish three crucial needs: (1) better staff retention, (2) persuading existing employees to work more hours and (3) recruiting new personnel.[1] To keep people in the care sector, what is required first and foremost is better working conditions. To encourage them to work more, it is important to increase both labour-force participation and the hours worked per person. And recruitment is about making care an attractive option for potential employees. For each of these three needs, clear targets should be set and a raft of concrete measures devised in their pursuit. Some of which might address more than one need. Take staff remuneration, for instance—a factor we look at in particular detail below. It can influence both recruitment and retention. Moreover, interactions are conceivable between labour-market policies and labour productivity; some measures affect both. Whilst higher productivity may lead to more stress and burnout, addressing the number of hours worked might actually reduce them.

Incidentally, it is important here to distinguish between quantitative and qualitative stumbling blocks in the labour market.[2] Achieving greater capacity, however it is done, in no way guarantees that the demand for care will be met any better. It is also important that the workforce in this sector be suited *qualitatively* to the changing demand for care in the future—and as we saw in Chap. 2, such change is more or less inevitable if only because health profiles are evolving. So even if staff work more, harder, more efficiently and for longer, the quality, accessibility and affordability of care may still decline because, for instance, employees have become too specialized and hence less easy to deploy flexibly or broadly. Which only compounds the problem of staffing sustainability.

## 6.1 Labour Productivity, Technology and Sustainability

### Labour Productivity and the Sustainability Challenge

Is it possible to address the sustainability challenges facing the care sector by using its workforce more efficiently? Labour productivity is about how much of a "product" a worker can produce per unit of time. In our case the "product" is care, so an increase in productivity means that fewer people are needed to deliver the same amount of care. Or that more care can be "produced" by the same number of people.

---

[1] This breakdown aligns with the challenges facing the labour market in care as identified by Professor Ronald Batenburg in his inaugural lecture (Batenburg 2019).

[2] After Batenburg (2019).

**Table 6.1** Total labour costs as a share of operating income in health and social care, 2018

| Domain | Labour costs (share) |
|---|---|
| Hospitals | 60% |
| Inpatient mental healthcare | 75% |
| Disability care | 70% |
| Residential child and youth care services | 72% |
| Non-residential child and youth care services | 73% |
| Nursing, residential and home care | 72% |
| Total: Health and social care | 67% |
| Total: All economic activities | 53% |

Source: CBS Business Accounts. For calculation, see online Appendix 5

This is closely related to the notion of staffing sustainability. After all, labour productivity determines how much care can be delivered by the available workforce.

Since personnel costs account for the majority of spending in a labour-intensive sector like care, this in turn has indirect implications for financial sustainability. In the Netherlands, on average those costs represent 67 per cent of expenditure across health and social care as a whole (see Table 6.1). This is well above the average of 53 per cent for all economic activities combined, with outliers downwards of 12 per cent in mineral extraction and 26 per cent in the energy supply sector. In a high-tech environment like a hospital, staffing's share of total costs is logically lower (60 per cent) than in, say, nursing homes (72 per cent) or inpatient mental health facilities (75 per cent).[3] There is also a link to financial sustainability through the so-called Baumol effect: if productivity growth in a sector lags behind the average for the economy as a whole, relative prices in that sector rise (see Chap. 2). This effect is typical for labour-intensive parts of the economy.

Finally, rising labour productivity can also be expected to exert indirect effects upon societal sustainability. After all, public concerns about the quality and accessibility of care correlate closely with worries about staff shortages (see Chap. 3). So if productivity growth can mitigate staff shortages, that could be good for societal sustainability.

From a sustainability point of view, then, there are good reasons to want to push for productivity growth in this sector. But it is important that this be done in a sustainable way. In the short term, for example, productivity can be increased simply by increasing workloads. But this affects not only the quality of care, but also the retention and recruitment of new staff—and so may actually harm staffing sustainability in the longer term. In this section we look at the potential for a productivity growth strategy in care. In doing so we first look at the historical background, internationally as well as in the Netherlands. Although past performance is neither a

[3] For details of this calculation, see online Appendix 5.

guarantee for the future nor necessarily a limiting factor, we can learn something from it as regards the extent to which productivity growth represents a realistic basis for care policy. After that we analyse how a commitment to enabling technology—in particular e-health—might help achieve productivity gains in care. In many other sectors, after all, greater productivity is closely associated with the use of technology. A carpenter can make more tables per hour with an electric drill than with a hand drill. If e-health allows nurses to supervise a larger number of patients,[4] then their productivity increases in a similar fashion: each worker is "producing" more care. In the context of labour productivity, this type of technology is therefore called "labour-saving". We look primarily at health and social care as a whole, but on occasions also draw conclusions about particular subsectors.

**Historical and International Productivity Growth**

We first look at the historical picture: how has labour productivity in care evolved in recent years and how does that compare with other sectors? Figure 6.1 shows the trend in value added per worker as a measure of labour productivity. Even at a glance we see that the care sector is lagging significantly behind the economy as a whole—its productivity rose by a total of just 1.7 per cent in the period 1995–2019, compared with 23.4 per cent for all economic activities combined—and manufacturing in particular (where the increase was 82.5 per cent).[5] According to the Netherlands Bureau for Economic Policy Analysis (Centraal Planbureau, CPB), labour productivity in the commercial sector rose by 32 per cent over the same period.[6]

This difference reflects a fundamental economic phenomenon. Productivity growth is largely determined by the potential within a given production process to apply division of labour (specialization) and capital intensification. The opportunities for both are particularly high in manufacturing industry, but far more limited in services. And especially so in personal services in general and care in particular, where the human aspect remains crucial and is also intrinsically important to patients. Moreover, processes in care are less repetitive than in other sectors and cannot be divided into standardized—and mostly automated—component parts in the same way.

[4] Hilbers-Modderman & De Bruijn (2013).

[5] These figures are per working person. Due to the decline in the number of hours worked in sectors other than care, the discrepancy by that measure is even starker: the increases in added value between three-year averages for 1996 and 2018 are 4 per cent for care and 26 per cent for the economy as a whole. Although we should here point out that whereas economic analyses measure growth in labour productivity in terms of income generated ("added value"), when it comes to care we are more interested in the volume of care "produced" using the available resources. That, after all, is what determines how much care people can use. Looking at that factor, we find that the increase in labour productivity in care is somewhat greater: 13 per cent for three-year averages between 1996 and 2018. Nevertheless, the gap with the commercial economy remains clear.

[6] CPB (2021) (core data table: commercial labour productivity per hour).

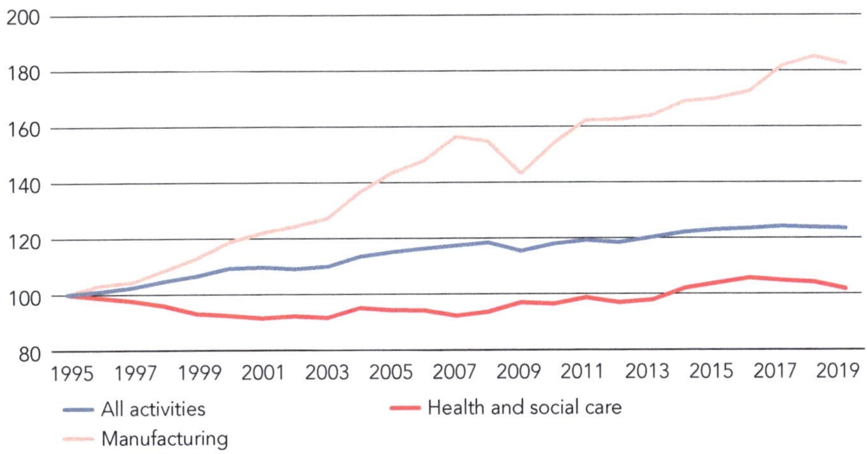


**Fig. 6.1** Value added per worker in health and social care, manufacturing and the economy as a whole, 1995–2019 (indexed: 1995 = 100). Source: CBS Statline (National Accounts)

Although only limited international comparative research is available on this topic, what studies have been undertaken suggest that the Netherlands is not unique. One conducted in the UK, for instance, puts total productivity growth in healthcare there during the period 1995–2016 at 7 per cent.[7] A comparative analysis of a number of other—mainly English-speaking—countries reveals similarly modest growth figures, and in some cases even contraction.[8] So not only does the phenomenon appear not to be confined to the Netherlands, but it seems that nowhere have the far-reaching technological changes of recent decades been able to substantially change the pattern of limited productivity growth in care.

**Productivity Growth Through Technology and e-health**

In Chap. 2 we discussed how sustainability issues are influenced by technological developments. It became clear that that influence can come from advances in both medical and enabling technologies. E-health is one example of the latter, as are process innovations. These are developments that change not so much the care on offer (in the way a new medicine does, say), as how it is delivered. Whereas medical technologies tend to put strong upward pressure on the costs of care, the picture is more diffuse when it comes to enabling technologies. So far the expectations they raise seem to have gone largely unfulfilled, but that does not alter the fact that such technologies could in principle have a positive impact for sustainability in the future. Below we elaborate upon the opportunities and obstacles surrounding the deployment of enabling technologies, as well as their potential future role in the sustainability of care.

[7] Charlesworth (2019).

[8] Sheiner & Malinovskaya (2016).

Digital information and communication technologies (ICT) have the potential to support or improve care.[9] For example, they could allow more treatments to be delivered remotely and so enable the elderly and other people in need of care to live at home for longer. Take GPS trackers, for example, or the so-called assistive robots which help people with dementia remember to take their medication or relay messages from a family carer.[10] ICT can also enhance the accessibility of care, as in the case of remote monitoring via sensors worn on the body. One example is the "smart patch", which can measure heart rate, breathing frequency and temperature. When it comes to improving quality, ICT has the potential to bring integrated care closer to realization[11] by, say, facilitating interaction with one's GP in respect of home care as well as harmonizing its delivery. In principle, this should save money as it would enable a shift away from expensive second-line care to cheaper first-line provision. Such innovations thus seem to open up opportunities to make care more efficient and less labour-intensive.[12] Especially in care for the elderly, this could offer a lifeline given that task's labour-intensive nature and the increasing pressure it is under due to ageing and staff shortages. In Japan, robotics and domotics are already heavily used and technological developments are seen as a way to organize long-term care sustainably.[13] Covid-19 has also driven up use of e-health in parts of the care sector, since the crisis put particular pressure on services for frail elderly and chronically ill people living at home and increased the need to be able to deliver them remotely (see Box 6.1). But whether these effects will last remains an open question.

**Box 6.1 E-health and Covid-19**

A study by research institute Nivel of more than 1400 Dutch general practices shows that three quarters of them have started to make more use of e-health applications.[14] The biggest change has been the rise in the use of video consultations, but there has also been a significant increase in online requests for repeat prescriptions. During the pandemic, 64 per cent of practices started conducting video consultations with patients for the first time. Of these, a quarter said they would continue to do so intensively after Covid-19 has passed. This indicates that a decline is to be expected at that point. Respondents cite the increase in the use of e-health as a major administrative burden, and online or video consultations are not viewed as saving time.[15] Meanwhile, an initiative with home oxygen use that included the telemonitoring of Covid-19 patients from the Maasstadziekenhuis hospital in Rotterdam proved safe and patient-friendly, and reduced both the length of hospital stays and costs.[16]

---

[9] Nictiz & Nivel (2019).

[10] See Van der Meulen (2020).

[11] Velez Lapao & Dussault (2017).

[12] Ishiguro (2018); Dethlefs & Martin (2006).

[13] Ishiguro (2018); Kruse et al. (2021).

[14] Van Tuyl et al. (2020a).

[15] Meurs et al. (2020a).

[16] van Herwerden et al. (2021).

**Barriers to e-health and Digital Care**

The Netherlands is not doing as well as countries such as Spain, Portugal, the UK and Sweden in adopting digital forms of care. In the most recent Digital Health Index, our nation ranks eighth. In a 2020 advisory report on futureproofing care, the Social and Economic Council of the Netherlands (Sociaal-Economische Raad, SER) identified some significant opportunities for e-health.[17] Use of this technology can deliver health benefits through better and more timely care. In addition, technology can strengthen the patient's position, enhance job satisfaction amongst health professionals, improve the transfer of information and cut red tape. Developments like artificial intelligence (AI) and big data have the potential to make care more personalized. For instance, telemonitoring can support self-management and virtual reality can offer an alternative to conventional care.[18] The Netherlands Court of Audit (Algemene Rekenkamer), however, observes barriers of several kinds still hindering the widespread implementation of e-health in care for the elderly. These occur at multiple levels and are interrelated.[19]

- *Human barriers.* Care users and providers regularly lack the time, knowledge and skills needed to take advantage of e-health, or an organization-wide vision of how it should be used.
- *Technical barriers.* There is often a mismatch between digital care applications and actual needs. For example, applications are too complicated for the relatively simple problems they are intended to solve. In many cases, moreover, the true effectiveness of an application is unclear, making it hard to choose from the multitude of alternatives available.
- *Financial barriers.* Claiming back the costs of e-health provision from insurers is not always possible because policies do not explicitly cover it, and providers are also sometimes unfamiliar with the funding options that do exist.

Such barriers play a role not only in care for the elderly, but across the sector. Other obstacles mentioned by the SER include patients and professionals not being familiar with e-health technology, a lack of standardization in data exchange, funding issues and a lack of direction.[20] As a result, many promising initiatives never go beyond pilots, living labs and local implementation. According the Court of Audit, there is a particular need for integrated forms of funding across different domains, as well as more possibilities to learn from others' experiences. This finding is in line with recommendations made by the Council of Public Health and Society (Raad voor Volksgezondheid en Samenleving, RVS) and the Dutch Healthcare Authority (Nederlandse Zorgautoriteit, NZA).[21] The NZA wants to promote digital care through a more integrated approach and better funding on the demand side, and by including agreements on its use in care contracts, especially those covering high-volume services like outpatient clinics.[22] Another idea is to lower the insurance

[17] SER (2020).

[18] SER (2020).

[19] Algemene Rekenkamer (2020c).

[20] SER (2020).

[21] RVS (2020b, c); NZA (2020a).

[22] Health insurers have started doing this to some extent. See ICT & Health (2021); Gibbels (2012).

excess for digital care in order to channel existing demand into this form of provision.[23] The SER, meanwhile, has identified a number of preconditions for successful implementation. First, the sector's ICT infrastructure has to be in order, including both well-functioning electronic patient records and a secure, user-friendly personal health environment. Only then can data be better utilized for novel applications such as AI. This also requires effective regulation, whilst examples of best practices and supraregional and thematic co-operation will be needed for a national rollout.[24] Above all, though, care professionals should be actively engaged with digitalization—by, for example, paying more attention to e-health in their training, as well as specifically considering those sections of the population at risk of exclusion due a lack of digital skills. The SER concludes that whilst expectations with regard to the digital transformation are high, especially when it comes to so-called "blended care" (combining conventional care with digital technology), its actual outcomes so far remain disappointing. Whereas digitalization in other sectors has major consequences for core processes, revenue models and productivity, such effects are only marginally discernible in health and social care.[25] Considerable policy effort and investment have been put into promoting e-health in the Netherlands, but it has still failed to catch on—at least until the Covid-19 pandemic.[26]

**E-health and Productivity Growth**

A substantial body of advisory literature is available on the barriers to e-health. But the fundamental question we face is this: if we were successful in removing those barriers, what would be the likely effects for labour productivity and hence for staffing and financial sustainability? That is a difficult question to answer, not least because that answer depends in part upon yet-to-be-developed technologies, the scale and scope of which are currently unknown. Another more general problem here is a lack of scientific research on the efficacy and efficiency of innovative interventions in health and social care.

Nevertheless, some studies have looked into this question. For example, by examining innovations that have succeeded in at least partially overcoming the technical, human and financial barriers mentioned above. Most of this research focuses upon the cost effects of new technology, and sometimes also its staffing impact.[27] Where e-health is implemented successfully, how costs are affected varies widely. On the staffing front, no consistent picture emerges with regard to reduced needs or improved labour productivity. Whilst real gains are often made in terms of quality or accessibility of care, and patients tend to be satisfied,[28] this does not mean that either efficiency or labour productivity have automatically gone up. Again, this

---

[23] NZA (2021).

[24] SER (2020).

[25] McKinsey Global Institute (2016).

[26] Nictiz & Nivel (2019). See also previous e-health monitors.

[27] For metastudies see, for example: Elbert et al. (2014); Mistry (2012); Steventon et al. (2013); Sanyal (2018); Velez Lapao & Dussault (2017).

[28] See also, for example, Meurs et al. (2020a).

result is not specific to the Netherlands: it applies to several Western countries. One important factor hampering the deployment of technology across the board—and not only in the care sector—is the lack of personnel with the requisite digital skills (see also earlier in this section).[29] Viewed from the sustainability perspective, these empirical results reinforce the historical picture: it remains very difficult to systematically accelerate productivity growth in a labour-intensive sector like care.

Recent research by Nivel shows that the Dutch population is for the most part positive about the use of e-health. At the same time, though, the pandemic has not shifted public opinion favourably with regard to the added value of digital applications when it comes to, say, contacts with providers, the cost of care and its delivery at or closer to home. Indeed, the experience of Covid-19 has made the Dutch more negative about the contribution e-health can make to the quality of care and to better control over one's health.[30] This technology's fundamental limitation remains the high importance for patients of the human factor, of having another person's time and attention. This touches upon issues of societal sustainability. A synthesis by the SCP of current knowledge concerning care for elderly people living at home shows that they accept the use of technology when it comes to diagnostics but are resistant to the deployment of care robots when these devices start taking over interpersonal contacts.[31] The need for a human component in the interaction makes introducing technology into care settings—and also into education, for instance—substantially different from process innovations in, say, industry.[32] In the latter case, the core purpose of the innovation is usually to save time. In care, by contrast, saving time is often seen as undesirable. This raises a substantial barrier to the deployment of labour-saving technology in care, and hence to its potential to increase productivity.

This does not mean that there are no gains to be made. The pandemic revealed, for example, that there is real potential for much wider use of techniques like video consultations (see Box 6.1). But what it does mean is that caution needs to be exercised in expecting technology to make staffing much more efficient anywhere in the health and social care sector. All things considered, we conclude that whilst the use of enabling technologies like e-health looks likely to make some contribution towards improving labour productivity, there is no good evidence that it will do so to such an extent as to meet the staffing sustainability challenges we face. There are some encouraging examples, and of course we can never be sure what will be developed in the more distant future, but the implicit expectation that new technology will somehow leave substantial productivity growth there for the taking is based more upon hope than evidence. That said, employers in the care sector and policymakers should still make every effort to organize work processes in less

---

[29] See, for example: OECD (2019a, d). Despite increasing digitalization, labour productivity is generally declining in OECD countries. Whilst the Netherlands has a high internet penetration rate, it lags behind Europe as a whole in terms of digitally skilled personnel.

[30] Meurs et al. (2020b).

[31] De Klerk et al. (2019); PWC (2017).

[32] Polder (2018).

labour-intensive ways. A number of recent advisory publications offer guidance on how this could be done.[33] Greater efficiency in health and social care can be achieved through the better utilization of human as well as material resources (see also Chap. 5).

**Key Issues—Labour Productivity, Technology and Sustainability**

- Historically, productivity growth in health and social care lags behind that in the wider economy. This is a consequence of the labour-intensive nature of the care "product".
- The pattern has not changed in recent decades despite the far-reaching technological advances achieved during that time.
- Enabling technologies like e-health offer some potential to improve productivity, but are highly unlikely to adequately mitigate the challenges of staffing sustainability in the near future.

## 6.2 Labour-Market Policies in Care: Finding More Staff

Besides a commitment to improving labour productivity, a number of other policy directions can help address staff shortages in the health and social care sector by increasing the number of people it employs—and especially the number of hours they work. As mentioned earlier, in this section we look at three crucial needs: (1) better staff retention, (2) persuading existing employees to work more hours and (3) recruiting new personnel. Another means to boost staffing in the care sector is through remuneration policy. This can influence both recruitment and retention and is a fourth angle we look at below.

### *6.2.1 Staff Retention, Workloads and Turnover*

Staff retention is really about nothing more or less than being a good employer. By addressing issues like workloads and personnel leaving their jobs, it should be possible to keep people already working in care where they are. Chap. 3 showed that there are currently significant staff shortages in parts of the sector and that the physical and psychological strain of the work involved is adding to capacity problems. Above-average rates of sick leave and of long-term absenteeism due to burnout are part of this. Almost half of all care workers consider their workload too high or even much too high.[34]

[33] SER (2020); RVS (2020b, c); NZA (2020a).

[34] AZW care surveys 2018 and 2019. Incidentally, perception of the level of autonomy afforded by being able to determine one's own working hours more independently did increase. See also https://www.cbs.nl/nl-nieuws/2016/46/werknemers-in-de-zorg-ervaren-hoge-werkdruk

A questionnaire-based survey by Nivel of nurses, professional carers, support workers and practice assistants active in first-line patient care (see Box 3.6 in Chap. 3) revealed that almost a quarter felt they were working in a "crisis situation" and trying to do too much too fast They also reported spending a lot of time on record-keeping and reporting, leading to perceptions of increased workloads and reduced professional autonomy. It is factors like these which are behind the relatively high rate of staff turnover in the care sector, especially amongst nursing personnel.[35] That rate is substantial across the board, with peaks of between 11 and 12 per cent in nursing, residential and home care and in child and youth care services.[36] Staff shortages further exacerbate workloads, of course, which can lead to a vicious circle and even more people leaving the sector.

One key factor here is the administrative burden. Staff spend too much time—as much as 30 per cent of their working hours, according to one estimate[37] –on process accountability, at the expense of patient-related activities. As the Nivel survey revealed, this is a major cause of high workloads, low job satisfaction and staff turnover. Excessive "red tape" is a problem for doctors too, as highlighted by initiatives like the campaigns "More time for the patient" ("Meer tijd voor de patiënt") by the National Association of General Practitioners (Landelijke Huisartsen Vereniging, LHV)[38] and "Let doctors be doctors" ("Laat dokters dokteren") by the Dutch Association of Medical Specialists (Federatie van Medisch Specialisten, FMS).[39] As we concluded in Chap. 5, an abundance of steering and control mechanisms is an inevitable side-effect of the complexity of the health and social care system, fuelled by the demands of health insurers and inspectorates, by risk aversion, by liability issues and so on. Such mechanisms not only engender high implementation costs, they also stretch staffing sustainability to the limit. This is by no means a new observation—it has been raised time and again in advisory papers in recent years[40]—but is no less critical for that.

In the light of obvious staff shortages, various policies have been put in place in the past few years to mitigate staff workloads, absenteeism and turnover. We concur with the SER and the RVS when they state that policy of this kind should be implemented more widely. Both advocate a firm commitment to staff retention through better staffing policies with a focus upon easing pressure in the workplace and

[35] WRR (2020b).

[36] On average over the period 2014–2019, the rate was 10.8 per cent in nursing, residential and home care and 12.1 per cent in child and youth care services. For care in general it was 9.4 per cent, for general hospitals 6.7 per cent and for university hospitals 7.7 per cent. Figures derived from CBS AZW Statline: https://azwstatline.cbs.nl/#/Azw/nl/dataset/24049NED/table?ts=1593595854441 and https://azwstatline.cbs.nl/#/Azw/nl/dataset/24017NED/table?ts=1620042632938

[37] In 2018 the Ministry of Health, Welfare and Sport launched "(Ont)regel de Zorg", a plan of action to "deregulate and sort out" care. Under this, a range of actors are working together to tackle the regulatory burden.

[38] LHV (2021).

[39] Medisch Contact (2018).

[40] In, for example: SER (2020); RVS (2020d).

creating more room for professional autonomy.[41] This opinion is shared by the Work in Care Committee (Commissie Werken in de Zorg). In short, job satisfaction in the care sector needs to rise. Front-line providers should be given more room to deliver actual patient care. At present they often lack the authority to shape the care they provide, or to influence their own working hours and processes.[42] In a separate report, the WRR has already called for greater "control at work" for professionals in care (and other sectors).[43] Means to achieve this include greater autonomy, more time for patients/clients and better recognition of their professionalism. On this latter point, the RVS notes that many professional carers and nurses lack attractive career prospects. For carers in particular, their financial remuneration and contracts are often so limited that they are not economically independent.[44]

A commitment to tackling the issues mentioned above can help reduce staff turnover and retain people in the care sector, thus alleviating the situation in the domains under the greatest pressure. Given the scale of the task, however, it is highly questionable whether better staff retention alone will be sufficient to meet the future demand for labour. Indeed, whilst turnover in this sector is relatively high it does not massively exceed the rates in other parts of the economy. Overall, the proportion of people in the Netherlands who change job in a given year, some 12 per cent of the workforce, closely matches the figure for care specifically.[45] This suggests that while there is potential for improvement, there are also limits to that potential.

### 6.2.2 Greater Labour-Force Participation

Can we persuade people already working in care to work more, and can we entice more people to work in care? Starting with the latter question, we first look in general terms at labour-force participation in the Netherlands. Average active participation in the economy as a whole has risen systemically since the mid-1980s and is

---

[41] SER (2020); RVS (2020d).

[42] RVS (2020d). See also https://www.venvn.nl/nieuws/merkbaar-beter-tijd-voor-meer-zeggenschap-op-de-werkvloer/. Trade union CNV Care and Welfare (CNV Zorg en Welzijn) and the Netherlands Association of Nurses and Professional Carers (Vereniging voor Verplegenden en Verzorgenden, V&VN) have launched the joint project "Noticeably Better" ("Merkbaar Beter"), in which they offer employers 50 interventions (training courses on workloads, for instance) with the aim of improving staff input, easing pressure and raising job satisfaction in health and social care.

[43] WRR (2020b).

[44] RVS (2020d).

[45] It is lower than this overall average in some specific sectors, such as manufacturing (8 per cent), public administration (7 per cent) and education (8 per cent), and higher in others—substantially so in the case of business services (20 per cent), for instance. Calculations derived from CBS data at https://opendata.cbs.nl/#/cbs/nl/dataset/71792ned/table?ts=1620045627298

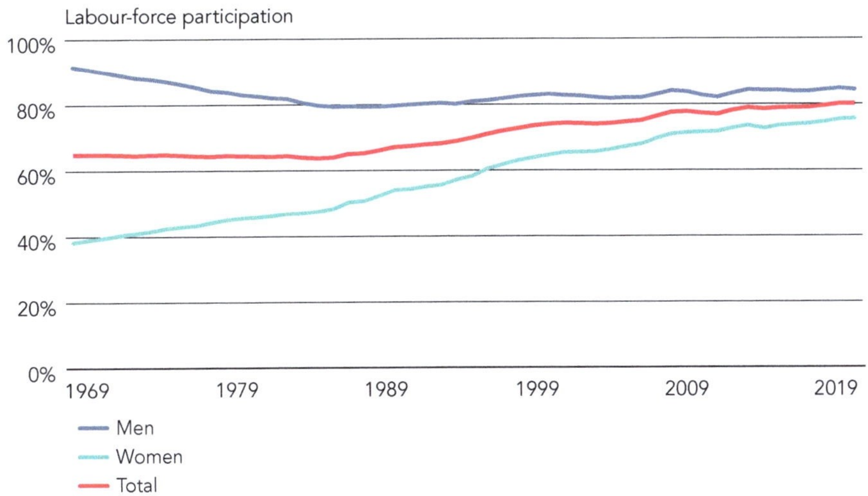


**Fig. 6.2** Labour-force participation by persons aged 15–65, 1969–2020. Source: CBS Statline

now above 80 per cent (see Fig. 6.2).[46] This increase is entirely attributable to increasing female participation in the workforce; the rate of male participation has remained stable throughout this period (see Fig. 6.2). Incidentally, these figures still say nothing about the number of hours people work: women are more likely to work part-time than men. But they do indicate that, although the employment rate amongst women could still go up further, the potential for it to do so has fallen sharply. In times of high levels of employment, as at present, any substantial increase in labour-force participation is likely to come at the expense of unpaid tasks (including informal care), which are thus pushed into the formal market. So it might actually lead to further shortages in the care sector.

How is the picture set to evolve in the future? In the final report of their project "Population Reconnaissance 2050" ("Verkenning bevolking 2050"), the Netherlands Interdisciplinary Demographic Institute (Nederlands Interdisciplinair Demografisch Instituut, NIDI) and Statistics Netherlands (Centraal *Bureau* voor de Statistiek, CBS) conclude that shrinkage of the working-age population can be prevented only through greater labour-force participation by both women and older workers, in combination with higher labour migration.[47] Greater participation by older workers would be particularly important for the care sector because some of its domains

[46] This figure is for the 15–65 age group. Influenced in part by the policy push for an increased level of labour-force participation, in recent years the upper age limit used in these measurements has been raised to 70. In the light of life expectancy and the official retirement age, however, this extension is irrelevant for earlier years and only distorts the figures and the trend curve. The active working population aged between 65 and 70 increased in number from 67,000 to 278,000 between 2000 and 2020, according to Statistics Netherlands, but still constitutes only 3 per cent of the total national labour force.

[47] NIDI & CBS (2021).

have a relatively high proportion of staff aged 55 or over who are heading towards retirement in the coming years. This is most true in nursing and residential care, where 29 per cent of nurses and professional carers fall into that age category.[48] We discuss labour migration in the next section, but now first turn our attention to female labour-force participation.

Given the high proportion of women working in care—about 80 per cent of the sector's workforce, the vast majority of whom (82 per cent) are part-timers[49]—increasing the number of hours worked by female staff in particular offers great potential to help overcome its staff shortages. According to NIDI and Statistics Netherlands, were the percentage of working women in 2050 to have reached the same level as the figure for men and were the male-female differential in part-time work to have halved, that would have a major effect upon the size of the workforce. By their calculations, it would have added between 500,000 and 700,000 full-time equivalents (FTEs[50]).[51] Since, as we have stated previously, by that time around one in three working people in the Netherlands would have to be employed in the care sector to meet demand for its services, that potentially represents an extra 200,000 or so FTEs for care. They would make a substantial contribution towards its future staffing sustainability, but would still not be nearly enough to meet the estimated shortfall of some 1.4 million workers in 2050 (see Table 3.4 in Chap. 3).

The NIDI/Statistics Netherlands figures nevertheless suggest that there is good reason to try to influence demographic trends by investing in participation. But how realistic is this? Female labour-force participation has only increased in recent decades because of policy moves to treat couples' incomes separately for tax purposes, to reduce the taxation of labour and so on. The latter effort, in particular, may be hard to maintain in the future. After all, the rising demand for care itself is putting increasing pressure on our collective finances. Moreover, the percentage of people in employment is already so high that there is now only very limited potential to increase it any further without straining other aspects of life, including such activities as childcare and informal care (see above). Realizing that potential, as NIDI and Statistics Netherlands also conclude, will thus require that several crucial preconditions are met: affordable professional childcare for all who need it as well as a shift away from traditional gender roles in the home. Enabling people to stay in work

[48] In the health and welfare category as a whole, 24 per cent of employees are aged 55 or older (compared with 20 per cent across all economic activities). Negative outliers include child and youth care services (16 per cent) and childcare (12 per cent). See CBS (2020e) (https://www.cbs.nl/nl-nl/longread/statistische-trends/2020/arbeidsmarktprofiel-van-zorg-en-welzijn/3-kenmerken-branches-zorg-en-welzijn)

[49] The average contracted working week in health and social care is 23.6 hours, whilst 28 per cent of contracts are for 20 hours or less. See Stichting het potentieel pakken 2020; Commissie Werken in de zorg 2020.

[50] FTE stands for "full-time equivalent" and indicates how many people would be on the payroll if the entire workforce were in full-time employment. Part-time positions are expressed as a proportion of full-time one (e.g. 0.5 FTE).

[51] NIDI & CBS (2021).

after the official retirement age is also not without its problems. Given the picture we have painted of high workloads and rates of long-term absenteeism through illness in care, staying on would probably be too heavy a burden for a significant proportion of older staff unless and until working conditions changed substantially for the better. Nursing, residential and home care has long had the sector's highest rate of long-term absenteeism, and across the board the rate is higher amongst employees aged 55 or over than their younger colleagues.[52]

From a historical perspective, the past few decades have been exceptional. Although population growth has halved since 1970, from around 1.2 per cent a year to an average of 0.5 per cent in the past decade, the size of the working population actually grew faster from the mid-1980s onwards (in absolute figures, from 6.3 to 9.0 million for the 15–65 age category). Half of this growth can be explained by the increase in labour-force participation. But now that the growth of the working population has come more or less to a standstill and the potential to further increase participation rates has largely been exhausted, the finite nature of the strategy with that aim is becoming more apparent than ever. The potential of a commitment to expand the number of hours worked also seems more limited in the long run than the NIDI/Statistics Netherlands estimates suggest. The number of hours in the average working year in the care sector was 1181 in 2019, less than in the economy as a whole (1440). Moreover, that figure has remained largely constant over the past 25 years (see Fig. 6.3). With several tens of thousands of jobs in care to be filled in

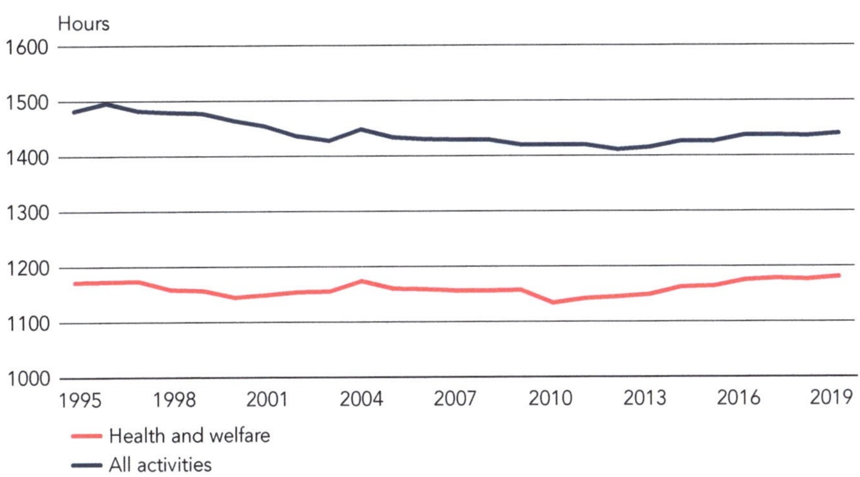


**Fig. 6.3** Hours worked per person per year in the health and welfare category and in the economy as a whole, 1995–2019. Source: CBS Statline

[52] See, for example: https://transvorm.arbeidsmarktinbeeld.nl/transvorm-artikel-ziekteverzuim-in-zorg-en-welzijnandhttps://www.cbs.nl/nl-nl/nieuws/2021/12/ziekteverzuim-verpleging-verzorging-en-thuiszorg-stijgt-tot-8-5-procent

the coming years, increasing individual workers' hours may offer some relief[53]—although the problem remains that this has the potential to exacerbate the issue of workloads and absenteeism rates highlighted in the previous section.[54] Above all, however, such an increase goes against the long-term trend in the wider economy: for a quarter of a century now, the number of hours worked per person per year in the Netherlands has been declining steadily. As we have become more and more prosperous, the relative value of work and income has decreased and that of leisure has increased. The care sector will find it hard to buck this trend.

Increasing the supply of labour in care is further complicated by the general trend in the field of taxes and their distribution. Having fallen from 1994 onwards, since 2005 the collective fiscal burden in the Netherlands has again been rising systematically—not least due to rapidly growing public expenditure on health and social care until 2013.[55] Taxes and other statutory levies have gone from making up 35 per cent of gross domestic product (GDP) in 2005 to more than 39 per cent now—a return to the levels of 1976 and of 1989–1990 (see Chap. 3 and Fig. 3.5 for more details). Because of the way higher taxation affects growth in the supply of labour, there is a direct trade-off here between financial pressure and staffing sustainability: as healthcare spending increases, and thus also its cost, it becomes harder to deliver sufficient growth in the supply of labour to keep pace with the rising cost burden.

Yet another problem is that the marginal pressure on labour—that part of an increase in gross income that does not result in an increase in disposable earnings—has been levelling off for some time, making it relatively high even for those on lower incomes. As a consequence, people earning as little as €23,000 a year see less than half of their additional gross pay for working extra hours actually reach their wage packet.[56] Looking to the future, easing this pressure could prove a promising incentive. Empirical research supports the idea that the current situation increases systemic inefficiency in the labour market: a rise in pay rates at the top end of the income distribution scale has only a limited effect upon the number of hours worked per person, whilst a rise at the bottom end actually acts as a significant deterrent to work.[57] As we noted in Chap. 3, an increase in the marginal tax burden primarily influences decisions on whether to work more or fewer hours.

---

[53] The Catching the Potential Foundation (Stichting Het Potentieel Pakken) is pushing to achieve this through its Contract Extension in Care (Contractuitbreiding in de zorg) initiative. See https://www.hetpotentieelpakken.nl

[54] Cf. McKinsey Global Institute (2018).

[55] All other things being equal, slower growth in public expenditure on care should result in either a lower overall tax burden or higher spending on other public services. Although whether this would actually have happened is of course speculative.

[56] See Ministerie van Financiën (2019). The marginal tax burden rises steeply above a personal gross income of around €13,000, reaching a level of 55 per cent from €25,000 onwards. At that point it levels out until gross income reaches just over €60,000. It then rises to 60 per cent, before falling gradually at €100,000 and beyond.

[57] Jongen et al. (2015). See also Commissie van Dijkhuizen (2013).

That said, other research shows that responses to financial incentives vary enormously and that their effectiveness is therefore highly reliant upon good design and targeting.[58] Generic tax relief achieves relatively little; labour-force participation by single people and by men cohabiting with a partner is fairly insensitive to financial incentives, whilst the opposite is true for mothers with young children.[59] Moreover, this approach appears more effective in influencing decisions whether or not to work than in encouraging people to increase the number of hours or days they work. On the other hand, policies that increase the income differential between those in work and not in work—examples being a more generous employment tax credit at the lower end of the income spectrum and limiting income support for low earners—yield relatively high participation rates. But this effect is offset by an increase in income inequality and by broader social repercussions (such as the impact upon informal care). Finally, the rather blunt workings of the Dutch system of tax allowances has an inhibiting effect upon the number of hours worked. As things currently stand, attempts to persuade nurses and professional carers, say, to work more hours by increasing their pay are often frustrated by the resulting cuts to their childcare, care and rent allowances, which on balance leave them earning very little—or even nothing—extra.

The effectiveness of policies aimed at increasing employment in health and social care thus has as much to do with general issues in the Dutch labour market as with the specific situation in that sector. Reforming the system of tax incentives might persuade existing care workers to work more hours, which is where the greatest scope for expansion lies, but on the other hand—and due in large part to spending on care itself—taxation overall is likely to remain under pressure. In any case, adjusting marginal pressures remains a political matter in which the broad distributional effects inherent in any such shift are hugely important.

### *6.2.3 Recruiting New Staff*

Besides retaining existing staff and persuading them to work more hours, a third option to expand employment in health and social care is to attract new workers. In this respect, factors like good working conditions and career prospects are important as they are with the other two approaches described above.

**Greater Commitment to Informal Care**

One possible way to meet future demand is with more unpaid informal carers. But this alternative has severe limitations (see Chap. 2), not least that group's lack of qualifications. In any case, more than four million people aged over 16 in the Netherlands are already providing some form of informal care—much of it both

[58] Jongen et al. (2011, 2015). See also De Boer et al. (2014); Blau & Kahn (2007); Saez et al. (2012).

[59] Mastrogiacomo et al. (2011).

long-term and intensive—to a total of about 750,000 beneficiaries.[60] Not only is there good reason to question how much further this commitment can be increased, but informal carers also constitute an important section of the cohort from which care professionals need to be recruited. Above all, though, the demographic potential of informal care is declining rapidly, especially in regions with ageing populations (see Chap. 2). This too is an international trend, the consequences of which have been apparent for some time. In a 2010 analysis, demographers François Herrmann, Jean-Pierre Michel and Jean-Marie Robine speak of a "dramatic decline in informal care resources available to the oldest old".[61]

For this reason, a more practical way to meet increasing demand is for new groups to choose to train and work professionally in care. Looking at the current composition of the sector's workforce, this means more young people and men in particular. Employers could also make efforts to attract staff from other sectors. For this recruitment drive to succeed, it is important that the training for care work be made more appealing. Another option is to bring in staff from abroad. We discuss all these alternatives in more detail below.

**More Appealing Training**

The Dutch government has made substantive efforts in recent years to stimulate the labour market in health and social care. These include targeted recruitment campaigns and incentive schemes such as the Work in Care Action Programme (Actieprogramma Werken in de Zorg), but also the facilitation of relevant education and training. Graduations from nursing degree and diploma courses have risen from a more or less constant level of around 6300 a year up until 2013 to some 10,000 since 2018.[62] Partly because of this, actual employment in the sector is increasing again (in hours worked since 2016, in people employed since 2017), more job vacancies are being filled, more students are choosing care-related courses and the staff shortages predicted for the coming years seem set to be somewhat less severe than previously feared. Looking to the longer term, however, it remains highly doubtful—given the scale of the challenge (see Table 3.4) and the demographic developments we have described—whether even continuing concerted efforts to make courses and careers in care more appealing will be enough to sustain the sector. After all, the demand for labour in other domains—private as well as public—is also persistently high.

---

[60] The qualifying definition in the underlying survey is "persons providing informal care more than 8 h per week for 3 months or more".

[61] Herrmann et al. (2010).

[62] The average for the period 2005–2013 was 6333 (2005 is the earliest year which data is available). In the 2016–2017 academic year it was 9380. At the same time, however, the number of medical graduates fell from 3742 in 2012 to 2717 in 2018. This was due in part to restrictions on admissions. See CBS Statline: https://www.cbs.nl/nl-nl/nieuws/2018/19/meer-verpleegkundigen-afgestudeerd; https://www.cbs.nl/nl-nl/nieuws/2019/19/aantal-verpleegkundigen-toegenomen

Incidentally, the qualitative aspect is just as important here as the quantitative one, namely the numbers of people completing training courses (see also the introduction to this chapter). For instance, there is now an increasing focus upon so-called "skill-mix" policy: optimizing the composition of the workforce in terms of functions and skills. The pandemic has shown that more is possible here than had previously been thought, an example being the use of medical students to perform certain interventions under supervision.[63] More generally, task shifting was introduced in the Netherlands a decade ago and is now practised in every aspect of health and social care.[64] In clinical medicine, for instance, this involves professionals such as nurse specialists and physician associates take over tasks previously entrusted only to doctors. Task shifting is regarded as an important tool in delivering "the right care in the right place". A number of studies have shown that it produces positive outcomes in terms of accessibility, quality of care and patient satisfaction, and also greater job satisfaction.[65] So far, however, it has not had a positive impact upon affordability—although the NZA considers the existing production-oriented incentives in the funding system partly responsible for that.[66]

Whatever the case, a phenomenon like task shifting illustrates that the staffing challenge in health and social care does have an important qualitative component; it is not just numbers of people which matters, those people also have to have the right skills—and they may change over time. More generally, the dynamic health profiles outlined in Chap. 2 combined with the developments around complexity and integrated care discussed in Chap. 5 mean that the workforce needs to be futureproofed in terms not only of its size but also its composition. Effective staffing is not just about deploying *more* people, it is about deploying them *differently* as well. This approach necessarily begins with different education, during both initial training and on-the-job training and upskilling. Courses have already made changes in this respect, but in practice the care sector can be set in its ways, maintaining a traditionally rather rigid, protected and hierarchical professional structure.[67]

---

[63] Bosveld et al. (2021).

[64] Task shifting is the systematic reallocation of tasks and their associated responsibilities to different professions. Its aim, as stated explicitly in the Outline Agreement on Specialist Medical Care (Hoofdlijnenakkoord medisch-specialistische zorg) and the report of the "Care in the right place" (Zorg op de juiste plek) task force, is to continue to provide efficient, high-quality and accessible care without incurring additional costs.

[65] Van Tuyl et al. (2020b).

[66] NZA (2019b).

[67] Interdisciplinary training has been introduced into all Dutch medical school curricula, with a focus upon lifelong professional development and network collaboration across disciplinary boundaries. See the 2020 "Medical Education Framework Plan" Raamplan Artsopleiding 2020: NFU (2020).

**Recruitment Abroad**

There are regular calls in the Netherlands for more recruitment of foreign health and social care workers. The discussion tends to focus upon two different groups: (1) migrants already in the country, such as refugees, and (2) personnel recruited overseas specifically to work in care.

Theoretically, the successful recruitment of refugee migrants into the care sector would create a win-win situation: they would be in work, giving them an income and promoting their integration into Dutch society, and their employers would fend off possible labour shortages. Nevertheless, this option has its snags, even for migrants who worked in care in their country of origin or had at least been trained to do so. Take the lengthy asylum procedure, for instance, the language barrier and potential problems around the recognition of foreign qualifications and professional experience.[68] Moreover, on average the employment rate of refugee groups in the Netherlands is very low. For a recent publication, Statistics Netherlands tracked a cohort of refugees granted asylum and a Dutch residence permit in 2014. Of this group, 43 per cent had a job (mostly part-time and on a temporary contract) by mid-2020.[69] Three-quarters of those jobs were in agency work, hospitality or commerce, and very few in the care sector.[70] Particularly relevant in light of the substantial overrepresentation of women in care work is the fact that female refugees are significantly more estranged from the labour market than their male counterparts and many have no interest in seeking work. Their absolute numbers are limited, too. In the period 2014–2017, for example, when the influx of asylum seekers into the Netherlands was at its peak, a total of 51,500 female refugees entered the country (including those arriving by arrangement under the family reunion scheme). Of them, only a minority eventually found work and very few have ever worked in care.[71] Of course, every refugee migrant who is eventually employed in that sector is one more worker for it. But despite that we feel justified in concluding that this option—the recruitment of refugee migrants—will never represent more than a drop in the ocean when it comes to overcoming the huge personnel shortages expected in the future.

Another possibility is to recruit staff overseas. Ageing populations are already causing major shortages of doctors and nurses in many Western countries, increasing their reliance upon personnel from other parts of the world. As a consequence, the migration of care professionals to, from and between European Union member states has been under way for some time and is steadily increasing.[72] Particularly in France and Italy, but also in the UK, many working doctors come from outside the

[68] Regioplan (2020); Van Liempt & Staring (2020); ACVZ (2021a).

[69] CBS (2021).

[70] See CBS (2020d). In the labour force as a whole (ages 15–75), too, the proportion of people with a migrant background working in a "health and welfare" occupation is lower than the figure for those with a Dutch background (CBS 2020b).

[71] This group represents a third of the total: far more men than women seek asylum in the Netherlands. See, for example, Razenberg et al. (2018).

[72] Wismar et al. (2011); Williams et al. (2020).

EU.[73] Many professionals are also leaving the EU to take up jobs elsewhere, particularly in English-speaking countries like the United States, Australia and Canada. By comparison with other European countries, the Netherlands has relatively few foreign-trained doctors and nurses. The figure for doctors was just 2 per cent in 2015/2016, compared with 12 per cent in both Belgium and Germany. And for nurses it was even lower: a mere 0.5 per cent (the OECD average is 6.4 per cent).[74] In short, there is plenty of global circulation of care personnel but the Netherlands is very much "out of the loop". A number of specific barriers may explain this. Consider, for instance, the relatively heavy emphasis the Netherlands places upon qualifications and registrations. Another possible factor is that the staff shortages in many other countries are even greater than those in the Netherlands. Then there is the fact that few other countries have as many people who have completed training for care-related occupations as here. This may make the need to "import" staff from abroad less urgent in the Netherlands than in other countries, at least up until now. None of these points is certain, though, so further research into the explanatory factors behind this situation would seem desirable. According to the Dutch Advisory Council on Migration (Adviescommissie Vreemdelingenzaken, ACVZ) in its exploratory study entitled "From asylum-seeker to care provider" (*Van asielzoeker naar zorgverlener*), finding a solution to migrant underrepresentation in the Dutch care workforce might help mitigate the sector's staff shortages.[75] More generally, it would certainly be valuable to explore what can be learnt from other countries which have already attracted care personnel from abroad on a larger scale. Have they found ways to avoid or to lessen the barriers to this group's employment (see below)?

Another controversial issue here is the impact of an exodus of care workers upon their countries of origin, specifically its potential to cause a "brain drain".[76] In many cases, after all, those nations have their own staffing difficulties because of an ageing population and increasing demand for care. Some central and eastern European countries suffered significant problems during the pandemic, for example, because so many of their care professionals were working abroad.[77]

Much of the attention in these debates centres on attracting foreign personnel to curative healthcare, but understaffing in long-term care is forcing many countries to extend international recruitment into that domain as well. Besides a shortage of professional carers and high staff turnover, in many cases another driver of that strategy is a growing shortage of informal carers looking after older people in their own homes. An international comparison of the sustainability of long-term care for

---

[73] ILO (2019).

[74] OECD (2019c); ACVZ (2021b).

[75] ACVZ (2021a).

[76] Adovor et al. (2021).

[77] *NRC Handelsblad* 2020, available at: https://www.nrc.nl/nieuws/2020/11/26/corona-legt-artsentekort-midden-europa-bloot-a4021537

the elderly undertaken for our report shows that this is the situation in Germany and the United Kingdom, for example.[78]

In the UK, which has major staff shortages in long-term care, the use of foreign workers is commonplace. Because of Brexit, however, recruiting them from other parts of Europe has become much harder. The German situation also stands out. Migrants, mainly from Poland, deliver a substantial proportion of both formal (nursing home) and informal care there. They are mostly middle-aged women on low wages, which are nevertheless higher than in their countries of origin. But there is little or no supervision of the service they provide, nor of their own working conditions. Due to the high demand for care and the shortage of other people willing to do these jobs, that lack of oversight is widely tolerated. And particularly so in rural areas, where the need is greatest. This is all the more striking since Germany imposes strict demands on migrants working officially in care, such as mastering the German language, including professional terminology, and obtaining a professional qualification in line with local standards.

Japan is another interesting case. Immigration is a sensitive issue there, and politicians have been keen to embrace technological innovation as an alternative. However, experts have come to the conclusion that they alone are not sufficient to make up for the substantial shortage of care personnel. Since 2020, Japan has therefore been offering permanent residence permits to care professionals from abroad. But to qualify, before they can start work these migrants must already speak good Japanese, know the country's "rules of daily life" and obtain the Japanese "care professional" diploma. These stringent requirements are important for public acceptance of the scheme, but at the same time have severely limited uptake.

The above examples reveal a number of obstacles to the employment of foreign workers in the care sector, on both the supply and the demand side. When it comes to supply, they include the validity of qualifications, language issues and cultural differences. These mean that considerable time has to be invested in a person before they become employable.[79] A lot of work in clinical healthcare in particular is highly skilled, and effective communication with patients and professionals is very important. Moreover, migrant workers often return to their country of origin sooner or later, making the return on these investments in human capital uncertain.[80] As for the demand side, across the board the care sector is already struggling to retain staff. In a recent advisory report, the RVS identifies this as a major problem.[81] The Work in Care Committee notes that 43 per cent of new workers in the sector leave it again within 2 years, more than the rate for care personnel as a whole.[82] Reasons include low starting salaries, high workloads, the working hours, poor career prospects and the absence of a culture of investment and learning. If anything, these factors apply

[78] Kruse et al. (2021).

[79] See, for example, Razenberg et al. (2018); Regioplan (2020).

[80] WRR (2020a).

[81] RVS (2020d).

[82] Commissie Werken in de Zorg (2019).

even more to staff brought in from abroad, especially if they are seen mainly as cheap labour (as in the German example above) and there is no substantial investment in them.[83] Other impediments they face in the Netherlands in particular include this country's strict attitude towards professional qualifications and registration.[84] The ACVZ cites the legal and regulatory issues around the recognition of foreign qualifications as a specific impediment, but also mentions the workplace culture here—such factors as hierarchy and etiquette, to say nothing of preconceptions and prejudice—as a further deterrent.[85]

NIDI and Statistics Netherlands have explored how migration is likely to affect the overall size and composition of the Dutch workforce in the years ahead, taking into account people with a migrant background[86] already in the country as well as future newcomers. In a scenario with high net immigration and a high rate of labour-force participation by these groups, the national workforce would increase by 150,000–300,000 FTEs between now and 2050.[87] Given the expectation that by that time around one in three working people in the Netherlands would have to be employed in the care sector to meet demand for its services, that potentially represents an extra 50,000–100,000 FTEs for care. Although, of course, that again is not nearly enough to meet the predicted shortfall of some 1.4 million FTEs. Moreover, these calculations are for a best-case scenario and the actual numbers are likely to be considerably lower in the light of the practical concerns mentioned above.

In short, recruitment overseas looks like an expedient option to overcome certain specific staffing issues in health and social care, especially shortages of specialist personnel like intensive-care nurses. But for this strategy to succeed, the impediments discussed will have to be addressed. And if the Netherlands, following Germany's example, starts to employ low-skilled foreign workers on a larger scale in such areas as home care, that will raise wider issues and cost much more. We also need to bear in mind the broader social and ethical questions associated with a policy of this kind, in both the host nation (will Dutch public opinion accept the widespread use of foreign nurses to care for our older people?) and the migrants' countries of origin (are we causing a brain drain in poorer nations?).

[83] Ruhs & Anderson (2010).

[84] To practise any kind of clinical profession in the Netherlands, a person must be inscribed in the Register of Professions in Individual Healthcare (BIG-register). Only then are they allowed to use their professional title and to undertake procedures reserved for members of their profession. According to the RVS, this requirement contributes towards inefficient working practices and staff shortages in healthcare; it argues that the law should be changed to place more emphasis upon professional skills and less upon formal qualifications (RVS 2019).

[85] ACVZ (2021a).

[86] In Dutch policy circles 'people with a migration background' is the term used to refer to residents with at least one parent born outside of the Netherlands. Thus, this also includes second-generation migrants.

[87] NIDI & CBS (2021).

### 6.2.4 Remuneration

A fourth way for the care sector to attract a greater proportion of the working population is through remuneration policy. This option can impact both recruitment and retention. In the public debate it is often intertwined with the closely related issue of pay levels in health and social care, and whether they are keeping up with other sectors. We look briefly at that topic in this section.

Historically, average wages in the care sector do not seem to have lagged behind those in other sectors. Since 2010, overall salary levels enshrined under collective agreements covered by the statistical category "health and welfare" have risen by 16 per cent. That is more than in the "market" and "education" categories. Figure 6.4 shows the evolution since 1969 of total remuneration per hour worked in various parts of the public sector and in the economy as a whole. Even when viewed over this extended period, half a century in all, pay levels in care appear to have kept pace with the national average. This is a very different picture than in education, say, where there is a clear negative differential. The so-called "OVA Covenant", in place since 1999, under which the government automatically contributes towards keeping pay levels in the care sector aligned with those in the economy as a whole, is an important factor explaining that discrepancy.[88] On the other hand, care does lag behind public administration. This is mainly because wages in that domain grew significantly faster than in the economy as a whole from the early 1990s onwards. From an international perspective too, according to OECD figures there appears to be little reason to believe that Dutch health and social care as a whole is the victim of systemic deficiencies in remuneration rates. At 1.18:1, the pay differential between hospital nurses and the nation's average worker is higher in the Netherlands than in most of the 31 countries surveyed.[89] All in all, then, there is no evidence of a structural deficit in remuneration for care work.

---

[88] "OVA" stands for "government contribution to labour-cost incrementation" ("overheidsbijdrage in arbeidskostenontwikkeling"), a term which covers increases to employer levies and incidental payroll costs as well as salaries. The level of the contribution, known as the "OVA margin" is calculated by the CPB from an estimate of the average expected wage increase for the whole of the Netherlands. Health insurers are required to include this incrementation in the contracted rates they pay care institutions. Through this system, the care sector is guaranteed government support to enable its rates of pay to move in line with those in the economy as a whole. Other parts of the public sector lack this degree of certainty. This is most obvious in its second-largest domain, education. Figure 7.4 shows that, as wage growth in health and social care has remained strong over the past two decades, so an ever-widening gap in relative average hourly pay has appeared between it and education (and latterly even between it and some market sectors).

[89] OECD (2019b). This refers to gross annual income including social security and income tax contributions payable by the employer.

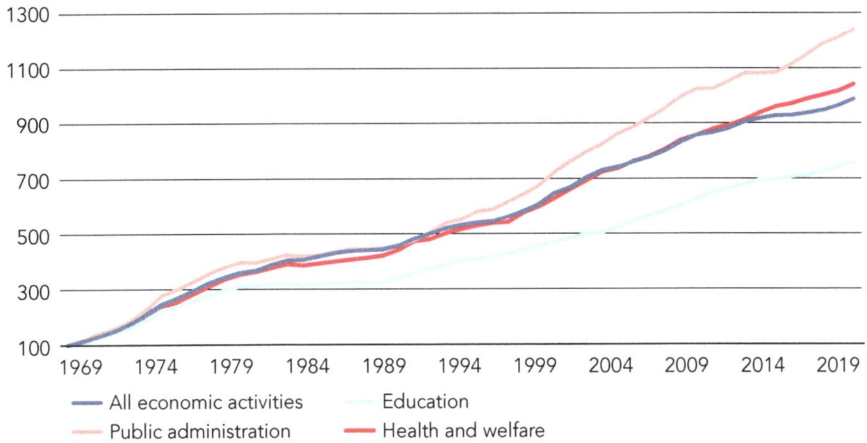


**Fig. 6.4** Wages in health and welfare, education, public administration and the economy as a whole, 1969–2019 (total remuneration per hour worked, indexed: 1969 = 100). Source: CBS Statline

Why, then, do so many people think that care workers in the Netherlands are underpaid? Above all, what seems to distort their view is the fact that whilst basic wages in this sector are broadly in line with market rates, its average employee works fewer hours than their counterparts with comparable educational qualifications in other sectors. Which leaves them with less money in their wage packet at the end of the month. As discussed previously, the reason why fewer hours are worked may be the pressure people experience in this kind of job. Besides this point, there is of course the normative matter of whether nurses and other care personnel should receive higher rates of pay anyway, in recognition of the particular demands of their professions—a question that has been brought into sharp focus by the pandemic.

In addition, factors *within* the remuneration system may affect staff retention and recruitment. To understand this phenomenon better, for a recent SER report the Netherlands Employer's Association (Algemene Werkgeversvereniging Nederland, AWVN) investigated remuneration issues in the care sector by comparing the salary scales in its collective agreements with those for equivalent positions in other sectors.[90] The key finding of this exercise was that the top pay grade in salary bands for positions in care requiring qualifications between professional further education

[90] SER (2021a); AWVN (2021).

and academic degree level (in the Dutch system, between MBO3 and WO) was, on average, 9 per cent below its equivalent in the private sector and 6 per cent below that in the public sector as a whole. Only in postgraduate degree-level positions and above do the pay grades in care exceed private-sector levels (and there maintain a constant differential). In other words, there is indeed a pay gap between relatively lower-skilled care personnel and their counterparts in comparable work in other sectors. Only at the top of the skills pyramid are care staff on a par with the rest of the economy or even earning more per hour. In a tightening labour market, this distributional inequity could well make it harder for care to recruit and retain its share of the workforce.

To enlarge that share on a lasting basis, systemically higher salaries would probably help. Especially at those levels where there is a like-for-like pay gap, as described above. The sector's size, however, combined with the proportion of its budget spent on wages, would make that a very expensive operation. According to CPB estimates, a 1 per cent pay rise across the board would cost €560 million per annum if awarded now.[91] And most likely more in the future, as employers in other sectors also strive to recruit enough workers in the face of increasing labour shortages. If higher salaries do indeed entice more people into care work, moreover, the rest of the economy will not only be less able to meet its own staffing needs but also face higher costs due to wage inflation: competitive effects which in turn will exacerbate the problem of financial sustainability. As well as highlighting how much the staffing and financial dimensions of sustainability are intertwined in health and social care, this also reminds us that both must be viewed as they relate to scarcity and in the light of demand for workers in other sectors, private as well public.

**Key points—Labour-market policies in care: finding more staff**

- Reducing workloads, increasing professional autonomy in the workplace and offering good career prospects can all help reduce the relatively high turnover of staff in health and social care.
- To increase the number of hours worked, consider the opportunities afforded by general tax policy (allowances and marginal pressure).
- To meet the increasing demand for care, new groups need to be "tapped" to train for and take up jobs in the sector. Possibilities include more men, refugee migrants and workers from abroad.
- Wider use of informal carers can be discounted as a long-term solution, primarily due to demographic trends.
- Recruitment abroad may be an expedient option to overcome certain specific staffing issues. But its use on a wide scale will require that a number of impediments are tackled first.

(continued)

[91] CPB (2020a).

- By international standards, care work in the Netherlands is not badly remunerated overall. Domestically, too, this is true by comparison with most other sectors.
- To ensure that a stable or larger proportion of the Dutch labour force chooses to work in care in the future, better remuneration is essential. The sector's size, however, combined with the proportion of its budget spent on wages, will make that a very expensive solution.

## 6.3 Possible Effects of Policies on Staff Shortages

In this section we provide a quantitative assessment of the various policy directions discussed above. Looking to the future, to what extent could they help mitigate the predicted staff shortages in health and social care? We should stress, though, that this exercise is no more (and no less) than a theoretical exploration of what would happen to those shortages if, say, the number of hours worked in the care sector increased to match the average in the economy as a whole. It also has plenty of pitfalls. For instance, we do not take into account the differences between the sector's various component parts. Nevertheless, we do offer a broad picture at the macro level of the general magnitude of the policy effects we have described.[92] What is the maximum achievable assuming that all barriers and obstacles also discussed in this chapter can be removed? In Table 6.2 we home in on two policy directions: expanding labour-force participation and increasing the number of hours worked.

Were successful policy efforts to succeed in maximizing the labour-force participation rate (to 85 per cent), then the originally estimated shortfall of 1.4 million full-time care workers in 2050 would decrease to around 1.0 million. And were the number of hours worked maximized (to 1440 per worker per year), the shortfall

[92] Reporting to the Ministry of Health, Welfare and Sport, the Advisory Committee on Medical Manpower Planning (Capaciteitsorgaan voor opleidingen van professionals in de zorg) assesses future staffing requirements in a total of 79 clinical professions. From those findings it then estimates the necessary intakes for the relevant training courses. Research institute Nivel has developed an estimation model for this purpose, to determine in policy terms how many more or fewer healthcare professionals need to be trained in order to balance the labour market and to keep it in equilibrium. The most important adjustable variable in this model is of course intake, but it also includes all kinds of other supply and demand parameters. Amongst them are the number of hours per FTE (changes to working hours), task shifting and substitution and, of course, demand for care itself (a function of the demographic, epidemiological, sociocultural and suchlike developments which will determine the required future supply); see Van Greuningen (2016). The committee's estimates are helpful in better matching supply and demand in a qualitative sense, but have little to do directly with the fundamental question we are discussing in this section in particular, as well as more broadly elsewhere this report: what needs to happen to find more staff for care, or to reduce demand for it?

**Table 6.2** Effects upon predicted care-sector staff shortages and employment structure of policy scenarios concerning labour-force participation and hours worked, 2019–2050

| | 2019 | 2030 | 2040 | 2050 |
|---|---|---|---|---|
| No policy change | | Number of persons × 1000 | | |
| Staffing shortfall at current share of labour force | | 360 | 858 | 1373 |
| Share of labour force needed to fill demand | 16.0% | 19.8% | 25.3% | 30.5% |
| Increased labour-force participation rate, of which one-third employed in care (2019: 75.8%) | | Number of persons × 1000 | | |
| Staffing shortfall at 80% participation in 2050 | | 284 | 727 | 1180 |
| Staffing shortfall of 85% participation in 2050 | | 215 | 592 | 972 |
| Share of labour force share at 80% participation | | 19.4% | 24.3% | 28.7% |
| Labour force share at 85% participation | | 19.0% | 23.3% | 27.0% |
| Increased hours worked in care (2019: 1181 hours per worker per year) | | Number of persons × 1000 | | |
| 1311 hours per worker per year in 2050 | | 304 | 749 | 1205 |
| 1440 hours per worker per year in 2050 | | 249 | 641 | 1039 |
| Share of labour force at 1311 hours per year | | 19.1% | 23.8% | 27,9% |
| Share of labour force at 1440 hours per year | | 18.5% | 22.4% | 25,7% |
| Increased labour-force participation rate and hours worked | | Number of persons × 1000 | | |
| Staffing shortfall at 80% participation and 1311 hours per year | | 228 | 618 | 1013 |
| Staffing shortfall at 85% participation and 1440 hours per year | | 104 | 375 | 638 |
| Share of labour force at 80% participation and 1331 hours | | 18.4% | 22.4% | 26.0% |
| Share of labour force at 85% participation and 1440 hours | | 17.1% | 19.7% | 21.9% |

Source: WRR estimates

would be cut to about 1.1 million. But if both targets were achieved simultaneously, the shortfall would be reduced to 680,000 people—almost halving the original figure of 1.4 million. In reality, however, that would only be possible by accepting some fairly extreme assumptions and with substantial repercussions for, say, the choice to work part-time and the ability to provide informal care. Even with the shortfall cut to between 680,000 and 1.1 million people, moreover, in 2050 about a quarter of the national workforce would still have to be employed in care—and that in a situation of extreme labour scarcity. On the other hand, this exercise does not consider all possible factors. For example, the potential offered by making greater use of foreign workers or by enhancing the appeal of training for occupations in care is nigh on impossible to estimate on a timescale of several decades. Nonetheless, the magnitude of the projected shortfalls above shows that tackling the staffing-related challenges in care requires multiple policy approaches and that, even accepting some rather extreme assumptions about their success, this factor remains a major constraint to achieving sustainability.

**Key Points—Possible Effects of Policies on Staff Shortages**

- If a successful policy effort were to maximize labour-force participation and hours worked per person, in theory the staffing shortfall in health and social care could be cut to 680,000 people as of 2050.
- In reality, however, this would only be possible by accepting some fairly extreme assumptions and with substantial repercussions for, say, the choice to work part-time and the ability to provide informal care
- Even with the shortfall reduced to somewhere between 680,000 and 1.1 million people, about a quarter of the national workforce would still have to be employed in care.
- The magnitude of the projected shortfalls shows that multiple policy approaches are required.

## 6.4 Conclusion: More Staff Are Essential But Not Enough

Although financial sustainability is a challenge already, and certainly will be in the long term, right now staffing is the most urgent and most challenging dimension of the sustainability of health and social care. To properly safeguard the sector's key public values, quality and accessibility, this aspect has to be in order. Which makes it important to focus upon all the pathways towards sustainability outlined in this chapter. Each, after all, has its own merits and potential. This means first of all—and in line with the recent opinions published by the SER and the RVS[93]—that the Netherlands should focus upon staff retention through better personnel policy, with less onerous workloads and red tape, greater scope for professional autonomy and more appealing career perspectives. An approach that should help reduce staff turnover and retain workers in the sector. Secondly, it is important to persuade care personnel to work more hours (after all, many currently work part-time)—an aim that could be achieved, at least in part, by updating the system of tax incentives and allowances to make extra work pay off for the average care worker. Although with the downside that this option would almost certainly reduce the availability of informal carers. Better working conditions with less pressure at work would have a positive effect in this respect, too, as would increasing pay levels relative to those in comparable jobs in other parts of the economy. Thirdly, there is the need to attract more people to enter the care sector. By making training for care-related occupations more attractive, say, or—although this is more controversial politically and socially—by recruiting workers from abroad to fields facing staff shortages. Whilst this strategy is being adopted by more and more Western countries for long-term care for the elderly in particular, as we have pointed out above there are a number of significant barriers to be overcome. Finally, employers will need to find less labour-intensive ways to organize their work processes and make better use of labour-saving technology.

[93] SER (2020), (2021a, b); RVS (2020d).

As shown in Chap. 3, if nothing changes policy-wise then 30 years from now a third of the entire Dutch workforce will have to be employed in care just to meet demand. The question is whether such a shift in the overall pattern of employment is feasible. The size of the national workforce is barely expected to increase in that time, so the scope to meet the rapidly growing demand for care (and for labour to provide it) solely through greater participation rates and longer working hours per person falls well short of the sector's overall needs. Labour-saving technology might fill the gap to some extent, but its future capabilities and acceptance remain uncertain. Moreover, there are still plenty of major obstacles to be overcome in that area as well. Once again, though, the real issue there is one of magnitude: even where it has already succeeded in breaking down barriers, as yet technology has had only a modest positive impact upon labour productivity.

All this means that, from a staffing perspective, it is going to become more and more difficult to provide the levels of quality and accessibility that the Dutch people expect from their care system. This situation is illustrated in Fig. 6.5: even if the effort to find more staff (by whatever means) proves successful—thus adding more people to the picture—in and of itself that remains highly unlikely to meet the full future demand for care and for people to provide it (leaving the "unfilled" positions on the right-hand side). A situation which is bound to have knock-on effects for workloads and, it is reasonable to assume, for the quality of the work being delivered. And hence for the societal sustainability of health and social care, as described in Part 1 of this report. On top of that, seeking to attract new staff on a large scale will strain the sector's financial sustainability and trigger competition with other parts of the economy, both public and private. And even if, through a combination

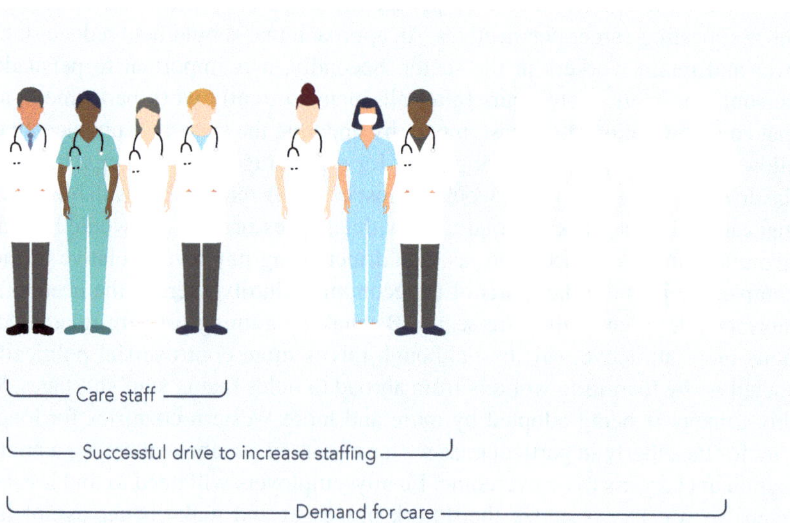


**Fig. 6.5** More care staff are essential, but not enough

of activities aimed at recruitment, retention and upping the number of hours worked, we were to succeed in finding enough staff, the question arises as to the impact this would have upon public values in other parts of the public sector. Could we, for instance, safeguard the accessibility and quality of our education system if one in three working people were employed in care? In other words—just as we concluded in the previous chapter on efficiency-driven policy—the scale of the challenge is such that more staff alone are not enough. Sooner or later, then, allocative choices will become unavoidable. We discuss this aspect in more detail in Part 3.

# Chapter 7
# Priorities and Distribution in Care

> The sustainability of health and social care is largely a question of making choices and setting priorities. At present, however, the way in which those choices are made is less than ideal from the perspective of health gains and safeguarding public values.

In the third part of this report we look at choices with regard to health and social care. In what ways can people and resources be distributed across sectors, organizations, treatments and preventive interventions? How do we divide our public resources between care and other goals? And how do we decide on such questions? Whereas our focus in the previous part was the organization of care and achieving effectiveness or productive efficiency—*how* to provide care—we now turn our attention to *what* to do? *What* care do we offer? And *how much* of it? Economists refer to this as *allocative* efficiency: to what ends should resources be allocated and what should attract fewer, or none at all? Allocative efficiency also concerns the extent to which that allocation is in line with society's wishes and preferences.[1] In other words, are we doing the right things? This is all about priorities, not to mention the practical limits we set to the growth of health and social care. And perhaps even more importantly, about how the choices are made.

[1] As opposed to productive efficiency, which is about whether we do things efficiently at the input-output level. In our case, in other words, are we using the fewest possible people and resources (input) to deliver the care we actually provide (output)? We noted in the previous part of this report that there is room for improvement here, but also that sustainability cannot be achieved through productive efficiency alone (see Chaps. 5 and 6).



G. Werner et al., *Financial, Staffing and Societal Sustainability of Dutch Health Care*, Research for Policy, https://doi.org/10.1007/978-3-031-58564-7_7

To answer these questions, in this chapter we look at the current organization of choice processes in the Dutch care sector and at the resulting distribution of resources—both within care itself and between it and other sectors. In particular, we examine whether these patterns are the most desirable from a health perspective. And we identify five impediments affecting choices within and about care. In the next chapter we further analyse the social, political and administrative backgrounds to those impediments and look at ways of tackling them.

## 7.1 Limits to Growth: A Matter of Choices and Priorities

When it comes to something as essential as care, why should there be any limits? Surely everyone is entitled to receive whatever they need. In an ideal world yes, but that is not the world we are living in. Ultimately, the sustainability challenge in health and social care is largely a question of allocating scarce resources. People always want better health or a longer life, and preferably both. But society's ability to satisfy that desire is limited. People and resources are finite, and so too is our collective willingness to devote them to the care sector.[2] In the first two parts of this report we saw that these limitations are set to become increasingly evident in the coming years, given the trends and developments society will experience (see Chap. 2). Demand for care is expected to continue to rise rapidly, whilst the expansion of the working population is stagnating and economic growth is also lagging behind care needs. The issue of scarcity and how to deal with it is therefore going to become increasingly important, since the sector just cannot continue to expand as it has been. The people needed to provide that level of care simply do not exist. This means that a gap is increasingly opening up between public expectations—that more and more care can be provided, ad infinitum—and the repercussions of that kind of growth.

Safeguarding the public values associated with care and keeping the three dimensions of sustainability in equilibrium means that the Netherlands is going to start having to make tough choices. It also means that the government and politicians will need to think carefully about where to draw the boundaries of growth, and thus what priorities to set. In a world where people and resources are increasingly scarce, after all, it is becoming more and more important to deploy them where they can best uphold the public values of quality and accessibility. And where they are in a position to deliver the greatest health benefits, specifically longer life expectancy in good health. All of which requires clear choices: where do the limits to growth lie, and by extension what care should remain collectively funded and what should not? Moreover, choices also need to be made about the criteria whereby that distinction is drawn. In short, priorities have to be set.

---

[2] Den Ridder et al. (2019), Kooijman et al. (2018). See also Chap. 3 of this report.

Choices concerning priorities are already made on a daily basis in thousands of places throughout the health and care sector, as well as in the associated policy domain. We cannot explore *all* of those countless choices in this chapter, so instead we single out the most important ones. They cover a broad spectrum. Some are very specific: should a particular medicine be reimbursed from the collective coffers, for example, or what treatment or diagnostics should a particular patient receive? Others are far more general, such as how much to allocate to the various aspects of health and social care? And at the highest level of all, government policy, there are choices about how we divide available human and material resources between care and other policy domains. Each of these choices is, in the final analysis, about comparing different options. Does money go to care or to education? Do we prioritize long-term care or prevention? Do we buy a surgical robot or hire more staff?

In the next section (Sect. 7.2) we look in broad terms at the prerequisites for care-related prioritization. We next home in on the way key choice processes in care are currently organized (Sect. 7.3). Here we start from the bottom up, with prioritization and limits *within* the various fields of care and in particular the two largest: curative medicine and long-term care. After that we turn our attention to the broad distribution of resources and people *between* fields, and then finally to their distribution across care and other public policy domains (Sects. 7.4, 7.5, and 7.6). Although it might seem more logical to begin at the top, so to speak, with choices about the overall allocation of resources to the care sector, we have adopted this "reverse" order because in fact the allocation patterns at the higher levels are largely determined by choices made lower down the ladder: decisions concerning the scope of collective insurance cover for all the various forms of care, for example, or those taken in the consulting room. In the Netherlands, implicit choices around "bigger" questions—such as the total amount of money spent on care—are more likely to flow from those made at lower levels than vice versa. Although in reality, of course, choices and decisions at all these levels influence each other—we describe them separately, but in a complex system everything is interrelated.

**Key Points—Limits to the Growth: A Matter of Choices and Priorities**

- Making choices in health and social care is about setting priorities.
- That is essential in order to be able to offer accessible and high-quality care.
- The choices are made in many different places: in the consulting room (between patient and practitioner), in the boardroom and in parliament.

## 7.2 Choices in Care: The Theory

In this section we look at the theory underpinning choices to limit the growth of the health and social care sector. That involves first assessing and comparing the benefits of the care available,[3] then weighing them up in normative terms: how important do we as a society consider them to be, what are we prepared to pay for them and how do we think they should be distributed?

### *7.2.1 Assessing the Benefits—What Are They?*

Either implicitly or explicitly, choices about limiting growth in the care sector always involve comparing different options. Not that the "alternative" is necessarily easy to identify: when deciding on the approval of a new medicine for a rare hereditary muscle condition, for example, we do not compare its performance explicitly with the possible benefits of a novel treatment for breast cancer. And we make decisions about the allocation of resources to nursing care for the elderly without specifically considering the requirements of preventive medicine—to fund mass screening for cancer, say—as an alternative. But such comparisons may well be implicit: choosing one option could preclude the other. Even if they are in no way similar. Or even simultaneous: the new medicine for breast cancer is available now, the one for the muscle condition not until next year, and even that is far from certain. Despite all their dissimilarities and their separation in time, in a world of scarcity these choices influence each other. Money and people already allocated to treatment A can no longer be used for treatment B, now or in the future.

One way or another, then, making choices in health and social care is a matter of comparing disparate options and their benefits for society.[4] To start with, these may be direct: a tangible individual health gain or improvement in the patient's quality of life. Benefits of this kind are assessed by comparing them with the health or quality of life that person would have experienced if the care in question had not been provided. Then there are indirect benefits. For example, the collective health gains derived from treating infectious diseases and carrying out vaccination programmes. These have received a great deal of attention in the past couple of years in the context of the Covid-19 pandemic. Or think of the economic benefits: working people are more productive when they are healthier.[5] And then there is public trust, the reassuring idea that good care will be available if we need it.

---

[3] The academic field concerned with care costs versus benefits is called Health Technology Assessment (HTA). This reflects the fact that its focus historically was the assessment of medical and other technologies, particularly pharmaceuticals. But its tools can also be used more broadly.

[4] Polder et al. (2020).

[5] Nevertheless, the same study concludes that health and social care spending across the board should not be regarded as an investment to generate economic benefits. This is a consequence of the fact that—at the macro level—the health benefits of the bulk of provision accrue to people who are not in work (or no longer are). See Polder et al. (2020).

However important such indirect benefits may be, ultimately they depend upon—and are a product of—direct health benefits. One widely-used measure in this domain is the QALY, or quality-adjusted life year (see Box 7.1). Taking into account both total life expectancy and quality of life during that time, this tool enables us to compare (to some extent at least) the benefits of otherwise utterly dissimilar treatments or interventions. QALYS are used mainly in curative medicine; other fields have their own methods, such as ICECAP (the Investigating Choice Experiments Capability Measure) in long-term care, where there is a greater focus upon quality of life than upon curing people. ICECAP measures how subjects rate their lives in terms of factors like attachment, security, autonomy and enjoyment.[6] Measures of this kind create a degree of comparability within part of healthcare by quantifying answers to the question, "What benefits does this form of care deliver?"

**Box 7.1: QALY: A Measure of Life Expectancy and Quality of Life**
The QALY, short for "quality-adjusted life year", is the most commonly used measure of the benefits of healthcare interventions. It is a way of expressing the outcomes of particular clinical or preventive treatments using what are generally regarded as their two primary goals: improving life expectancy and quality of life. QALYS capture both in a single measure and try to do justice to the widely-held notion that good care is not just about living longer but also about living a good life.[7] A treatment that extends life by one year in full health generates one QALY. A year of life gained with a lesser quality of life counts for less—say 80 per cent (0.8 QALY).

### 7.2.2 *Weighing Up the Benefits—What Is Important?*

Once the health gains and costs of a treatment are known, the next step is to weigh up its potential benefits. What do we as a society consider important? To be able to take decisions concerning the limits of care that are legitimate in the public eye, we need to reach a certain degree of consensus on this point. So in this step we look not only at what care is able to "deliver", but also at how those outcomes are distributed: who ultimately benefits? Ethical philosophers have developed a number of principles of so-called "distributive justice" which can help us here; some of those most frequently used in the context of health and social care are summarized in Table 7.1.

Utilitarianism is about optimizing potential health gains for the entire population.[8] After comparing possible treatments, the one which helps achieve the greatest health gain per invested euro is chosen. In fact, then, this approach only optimizes

---

[6] Coast et al. (2008).

[7] Weinstein et al. (2009) and Whitehead and Ali (2010).

[8] Emanuel et al. (2018) and Bognar and Hirose (2014).

**Table 7.1** Principles of distributive justice for prioritization in healthcare

| Principle | Objective | Implication |
|---|---|---|
| **Utilitarianism** | Optimize overall health. | Every health gain counts equally; distribution plays no role. |
| **Rule of rescue** | Prioritize the most urgent conditions. | Priority is given to health gains in life-threatening situations. |
| **Fair innings** | Minimize differences in longevity. | Priority is given to health gains for young people. |
| **Absolute shortfall** | Prioritize greater absolute loss of life years. | Priority is given to health gains for young people and those with serious conditions. |
| **Proportional shortfall** | Prioritize greater relative loss of life years | Priority is given to health gains for those with serious conditions. |
| **Prioritarianism** | Optimize the health of the worse off. | Priority is given to health gains for the economically disadvantaged. |

efficiency and seeks to offer as much *overall* health gain as possible with a given budget. Other considerations, such as the health status of the people to whom the gains accrue or the distribution of care provision across the population, are disregarded. As the example of Oregon (see Box 7.2) shows, however, making choices purely on this basis leads to outcomes that society may regard as unjust.

**Box 7.2: Systematic Prioritization in Oregon**

In the early 1990s the US state of Oregon became one of the first jurisdictions to conduct an experiment to tackle clinical priorities in a systematic and objective manner.[9] As initially proposed, the scheme was based solely upon QALYS gained versus costs incurred. In other words, it was strictly utilitarian in its approach. With the result that extracting wisdom teeth would have become one of the state's top ten clinical priorities, whereas intensive care for premature babies with a very low birth weight was well down the list. This led to widespread dissatisfaction with the system and the criteria used.

From a purely utilitarian point of view, however, it was an understandable outcome. The treatments available at the time for very premature babies had a relatively low chance of success, so the expected health gains were small. But the public response aptly illustrates the fact that the distribution of those gains—whose health improves?—is also important to people. Factors such as the severity of a patient's illness, their age and their expected loss of life years do matter to them. As a result, Oregon never introduced its original, entirely utilitarian list. Instead, a number of other considerations were taken into account when determining the eventual prioritization.

[9] Honigsbaum et al. (1995).

The other principles of distributive justice listed in Table 7.1 can all be regarded as corrections to or variations on utilitarianism.[10] All in some way or another weigh[11] certain forms of health gain more heavily than others, and thus consider more factors than just the *overall extent* of the gain. Take the "rule of rescue", for instance. According to this principle, we should consider not only health potential but also the urgency of treatment. Potential health gains for acute patients thus outweigh the *same* gains for less acute ones. Under the "fair innings" approach, the same gain is given more weight for a younger person than an older one. During the Covid-19 crisis, almost all of these principles were applied to some extent in the Netherlands (see Box 7.3).

**Box 7.3: Normative Justification of Covid-19 Prioritization**

At several points during Covid-19, fears arose in the Netherlands that there would be an acute shortage of intensive-care beds for critically ill patients requiring ventilation. This brought the issue of prioritizing scarce medical resources to public attention, in a far more acute way than in the context of sustainability. The underlying principles at play, however, are similar.

At the beginning of the crisis in March 2020, the Dutch Society of Intensive Care (*Nederlandse Vereniging van Intensive Care*, NVIC) issued a triage guide describing how ICU capacity should be allocated during an acute emergency phase.[12] The inclusion criteria were essentially a form of the "rule of rescue": only patients with an urgent and acute need for ventilation would be eligible for admission.

The exclusion criteria applied at the time can be viewed as a mix combining elements of the "absolute shortfall" and "fair innings" principles. For example, advanced age (over 80) as the final criterion was in line with "fair innings". But a number of situations with a low probability of survival and a short life expectancy were also listed, such as metastatic cancer. That is a form of "absolute shortfall", since those patients were not expected to live much longer anyway. The limited likely benefits of ICU treatment for them meant that they were given a lower priority than other categories. In the political and public arenas, the "fair innings" aspect of this triage proved particularly controversial.[13] It even triggered an initiative to ban by law the use of age alone as a criterion for treatment, although that was later withdrawn in the face of protests from the medical profession.

---

[10] Weinstein (1998).

[11] This different weighting can be either implicit or explicit and quantitative.

[12] Nederlandse Vereniging voor Intensive Care (2020).

[13] This public debate was triggered primarily by a later advisory document drawn up by doctors and ethicists (FMS & KNMG, 2020).

**Dutch Preferences Regarding Prioritization**

What are the Dutch public's preferences when it comes to prioritization in healthcare? Research[14] shows that, broadly speaking, people here feel that health gains for conditions with a high burden of disease should cost more. This is in line with both the "proportional shortfall" and "absolute shortfall" approaches. The Dutch also tend to support measuring the burden of disease according to the "proportional shortfall" principle (see Table 7.1). In addition, there is reasonable enthusiasm for principles along "fair innings" lines, meaning that health gains for the young should prevail over gains for the old. These findings support the approach adopted in the Netherlands in defining the basic statutory health insurance package, whereby higher maximum costs per QALY are applied to serious diseases.[15] Similar outcomes emerged from the citizens' forum Choices in Care (*Keuzes in de Zorg*), at which 24 lay participants debated the scope of the basic health insurance package over three weekends.[16]

**Procedural Justice**

The normative frameworks listed in Table 7.1 are forms of distributive justice. There are also theories that focus not so much upon substantive considerations but rather upon the process whereby they are weighed up—"procedural justice".[17] Proponents of this kind of approach argue that general frameworks such as "fair innings" are not specific enough to enable truly practical choices.[18] More fundamentally, they also object that it will never be possible for society to agree on any single framework because people disagree at root about the importance of the underlying principles. It follows from this that they believe it illusory to think that any theory of distributive justice can ever lead to decisions that enjoy universal legitimacy. It is therefore more important to institute a fair procedure that ultimately leads to legitimate decisions with regard to prioritization. With, at its heart, an open, deliberative process accessible to ordinary citizens or their proxies (public participation with appeal rights). Such a process helps articulate views and preferences and to hone them through contact with other opinions. By its deliberative nature, moreover, the process should bring equilibrium to the conflict of interest inherent in citizens' dual role within the system, as both its benefactors (through taxes and insurance premiums) and its beneficiaries (as patients, now or in the future).

In practice, the distributive and procedural approaches are complementary. To reach consensus concerning a principle of distributive justice, for example, public debate is essential—either in the political arena or through various forms of citizen participation. We look at this interaction in more detail in the next chapter.

---

[14] Reckers-Droog et al. (2018, 2019) and Stolk et al. (2005).

[15] The ZiN uses the following upper limits for additional costs per QALY: €20,000 for a burden of disease of 0.1–0.4, €75,000 for a burden of 0.41–0.7 and €80,000 for a burden greater than 0.7. The cost of achieving the same health gain can thus be higher for a more severe condition than for a milder one. This is in line with Dutch public opinion, although we do not know whether these specific figures align with it.

[16] Baltussen et al. (2018).

[17] Derived from the famous book *A Theory of Justice* by the philosopher John Rawls.

[18] Fleck (2009) and Daniels and Sabin (2008).

**Choosing Care—Or Something Else?**
Finally, we need to broaden our outlook even further. Up until now we have confined ourselves to prioritization *within* health and social care—treatment A or treatment B, curative or preventive medicine? The issue of sustainability, however, is also about whether society prefers to deploy people and resources to this sector or to other public policy domains, such as education. This makes measuring and comparing the benefits even more complex. Even within the sector, making comparisons is hard enough because of the wide disparities between the returns generated by different forms of care. It becomes truly daunting when the broad gains to be had from investing in defence, education, culture or social security are set against those we can derive from enabling care to expand further. The challenge becomes a little more manageable, however, if we look only at the *health* benefits delivered by domains other than health and social care. After all, we know that activities like education, combating poverty, design of the physical environment and public welfare deliver considerable health benefits in their own right, in the form of preventive effects.[19] Whilst their impact is impossible to quantify exactly, in all probability such factors as housing, working conditions, the environment and social cohesion are more significant determinants of general health than actual care in the narrow sense.

**Choices in Practice—What Do We Actually Do?**
So much for the theory behind choices in care. That is simply a matter of assessing the benefits of all the various kinds of care, then reflecting in an open public discourse upon the principles used to weigh them up and upon their true worth to society. The next step is to apply this process to all forms of care that can be provided collectively.[20] The result is choices and priorities that society is able to support. This outcome makes it clear what care will and will not be provided, and hence where the limits to the sector's growth lie. But that is not how things work in practice, of course. There are all kinds of reasons for this, from institutional barriers to lack of knowledge, normative objections and differences between social groups in their ability to organize themselves. In the rest of this chapter we look at how choices about the prioritization and allocation of care are made at three different levels in the Netherlands.

**Key Points—Choices in Care: The Theory**
- To be able to choose between alternative interventions, as far as possible their respective benefits should be measurable and comparable.
- Although there are tools available to help with this, such as the QALY, it is never possible to measure benefits in a completely objective way.

(continued)

[19] Broeders et al. (2018), WRR 2020b, and Polder et al. (2020).

[20] In essence, this process can be seen as a form of social cost-benefit analysis (SCBA) of the kind also used when making choices in other public policy domains.

- In order to arrive at a choice, benefits and costs should not only be assessed but also weighted. This involves the inherently normative question of what we as a society consider important and just.
- Various principles of distributive justice that can help us with the process of making choices. And in the interests of procedural justice, we also need to ensure that the process itself is fair.

## 7.3 Choices in Practice: Prioritization in Different Fields of Care

To consider prioritization within health and social care in more detail, we separate the sector into a number of broad fields. Within these we look in particular at the assessment framework for prioritization (what criteria are used?), but also at institutional embedding (which actors are responsible for the assessment?) Because they are closely linked, we discuss both aspects together.

We focus mainly upon curative medicine and long-term care because these fields constitute the bulk of the sector by both current volume and expected contribution to future growth (See Chap. 2). From the sustainability point of view—especially in its financial and staffing dimensions—it is therefore vitally important that clear choices be made within these two domains. As a hypothetical example, if an unequivocal choice were made to reduce the forecast annual growth in hospital provision by 0.5 per cent, in 2060 that would save more than 15 times the total estimated expenditure on municipal health services in that year.[21] In other words, by making better choices within the two dominant fields of care it soon becomes possible to free up a lot of human and material resources for other purposes, either within the care sector or elsewhere.

### 7.3.1 *Curative Medicine*

Curative medicine aims to successfully treat and cure acute and chronic illness. In the Dutch system, it largely coincides with the provision financed under the Healthcare Insurance Act (Zorgverzekeringswet, Zvw; see Chap. 4). The fact that government has a duty to ensure access to a comprehensive range of high-quality curative

[21] Calculation based upon the underlying data for figure 4.11 in Vonk et al. (2020). The forecast average annual growth rate in spending on hospitals in the period 2020–2060 is 2.9 per cent. If that is reduced to 2.4 per cent throughout the whole period, total expenditure up until 2060 will amount to €79 billion rather than the predicted €96 billion if the status quo is maintained. On an annual basis, that is more than fifteen times the estimated budget for municipal health services in 2060 (€1.1 billion).

medicine is generally uncontroversial in the Netherlands; debate focuses more upon the limits of that responsibility. In other words, what forms of care should and should not be covered. Choices made in that respect have direct implications for the human and financial sustainability of care; after all, a larger package of insured benefits requires more people and resources than a small one. Any decision concerning priorities *within* care thus involves an implicit choice about the sector as a whole: how much money goes to it and how much is left over for other public services?

In the Netherlands, ultimately it is the government which decides what care is and is not covered under the basic statutory health insurance package. The National Health Care Institute (*Zorginstituut Nederland*, ZiN) provides advice, both solicited and unsolicited, on the composition of that package.[22] In doing so it considers the principles of procedural justice—providing for public consultations, for instance—and to some extent distributive justice as well (see Table 7.1). In general, new forms of care are "admitted" to the package in one of two ways: through a so-called "closed" system involving a formal authorization procedure (see Box 7.4) or through the "open" system, whereby an effective treatment is accepted automatically. The vast majority of new treatments follow the "open" route.

**Box 7.4: Authorization of Medicines Using the Closed System**

The "closed" authorization system applies in particular to medicines available at pharmacies and to a number of expensive drugs only dispensed in hospitals.[23] These are reimbursed under the basic statutory health insurance package only once they have successfully undergone a formal procedure to check their compliance with four basic criteria: necessity, clinical effectiveness, cost-effectiveness and feasibility.[24] First of all, in other words, does the disorder in question actually require medication-based treatment (necessity)? Will the new treatment deliver sufficient health gains (clinical effectiveness)? Do those gains outweigh its cost (cost-effectiveness)? And is it actually possible for clinicians in the Netherlands to provide the treatment (feasibility)? New medicines are assessed by the ZiN's Insured Package Advisory Committee (*Adviescommissie Pakket*, ACP), made up of medical specialists, ethicists, economists and other experts. It compiles a draft recommendation, which is submitted to various interested parties (patient organizations, pharmaceutical companies and so on). After a public session to hear their feedback, the ACP draws up its final recommendation concerning the drug's authorization.

---

[22] Zorginstituut (2017).

[23] As a rule, under the "open" system (see below). But very expensive ones may have to undergo the "closed" authorization procedure. Nevertheless, the proportion of the overall cost of specialist medical care accounted for by these expensive drugs has been rising rapidly in recently years, at rates of between 5.5 and 12.1 per cent annually. And in absolute terms from just under 7 per cent in 2012 to almost 10 per cent in 2018. See NZa (2020b).

[24] These are based upon the so-called Dunning funnel from 1991 (see also Chap. 4). Its criteria (formulated for a somewhat different purpose) were necessity, effectiveness, efficiency and individual responsibility. The last of these has been replaced with feasibility.

The ZiN advice to the Minister of Health is based upon the outcome of the procedure conducted by its ACP (see Box 7.4). The minister is not obliged to adopt this, however, but can instead make his or her own assessment. He or she can also take decisions concerning the basic insurance package without prior advice from the ZiN. Ultimately, then, those decisions are a political matter. That is not always the case in other countries. We look in more detail at some of their alternative arrangements in the next chapter.

From a sustainability perspective, cost-effectiveness is the most essential of the four criteria applied by the ZiN. In this context, it basically expresses how much society is prepared to invest to achieve a year of "good" life (a QALY)—at least through the forms of care covered by this procedure (primarily medicines). The ZiN's advice is not necessarily confined to a recommendation on whether or not to authorize the drug: it can also suggest that the minister negotiate regarding its price. This is usually done when a treatment has been deemed clinically effective—that is, it does deliver health gains—but not (or not yet) cost-effective. If the price drops far enough, after all, any therapy that works eventually becomes cost-effective.

Whilst this "closed" authorization system applies to certain specific forms of treatment, medicines in particular, as stated above the vast majority—95 per cent—follow the "open" route (see Fig. 7.1).[25] This effectively includes all therapeutic

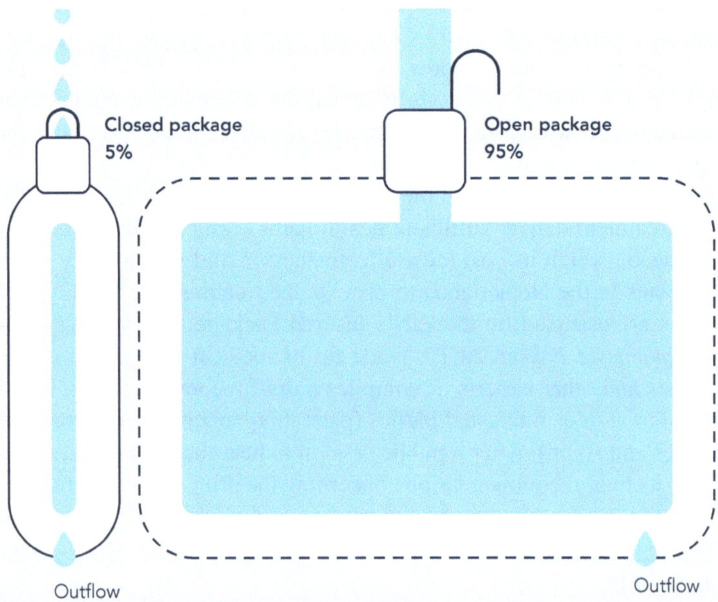


**Fig. 7.1** Schematic diagram of statutory health insurance package management in the Netherlands

[25] Van der Wilt et al. (2018).

provision not involving a medicine—medical devices and aids, for instance.[26] In their case healthcare providers and insurers decide between themselves, without following a formal procedure, whether a solution falls within the scope of statutory insurance cover. There are still set parameters, however. First and foremost, the treatment has to be clinically effective. In other words, it must deliver health gains. More specifically, it needs to be in line with the current "state of the art" in medical science and clinical practice. If there is any uncertainty on that point, health insurers, care providers or members of the public can request a so-called "standpoint" from the ZiN. This only states whether or not the treatment has been found to be clinically effective, however, and says nothing about its cost-effectiveness. This open access route thus has a very fundamental implication from a sustainability perspective. Across the vast majority of the statutory package, any new treatment that is more clinically effective than the existing one is authorized automatically. In other words, improvements to the quality of care are implemented immediately and without any explicit decision, political or otherwise, concerning their admissibility or any consideration of the costs involved.[27]

**Outflow**

When it comes to sustainability, "outflow" from the statutory health insurance package—forms of care it ceases to cover—is at least as important as the "inflow" of new treatments. As science and technology advance, a solution may no longer satisfy the requirements for inclusion. For example, because further research has shown that, in practice, it fails to yield the hoped-for health gains. In the Dutch package management system, formal outflow mechanisms exist only to a very limited extent. Only expensive intramural medicines (those administered solely at hospitals) can be granted provisional authorization within the terms of the "closed" procedure described above. Other treatments may or may not be reassessed on an ad-hoc basis, and then possibly excluded from the package—as happened with a number of over-the-counter medicines with effect from the beginning of 2019.[28] For other forms of care, the "state of the art" criterion applies. In other words, it must be clear from scientific research or clinical practice that a treatment is no longer appropriate and so should not be reimbursed any more. Formal exclusions from the package are therefore very infrequent. Moreover, their financial impact is limited. According to the Netherlands Court of Audit (*Algemene Rekenkamer*), explicit outflow decisions between 2007 and 2013 were expected in advance to result in cumulative annual savings of €0.5 billion, but in the end achieved only half of that figure.[29] A very modest amount when set against the €13.4 billion increase in Zvw-related healthcare spending in the same period.

---

[26] A conditional authorization procedure for expensive medical devices, known as the "lock" (as in a canal), is currently under consideration. This would be similar to the procedure for expensive intramural medicines. See Oosterkamp et al. (2021).

[27] Studiegroep Begrotingsruimte (2020) and Kersten et al. (2021).

[28] These include high-dose paracetamol (1000 mg), vitamins and minerals. Zorginstituut (2016a).

[29] Algemene Rekenkamer (2015).

**Choices in the Consulting Room—Appropriate and Inappropriate Care**
Thus far we have discussed prioritization in curative medicine solely as a matter of whether or not to include a particular treatment in the basic statutory health insurance package. In a large number of situations, however, the picture is not so clear-cut. Rather, it is a matter of identifying subgroups of patients for whom the solution is both clinically effective and cost-effective. In practical terms, this shifts the decision about whether or not to use it from the system level to the consultation level: does this particular patient fall within the group proven to benefit from the intervention? But it also highlights major obstacles to the actual provision of appropriate care in this way.[30] Underlying these is a whole raft of processes, often behavioural in nature. In clinical practice, for example, treatments of various kinds are often prescribed more and more widely as time passes—often even when there is no scientific proof that the patient concerned will benefit. It is estimated that 40 per cent of all care provided within the statutory package is not known to be evidence-based, whilst 10 per cent is demonstrably inappropriate.[31] In the Dutch system, delivering the right form of care for the patient and their condition is ultimately the shared responsibility of the parties "in the field", especially practitioners and insurers: the former on the basis of their duty as medical professionals, the latter in their capacity as pilots of an efficient system steered by their purchasing policies—meaning that they should avoid reimbursing non-appropriate care. However, a recent evaluation by the Court of Audit raises serious doubts about the effectiveness of this mechanism.[32] It shows that some forms of care continue to be offered even when there is good evidence that they are not appropriate.

**Implicit Choices and Displacement**
In addition to the explicit choices within curative medicine described above, prioritization can also take place in an implicit fashion. In a world where people and resources are scarce, the provision of one form of care can lead to others effectively being supplanted. Such implicit displacement often takes place at a lower level within the system; for example, when a healthcare institution sets its priorities.[33] A study commissioned by the ZiN analysed six cases in the field of curative medicine and found that the pressure on providers' budgets caused by the introduction of new medical technology probably leads to other aspects of care being pushed aside—with possible negative net health outcomes as a result. For example, the purchase of an expensive device like a surgical robot may indirectly leave a hospital with a smaller budget for staffing. However, such displacement is hard to demonstrate on a one-to-one basis.[34] Protocols like the outline agreements in which stakeholders

[30] Other terms used in Dutch policy circles to describe similar concepts are "sensible care", "appropriate use" and "evidence-based medicine".

[31] Kiers (2021).

[32] Algemene Rekenkamer (2020b).

[33] Maybin and Klein (2012).

[34] Adang et al. (2018).

agree to limit cost increases within a sector (see Chap. 5) only raise the potential for effects of this kind,[35] though, because they tighten institutions' budget constraints. These agreements can therefore be regarded as a means of imposing implicit prioritization choices,[36] but the question is always whether the resulting trade-off is the one that delivers the greatest health benefits.

### 7.3.2 *Long-Term Care*

The core purpose of long-term care is to provide nursing and support, if necessary on a full-time basis, rather than working towards a cure and recovery. Medical interventions are only a limited part of this; much of the work is about helping people with their day-to-day functioning (washing, assistance with dressing and so on). Users of long-term care are often vulnerable, such as those who have difficulty leading an independent life due to severe physical or mental disability, dementia or the like. As with curative medicine, there is debate here as to what provision should and should not be a collective responsibility. But whereas choices in that field relate mainly to innovations (new medicines, medical devices and technologies) and their inclusion (or not) in the basic statutory health insurance package, that factor plays much less of a role in long-term care. After all, far fewer "new" forms of care are developed in this domain. Which makes the normative aspects of the decision-making process all the more important. For instance, should the package cover services like cleaning and preparing meals? And how much responsibility for a person's care rests with their own social network: family, friends, neighbours and so on?

In principle, long-term care provision—like the "open access" component of curative medicine—must comply with strict scientific and practical criteria concerning its clinical effectiveness. In practice, however, there is no great tradition of demonstrating such effectiveness in this field.[37] That is due in part to its lack of a research culture and systematic research funding. But also because its outcomes are harder to measure objectively. Long-term care is largely concerned with preserving quality of life, which more than curative care is about the client's own subjective perceptions preferences. And that makes it even more difficult to define clear boundaries. Nevertheless, tools are being developed to measure the benefits of long-term care, amongst them the ICECAP method mentioned earlier.

Despite these limitations, there are implicit forms of prioritization in long-term care. Since a reform of the Dutch system in in 2015, for example, only people suffering the greatest burden of disease are now eligible for permanent residence in nursing homes. As a result, their capacity has been reduced, more people are remaining in their own homes for longer periods of time and those who are in

35 Van der Wilt et al. (2018).

36 Van der Wilt et al. (2018).

37 Zorginstituut (2016b).

residential care tend to be in poorer health. A comparative analysis of long-term care for the elderly in other countries has revealed a similar trend elsewhere, although in some cases that has since reversed, causing a pendulum effect.[38] One reason for those turnarounds is that it had not become evident that the shift to home-based provision was leading to any improvement in staffing or financial sustainability. After all, care at home does not necessarily require fewer personnel, nor is it bound to be cheaper. Research in the Netherlands has shown that savings on long-term care have been offset by higher expenditure on curative medicine and home care.[39] For precisely this reason, the trend towards home care in Japan has been partially reversed. In Denmark less so, but there a highly advanced system of home care provision had to be put in place to make the shift possible.[40] In the Netherlands, moreover, the increased prevalence of home care has unintentionally led to what is known as the "wrong bed" problem. As residential care capacity is reduced, patients needing long-term care sometimes end up staying in hospital for extended periods,[41] which leads to higher costs. The same phenomenon has also been observed in Japan, where the population has been ageing rapidly.[42] This is a prime example of how prioritization within one field can have unexpected repercussions for another—and how they are not necessarily ideal for the health and social care system as a whole. Similar unintended allocation effects have occurred in other places as well (see Box 7.5).

**Box 7.5: Quality Framework for Nursing Homes**

One topic to have received a lot of attention in the Netherlands in recent years is the quality framework for nursing homes. Following a public campaign, there was huge political pressure to improve the standard of care in these institutions. In 2016, the government asked the ZiN to draw up a new quality framework for and in consultation with the homes. But after discussions broke down, the ZiN's Quality Council went on to compile a framework unilaterally. The cost of implementing this turned out to be €2.1 billion annually, a sum the government was forced to provide since it had committed itself to funding the framework[43]—although some of that money could subsequently not be spent due to a shortage of staff.[44]

[38] Kruse et al. (2021).
[39] Wong et al. (2018).
[40] Wong et al. (2018).
[41] Van der Geest (2019).
[42] Kruse et al. (2021).
[43] Schakel et al. (2018).
[44] Algemene Rekenkamer (2019).

The course of events surrounding the quality framework for nursing homes (see Box 7.5) raises a number of questions about how resources are deployed within long-term care for the elderly and other groups. First of all, whether cost-effectiveness was rightly excluded from the quality framework; should it not in fact be a core consideration when developing instruments of this kind?[45] Secondly, whether it is right for the ZiN and providers themselves to be solely responsible for that decision; should including (or excluding) quality as a criterion not be a political choice? This question has since been partially answered with the introduction of a so-called "emergency brake", which allows politicians to intervene in the event of a very substantial expected increase in expenditure.[46] But the broader question remains as to whether this political assessment should not be more wide-ranging and take place at an earlier stage. Thirdly, this story highlights the fact that financial resources are not the only limiting factor: staffing issues also play an important role (see 3.3). Showing once again how important it is for healthcare policy to consider all three dimensions of sustainability, and keep them in equilibrium.

### *7.3.3 Child and Youth Care and Mental Healthcare*

Finally, we look briefly at prioritization and allocation within child and youth care services and in mental healthcare. Although these fields are limited in scale size at a macro level (see Fig. 1.4), clear shifts in their implicit prioritization can be observed. Moreover, all aspects of child and youth care are experiencing rapid growth (see Chap. 4). Rigorous consideration of the way priorities are set within these fields is particularly important because—as we saw earlier in this report (see Chap. 4)—parts of both currently fail to meet basic standards with regard to quality and accessibility.

In respect of prioritization, we see similar constraints here as in long-term care: benefits are not as easy to measure or quantify objectively as in curative medicine, largely because they are linked more to quality of life than to health gains. And often also to the client's situation outside the care setting (housing, work and so on).

Looking at distribution patterns in recent years, a few things nevertheless stand out. In mental healthcare, for instance, growth has been far stronger in basic provision—the treatment of milder disorders—than in specialist services. In the period 2015–2018, the number of patients receiving basic mental healthcare rose by 11 per cent. In specialist care the figure was 2.9 per cent. Spending rose by 22.6 and 10.7 per cent respectively.[47] In the preceding period, 2011–2016, expenditure on

---

[45] Algemene Rekenkamer (2019).

[46] Under the Financial Assessment of Proposed Quality Standards Act (*Wet financiële toetsing voorgedragen kwaliteitsstandaarden*).

[47] NZa (2021).

specialist mental healthcare actually fell by 6 per cent in absolute terms.[48] Compared with other parts of the health and social care system—and curative medicine in particular—this picture bucks the general trend. Which is especially striking given the high and increasing demand for these forms of care and the persistent waiting lists for more serious forms of mental healthcare (see Chap. 4). Within child and youth care, too, client numbers went up from just over 350,000 a year to almost 450,000 between 2015 and 2019. Most of the increase was in use of relatively light-touch support services; the numbers of child protection and judicial referral cases during that period remained roughly the same, at about 40,000 and 9000 respectively.[49]

**Key Points—Choices in Practice: Prioritization in Different Fields of Care**

- In only a relatively limited part of the Dutch health and social care sector are benefits explicitly weighed against costs.
- Most new forms of care (quality improvement) in curative medicine are introduced automatically: about 95 per cent enter the basic statutory health insurance package via the so-called "open" route.
- In long-term care, mental healthcare and child and youth care services, too, there is only limited explicit testing and delineation of insured cover (package management) in terms of clinical and cost effectiveness.
- So-called "outflow" (the exclusion from the package of forms of care that are not or are no longer appropriate) is intermittent and is not organized systematically. As a result, for some 40 per cent of the care included in the package we are unable to determine whether or not it is appropriate.
- The growth of resources and users in child and youth care services and in mental healthcare is related mainly to relatively minor problems.

## 7.4 Choices in Practice: Distribution Between Fields

Having discussed prioritization *within* various fields of care in the previous section, we now look one level higher: at how resources—and hence people—are distributed *between* different fields in the Netherlands. We have already noted in the first chapter of this report that the bulk of resources go to specialist medical and long-term care.

[48] The period 2011–2016 saw both a decline of 6 per cent in spending on specialist mental healthcare (from €3.2 billion to €3 billion) and a doubling of expenditure on basic mental healthcare (from €104 million to €197 million). See KPMG and Vektis (2018).

[49] AEF (2020). The number of child protection cases fell slightly, from 42,318 in 2015 to 41,249 in 2019. Judicial referrals saw a decrease from 11,420 to 9170. See also Chap. 2 of this report.

In this section we further unravel the choice processes underlying this allocation. How is it determined and how does it change over time? What dials can policymakers turn? We focus in particular upon the distribution of resources; although this does not coincide entirely with the distribution of people, the two are closely related.

In the Dutch context, the most useful approach to this question is through the so-called "system laws" governing the funding and provision of health and social care. Overall spending under the Healthcare Insurance Act (*Zorgverzekeringswet*, Zvw)—covering, roughly speaking, all forms of curative medicine—is primarily demand-led, in line with the scope of the care included in the basic statutory insurance package. The dynamics of the inclusion process (the inflow and outflow described earlier in this chapter) thus indirectly determine the total demand for resources. Insurers are free to set the premium they charge policyholders directly for the package, whilst the income-dependent contribution is determined by central government. In the case of the Long-Term Care Act (*Wet* langdurige *zorg*, Wlz), both premiums and payments—and hence total expenditure—are regulated by the government. As for the Social Support Act (*Wet maatschappelijke ondersteuning*, Wmo) and the Child and Youth Act (*Jeugdwet*), total expenditure depends upon the policy choices made by the individual local authorities with respect to the services they provide.

Within the scope of all the system laws, in practice there is a complex interaction between public expectations concerning the quality and accessibility of provision and what is actually delivered. Governments—national and local—in theory usually have the freedom to set and to vary budgets, but in the real world their room for manoeuvre is limited because any changes very quickly impact services on the ground. One example is the effects of budget cuts in the wake of the financial crisis upon employment levels in mental healthcare, child and youth care services and nursing and personal care, and the resulting problems with waiting lists and quality (see Chaps. 3 and 4).

Looking at the historical distribution of resources to various types of provider (see Fig. 7.2),[50] we find that specialist medical care has accounted for the largest share of expenditure over the past twenty years. Moreover, that share has increased gradually from 27 per cent at the turn of the century to well over 30 per cent today. More generally, as revealed by the relatively "flat" lines in Fig. 7.2 the broad pattern of allocation changes only very slowly. This reflects a high degree of path dependence: to a great extent, the distribution of resources is determined by historical factors. To some degree this is inevitable—the underlying demographic, social and technological trends are slow as well. A "supertanker" like the health and social care sector cannot change course too suddenly, and it is questionable whether that would be desirable.

---

[50]As we have seen in Chaps. 1 and 2, total spending rose substantially between 1998 and 2019. This increase is not apparent in Fig. 7.2, which shows only the distribution of that expenditure across various types of provider.

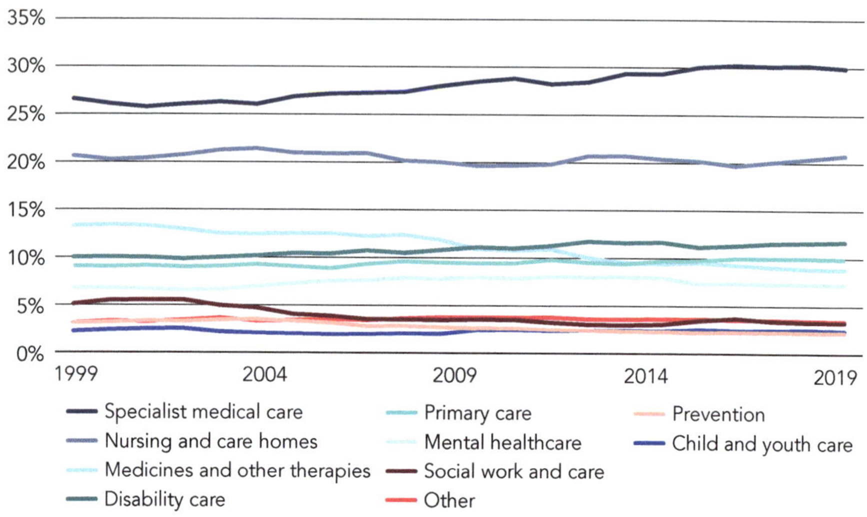


**Fig. 7.2** Relative distribution of expenditure by eight types of health and social care provider, 1998–2019. (Some of the shifts observed can be explained by the transfer of care budgets from one field to another. In 2012, for instance, the "expensive medicines" budget was reallocated to hospitals. The categories in this diagram correspond with the main headings in Fig. 1.4, with two exceptions: (1) "long-term care" is subdivided into disability care and nursing and care homes; and (2) "policy and management organizations" are omitted because our focus here is care providers)

### *7.4.1 Limited Commitment to Prevention*

Regardless of the speed of the shifts within it, the distribution of resources seems to bear fairly little relationship to where in the system we know that health gains can be achieved, quality of life improved and public values upheld. This is problematic given the sustainability challenges we face. The increasing scarcity of people and resources within the care sector means that the issue of displacement is becoming more and more acute,[51] which in turn makes it all the more important that they be deployed where quality and accessibility require the greatest support and where health gains can be achieved in a relatively efficient manner. It is precisely when scarcity is an issue, after all, that society needs to receive sufficient benefits in return for its efforts.

---

[51] As it also is in allocations to health and social care versus other sectors. We return to this point in Sect. 7.6.

Why do we think that more people and resources should be directed towards those points in the system where health gains can be achieved and public values upheld? One reason is the relatively limited spending on preventive medicine and interventions over several decades; together with child and youth care services, these activities are allocated the least resources overall (see Fig. 7.2).[52] Despite repeated calls over many years for greater commitment in this area,[53] its share of spending has fallen steadily since the turn of the millennium. Yet research shows that a whole range of preventive intervention can achieve tangible health gains at relatively low social and financial cost[54] (see Table 7.2 and Box 7.6)—certainly when compared with some forms of curative medicine. Moreover, effective prevention could also bolster the sector's societal sustainability. Take the pressure on solidarity associated with lifestyle-related ailments, for instance (see Chap. 3): these are perfect examples of conditions that preventive measures can help avert or suppress. And in some forms, such as excise duties and so-called "sin taxes", these actually generate money rather than costing it (see Table 7.2). This does not mean that investing in prevention will automatically result in financial savings, but it does mean that this approach offers great potential to achieve health gains—and often at relatively low cost compared with those attainable through other forms of intervention (see Box 7.6).

[52] Incidentally, Fig. 7.2 only includes spending on forms of prevention that fall within the domain of health and social care, most notably disease prevention and health promotion activities by municipal health services and other institutions as well occupational health and safety work, screening programmes for cancer and so on. Statistics Netherlands reports that the expenditure shown in Fig. 7.2 amounted to almost €2 billion in 2015. If we take a broader view of preventive health, however, outlay is much higher. In that same year, in fact, it totalled some €9.5 billion. By far the largest constituent item in this sum was sewerage (€3.2 billion), followed by drinking water and air quality (€1.4 billion each), waste disposal (€1.2 billion) and road safety (€1.2 billion). By comparison, broadly defined expenditure on disease prevention in 2015 was €2.4 billion and that on health promotion €0.6 billion. Even under the broadest interpretation of preventive health, however, expenditure has fallen: adjusted for inflation, by 17 per cent between 2007 and 2015. For more information, see Van Gils et al. (2020) and Volksgezondheidszorg.info ("Kosten van Preventie").

[53] For an overview, see Broeders et al. (2018).

[54] Polder et al. (2020).

**Box 7.6: Does Prevention Save Money?**

There is often an implicit expectation that preventive medicine and interventions save money and so, by extension, that investing more in these activities will reduce overall healthcare spending. After all, "prevention is better than cure". If a person stays healthy, surely that costs nothing? Unfortunately, things are not always that simple. And for various reasons.[55] One is the fact, discussed earlier in this report (see Chap. 2), that a large proportion of the expenditure is incurred just before death (see Chap. 2). Prevention does not necessarily change this, it just defers those costs. Another is that prevention can extend life expectancy, but in some cases with much of that extra time spent in poor health ("expansion of morbidity"). Then there is the possibility that the burden of disease simply shifts. Fewer smokers means a lower prevalence of lung cancer, for example, and so more people living longer, but some of them will go on to develop dementia later in life. That "surrogate" condition may be cheaper to treat, but it could also prove more expensive.

So the net effect of preventive medicine is not always clear in advance, is shrouded in uncertainties and varies greatly between interventions. One of the preliminary studies for this report summarizes its benefits and those of other forms of care.[56] The broad picture is that it cannot be said that "prevention" in general reduces care costs. What is apparent is that many preventive interventions are by far the least costly way to generate extra healthy years of life. And in many cases prevention is simply the most effective means to improve the health of a large group of people, notwithstanding the cost.

However, a greater commitment to prevention is not just a matter of investing more money. Many preventive interventions cost little or nothing, and some even generate revenue—quite apart from the health benefits they bring. These are often legislative measures such as the so-called "sugar tax" (see also Table 7.2); the preliminary study by National Institute for Public Health and the Environment (*Rijksinstituut voor Volksgezondheid en Milieu*, RIVM) provides a list.[57] The issue with instruments of this kind is not so much one of resource allocation or distribution, then, but more normative: to what extent can and do we restrict people's individual freedom in the interests of their own future health? Effective, well-designed incentives and deterrents are an important factor here, and sometimes also the

[55] Cohen et al. (2008), Goetzel (2009), Russell (2009), Woolf (2009), Licher et al. (2019), and Wouterse (2020).

[56] Polder et al. (2020).

[57] Polder et al. (2020) and Van der Vliet et al. (2020).

**Table 7.2** Examples of potential health gains and cost-effectiveness

| Interventie of behandeling | Totaal te winnen gezonde levensjaren | Kosten/ qaly (icer) | Totale kosten |
|---|---|---|---|
| **Voorbeelden kosteneffectieve preventieve maatregelen** | | | |
| Verbod op tv-reclame voor ongezond eten gericht op kinderen | 29.229 jaar | € 3 | € 101.337 |
| Screening huisarts op overmatige alcoholconsumptie | 65 jaar | € 681 | € 44.360 |
| Verlaging max. snelheid in dichtbevolkte gebieden naar 80 km/h | 143 jaar | € 1.500 | - |
| Financiële prikkel meer bewegen op werk | 542 jaar | € 3.196 | € 13 miljoen |
| Screening huidkanker risicogroep | 126.880 jaar | € 12.291 | € 1,5 miljard |
| **Ter vergelijking, recent pakketadvies** | | | |
| Osimertinib (longkanker) | | € 134.575 | |
| **Kostenbesparende preventieve maatregelen** | | | |
| Accijnsverhoging ongezonde voeding (10% prijsstijging) | 522.907 jaar | | € 2,9 miljard opbrengst |
| Verplichte zoutreductie voedsel | 65.718 jaar | | € 217 miljoen opbrengst |
| Accijnsverhoging suikerhoudende dranken | 42.953 jaar | | € 75,3 miljoen opbrengst |

Sources: Polder et al. (2020), Van der Vliet et al. (2020), and Zorginstituut (2020a)

realization that we have to override short-term concerns for the sake of long-term health gains.[58] We look in greater detail at the social and institutional barriers to more widespread prevention in the next chapter.

[58] RIVM (2018a, b), Van Giessen (2020), and Van Giessen et al. (2021a, b).

### *7.4.2 Commitment to Public Values*

Illustrative of the lack of systematic prioritization between different fields in health and social care is the position of those where public values are not being sufficiently upheld. In Chap. 4 we showed that quality and accessibility are under particular pressure in child and youth care services, specialist mental healthcare and care for vulnerable elderly people. Yet looking at the first two of these, there are no signs that their financial situation is improving or that they are being prioritized for more resources (see Fig. 7.2). Their relative share of overall funding has remained remarkably constant for decades, and indeed actually declined due to the budget reductions accompanying their decentralization to local authorities in 2015. We have also seen (in Chap. 3) that substantial staff reductions occurred during the same period. On the other side of the coin, examination of the longer-term trend reveals a steady growth in the relative weight of hospital care—a field that performs well in terms of quality and accessibility as measured by OECD standards (see Chap. 4). According to the prognoses, this will remain so in the decades to come as growth within the sector, in both absolute and percentage terms, is concentrated in curative medicine and care for the elderly (see Chap. 2).

Investing in prevention is not only a generally effective and efficient way to achieve health gains, it can also help safeguard public values in fields where they are at risk. As we saw earlier in this chapter, the proportion of users with relatively minor complaints is currently on the rise in these fields, child and youth care services and mental healthcare amongst them. A stronger commitment to preventive interventions might actually reduce the influx of such straightforward cases, freeing up human, material and administrative resources for more patients with serious conditions. One example is measures to avoid the occurrence and aggravation of mental disorders (see Box 7.7) and of the need for youth care. Much the same applies in care for the elderly: to enable them to continue living at home, it is very important that they have a social network and remain mobile. In this respect, providing them with an exercise regime and fall-prevention measures are obviously beneficial interventions. It is also important to identify increased frailty over time, cognitive and mental as well as physical. However, the RIVM has found that there is still insufficient co-operation between care and assistance providers when it comes to early signalling of issues of this kind.[59]

[59] Buist et al. (2018).

**Box 7.7: Strengthening Preventive Interventions to Combat Mental Disorders**

A growing body of data shows that it is possible to prevent mental disorders like psychosis, depression, alcohol dependence and suicide.[60] A meta-analysis of fifty randomized controlled trials[61] involving people who had not been diagnosed with depression at the start of the trial and who then received either "preventive" cognitive behavioural therapy or "usual care" found that after one year the active intervention had led to a 19 per cent reduction in the risk of developing depression[62]—albeit with the rider that it had a low absolute effect upon incidence and limited reach.[63] In addition to being clinically effective, the intervention also appeared to be cost-effective.[64]

Both the lack of commitment to preventive medicine and the limited allocation of people and resources to parts of the care sector where public values are under pressure are, to a certain extent, the flip side of implicit prioritization decisions in other fields. Consider, for example, the strain on budgets discussed earlier in this chapter that results from automatically accepting quality improvements across much of curative medicine—and only exacerbated by the rapid development of medical technology (see Chap. 2). Or the increase in expenditure on long-term care for the elderly being driven by demographic factors. One-to-one substitution cannot be proven, but in a world of scarce people and resources all the various aspects of health and social care end up fishing in the same pond.

[60] Cuijpers and Beekman (2018).

[61] Of these 50 trials, 16 were in indicated prevention (with subjects who have some symptoms but do not meet the clinical criteria for depression), 33 in selective prevention (members of high-risk groups, such as children of parents with depression or people who are unemployed) and one in universal prevention (covering the entire population regardless of whether there was a known risk factor for depression).

[62] Cuijpers et al. (2021).

[63] Cuijpers and Beekman (2018).

[64] Cuijpers and Beekman (2018).

**Key Points—Choices in Practice: Distribution Between Fields**

- The broad distribution of resources between the different fields of health and social care in the Netherlands is determined primarily by historical patterns.
- Preventive medicine and interventions can achieve relatively substantial health gains at relatively low cost, but efforts in this field have remained at a fairly constant low level for more than two decades.
- Despite overall growth in the sector's resourcing, fields where the quality and accessibility of provision are at risk—including specialist mental healthcare, child protection and youth care under judicial referral—have largely missed out.
- Preventive medicine and interventions can help curb the influx of care users and bolsters public values, especially in the fields where these are under pressure.
- The allocation of resources and people between and within sectors is only driven to a very limited extent by the potential to achieve health gains or to uphold public values.

## 7.5 Choices in Practice: Collective Versus Individual

So far, this chapter has dealt with the distribution of resources in health and social care. But another way in which boundaries can be drawn is from the funding side. Should people who use care be expected to contribute directly towards it themselves, and to what extent? Or should the entire cost be borne by the collective? The degree to which responsibility is invested in the collective is important for the sector's financial sustainability, since it has a direct impact upon the financial burden that care places on collective resources. There are also potential indirect repercussions for human and financial sustainability, as out-of-pocket contributions such as co-payments can reduce the use of care provision (a behavioural effect).[65] Of course, the extent to which care use is charged for in this way may also affect the financial component of accessibility, although here much depends upon the exact pattern of distribution: who is expected to make contributions and what are their personal circumstances? Finally, there are potential effects for societal sustainability. These can be either negative or positive: negative if people are concerned about the consequences for the financial accessibility of care, positive if they consider it fair that the users of care should at least partly bear the costs themselves (see also Chap. 3). The net impact of these effects across the board is unknown.

[65] This is referred to as the "brake effect". When this goes so far that people fail to take up care that is medically necessary, the term "care avoidance" is used.

The Dutch care system features direct charges in a number of areas, in particular a compulsory excess built into the basic statutory health insurance package under the Zvw, covering mainly curative medicine, and personal contributions for long-term care (Wlz) and social support (Wmo).[66] The Zvw excess is currently €385 per annum,[67] whilst the Wlz contribution is means-tested[68] and the Wmo requires a monthly "subscription fee" of €19 per beneficiary household. All of these charges are the subject of controversy in the public debate because they represent mandatory out-of-pocket fees for essential basic provision, and hence are unavoidable for patients in need of the treatment, care or support in question. Other forms of direct personal payment within the Dutch system, such as premiums for optional supplementary health insurance cover, are less contentious because the provision concerned is not generally regarded as essential.

**Box 7.8: Amounts and Types of Direct Charge in the Netherlands and Elsewhere**

Direct charges are an integral part of other nations' health and social care systems, too. One variable we are able to compare internationally is the ratio of out-of-pocket payments to collective financing. In general terms, the proportion of direct charges in the Netherlands is slightly lower than the OECD average (see Fig. 7.3). In most neighbouring countries, with the exception of France, it is marginally (Germany, United Kingdom, Norway) or considerably (Belgium) higher.

A WHO comparison shows that the Netherlands has the lowest level of out-of-pocket payments in Europe, 5.2 per cent, followed by France (6.3 per cent) and the United Kingdom (9.7 per cent).[69] Unlike in many other countries, moreover, the Dutch excess for curative medicine (under the Zvw) has a clearly specified upper limit. This protects lower income-earners with chronic conditions, in particular, against the "stacking" of care charges.

Compared with citizens of other Western countries, the Dutch incur relatively low direct charges (see box 7.8 and Fig. 7.3). Furthermore, their overall level has actually decreased over the past few decades (see Fig. 7.4). In recent years, too, the

[66] For the sake of clarity, when we refer to "direct charges" we are not talking about health insurance premiums. They, after all, are a mandatory contribution paid by everyone—effectively a tax—and unrelated to actual use of care provision.

[67] The excess was originally set at €150 when the current system was first introduced in 2008 and was subsequently increased in steps.

[68] Capped at €2469.20 per month in 2021.

[69] See https://gateway.euro.who.int/en/indicators/h2020_29-out-of-pocket-expenditures/visualizations/#id=21528&tab=table. The exact percentages differ between the studies cited because they use different terms of reference; for example, on how to deal with compensatory measures like the Dutch care allowance. Nevertheless, the broad picture with regard to countries' relative positions is robust.

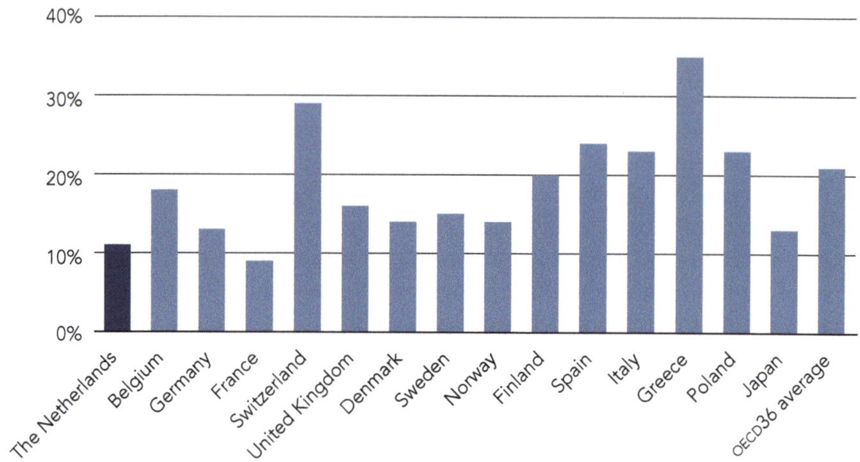


**Fig. 7.3** Total share of direct charges within health and social care financing in the Netherlands and other OECD countries. (Source: OECD, 2019b)

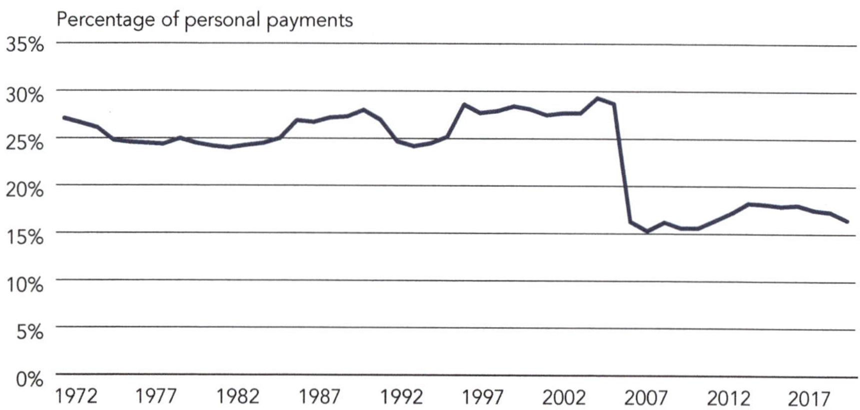


**Fig. 7.4** Percentage of personal payments in Dutch health and social care. (Source: CBS Statline)

trend has been downwards. The Zvw excess, for instance, has barely increased since 2013, when it reached €350 per calendar year, and not at all since the current figure of €385 was set in 2016. In real terms this means that it has been decreasing slowly for almost a decade. The introduction of the Wmo "subscription" model in 2020 has also reduced the extent of out-of-pocket fees. None of this, however, alters the fact that these charges can be a substantial outgoing, especially for low-income households.

As well as their overall level, the manner in which direct charges are levied is also important. In particular, the extent to which the amount payable is directly related to the use of insured care. Two common methods are illustrated in Fig. 7.5.

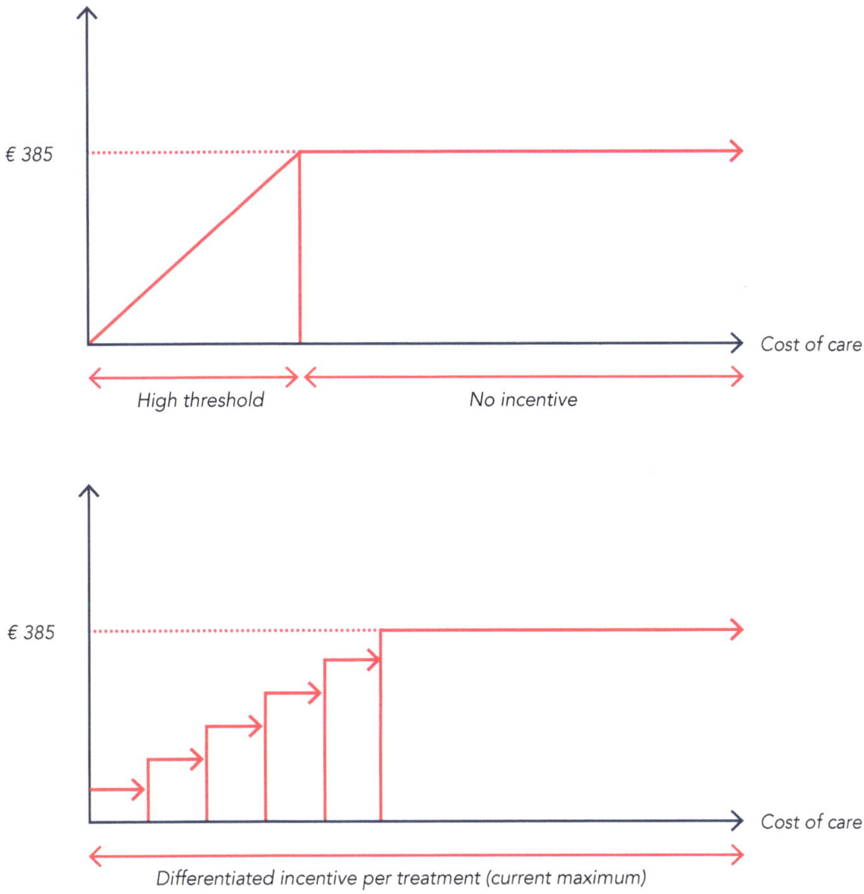


**Fig. 7.5** Two models for levying direct payments for insured care: with fixed annual excess (top, the current Dutch Zvw system) and with set co-payments per treatment (bottom, as used in Germany, Belgium and other countries)

The x-axis shows a person's total spending on care in a given year, the y-axis how much of that they have to pay out of pocket. In a system with a fixed annual excess (as under the Dutch Zvw), the patient first pays that amount in full but nothing more thereafter. Where there are so-called "co-payments", by contrast, they pay a set amount for each new intervention. Under this arrangement the costs for the individual rise less quickly when he or she uses care, but there is a longer braking effect.

How direct charges are structured shapes the kind of behavioural incentive (or disincentive) they create. The situation under the Dutch Zvw—a relatively low excess by international standards—makes the threshold for the initial use of care relatively high, but as soon as that is crossed there is no longer any deterrent effect. In practice, this means that that effect is never a factor at all for most chronic patients because they know full well in advance that they will "use up" their entire policy excess in a given year. By contrast, a co-payment model along German or Belgian lines—possibly in combination with the same annual maximum contribution of €385 (the scenario depicted in the bottom diagram in Fig. 7.5)—would maintain the braking effect for longer. Another way to achieve a similar outcome is through a so-called "shifted" excess, whereby the patient only starts contributing personally once they reach a certain expenditure threshold (€400, say).[70] Depending upon the way co-payment is arranged, it can be more predictable for the patient because it is not linked to the total costs incurred by the insurer "behind the scenes"—information that is not very transparent for the patient and not easy to foresee—but only on the number and, perhaps, type of interventions undertaken. Such predictability can be especially important for those on very low incomes. Potentially, it might also bolster societal sustainability. Unfortunately, though, little is known about how various forms of co-payment affect this dimension; recent analyses only provide estimates of the overall financial and distribution effects of different ways of calculating co-payments.[71]

A third important factor with regard to the design of direct charges is the question of who should and should not pay them, and how much they should be. In the Netherlands, their levels under the Zvw and Wmo depend only upon the care received[72] and not upon any other payer characteristics such as their age, gender or income.[73] In short, everyone using care pays the same for it.[74] In the case of social support (covered by the Wmo), this is a recent development: until the introduction of the "subscription" model in 2020, personal contributions were income-dependent.[75] Since the change the median income of families receiving youth support has been rising, presumably due to a pull effect on higher income-earners who are now asked to pay only a (lower) flat monthly fee.[76]

On the other hand, personal contributions for long-term care (under Wlz) are still means-tested. Both income and assets are taken in account.[77] A wealthier user thus pays more than a poorer one for the same care. Similar arrangements are also common in long-term care in other countries. An international comparison of systems to fund care for the elderly, for example, showed that all the countries examined

---

[70] Boone and Remmerswaal (2020a).

[71] Boone and Remmerswaal (2020a, b).

[72] Under the Zvw, for example, not all care counts towards the excess. One of the exemptions is GP appointments.

[73] There are limited exceptions to this rule. For example, children under 18 have no excess.

[74] Under the Zvw there is an indirect income-dependent effect through the earnings-linked care allowance, but that is not related in any way to actual use of care.

[75] However, local authorities are still free to charge some or all of their residents a lower fee. This facility is used mainly to relieve the financial burden for those on the lowest incomes. When applied in this way, it reintroduces an income-dependent component—albeit a limited one—to the contributions.

[76] AEF (2020).

[77] And to a limited extent age as well, specifically whether or not a person has reached the official retirement age.

impose direct charges with income and/or asset-dependent components.[78] The most modest are in Denmark, where users only pay an income-related fee for board and lodging whilst the government funds all care proper from the collective coffers. The most stringent means-testing is in the United Kingdom; an elderly person there only qualifies for publicly-funded care if their total net assets are worth less than £23,250 (just over €26,000; 2020 figures). Such a low and absolute cut-off point implies that collective provision of long-term care for the elderly in the UK exists only as a last-ditch safety net, not as a broad service accessible to a significant proportion of the population.

Other criteria for means-tested payments, such as a higher or graduated upper limit, need not have this implication. Ultimately, society pays for all care in some way or another, but the way those costs are distributed is important. The precise function and form of means-testing is a political question, and the answer can and will be different for different aspects of health and social care. But before coming to that there is the matter of direct charges and the role they should play. Are they primarily a way of in inhibiting the uptake of care (the brake effect)? A means of distributing its costs fairly across different income and wealth groups? Or a way to give individuals a say in the type—and possibly quality—of care they receive, in line with their personal and economic circumstances? Here again, the socially desirable answers to questions like this will vary according to the nature of the care in question. In general terms, however, levels of direct charges and the precise form they take should be determined only once we have answered a more fundamental question: what is their purpose? Unfortunately, that is not the case at the moment, since in the Netherlands at any rate the public debate seems to centre solely on their amount and form.

**Key Points—Choices in Practice: Collective Versus Individual**

- Compared with other countries, direct charges for health and social care in the Netherlands are relatively low and their share in covering its overall costs has been declining in recent decades.
- The form direct payments take—who pays them and for what, whether they are means-tested and so on—is important due to their potential impact upon access to care.
- Direct charges in the Netherlands are generally linked only to the nature of the care concerned, not to other payer characteristics (especially their income or assets). The exception is the means-tested personal contribution for long-term care (under the Wlz).
- Direct charges can serve various purposes, from inhibiting the uptake of care to redistributing its costs.

[78] Kruse et al. (2021).

## 7.6 Choices in Practice: Care Versus Other Sectors

Up until now we have looked only at the prioritization and distribution of resources within health and social care: should we reimburse treatment A or treatment B, invest in preventive medicine or long-term care and so on. But there is also a broader question, and one equally important for sustainability: how much do we allocate to care as a whole, rather than other public services? To a great extent the answer to this question is derived from the choices and decisions made within the sector, as discussed above: what provision is covered by the basic statutory health insurance package, how generous are defined rights and entitlements to long-term care and what do we expect patients and users themselves to contribute? All of these factors help shape spending on care.

Moreover, the level of that spending is closely related to the fact that, compared with other policy domains, the care sector in the Netherlands is in a unique situation with regard to its budgeting processes.[79] Other domains are allocated financial resources in each new government's coalition agreement, in line with its political priorities and ambitions, and these amounts are then adjusted and honed during subsequent annual budget cycles. But that is not the case with health and social care.[80] Instead, the Netherlands Bureau for Economic Policy Analysis (*Centraal Planbureau*, CPB) forecasts the sector's expected expenditure based upon a model that incorporates such factors as demographic developments and historical spending trends, including past growth as a result of the introduction of new forms of care and technologies. From this the CPB generates a so-called "baseline", from which politicians can deviate in their decision-making, either upwards (more investment in care) or downwards (less investment). This is known as an "accommodating budget" since, rather than reflecting an outlook or political aspiration like the spending allocations in other policy domains, it "accommodates" what the care sector itself is expected to do.

We have described the underlying reason for this deviation from standard procedure earlier in this chapter. Across large parts of the sector—certainly those consuming the bulk of its resources—the government has only limited scope to "steer the ship" directly. In curative medicine, for instance—the main field governed by the Zvw and by far the largest in the sector—total spending, the volume of care provided and prices are determined largely[81] by public demand and by interactions between patients, providers and insurers. The government does have some means to exert control in these areas, but to be realistic these are modest in their reach (adjusting the composition of the basic insurance package, for example) or not legally

[79] Studiegroep Begrotingsruimte (2020) and Kersten et al. (2021).

[80] Of course, there are also practical and political constraints in other public policy domains which prevent their budgets being varied with complete freedom. But the exact amount is an explicit political decision.

[81] "Largely" because, for example, the Zvw does provide for forms of tariff regulation in some areas.

enforceable (outline agreements), or their effectiveness at the macro level is hard to predict and in practice often disappointing (as with substitution to promote cheaper forms of care and other efficiency measures—see Chap. 6). Similar dynamics are at play in other parts of the sector, too. Because much of social care has been devolved to local government, for example, "The Hague" is limited in its powers to intervene there as well. And since the CPB generates a baseline spending forecast only once during a government's term, when it first takes office, it can only use its limited options relatively rarely.

The unusual budgetary procedure in the care sector has a number of practical and political consequences. For instance, it creates an implicit normative effect with regard to spending and volume growth because the baseline issued by the CPB serves as its frame of reference. This establishes a dynamic whereby that growth is not a conscious political choice but an automatic process. Downward deviations from the baseline are perceived as spending cuts even if there is a substantial increase in absolute expenditure. In recent decades the baseline increase in expenditure has systematically exceeded economic growth.[82] Consequently, the political judgement as to whether rapidly rising spending on care is actually in the best public interest, or would these resources be of better use in other public policy domains, is not always aired explicitly.

**Key Points—Choices in Practice: Care Versus Other Sectors**

- Unlike expenditure in most other public policy domains, total spending on health and social care is estimated rather than budgeted.
- This puts the sector in a relatively dominant position in the overall policy arena. Deviations from the baseline estimate are perceived as cuts, even if actual expenditure increases.
- With regard to total spending on care and the allocation of resources within the sector alike, political and policy options to exert control are limited in both a formal and a practical sense.
- Consequently, the political judgement as to whether the public interest is best served by the existing system and the current distribution of resources within the sector is not always aired explicitly.

[82] This has not necessarily been the case in every individual year, but it does apply to the long-term average. In recent years, however, the baseline has again dropped below the forecast rate of overall economic growth. This is due largely to predicted spending reductions in curative medicine as a result, in part, of the outline agreements in that field (see also Chap. 5) and their extrapolation into the future in the forecasts. In reality, however, it is highly questionable whether those reductions will be sustainable—particularly in the light of prognoses by the likes of the RIVM which foresee continuous growth (Vonk et al., 2020). This illustrates a downside of extrapolating future estimates from data covering a relatively short time period: the resulting picture can be relatively strongly coloured by recent policy developments and other trends.

## 7.7 Impediments Affecting Choices and Allocation

This chapter centres on choices in the health and social care sector, both theoretical and practical. We have so far addressed a number of distribution-related questions. For example, how do we allocate people and resources within the sector? What treatments and other interventions do we choose? How much responsibility, financial and otherwise, do we place upon the individual? How much do we invest in care at the expense of other public services? And for all of these questions, how do we decide? From the sustainability perspective, our analysis of choice processes in Dutch health and social care produces a number of interrelated conclusions—all linked to the single observation that, given the increasing role being played in this sector by scarcity, the three dimensions of sustainability will in the future require that priorities and choices associated with that scarcity be determined in a better manner. Because the implications and effects of these choice processes extend to and often aggravate sustainability-related issues, we formulate the conclusions below in terms of impediments to good choices with regard to the allocation of people and resources in health and social care. In order to identify those impediments, we sometimes refer back to earlier chapters in this report.

**Impediment 1—Automatic Inflow of New Care**
Firstly, in curative medicine only a very small proportion (5 per cent) of new forms of care and treatment covered by the Dutch statutory basic health insurance package are subject to an explicit advance authorization procedure to test their health benefits against their cost (cost-effectiveness). The vast majority are admitted via the so-called "open" route, effectively meaning that quality improvements are generally accepted automatically for reimbursement from collective funds. This puts healthcare in a unique position within the public sector. In education, for example, new technologies and other innovations with potential quality benefits require explicit political consideration before they are implemented.[83] Since the bulk of care-related advances in the real world are in curative medicine, this impediment also has repercussions for relationships *between* the various aspects of health and social care: it strengthens the position of rapidly improving fields like curative medicine at the expense of those where the rate of progress is more sedate. They include child and youth care, mental healthcare and care for the elderly.

**Impediment 2—No Systematic Outflow Management**
Secondly, managing outflow from the statutory package—the exclusion or abandonment of forms of care and treatment no longer deemed appropriate—appears to be just as tough a challenge as regulating inflow. From the sustainability perspective, both are equally problematic; after all, a comprehensive yet efficient package can only be maintained by keeping a constant eye out for "obsolete" interventions that can be dropped from it. In part, the problem here is lack of information: for a

[83] Kersten et al. (2021).

very substantial proportion of all care provided within this package—thought to be about 40 per cent—we simply do not know whether or not it is appropriate.[84] But even when it is actually known to be inappropriate, which applies to an estimated 10 per cent or so of the total, in practice outflow does not necessarily follow. This is due to a combination of disincentives, habit and vested interests. And what it shows is that making sustainability-related choices in healthcare is an issue not only for the world of policy, politics and public administration, but also one influenced to some extent by decisions taken in the consulting room. Obviously, this situation is particularly undesirable from the patient's point of view; by definition, after all, inappropriate care is not in their interest. But it also has sustainability implications, because such care makes claims on people and resources that are not—or not sufficiently—offset by benefits. This can result in the implicit displacement of other, more effective care. Which, in essence, is a form of allocative inefficiency.

**Impediment 3—Limited Knowledge of Clinical, Therapeutic and Cost-Effectiveness**

Thirdly, in large parts of the sector assessment of clinical or therapeutic effectiveness of the care provided—and by extension its cost-effectiveness—is limited. In fields like long-term care, but also certain aspects of mental healthcare and child and youth care, systematic evaluation is even less common than in curative medicine. Measuring and objectively appraising therapeutic effectiveness—and hence cost-effectiveness—are inherently more difficult in these fields because the benefits are harder to quantify. Moreover, their research culture is less well-developed and the use of available instruments such as ICECAP is limited. Across much of the sector, therefore, we have little insight into whether people and resources are deployed prudently from the sustainability point of view. This creates the risk that they are diverted into forms of care that generate only limited health gains or improvements in quality of life.

**Impediment 4—A Sustainability Imbalance: Financial Considerations Dominate**

A fourth impediment is that choice processes in health and social care often upset the equilibrium between the instruments put in place to guide the three dimensions of sustainability, or between sustainability and public values. In most cases this imbalance involves financial considerations overshadowing the other factors. One example, already discussed in Chaps. 3 and 4, is the drastic staffing cuts undertaken in mental healthcare, in child and youth care services and in nursing, residential and home care as a result of the pressure to make cost savings. Financial considerations can quickly come to dominate political and administrative decision-making because they are easy to measure and often relatively straightforward for policymakers to direct. As the issue of staffing sustainability becomes more acute, however, manpower will also become a constraining factor. Indeed, we have this occur already in

---

[84] The ZiN's Care Evaluation and Appropriate Use (Zorgevaluatie en Gepast Gebruik, ZE&GG) programme is attempting to address this issue by strengthening the evaluation of care.

the case of the quality framework for nursing homes discussed above, under which resources were released to improve quality but the staff needed could not be found.

**Impediment 5—Short-Term Policies Dominate Choice Processes**
One final impediment is the prevalence of short-term thinking in politics and public administration. It is not so attractive to invest in forms of care with benefits that will only materialize in the longer term, and if you do they are prone to cutbacks further down the line. Preventive medicine is a classic example. In many cases, its positive outcomes only emerge years—sometimes even decades—later. This makes it less appealing than forms of care that yield results much sooner. Another related aspect is the visibility of a health problem and the gains to be achieved from tackling it. Some conditions are relatively invisible to the general public; various kinds of mental disorder, for instance, are responsible for a large burden of disease but less apparent than with obvious physical ailments. We look at this impediment in more detail in the next chapter.

**Choices in Care as a Sustainability Issue**
The current distribution of people and resources across the health and social care sector is less than ideal when it comes to delivering health gains, improving quality of life and safeguarding public values. This is largely down to the impediments listed above. So they are what politicians need to address in order to achieve greater health gains and to safeguard public values. In particular, that means actively strengthening their commitments to preventive medicine and to those aspects of care where public values are under pressure.

But what does this analysis have to do with the sustainability of health and social care? The link is the scarcity factor discussed earlier: the ever more stringent financial, staffing and societal constraints on the sector's growth. We began this chapter with the notion of allocative efficiency: are we doing the right things? With scarcity on the rise, the impediments to the process of making choices in that respect are becoming more and more significant. Which in turn makes it increasingly important to ensure that the choices are made in a better way. This does not mean aiming to shrink the sector, but rather that we need to pursue more selective growth. This issue of prioritization in care is intrinsically normative in nature. After all, it is ultimately about what we as a society regard as fair and important. For example, to say that it is problematic that the quality and accessibility of care in some fields have fallen below par is a normative judgement. It is therefore important to emphasize that the underlying motive for making better choices is not financial; in fact, the aim is to safeguard the quality and accessibility of care within the parameters of the available people, resources and public support, not to save money as an end in itself. It is precisely in order to be able to continue to uphold these public values that it is inevitable that choices will have to be made, so that people and resources are freed up for the parts of the system where those values are under pressure. Sometimes those will be tough choices. Not everything that is possible technically and medically will actually be done. The next chapter therefore addresses the difficult question of how to deal with this dilemma.

# Chapter 8
# Towards Better Choices in Care

> To make better choices about health and social care, we need to find sensible ways to overcome psychological barriers, conflicts of interest, design issues, short-term thinking and legitimacy concerns.

In the previous chapter we noted that the way choices are made in health and social care in the Netherlands, and thus the results of those choices, is not always ideal. Greater health gains could probably be achieved by deploying people and resources more effectively than is currently the case. The quality and accessibility of care could also be better assured, especially for vulnerable groups. Where limits are imposed upon the growth of care, this is not always done in the most prudent way. We also discussed five impediments to good choices and distribution in care.

In this chapter we approach the question of why such choices are so difficult from various angles. And perhaps even more importantly, we ask why drawing boundaries is so difficult. We adopt psychological, institutional, social and political perspectives, look at the timing of choices and identify barriers to better ones. In doing so we present illustrative examples; these are drawn from curative medicine because that is where the most research is available, but the points they highlight apply in a general sense to all fields of care. And in some cases also to the trade-off between care and other domains.

One central theme to recur implicitly in all our perspectives is the notion of legitimacy. Prioritization in healthcare can only be successful if it is undertaken in a legitimate way, with broad public support. Otherwise, the choices made are not socially tenable and, one way or another, will eventually be reversed or subverted. There is even a risk that they could undermine public backing for the system more generally. After all, it is not inconceivable that boundaries set too strictly might be regarded as unjust, callous even, and so damage public confidence and hence the societal sustainability of care. At the same time, though, the WRR views well-considered prioritization as an effective way of guaranteeing sustainability. Without



G. Werner et al., *Financial, Staffing and Societal Sustainability of Dutch Health Care*, Research for Policy, https://doi.org/10.1007/978-3-031-58564-7_8

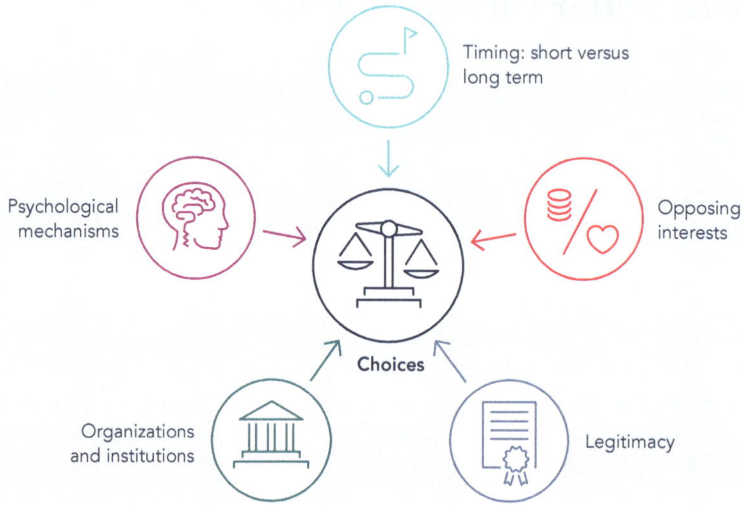


**Fig. 8.1** Five perspectives on making choices about care

clear choices, after all, the tide is sure to turn: the limits of staffing and financial sustainability will be reached and the quality and accessibility of ever larger swathes of the care system will come under unacceptable pressure as a result of displacement. In the long run, this too will be detrimental to societal sustainability. To a large extent this is also a problem of social expectations—there seems to be a clear disjunction between people's presumption that the sector can continue to grow at current rates and the adverse consequences, for care and for other domains, of the displacement that growth inevitably entails.

So there is a dilemma here too: limits have to be imposed upon growth, by making better choices, but this needs to be done in such a way that self-imposed constraints are not more damaging to public support than the absolute financial and staffing limits they seek to forestall. Before exploring this challenge, we look first at choices and limits in care from a number of different perspectives (Fig. 8.1). For the sake of clarity we treat each of these separately, but in practice they build upon and reinforce each other and the insights they deliver should not considered in isolation.

## 8.1 The Psychological Perspective

We look first at the psychological perspective. Making choices in health and social care and imposing limits on the sector's growth is almost bound to encounter public resistance. In part, this can be explained psychologically. We focus here upon two relevant phenomena in this regard: "taboo trade-offs" and "statistical lives".

### 8.1.1 Health as a "Sacred Value"

The American psychologist and political scientist Philip Tetlock explains why choices in sectors like care are so controversial by stating that health and life are so-called "sacred values".[1] Meaning that people consider them so essential that they cannot be traded off against other values and goals. Other sacred values include love, honour and justice. On the other side of the coin are less essential "secular values"—money being a classic example. If a sacred value has to be weighed directly against a secular one, that results in great psychological discomfort and hence resistance. The term used to describe this situation is "taboo trade-off": even just considering such a deal is a major social taboo.

Taboo trade-offs are perhaps most pronounced when they involve a clash between a concrete, identifiable detriment and a more abstract concept such as (financial) sustainability. Society generally finds it acceptable not to include a treatment in the standard health insurance package because it has limited benefits, but is distressed when specific patients are denied an effective but expensive treatment that has been excluded on cost grounds. This, after all, exposes the great taboo: a person has to suffer solely because it is too expensive to help them. The sacred value "life" here clashes directly with the secular value "affordability"—and in a visible, personal way to boot. Most people find this unacceptable, as the case of the drug Orkambi illustrates (see Box 8.1).

**Box 8.1: An Authorization Dilemma in Dutch Healthcare**

When a drug has little effect, deciding whether or not to reimburse it from collective funds is not much of a normative dilemma. Things become more difficult when a treatment is definitely *clinically effective* (it delivers health benefits) but not *cost-effective* (those benefits do not outweigh the financial investment required). When it was first introduced, the cystic fibrosis drug Orkambi (lumacaftor/ivacaftor) seemed to fall exactly into this category. But the proposal that it therefore be excluded from the Dutch basic statutory health insurance package sparked a public outcry, leading to parliamentary questions and direct appeals to the responsible minister.

Because the cost of the drug was estimated at €400,000 per quality-adjusted life year (QALY, see Box 7.1), the National Health Care Institute (*Zorginstituut Nederland*, ZiN) advised the minister to negotiate on the price. After several rounds of talks with the manufacturer, Orkambi was eventually included in the package from the end of October 2017. Its final price, and hence its cost-effectiveness, has still not been revealed.

This example shows that, despite broad support amongst the Dutch public for the general principles behind prioritization, controversy can arise over its application in specific cases.

[1] Tetlock (2003).

Yet sometimes there is no alternative to such choices. After all, we have established that the resources we can or want to spend on care are finite. As they are in other public policy domains. So choices have to be made somewhere, and someone will suffer as a result.

Nevertheless, people are generally willing to go a long way to avoid taboo trade-offs. And when they are unable to, they have a strong tendency to deny it; for example, by emphasizing other factors they have taken into consideration ("the benefits are only small, and very uncertain"). This is essentially dressing it up as a "routine trade-off"—the kind of judgement policymakers face on a daily basis. Another way to make a taboo trade-off more acceptable psychologically is to think of it as a more or less inevitable conflict between two sacred values, what we call a "tragic choice"[2] or "tragic trade-off".

Not long after the high-profile Orkambi controversy, the drug Spinraza came onto the market for the treatment of a rare hereditary muscle disease. Its cost per QALY is even higher than Orkambi's: between €600,000 and €1.7 million.[3] And it is part of a trend. More and more drugs that are clinically effective but place a substantial—possibly too substantial—financial burden on society are in the pipeline (see Chap. 2), and hence so are more and more potential taboo trade-offs.[4] How are we going to deal with them? Roughly speaking, there are two possibilities.[5] One is to explain to the public that such trade-offs are unavoidable and are in fact made in all kinds of policy domains, then count on their understanding. The other is to view such trade-offs as inherently "tragic" and to present them as such. Although people suffer and so a sacred value is violated by not paying for the treatment, the same would happen if its cost were covered. Because then a choice, explicit or implicit, might have to be made to divert funds away from other treatments or forms of care. Which could be detrimental to the health of other groups—by, for example, undermining care provision for vulnerable people (see Chap. 7). This logic of implicit choices in a context of scarce resources is one of the key messages of this report. The decision here is therefore not just about care versus cash, but ultimately also about care versus care. As we saw during the recent pandemic over the issue of scaling down "regular" care in favour of urgent "Covid care", this will always be a tough call, especially if the implications of one of the two options are less visible.

---

[2] Calabresi and Bobbitt (1978).

[3] In the end, the drug was admitted conditionally to the statutory basic health insurance package for all patients with the disease in question (https://www.zorginstituutnederland.nl/actueel/nieuws/2018/02/07/zorginstituut-nusinersen-spinraza-tegen-huidige-prijs-niet-in-basispakket), subject to the prerequisite is that they participate in a study of its efficacy. See www.zorginstituutnederland.nl/publicaties/adviezen/2019/12/02/vervolgadvies-voorwaardelijke-toelating-van-nusinersen-spinraza.

[4] In recent years we have seen a rapid rise in the cost of "expensive" medicines, from more than 7 per cent of the total expenditure on specialist medical care in 2013 to about 10 per cent in 2020 (NZA, 2020b).

[5] Tetlock et al. (2017).

### 8.1.2 *Statistical and Actual Lives*

This observation brings us to another psychological phenomenon: the visibility of those who benefit from an intervention. Choices are easier when they concern a so-called "statistical life" rather than a real person.[6] Suppose we have to decide how much we want to spend on measures to improve air quality in the Netherlands. We can predict with reasonable accuracy how many lives we would save, but can never identify whose lives they would be—which individuals would have died if we had not acted. Their lives may have been prolonged by the measures, but they remain statistical, unidentifiable individuals. Something similar often happens in preventive medicine: much of the health gain is statistical in nature, and hence so are many of the lives saved. We know that, on average, universal prevention benefits the entire population, but we cannot pinpoint a specific individual it has helped. Were a so-called "fat tax" to be introduced, for example, we could never ascertain who did not have a heart attack as a result. This abstract outcome is fundamentally different from that brought about by the kind of care provided at hospitals, by GPs or in nursing homes, say, in response to the specific needs of a specific person.[7] This gives rise to what it known as the "identified lives effect"[8]: despite there being no good moral justification for doing so, people have greater empathy with real human beings they can put a name to, as it were, than with the anonymous lives reported in statistical data. That is because they feel more connected to those "identified lives".

One final, related phenomenon is the urgency of a choice. In the previous chapter we discussed the rule of rescue—the normative principle that health gains in urgent cases should be given priority. This approach is in keeping with the way things are done in emergency situations, such as a major traffic accident. In those circumstances, triage is carried out according to the urgency of the patient's condition. But when it comes to prioritization decisions at the policy level (over the contents of a collective insurance package, for example), it is less obvious why more value should be attached to potential health gains for acute patients than to the same amount of gain for less acute ones.[9] Although we have good reason to assume that people actually prefer other prioritization principles—certainly after proper reflection (see Chap. 7)—urgency often turns out to have a consequential or even decisive effect in decision-making. This was the case during Covid-19, for instance, when in practice policy was directed mainly towards preventing immediate and obvious damage to health. As with the identified lives effect, we tend to notice and understand urgent health problems more readily, which potentially gives them an advantage when policy is being shaped.

---

[6] Thaler and Rosen (1976).

[7] Polder et al. (2020).

[8] Cohen et al. (2015).

[9] Mckie and Richardson (2003).

**Key Points—The Psychological Perspective**

- Making choices in health and social care is always difficult because there is a social taboo against juxtaposing good health versus financial sustainability (the taboo trade-off).
- Another challenge is that the benefits of preventive medicine, say, are often statistical in nature and cannot be traced back to actual identifiable individuals (the identified lives effect).
- Considering trade-offs as inherently "tragic" choices, a conflict between two valid claims to care, can increase their social acceptance.

## 8.2 The Perspective of Opposing Interests

In this section we look at the role played by vested interests, of all kinds, when making choices in health and social care. How do the interests of voters, patients and users, suppliers, politicians and other groups influence prioritization? We look in particular at the effect that opposing interests can have within the political arena and upon decision-making processes. After all, making choices in care is a political matter as much as anything else. Even though politicians have no direct powers in respect of certain choices, they are still called to account if one becomes the subject of public controversy.

### *8.2.1 Voters, Voting Behaviour and Majorities*

In a democracy, politicians' room for manoeuvre can be explained to a large extent by the preferences and expectations of the electorate, their potential voters. Models that take this perspective therefore view political behaviour primarily as an effort to maximize votes.[10] This does not mean, of course, that politicians' own ideals and convictions do not guide their actions as well, but it does mean that the scope of those actions is limited in practice. Not least, simply because they have to be elected or re-elected in order to actually translate their ideals into policy. One influential model in this respect is the median voter theorem, although it is almost certainly oversimplistic in the context of Dutch multiparty and coalition politics. Nevertheless, it can help to understand some aspects of choice processes in care. In a more complex political context, for example, the need for governments to secure the backing of certain dominant electoral groups, like "the middle class", also plays a role. This means that politicians have an incentive to focus primarily upon the interests of those groups. When it comes to health and social care specifically, the implication is that forms of provision the "median" voter expects to use are in a stronger

[10] Tuohy and Glied (2011) and Hauck et al. (2004).

position than others to attract political support, even though their prioritization would not necessarily be justified in terms of health gains or upholding public values. Furthermore, it follows on from this that the "favoured" provision tends be the most heavily used. Dutch hospitals, for example, treat more than 8 million patients annually,[11] so almost everyone knows someone who had to go to hospital in a given year—and thus "sees the need" for them. The situation is very different for specialist mental healthcare and child and youth care services, both of which have "only" about half a million users a year.[12]

At an even more fundamental level, this analysis is about the expectations a typical voter has of the welfare state—and of health and social care within that state. As we saw in Chap. 2, these expectations are also linked to the nation's demographic characteristics: an affluent and ageing population will be more willing to invest in care than a young, poor one. It will also want to distribute resources in a manner that suits its own interests—by ploughing more into care for the elderly, for instance. In recent decades, moreover, society has come to expect that use of care will increase rapidly and that quality improvements—in curative medicine especially—will be included immediately and in full in the standard package of entitlements (see Chap. 7). Previous attempts at reforming other aspects of the welfare state, as such as pensions and social security, show that it takes a long time and a shared information base before suppositions of this kind shift.[13] In the care sector, too, public perspectives and expectations—normative and otherwise—ultimately determine whether reforms are successful. And it can take years to build broad support for them.[14]

### *8.2.2 Avoiding Blame*

In a classic article, the American political scientist Kent Weaver analysed the behaviour of politicians. He came to the conclusion that one of their most important motivations is to avoid being blamed for unpopular decisions.[15] This is because voters have a so-called "negativity bias"[16]: they are more sensitive to actual or perceived negative aspects of policies than to positive ones. Politicians' electoral ambitions therefore dictate that it is in their interest not to be held responsible for effects perceived as disadvantageous—even more so than being acknowledged for positive outcomes. This is particularly true in situations where an existing right is at stake. Politicians use a range of strategies to avoid the blame for its loss, or to neutralize

[11] https://ziekenhuiszorgincijfers.nl/geleverde-zorg-in-ziekenhuizen

[12] https://www.nza.nl/zorgsectoren/geestelijke-gezondheidszorg-ggz-en-forensische-zorg-fz/kerncijfers-geestelijke-gezondheidszorg-ggz

[13] van Zanden (1997), van Ark et al. (1996), Goudswaard et al. (2010), and CPB (2004).

[14] Kruse et al. (2021).

[15] Weaver (1986).

[16] So underlying this behaviour on the part of politicians is also a psychological phenomenon amongst voters. Their "negativity bias" is linked closely with the notion of "loss aversion".

the impact of that accusation. Examples include keeping an unpopular policy choice off the agenda as much as possible, redefining the issue in such a way that the "losers" are less visible, finding a scapegoat, shifting the choice or postponing it. This explanatory model is also used in the context of choices in care.[17] In fact, it goes some way to explaining why it is so difficult for politicians to take negative decisions in concrete cases. And why they are so sensitive to accusations that they are "cutting back" on care, even if expenditure is actually increasing (see Sect. 7.6, on forecasts and the normalizing role played by the baseline). Particularly in a context where the choice before us has elements of a taboo trade-off, avoiding blame quickly becomes a compelling motivation for politicians. This is one key reason why choices that are unpopular but have to be made in the public interest are so often delegated to unelected bodies. We return to that topic later in this chapter.

### *8.2.3 Interest Groups and Organizational Strength*

Other explanatory models look at the power of organized interest groups.[18] The most important of these in health and social care are patient and user organizations, care providers and their organizations, suppliers (pharmaceutical companies, manufacturers of medical devices and so on) and the buyers of care (governments and insurers). The central assumption in these models is that the interests of such groups never coincide with those of the collective[19] and that they therefore organize themselves in order to align decision-making with their own perspective. Sometimes they do this behind the scenes (lobbying), in other cases by influencing public opinion (publicity campaigns and the like) and often through a combination of the two. The degree to which they achieve their objectives depends upon such factors as their organizational strength, internal coherence and social authority. Interest groups tend to be particularly successful when the benefits of a policy are highly concentrated within a specific, usually small group, whilst its costs are diffuse and spread more widely.[20] Small groups with a lot to gain are strongly motivated to pursue that end and, due to their limited size and lack of internal conflicts of interest, are able to organize themselves relatively easily around their objective—all the more so when it is a narrowly defined goal.[21]

---

[17] See, for example: Ham and Coulter (2001), Landwehr and Bohm (2011), Garpenby and Nedlund (2016), and Fredriksson et al. (2019).

[18] Contandriopoulos (2011).

[19] Buchanan and Tullock (1962).

[20] Olson (1971) and Tuohy and Glied (2011).

[21] One example is an ultimately successful attempt to reverse a negative recommendation by the ZiN's predecessor concerning the inclusion in the statutory basic health insurance package of expensive medicines for Pompe and Fabry diseases.

One not uncommon example in healthcare is lobbying for collective insurance coverage of an expensive medication for a rare disease. Both the drug's manufacturer and the patients concerned have a strong stake in achieving this, whilst the more abstract, diffuse interests of financial sustainability and affordability are opposed. Through a combination of behind-the-scenes persuasion and public campaigning, the lobby hopes to coax politicians and other decision-makers into shaping policy more to suit its own wishes. And often justifiably: a classic study in the United States found that drugs for conditions with active and well-funded patient organizations are approved more quickly.[22] This is a situation fundamentally different from that in other fields of health and social care, especially preventive medicine. There are hundreds of patient organizations in the Netherlands, for instance, but no "Dutch association of prevention users". On top of that, much of prevention is essentially about changing behaviour, such as taking more exercise and eating, drinking or smoking less—and whilst those activities might be unhealthy, they are also linked to massive economic interests. Viewed through the lens of interest-group theory, these factors help explain why the lobbies against some forms of prevention are well-organized and those in favour weak.

### 8.2.4 *Visibility and Exit Options*

Finally, using the "exit, voice and loyalty" theory[23] described previously (see Chap. 3) it is possible to arrive at a similar conclusion from the perspective of the "end user" of health and social care—the patient or "client". If the quality of a public good like care is substandard, users essentially have two options. They can either switch to another provider (exit) or voice their complaints in public, with their choice determined by their loyalty to the provider in question and the available scope to find another. In large parts of the Dutch care sector the exit options are limited, although there is some choice in the markets for health insurance and provision, most especially curative medicine. This may in part explain why quality and accessibility are best in that field (Chap. 4)—the possibility that users will switch creates an incentive for providers and buyers to perform well. In much of the rest of the sector, however, the only option available is "voice". In a collective domain of this kind, as often as not that means pushing the issue on the political or policy agenda. Again, this is easier to accomplish if it involves a specific and narrowly defined interest. More importantly still, groups that understand how the system works and are able to make their perspective seen and heard through lobbying or public campaigns are more successful in these efforts (see Box 8.2). This may partly explain why issues surrounding the quality and accessibility of care in certain fields serving socially vulnerable groups—specialist mental healthcare, child and youth care services, care for the elderly and so on—are often only picked up relatively slowly.

---

[22] Carpenter (2002).

[23] Hirschman (1970) and Dowding (2015).

**Box 8.2: Lobbying and Visibility During Covid-19**

The public battle that broke out in early 2020 regarding the Dutch authorities' prioritization of coronavirus vaccinations illustrates the importance of visibility and organizational strength for an interest group. In a number of advisory reports, the Health Council of the Netherlands (*Gezondheidsraad*) had recommended that vulnerable elderly people be vaccinated first as that would maximize the health gains. Yet various social groups subsequently succeeded in rearranging the order of priority by means of appeals in the media. This shows how a relatively heterogeneous group with little voice can be put at a disadvantage when it comes to allocation questions in health and social care.

### *8.2.5 Interests Versus Ideals*

In this section we will look at choice processes in care, and the associated politics, from the perspective of vested interests. But this does not mean that we claim that interests *alone* shape people's behaviour. We have already seen (in Chap. 3) that there is broad public support in the Netherlands for the principle of solidarity, even when it is not in people's own interests. And if our society had not also put that principle into practice, its health and social care system would have collapsed long ago. Citizens, politicians and other actors in the care sector do thus uphold their ideals, over their own best interests. But that does not mean that vested interests should be written off completely. They do play a role in the choices made in care, and we cannot always understand the outcomes if we do not take that role into account.

**Key Points—The Perspective of Opposing Interests**

- Politicians have an incentive to invest in aspects of health and social care that are used and considered important by a broad section of the public, even if quality and accessibility are already relatively good in those areas.
- Avoiding blame for unpopular decisions can be an important motivation for politicians.
- Interest groups are more successful at influencing policy if the benefits are concentrated within a relatively small, homogeneous group.
- Some societal groups are less successful in making their voices heard in the political arena and public debate.

## 8.3 The Institutional Perspective

Another scientific tradition looks at the institutional context within which policy choices are made. The question here is how the design and structure of the institutions concerned help shape those choices. The word "institutions" can be used here in both a narrow and a broader sense. In the former it refers to the formal government bodies that take decisions, and their powers; for example, parliament or regulators such as the ZiN and Dutch Healthcare Authority (*Nederlandse Zorgautoriteit*, NZa). What are they legally allowed to do and what is beyond their remit? More broadly, by "institutions" we also mean the informal customs, conventions and agreements which affect and restrict those actors in their freedom of action. In this section we look at a number of important institutional aspects of choice processes in Dutch health and social care and compare them with other countries. First, though, we take a look from a theoretical perspective at the question of what responsibilities surrounding choices in care belong in the political domain, and which belong elsewhere.

### 8.3.1 Responsibility for Choices—Distant or Close?

At an elemental level, prioritization in care is a normative—and hence inherently political—activity. After all, it is about the issue of what we as a society find most important. At the same time, as we saw in the previous chapter, it is also an activity requiring a high degree of technical expertise: who benefits from what care under what circumstances? In addition, as pointed out earlier in this chapter, it is an activity loaded with psychological baggage: how should politics deal with the complex considerations involved, and where should responsibility for the choices made lie?

The trend in the Western world in recent decades has been to distance certain aspects of public policy and their implementation from the political arena.[24] In the academic literature this process is called "delegation", and the organizations that exercise the delegated powers are often referred to as "non-majoritarian institutions" (NMIs).[25] Think of independent central banks that are allowed a considerable degree of freedom within a certain mandate (since the 1990s, usually an inflation target). At the European level too, a variety of NMIs have been established since the 1980s, amongst them the European Medicines Agency (EMA)—which attracted considerable public attention during Covid-19 over vaccination issues.

At the theoretical level, there are a number of reasons for delegating executive responsibilities from political actors to NMIs.[26] One of the most important is the provision of information, and its asymmetry, in policy domains where technical knowledge is crucial. Another is speed and efficiency: by setting up arm's-length organizations to respond to specific issues, politicians can concentrate upon general policy. Thirdly, there is the blame avoidance factor discussed earlier. NMIs can be

[24] Thatcher and Sweet (2002, 2003).

[25] NMIs in the Netherlands often take the form of a so-called "autonomous administrative authority" (*zelfstandig bestuursorgaan*, ZBO), a legal entity that is part of central government but not hierarchically subordinate to a minister. Delegation as a phenomenon does not coincide precisely with the ZBO structure, however, and so can also take other legal forms.

[26] Thatcher and Sweet (2002).

useful vehicles for decisions that politicians fear will be unpopular, but are nevertheless necessary for the common good (the term "depoliticization" is sometimes used in this regard). Related to this is the issue of credibility—in some cases people find the promises made by NMIs more believable and consistent than those of political actors who are more directly exposed to public pressure. And finally, for the same reason, in some cases these institutions are considered to more likely than politicians to avoid deferring costs and risks. The latter two mechanisms come into play, for example, in the role entrusted to central banks in controlling inflation.

In recent decades, various responsibilities in the health and social care sectors in the Netherlands and other countries have been transferred to NMIs. In the Dutch system, the most prominent are the ZiN—now responsible for advising on collective insurance package management and quality standards—and the NZa, which is supposed to act as the "superintendent" of the care market. Abroad, the National Institute for Care and Health Excellence (NICE) in the United Kingdom is a well-known example. It was set up in 1999, initially to improve the quality of care and in particular to combat so-called "postcode medicine".[27] Its remit was later expanded to include package management and health technology assessment.[28] Similar bodies exist in France, Germany, Italy, Sweden, Poland and Spain.[29]

To a greater or lesser extent, all of the above reasons for distancing executive responsibilities from politics apply to these organizations. For instance, many of the activities delegated to them—and certainly those related to package management—have an important medical and/or technical component for which specific expertise is indispensable (advice concerning the composition of the collective insurance package in the Netherlands is a task for the ZiN's Scientific Advisory Board). Their distance from the political decision-making process can strengthen their credibility and facilitate unpopular choices by shielding politicians from direct responsibility for them in the eyes of the public. And they boost the speed and efficiency of decision-making—even if they had the will and the necessary know-how, after all, political actors simply have no time for the countless prioritization calls that have to be made each year in health and social care.

Not that delegation to NMIs is without its drawbacks, though. Or that in specific cases there may not still be a public clamour for politicians to intervene. In England, for example, arm's-length package management has sometimes been thwarted by political pressure. In 2020 the government there decided to establish a dedicated Cancer Drugs Fund with a more lenient appraisal process than for other medicines.[30] This example illustrates how the line between the fundamental political considerations and (technocratic) implementation is not always clear-cut, and indeed is often controversial in itself.

[27] The phenomenon whereby access to certain forms of care depends upon the beneficiary's place of residence (their "postcode").

[28] Timmins et al. (2016).

[29] Angelis et al. (2018).

[30] Timmins et al. (2016).

### 8.3.2 *To Cover or Not to Cover? Collective Package Management in an International Context*

Delegating responsibilities is not an absolute, binary phenomenon. NMIs in the care sector and elsewhere enjoy varying degrees of formal and de-facto autonomy. Some have a narrowly defined remit, others are allowed more latitude. Some confine themselves to providing advice, whilst others take real decisions. Their independence at the governance level also makes a difference. Board appointments, for instance, may or may not be kept at arm's length from the political process. Moreover, autonomy is a factor not only vis-à-vis the government—the NMI's ultimate "client"—but also with regard to the regulated actors within its purview (manufacturers and suppliers, care providers, insurers and so on).

As a case study, we have compared collective health insurance package management in the Netherlands and other European countries from the perspective of delegation (see Box 8.3). Especially when it comes to curative medicine, this is a good topic for closer examination because technological developments will be largely responsible for the growth expected here in the coming decades (see Chaps. 2 and 7), so the extent to which they can be managed in a prudent manner is going to be decisive for future financial—and indirectly societal—sustainability.

Issues of collective package management extend far beyond curative medicine, however. Other fields of health and social care have their own "guaranteed" provision as well, after all: a set of interventions, amenities and other services funded from collective coffers that eligible citizens are entitled to make use of. Looking to the future, this is going to come under huge pressure—in long-term care in particular. Nevertheless, package management in curative medicine remains a good case study because it is an aspect of the choice process around prioritization in care which is relatively easy to compare internationally and relatively widely researched. This increases the likelihood that we can learn something from it in a general sense, with regard to the institutions needed when making choices in care. Furthermore, it is very possibly the aspect of the sector in which the challenges around such issues as taboo trade-offs, opposing interests and real people versus abstract values are most visible.

**Box 8.3: Collective Package Management Institutions Internationally**

All countries with any form of collective healthcare system are faced with the question of how to define its basic insured health package, and by extension how to weigh up patient interests versus sustainability considerations. Comparing the way these decisions are made in the Netherlands, Germany, the UK, France and Sweden, we find considerable variations in assessment frameworks (what is taken into account?), reach (what is and is not decided formally?) and institutional embedding (what public, semi-public or private

(continued)

**Box 8.3** (continued)

actors have what roles and responsibilities?).[31] So the overall criteria differ widely between countries. Understandably, clinical effectiveness (does the treatment work?) plays a role everywhere. But Germany and France do not explicitly consider cost-effectiveness. Another source of variation is the procedure's reach: what forms of care are assessed and which are not? Its approach also differs: some countries use a "positive list", meaning that in principle treatments are only reimbursed if they are on that list, others a "negative" one: in principle everything is covered unless specifically excluded. For extramural (pharmacy-dispensed) drugs, for instance, the Netherlands, France and Sweden have positive lists. With regard to the political and social debate that may arise around package management decisions, one relevant variable is whether the managing body's appraisals take the form of advice to a political actor (the responsible minister), as in the Netherlands, or are decisions in their own right—as in Germany and, to some extent, the UK. In the latter situation politicians can still intervene, but the threshold to do so is higher than in countries where appraisals are advisory only.

There is considerable institutional variation in the organization of collective package management across Europe (see Box 8.3). From a sustainability perspective, one important question here is how these differences affect outcomes. This issue has been examined in a number of comparative international studies.[32] They include an extensive and systematic investigation of the authorization of eleven medicines for four conditions (osteoporosis, multiple sclerosis and two forms of cancer) within the OECD,[33] with policy in that regard interpreted as a measure of the "generosity" of a healthcare system—at least as far as curative medicine and drugs are concerned. Authorization is not a binary, "yes or no" process in all countries, but can also be conditional, temporary or partial (only part of the drug's cost is reimbursed). Summarizing the results of this study, Fig. 8.2 shows that there are considerable variations between countries, and between the drugs, in their authorization outcomes. The Netherlands emerges as a relatively generous nation (yellow bars towards the top), whilst others are far stricter (horizontal red rows towards the bottom). Some of the drugs achieve reasonably consistent authorization outcomes internationally (predominantly yellow or red columns), but for some the picture is more mixed (columns in the middle with a variety of colours). Contrary to their expectations, the authors of this study found that a nation's wealth and its care budget did not significantly influence its decision-making in respect of collective package management: wealthy countries are not systematically more generous than poor

[31] See Online Appendix 6 on the WRR-website (available in Dutch only) for more details.

[32] Böhm et al. (2014), Vreman et al. (2020), Landwehr and Bohm (2011), and Landwehr (2016).

[33] Böhm et al. (2014) and Vreman et al. (2020).

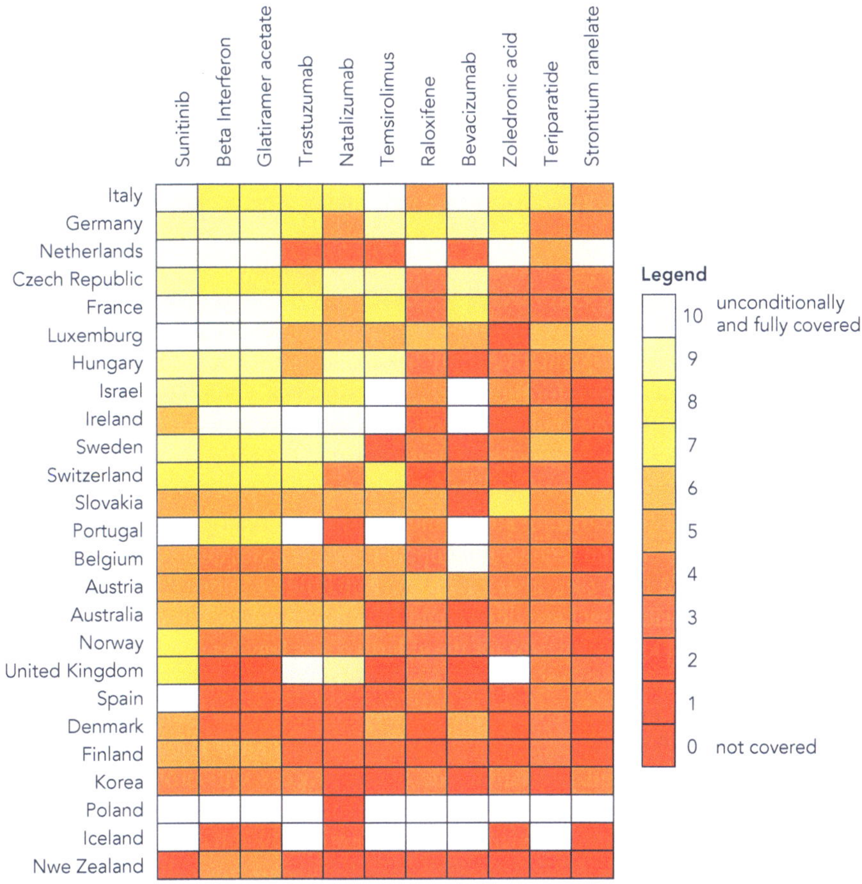


**Fig. 8.2** Inclusion of eleven medicines in the basic insured health package in 25 OECD countries. White indicates no data. (Source: Böhm et al., 2014)

ones. The nature of the healthcare system does have some effect, though: those funded to a greater or lesser extent through social insurance schemes, as found in the Netherlands and Germany, are more generous than those financed from general taxation like the National Health Service in the UK (see Chap. 5 for more on the different types of system). The institutional aspects of package management are also a factor. Countries where a treatment is not reimbursed as a matter of course unless a specific decision has been made to include it in the package (that is, with a positive list—as the Netherlands has for drugs) are more generous than ones with a negative list. The explanation for this is that a negative list entails an explicit and possibly unpopular decision to exclude a treatment by adding it to the list, whereas a positive list makes non-inclusion the default position and so that decision is avoided. Then there is the degree of delegation to the authorizing body, as well as its autonomy with regard to both government and regulated actors, in this case those in the field of healthcare. In general, the more independent the institution, the more stringent its decisions are. Transparency, meanwhile, is associated with more generous decisions. These two results can be attributed to blame avoidance. Finally, the inclusiveness of the authorizing body—the degree to which various social and interest groups are represented within it—was expected to increase generosity, but in fact no effect was observed. Another study, a quantitative analysis of package management decisions in different European countries, has shown that taking cost-effectiveness into account leads to a higher percentage of negative recommendations.[34]

Unfortunately, no analogous quantitative or semi-quantitative international comparative research findings are available concerning the organization of package management in such fields as long-term care, child and youth care services or mental healthcare. One more qualitative study has found that when it comes to the sustainability of long-term care for the elderly, it is particularly important to formulate a strategic vision with broad public support addressing the future role of this provision and so also society's requirements with regard to the collective package delivering it.[35] Cultural and normative aspects of the choice process probably weigh more heavily in this field than in some others, not least because new technology—and hence the medical and technical component of the assessment process—plays only a limited role here (see also Chap. 7). But little is known about what this implies for responsible package design and implementation. Given the substantial expected growth in long-term care for the elderly,[36] this leaves an unanswered question. In general terms, however, we have no reason to assume that principles similar to those applicable in curative medicine (the importance of the "standard", of delegation to a non-political actor, of autonomy and so on) should not also apply here. Although the cultural and normative side of the process will probably require a firmer grounding, even if a strategic vision of the kind mentioned above is available. It is also likely that with the increasing development of e-health solutions and robotics for fields like care for the elderly and mental healthcare, the technical aspect of their package management will increase in importance.

**Key Points—The Institutional Perspective**

- The institutional context is important for the outcome of choice processes in health and social care. Collective health insurance package management, especially with regard to medicines, is a good example of this.
- Choices are distanced from the political arena (delegated) for reasons of technical expertise, efficiency, credibility and to avoid responsibility for unpopular decisions.
- Package management is stricter in countries with more autonomous managing bodies.

[34] Vreman et al. (2020).

[35] Kruse et al. (2021).

[36] Vonk et al. (2020), Chap. 2.

## 8.4 The Timing Perspective

A classic dictum has it that politics is about "who gets what, when, how?".[37] Up until now, we have focused mainly upon the distribution question: who gets what? But choices in health and social care also have an important timing component. Actions we take now have consequences later—although sometimes only decades in the future.

### 8.4.1 *Choosing for the Long Term in Care*

One important question is how societies deal with situations where the costs and benefits of public policy play out over different time spans.[38] Think of pension reforms, for instance, which involve short-term costs while the benefits only take full effect in the longer term. Other examples include environmental and climate policy, where again the economic price (of reducing emissions, for example) is more or less immediate but we only reap the fruits later. Or reducing government debt: in the short term costly for today's taxpayer, but a boon for future generations. So the costs and benefits of a policy are distributed not only between groups and individuals in a society (as a horizontal investment), but also temporally[39]: from the now to the future (a vertical investment). From the perspective of debt avoidance and the electorate's generally short-term outlook, and in light of our previous discussion about interest and voter groups, we might expect that democratic governments would be reluctant, or even unable, to impose short-term costs in this way, with the promise of a return only at some (often vague) later date. But that would be jumping to conclusions. In reality, on occasions governments do all these things to a greater or lesser extent: they reform pensions, implement environmental policies and moderate national debt—all with an eye to the future.

The relevant question here, then, is what enables them to make forward-looking decisions of this kind. First of all, there is one quite simple explanation: voters sometimes do actually care about the long term—even when something is not in their own interest, they do think of the next generation. And they may well also be prepared to incur short-term costs and to exert pressure on politicians to act now with the future in mind. One obvious example is the increasing public support for strategic climate policy. A second important aspect is that vertical investments are more likely than horizontal ones to generate a positive-sum outcome. That is, one where those bearing the costs eventually also reap the returns—as opposed to a zero-sum situation, where one group benefits at the expense of the other.

[37] This quote comes from the title of a 1936 book by American political scientist and psychologist Harold Lasswell, *Politics: Who Gets What, When, How?*.

[38] In practice, many policies have elements of both.

[39] Jacobs (2012, 2016).

Preventive medicine is a good example of where this is possible, if the group making the investment shares in the health gains it ultimately achieves.

Nevertheless, we can also identify a number of barriers to long-term policymaking.[40] First, the electoral risks involved—which in turn are related to the extent to which voters pay attention to future benefits. Then there is the predictability (or otherwise) of a policy's effects in the long term: how confident can we be that the promised benefits will ever actually come to fruition? And finally there is the question of institutional capacity, and in particular the rooting that binds interest groups to a strategic goal. Each of these factors can be influenced, however, to increase the chances of securing commitment to a vertical investment.[41]

In health and social care, the temporal aspect is particularly relevant to preventive medicine and efforts to improve public health. After all, investments made now often only generate returns in years to come. But it also plays a role, albeit to a lesser extent, in the training of care personnel and in major capital investments, such as building suitable housing for large numbers of elderly people who are living independently for longer.[42] As we have seen earlier in this report, it is difficult to apply a long-term perspective to choices of this kind. This is evident, for example, from the low levels of investment in preventive medicine over a period of decades now (see Chap. 7), as well the sometimes massive policy swings when it comes to attracting and retaining staff (see Chap. 6). In other public policy domains, the Netherlands is already working very explicitly to create and maintain institutions which strengthen the long-term policy and investment outlook. These range from robust pension funds to the various incarnations of the so-called Delta Commission, set up to advise on the nation's strategic approach to water management. In the care sector, by contrast, relatively little attention seems to have been paid to the development of institutions with this kind of far-reaching perspective. Not that that is entirely lacking: the legislation governing the licensing of special medical procedures, for instance, takes into account expected future demand for these interventions and the infrastructure they will require.[43] Overall, however, the long-term outlook in health and social care would benefit from a strengthening of such institutions. Through them the public might then exert pressure—e.g. by means of citizen participation initiatives—to adopt more forward-looking policy (see also Sect. 8.5) in line with our previous observation that voters do in many cases look beyond their own interests and consider the long term as well.[44]

---

[40] Jacobs (2012, 2016).

[41] One example is the creation of a structure that makes it more visible and difficult to return to previous policies and thus increases the likelihood that the intended future benefits will actually be generated. For example, by investing resources in a special fund (possibly at arm's length from the political arena) so that future policymakers are less likely to be able to divert them for other purposes.

[42] Kruse et al. (2021).

[43] Special Medical Procedures Act (Wet op bijzondere medische verrichtingen, Wbmv). See https://wetten.overheid.nl/BWBR0008974/2019-04-02/0/informatie

[44] Jacobs (2012, 2016).

Bolstering the long-term perspective in care policy is especially important when it comes to preventive medicine, because the benefits often lie years or even decades in the future. This raises a fundamental barrier to effective investment in primary prevention (combating disease before it develops) by private actors like health insurers and care administration bureaus: the returns are beyond their time horizon. In such cases, it becomes a public task to make or require the necessary investments. That barrier is not so high when it comes to secondary and tertiary prevention (respectively, early detection of an existing condition and reducing the impact of an established one), because there the return on the investment is more immediate.

**Key Points—The Timing Perspective**

- Making choices in health and social care is also a question of timing: costs incurred now generate benefits (health gains) later. This is especially true when it comes to preventive medicine.
- The way institutions are organized can increase the chances that policies and investments are made in the long-term interest.

## 8.5 The Legitimacy Perspective

We pointed out earlier in this chapter that it is important that choices in health and social care be legitimate. In theory, citizens in a democratic society express their views on this matter at the polls and societal legitimacy thus arises from the mandate of the representatives they elect.

In reality, though, it is often difficult to anchor such legitimacy entirely in the regular democratic process. The reasons for that are also discussed above: politicians' tendency to avoid blame, for instance, and taboo trade-offs. One potential solution to this problem is for choices in care to derive their legitimacy from even more direct forms of citizen participation in the process. This possibility is at the heart of our final perspective on making those choices.

The underlying idea in this discussion is that the legitimacy of a choice process is a product not only of the quality (actual or perceived) of the resulting policy, but also of the groups involved in the process. We refer to the first of these aspects as "output legitimacy" and to the second as "input legitimacy".[45] By involving the right groups—ordinary citizens as the users of care and its funders, for instead, but perhaps also other stakeholders—in the process, the final decision it generates will be considered more legitimate. This perspective is closely linked to the normative basis of some forms of procedural justice, namely that a just prioritization decision can only be made if all relevant perspectives have been taken into account (see Sect. 7.2).

---

[45] Landwehr and Bohm (2011), Thatcher and Sweet (2002).

Citizens and other stakeholders can be engaged in different ways with the choices made in health and social care.[46] The specific form this takes matters for expected outcomes, and possibly for the effect upon their legitimacy as well. First, for example, there is the issue of the choice people are actually being involved in. Does this concern a specific decision—like what treatments to include in a collective insurance package—or is it about broader, more general priorities such as the extent to which society should focus upon preventive medicine or upon care for the elderly? One related factor in this respect is the duration of the citizen participation project: is it a temporary initiative or a more permanent scheme? Then there is form it takes: is it purely advisory, or are participants given a formal role in the choice process—for instance, as voting members of a committee entrusted with delineating the collective insurance package? A third relevant variable is who exactly takes part: do people register themselves, are they chosen (at random or otherwise) from the general population or are they selected as representatives of particular interest group? Finally, the degree of interaction with other perspectives discussed earlier in this chapter is also important: can and do citizens actually want to be involved in making choices of this kind, or are the taboo trade-offs too strong?

Let us begin with the latter aspect. In 2018 Radboud UMC, a teaching hospital in the Dutch city of Nijmegen, organized a citizens' forum under the title "Choices in Healthcare" (*Keuzes in de Zorg*). This exercise revealed that, with explanation and information about the costs and benefits of care and about relevant normative frameworks and practical considerations, even lay people are willing and able to make difficult choices about prioritization in this domain.[47] The forum comprised a representative group of ordinary citizens who were asked to think about priorities in healthcare, focusing upon on a range of treatments that might or might not be reimbursed collectively. They were also asked to think about the principles underlying their choices. In an earlier example, a so-called "Citizens' Lab" in Belgium was asked to address the broader issue of prioritization in healthcare.[48] It spoke out in favour of a greater emphasis upon preventive medicine, health promotion and health education, as well as for more focus upon quality of life rather than prolonging life. Both of these examples show that, with good, neutral guidance and the provision of structured information, the existence of taboo trade-offs need not be an impediment to citizen participation—and certainly not if this deals with broader principles and takes an advisory form. The crucial factors here are neutral guidance and structured information, as without them participants lack the relevant facts they need.

In a recent report the OECD analysed almost 300 examples of deliberative citizen participation projects in healthcare and other sectors.[49] Amongst them were Ireland's citizens' assemblies on abortion, climate policy, the ageing population and the electoral system, which have been instrumental in addressing controversial issues in Irish society.

---

[46] OECD (2020).

[47] Baltussen et al. (2018) and Bijlmakers et al. (2020).

[48] http://www.burgersengezondheidszorg.be/

[49] OECD (2020).

With regard to healthcare more specifically, some countries have established participatory initiatives to consider questions like how to deal with expensive medicines or what normative principles to apply when taking decisions about the collective insurance package. These include the so-called "citizens' councils" set up by NICE in the UK. Even more far-reaching is the permanent inclusion of lay members in the committees that take package decisions. The idea behind this is that their contribution increases the input legitimacy of those decisions, since they have been arrived at with backing from ordinary members of the public. The Netherlands, however, has yet to reach this level: citizen participation in care-related choices here remains limited to the right to attend and contribute to public meetings of decision-making committees.

Moreover, there are also potential downsides to this form of citizen participation. Indeed, it can actually harm the effectiveness and ultimate legitimacy of choice processes. One important aspect in this respect is the extent to which lay participants act—and are seen—as representatives of the general interest rather than a sectional one. In the light of the theory of interest groups discussed earlier, this is especially the case when stakeholders (or their proxies) are given a role in the choice process, or when they are more motivated or better able to take advantage of the opportunities they are afforded. And even more so when they are entrusted with real decision-making power—an actual vote, say, rather than just an advisory role. In its extreme form, the literature describes this phenomenon as "regulatory capture": that is, when a regulatory body (an NMI, for instance) is "hijacked" by the very interests it is supposed to be monitoring and regulating.[50]

Here lies a source of tension between two competing objectives. From the input-legitimacy perspective, it may be desirable to give stakeholders or their proxies a major role in choice processes. But when it comes to safeguarding the general interest, there lurks a danger here. As we have already noted, after all, the literature shows that activities like the management of collective insurance packages should be independent not only of government, but also of the various other stakeholders with an interest in issue at hand. To strengthen true citizen participation, then, it therefore seems advisable to ensure that it involve "ordinary" citizens drawn from the general population by means of a representative selection procedure rather than either implicitly or explicitly choosing those with a particular motivation to take part in the process. And particularly so when the focus is broad priorities and the criteria whereby they are defined, as was the case with the Dutch "Choices in Healthcare" forum. Furthermore, it is better that initiatives of this kind be anchored firmly within the overall management structure of the care system, as NICE does with its citizens' councils. In the Netherlands, such an institutionalization of citizen participation would better guarantee ongoing public engagement with general principles, priorities and criteria than the current ad-hoc approach. On the other hand, giving stakeholders with vested interests a greater direct role in the practical process

[50] Stigler (1971) and Tuohy and Glied (2011).

of making concrete priority choices would be far riskier, especially if that role were to go hand in hand with a say in formal decision-making. In this regard, it seems more advisable to retain the current opportunities for stakeholders to make submissions to decision-making committees so that all relevant perspectives are considered at face value.

**Key Points—The Legitimacy Perspective**

- Citizen participation can strengthen input legitimacy for choices in health and social care.
- Research shows that, with structured information, lay people are able to properly consider normatively difficult questions and taboo trade-offs.
- Citizens can participate in the consideration of general principles, priorities or criteria, but they may also have a valuable role—either advisory or with an actual say in decisions—when it comes to more specific choices such as those related to the content of the collective health insurance package.
- There is potential tension between strengthening input legitimacy for choices in care on the one hand and, on the other, upholding institutional autonomy and the public interest.

## 8.6 Towards Better Choices in Care

As we have seen in this third part of our report, choices in health and social care—by which we mean matters of allocation and distribution—could probably be better. To achieve the greatest possible health gains, it is important that future growth in this sector be steered more towards preventive medicine than we would expect under the present status quo. In order to uphold public values, moreover, the same applies to those aspects of care in which quality and accessibility are currently falling consistently short of the mark (see Chap. 7). All this means that we need to dare to set limits on growth, in so doing allowing ourselves to be more selective in where that growth occurs.

Why is this so difficult? In this chapter we have analysed that question from various perspectives, which to a great extent underlie the five impediments around choices in care that we identified in Chap. 7.[51] Is it now possible, based upon the resulting insights, to make any recommendations and to offer a recipe for "better choices" in our care systems? We will not do that directly here, but we do have a few tips for guidance. In fleshing them out, we refer back not only to the perspectives

[51] As a reminder, these are: (1) automatic inflow of new care; (2) no systematic outflow management; (3) limited knowledge of clinical, therapeutic and cost-effectiveness; (4) a sustainability imbalance—financial considerations dominate; and (5) short-term policies overdominate choice processes.

outlined above but also to earlier chapters and to a number of background documents.[52]

The issue we are faced with here begins and ends with broad public support for the choices to be made in health and social care. Or, to use our terms of reference, its societal sustainability. In turn, that support largely depends upon the perceived urgency and inevitability of the choices in question. After all, there is always considerable normative and psychological pressure to avoid making tough choices in a field as sensitive as care—and especially so if they might limit its growth. A pressure which is reflected in political and institutional decision-making processes. The most important step that needs to be taken, therefore, is to increase public awareness of the inevitability of choices in care and to create new, more realistic expectations of the sector as a whole and its future growth patterns.

Through this report the WRR is endeavouring to make its contribution to that change of outlook by outlining what will happen if choice processes in health and social care do not improve. The current manner in which care in the Netherlands is organized is expected to engender its rapid growth for some time to come, with all kinds of not insubstantial negative repercussions—both outside the sector, by putting other public policy domains under pressure, and within it by "squeezing" certain forms of care. The fact is that the staffing and financial constraints facing the sector are not going to disappear, even if we as a society continue do our utmost—as we must—to mitigate them. Due to rapidly rising demand, care is becoming increasingly scarce and it is up to society to learn to deal with that and to make choices about it.

This situation demands better choices at all levels—in government, "in the field" and by individual citizens. At present, decision-making at all levels with regard to limiting growth is mostly implicit. This, however, puts at risk the public values associated with care. So what should be done? First, the government needs to take an explicit political decision concerning the growth of health and social care expenditure; it can no longer allow this to increase automatically and unchecked, in line with the demand for care. Only by making explicit choices is it possible to protect spending on other public policy domains from being displaced by the demands made by the care budget. At the same time, that cannot be the whole story. By imposing constraints only from the top down, we run a huge risk that the bill will simply end up being presented at a lower level, directly to the most vulnerable in society. Better monitoring limits to growth should not compromise the public values associated with care. This requires active political intervention in the sector, at the level of broad prioritization across its various fields. The WRR therefore argues for a greater focus upon preventive medicine and upon those areas in which quality and accessibility are currently falling below acceptable minimum standards on a regular basis.

[52] Kruse et al. (2021), Vonk et al. (2020), Polder et al. (2020), and Bertens and Palamar (2021).

To make these changes possible, some things will have to be done less. This leads us to the question of what forms of care we still want to guarantee and finance on a collective basis. Some limits to growth will have to be delineated more sharply and their boundaries better guarded. This does not mean that we are arguing for cuts compared with the current situation, nor that we advocate restricting innovation in care. What the WRR does favour is limited and, above all, more selective growth in certain parts of the health sector. In quantitative terms, this can only be achieved—given the current prognoses (see Chap. 2)—by moderating the growth of curative medicine and care for the elderly.

In the case of curative medicine, this primarily means more active management of the "inflow" of new forms of care and treatment into the statutory basic health insurance package and of the "outflow" of obsolete or ineffective forms—effectively creating a "control knob" that can be adjusted as part of the package management process. Technological innovation plays a far smaller role when it comes to care for the elderly, so the main issue there is what should constitute the core of collectively guaranteed care. To what extent, for example, does this include housing provision? The distribution of costs between the collective and the individual user of care will have to remain a subject of discussion. More generally, it is going to be necessary to work on a long-term vision of the role and scope of care that is supported by society, and to involve citizens in prioritizing its provision.

**Recommendations Linked to Three Pillars: Society, Politics and Implementation**

Ultimately, limiting the growth of health and social care remains a difficult normative consideration. In the final chapter of this report we formulate a series of recommendations, which we link to three broad pillars for better choices in care. The first of these is the societal perspective: in order to make better choices, we as a society have to face up to the fact that choices are unavoidable and that we need a clear vision of the dilemmas associated with the growing scarcity of care. The second pillar is the political perspective: where does political responsibility for choices in care lie, and how can it be handled better than at present? Finally, the third pillar is implementation: how can the question of what should and should not be offered collectively be answered in practical terms? And what institutional changes will this require? These three aspects are interrelated. For example, politicians cannot be expected to protect other public policy domains from being displaced by a growing care sector without at the same time considering better ways of demarcating provision *within* that sector. And they in turn have little chance of success unless there is an accompanying societal vision of the sector's aims and priorities and of the role different forms of care should play within it.

# Chapter 9
# Choosing Sustainability: Conclusions and Recommendations

Good health and social care for all means making choices. To guarantee its accessibility and quality, care must be sustainable in financial, staffing and social terms. But these three dimensions of sustainability are coming under increasing pressure. In this report the WRR calls for well-considered, clear and sometimes uncompromising choices in the interests of accessible, high-quality care and broad health benefits. Deciding the priorities in this domain is first and foremost a political responsibility, but also one for providers across the sector as well as citizens themselves.

When the Dutch are asked what they consider important in life, one of the first answers is invariably "good health". Sooner or later, however, we all face health problems. When that time comes, we trust that care will be available and that it will be good, close at hand and affordable. Only recently, the Covid-19 pandemic has reiterated how much we rely upon that provision. The WRR therefore regards quality and accessibility as the most important public values associated with care. So they need to be safeguarded, now and in the future. At the same time, despite the ever-increasing need for care and hence for people and resources to deliver it, it is important to avoid compromising other public policy domains. To achieve that, our health and social care system needs to remain sustainable regardless of what demographic, social, technological and economic developments lie ahead.

The WRR works on the premise that sustainability has three dimensions: a financial, a staffing and a societal one. In other words: do we have the means, the people and the public support needed to maintain a viable care sector? Only when all three of these elements are up to par and properly balanced can we describe the system as sustainable, because only then can we guarantee that the public values of quality and accessibility will be upheld in the long term. Only then will we still have enough human and material resources for other public services as well. And only then will solidarity with and trust in the system remain intact.



G. Werner et al., *Financial, Staffing and Societal Sustainability of Dutch Health Care*, Research for Policy, https://doi.org/10.1007/978-3-031-58564-7_9

We began this report by asking whether health and social care in the Netherlands is sustainable. To answer this key question, we looked first at causes and effects of the sustainability challenges we currently face, both within and outside the care sector, and then at existing policy agendas to deal with those challenges. We also investigated the extent to which quality and accessibility are currently safeguarded across the sector. In most areas, this is indeed the case: generally speaking, care services in the Netherlands are performing well. Both their direct benefits in health terms and, as a consequence, their indirect ones for our economy and labour market are considerable.[1] But that does not mean that there are no impediments to ongoing sustainability, and we have highlighted them as well.

In this final chapter we make a number of recommendations, all related to the notion of "making better choices" in health and social care. This approach ensues directly from the nub of our analysis: that there is room for improvement in the way choices around care are currently made. In particular, those about how to deploy people and resources in the future. By default, that will mean setting priorities and redefining the role and scope of care in our society. In concrete terms, making better choices means steering the sector's future growth in the direction of provision and preventive interventions that achieve broad health gains[2] whilst at the same time continuing to guarantee the quality and accessibility of care for all. It also means improving the way we set priorities, so that they are properly considered, clear and sometimes uncompromising. And from a wider perspective it means thinking about the role played by interests and considerations other than those related to care. Finally, making better choices is about achieving better outcomes—that is, better health and quality of life and thus greater well-being for society as a whole.

Before making our final recommendations, we begin this concluding chapter with a summary of the analysis from our report. Our aim is not to offer ready-made policy recipes, but rather to outline paths to keep health and social care sustainable, now and in the future, by building upon three distinct pillars. Naturally, specific policy considerations, choices and decisions remain a political responsibility.

## 9.1 We Face Major and Urgent Challenges in All Three Dimensions of Sustainability

The sustainability of the Dutch health and social care system is coming under increasing pressure. That is the first key conclusion of this report (see Part 1). In concrete terms this means that—given the expected future growth in demand for care—we will no longer always have either the people or the resources needed to

[1] Polder et al. (2020).

[2] By this we mean the number of years of healthy life expectancy they can achieve. This is often expressed in terms of quality-adjusted life years (QALYs). See also Chap. 7 and Broeders et al., (2018).

guarantee the quality and accessibility the Dutch public expects. Or the sector will no longer enjoy the broad support it needs to muster the necessary people and resources. The challenge is both major and urgent, and it involves all three dimensions of sustainability: financial, staffing and societal.

### 9.1.1 Growth Has Various Underlying Causes

What trends and developments underlie this conclusion? A number of fundamental and interconnected forces are driving up the use and price of care (see Chap. 2). We recap the most important of them here.[3] The first is the changing composition of our population (demographics): the proportion of elderly people is set to rise in the coming decades, and they make use of health and social care on a relatively large scale. As a result, overall demand will increase. Then there are technological innovations—more advanced diagnostic capabilities, new drugs, improved medical devices, better therapeutic interventions and so on—which enable more patients to be treated than was previously possible. And thus increase the use of care services. Thirdly, our collective state of health is changing: people are living longer, more of them have chronic diseases and they are more likely to have several conditions at the same time (multimorbidity). This leads to greater and more complex demand for care. Fourthly, rising prosperity is driving a shift in preferences: as we become more affluent, the amount of care we demand increases disproportionately. Fifthly, because the human factor remains crucial in health and social care there is less opportunity for automation and standardization than in other sectors. This so-called Baumol effect causes the price of care to rise faster than that of other products and services.

The extent of these effects varies, but the broad picture is clear: if we do nothing, the developments just listed will result in the use of care provision rising faster in the coming decades than the rate of economic growth—and far faster than the size of workforce can keep up with. The margins of uncertainty in the long-term prognoses are considerable, but this general conclusion holds true regardless of the precise assumptions and methods used. Annual spending on health and social care is projected to rise to between 20 and 25 per cent of gross domestic product (GDP) by 2060, compared with 13 per cent today. The vast majority of the projected growth, both financial and in staffing, is being driven by two parts of the sector: hospital care and care for the elderly.[4] Between 2020 and 2060, together they are expected to account for 60 per cent of the total increase in expenditure (hospital care 34 per cent, care for the elderly 26 per cent). Combined, the other 12 domains making up the health and social care sector will be responsible for the remaining 40 per cent.[5]

[3] Here we highlight the quantitatively dominant factors, but these are not the only ones driving up the use of care. See Chap. 2 for a fuller overview.

[4] Vonk et al. (2020).

[5] Calculation based upon Vonk et al. (2020), data from Figure 4.11.

In the case of care for the elderly, the primary drivers of increased spending are the ageing population, higher prices due to Baumol effects and the relative scarcity of labour. When it comes to hospital care, demographic factors are playing a role but the main impetus comes from new diagnostic methods and treatments as a result of technological innovation. Baumol effects do occur here as well, although to a lesser extent than in long-term care.

### 9.1.2 Sustainability in Three Dimensions

We are facing a demand for health and social care that is already growing faster than our national wealth and our workforce, and will do so even more in the future. But why is that going to strain the sustainability of care? If we want to, why can we not just spend a quarter of our wealth on that provision? Or employ a third of our people to deliver it? We looked in detail at the financial, staffing and societal sustainability of care in Chap. 3 of this report.

Turning first to the financial dimension, there is no fixed monetary limit beyond which care suddenly becomes unaffordable. As a society we can indeed choose to allocate more and more resources to it. And some countries are already doing just that, amongst them the United States and Switzerland.[6] This option, however, entails real and ever-increasing social costs—what economists call "trade-offs". As we discuss in more detail later in this chapter, for example, spending more on care inevitably draws down investment in other public policy domains. Already, any real growth in wages in the Netherlands in the coming years is expected to be offset almost entirely by rising care costs, payable through both insurance premiums and taxes.[7] In other words, the Dutch population will have to spend the vast majority—if not all—of the extra wealth it accrues through economic growth on more or better health and social care. Over time, this greater financial burden may even negatively affect the nation's broad economic dynamics and growth prospects. Which could in turn undermine the care sector's funding base.

There is no hard limit when it comes to staffing sustainability, either. At no one specific moment does the situation go from being sustainable to unsustainable. But the prognoses look problematic. Under reasonable assumptions, national demand for care personnel seems set to increase from about one worker in seven today to more than a quarter of the workforce in 2040. And perhaps even to a third or more in 2060.[8] This is partly a consequence of the increasing demand for care, but also

[6] Using the OECD definition, which enables international comparisons but excludes items such as some aspects of care for the elderly and social support, the exact figures are 17.0 per cent of GDP for the United States, 12.1 per cent for Switzerland and 10.0 per cent for the Netherlands.

[7] Zeilstra et al. (2019).

[8] See Chap. 3 and online Appendix 3 for more details. This is a "no policy change" scenario based upon past trends and demographic and other prognoses.

due to stagnation in the size of the workforce itself. Such a large draw on the labour market will inevitably lead to competition for scarce personnel with other sectors, both public and private, and so to staff shortages in them. It thus represents a fundamental change in the Dutch economy, and one with far-reaching implications for health and social care in particular, as the nation's fastest-growing semi-collective sector. Alongside this issue, moreover, a far more urgent short-term problem is the acute lack of staff in certain parts of the sector, especially nursing, residential and home care. Whilst the impact of this phenomenon at present is being felt mainly within formal provision, in the form of increasing workloads and an inability always to guarantee quality or accessibility, it is also beginning to put more pressure on various forms of informal care.

Finally, there is societal sustainability. That is, the extent to which the health and social care sector enjoys public support. Is it providing in what people expect of it, and do they feel that it is delivering value for money? This dimension of sustainability involves perceptions of quality and accessibility on the one hand, and on the other the notion of solidarity: willingness to contribute to the care others receive through insurance premiums and taxes. And it is about how these aspects vary between different groups in society (see Chap. 3). What we actually see here in the Netherlands, first of all, is generally high levels of satisfaction with care providers as well as broad satisfaction with the care people receive. At the same time, though, there are significant concerns with regard to the quality and accessibility of certain parts of the sector—most notably some aspects of care for the elderly, mental healthcare and child and youth care services—although these focus more upon institutions (such as health insurers and some other organizations) than front-line providers. And there are issues with solidarity, too: it seems to be vulnerable precisely on those points where, given current epidemiological developments, it will remain most needed. With regard to lifestyle-related conditions, for instance. People appear less willing to contribute towards costs resulting from smoking or overeating or drinking than from, say, hereditary diseases. They also feel that the sector wastes substantial amounts of money, and they do not always trust its institutions. They would like to see more funds allocated to care—especially for more "hands at the bedside"—but believe and hope that this cash can be freed up by reducing waste. As we shall see later, this desire is not actually that realistic given the increasing scale of overall demand for care. Even if all waste could be eliminated, the extent of the sector's projected growth makes greater financial contributions from its users—whether through insurance premiums, taxes or direct charges—unavoidable. But they are also sure to put solidarity under even greater strain.

In short, we can encapsulate the broad picture with regard to societal sustainability as featuring real confidence in the people working in health and social care but less support for its institutions and "the system". Not to mention risks to solidarity. The danger, then, is that in the future we will see an ever-widening gap between the perceived benefits of our care system and the amount people feel it is costing them.

### 9.1.3 Maintaining and Balancing the Dimensions of Sustainability

The three dimensions of sustainability are closely intertwined. This implies that in many cases achieving and maintaining sustainability is primarily a matter of trade-offs. Cost savings, for instance, can be made at the expense of working conditions or recruitment—thus bolstering financial sustainability but damaging staffing sustainability. Conversely, increasing wage competition with other sectors for scarce personnel accelerates the challenge to achieve financial sustainability. In short, an excessive focus upon one of the dimensions can quickly become counterproductive due to its interconnectedness with the others, resulting in a "pendulum" effect for policy as the adverse consequences subsequently need to be countered. One specific Dutch example is the financially driven staffing cutbacks in nursing, residential and home care,[9] child and youth care services and mental healthcare between 2013 and 2016, which increased workloads for the remaining personnel and so prompted more of them to seek alternative employment, thus further undermining staff sustainability in areas where it was already under pressure. Since it also generated a need to train new staff in subsequent years, the departure of those workers entailed capital destruction as well. Another example is the 2017 quality framework for nursing homes, which focused heavily upon improving quality in order to bolster societal sustainability. Initially, however, this was done without adequately monitoring costs and staff embedding.[10] As a rule we observe that policymakers view the issue of sustainability too much through a financial lens, whereas in fact all three dimensions need be kept up to par and in mutual equilibrium.

### 9.1.4 Growing Demand for Care Is Challenging Sustainability

In short, there are no hard and fast limits to financial, staffing or societal sustainability. That said, the ever-increasing social costs associated with the growth of the care sector make trade-offs and adverse effects for the economy, the labour market and society as a whole inevitable (see Chap. 3). And, as we shall see later, they also put pressure on public values within certain parts of the sector. It is these trade-offs and effects which ultimately determine where the political and social boundaries to the sustainability of care lie. Sustainability is not a binary state, then (a situation is either "sustainable" or "unsustainable"), but rather a gradated phenomenon.

---

[9] "Nursing, residential and home care" is a category used by Statistics Netherlands in its labour-market statistics for the care sector. It includes provision governed by the Long-Term Care Act (Wlz) and by the Social Support Act (Wmo, covering home care as well social support).

[10] Algemene Rekenkamer (2019).

All things considered, the WRR concludes the Netherlands now faces a wide-ranging and urgent sustainability challenge in health and social care, encompassing all three of the dimensions we have been discussing.

In essence, this is an issue of scarcity. We as a society, including our politicians and government, must prepare ourselves for an era in which scarce resources are going to play an increasingly important role in the care sector. In facing up to this challenge, it is important to avoid reacting with ad-hoc policy corrections and thus creating a pendulum effect—which in many cases is likely to end up with policies overshooting their objectives. In the short term, staffing sustainability in particular looks set to come under serious pressure. And given expected demographic developments, most notably the stagnating workforce combined with the progressive ageing of the population, this dimension will probably remain a major stumbling block in the longer term as well. But the core underlying problem for all three dimensions is that the care sector is simply growing faster than the available resources (financial sustainability) and people (staffing sustainability) will allow, and that our expectations as a society have not adjusted sufficiently to this situation (societal sustainability). So the big question our problem analysis presents us with is this: how do we fit the growing demand for health and social care within the financial, staffing and societal bounds we have identified?

**Key Points—Major and Urgent Challenges in All Three Dimensions of Sustainability**

- Safeguarding public values, in health and social care as in other domains, requires financial, staffing and societal sustainability.
- Sustainability is coming under increasing pressure. The most pressing concerns are in the staffing dimension, but all three face major challenges.
- Policy tends to focus upon financial sustainability, but in the long term all three dimensions need to be maintained and balanced.
- Sustainability is important not only just for the care sector itself, but also for other public policy domains, the wider economy and society as a whole.

## 9.2 Commitment to Efficiency and Staffing Is Essential But Not Enough

Can we meet the rising demand for health and social care by working more efficiently or by recruiting more staff? Our second main conclusion is a sobering one: a greater commitment to both efficiency and higher staffing levels remains as essential as ever, but on its own will not be sufficient to overcome the sustainability challenges we now face (see Part 2).

### 9.2.1 Sustainability Through Efficiency?

In the context of health and social care, efficiency means achieving health gains or improving quality of life using the fewest possible human and material resources. It is therefore sometimes viewed as synonymous with "eliminating waste". By continuing to organize its provision more and more efficiently, we should theoretically be able to accommodate the rising demand for care within the boundaries of human, social and financial sustainability. This has consistently been a central goal of Dutch policy in recent decades, on occasion prompting radical changes to thoroughly reform parts of the system. The prime example is the Health Insurance Act (*Zorgverzekeringswet*, Zvw) of 2006, which was supposed to create an incentive for the more efficient delivery of care by introducing regulated market forces to the system in the form of competition between health insurers and between healthcare providers. But it can also involve far more modest changes, primarily affecting administrative and/or executive structures but not substantially altering the roles and responsibilities of the actors concerned. One example of this is the preference policy for medication, which dictates that health insurers may only reimburse the cheapest variant (the "preferred medicine") in a group of drugs with the same active component. As a result, the same health gains can be achieved but at lower cost. A third example which lies between these two extremes is the series of initiatives that has been under way for some decades now to shift the delivery of particular forms of care to different institutions or providers (from hospitals, say, to primary care services). Recently, this policy has been dubbed "The Right Care in the Right Place".[11] From our analyses in this report, it is clear that an even greater commitment to efficiency remains essential now and in the future. But that alone will not be enough to resolve the sustainability challenge facing the Dutch care sector (see Chap. 5)—its scale is simply too great.

### 9.2.2 A Reformed System Would Be No More Efficient

The first argument in support of this conclusion is that there is no good evidence that any other model, any change of system, would substantially improve the sustainability of the Dutch health and social care sector or its various component parts (see Chap. 5). All Western countries, regardless of their sometimes very different systems, currently face very similar issues when it comes to sustainability. Without exception, they share the same underlying trends: an ageing population and longer life expectancy, technological progress and growing prosperity. And although they have put very different systems in place to deal with these challenges, the results of

[11] In the context of care policy, historically the word "substitution" has generally been used for such shifts.

an international comparison give us no reason to believe that a fundamental redesign of ours would make the organization of care as a whole in the Netherlands substantially more efficient, and thus resolve the sustainability issues we face. On top of that, any overhaul would entail high administrative and social transaction costs, as well as taking years to prepare. The groundwork for the reform of curative care in 2006 (the introduction of the Zwv), for instance, last more than two decades. Likewise, more recent changes affecting long-term care and social support also had lengthy lead times. In fact, such transformational processes can distract from the improvements to sustainability achievable within the existing system.

### 9.2.3 Complexity as a Constraint

When we look across the board at the benefits of policies intended to improve efficiency, we find first of all that the broad returns often turn out to be disappointing by comparison with prior expectations. In many cases this is due to phenomena like infill effects (the "released" capacity is used anyway) or waterbed effects (demand shifts, but does not decrease overall).

Secondly, efficiency measures tend to lose their edge over time or start having unwanted side-effects as actors in the system adjust their behaviour. Thirdly, even the expected returns are often relatively limited when compared with the scale of the sustainability challenge as a whole. All of these conclusions are linked to the complexity of care. People are diverse, and so are their care needs. A complex pattern of interactions and dependencies—between patients, care providers, institutions, buyers, regulators and policymakers—makes the actual outcome of any measure unpredictable and often triggers unexpected side-effects. Vested interests also come into play here, as they never coincide perfectly with the objectives of the system as a whole. Whilst there is certainly some scope to reduce complexity, it is an illusion to think that this can be done to any great extent. Nor is it desirable, for many reasons. After all, complexity in health and social care is largely an expression of a high degree of development and a response to the need for highly skilled, specialized services. Governing an advanced care system is never going to be easy. Its degree of complexity requires that we be realistic about the extent to which the system's direction of travel can be controlled in a predictable manner, as well as about how possible it really is to achieve substantial efficiency gains within it.

### 9.2.4 Constraints to Productivity Growth

The pressure on each of the three dimensions of sustainability is closely related to labour productivity (see Chap. 6). In economic terms, this raises this question of how many people are needed to deliver a certain volume of care. And can that number be brought down? One specific example is with the help of the so-called "smart patch", which allows a nurse to monitor more patients simultaneously.[12] As with many other labour-intensive services, especially in the public sector, productivity growth in health and social care is systematically lagging behind the rest of the economy. This has a direct impact upon staffing sustainability since higher productivity makes it possible to provide more care with the same number of people, but also affects both societal sustainability (due to pressure on the accessibility and quality of care) and financial sustainability (through the Baumol effect).

Hopes of boosting labour productivity focus in particular upon the role of technology. Above all, better enabling technology or process technology (see Chap. 2). Rather than improving a product or service in itself, this intended more to change the way in which we deliver it. Examples include e-health: the provision of care by digital means.[13] Since the first wave of Covid-19, for instance, video calling has boomed in the medical world as it has in other sectors. Whilst this shows that there is certainly potential for further digitalization within health and social care, there are still questions to be asked about the extent to which wide-ranging productivity growth can be expected as a result. The success of process technology in industry is very much based upon time-saving and standardization, aspects that healthcare professionals and patients definitely do not always consider desirable. After all, they regard personal attention and time as an essential component of good care. When it comes to patient satisfaction, video calling has been a success. But efficiency gains are not an obvious part of that. In many cases a video consultation costs the provider the same amount of time as a face-to-face one, and hence the same in labour costs[14]—the largest component of care spending. At the same time this innovation certainly does have clear benefits for some patients at least (eliminating the need to travel, for instance), and these too are important.[15]

There is thus a strong case for sustained productivity growth in the care sector. Not only would that make it more efficient, but probably also more sustainable. We cannot predict how technology will develop in the future, or how it might be deployed, especially if the expected growing scarcity of human resources amplifies the incentive to use it as a substitute. As has been pointed out in other recent recommendations, it is therefore important to continue to strengthen and accelerate the adoption of e-health in order to maximize effective use of the available workforce.[16] That said, to date it has never proven possible to systematically boost labour productivity in the care sector at the same rate as in the rest of the economy. Moreover, there are fundamental reasons to doubt that this situation will change into the future.

---

[12] The patch contains sensors which continuously monitor the wearer's heart rate, breathing and temperature. For the most part this technology is still in the clinical validation and testing phase (Leenen et al., 2020).

[13] Expertise centre Nictiz formally defines e-health as "the application of both digital information and communications to support and/or improve health and healthcare" (van Lettow et al., 2019).

[14] See, for example, Meurs et al. (2020a, b).

[15] See, for example, Barsom et al. (2021). See also Chap. 6.

[16] See SER (2020) in particular for recommendations to accelerate and promote the "digital transition" in care and to remove barriers to e-health; see also RVS (2017b, 2020b, c). For factors facilitating and constraining the digitalization of the economy in general, see OECD (2019d).

In short, whilst it remains important to continue to invest in e-health and enabling technology, the sheer scale of the sustainability challenge makes it is highly unlikely that such efforts alone will be sufficient to resolve it.

### 9.2.5 *Attracting, Recruiting and Retaining More Staff*

Alongside recruiting new people, concerted efforts to retain existing staff or entice them to work more are a crucial strategy to address staffing sustainability. By redesigning tax incentives, for instance, putting in more hours could really pay off for the average care worker. In this sense, staffing problems in the care sector are strongly linked to general labour issues. Better personnel management—allowing more room for autonomy and personal responsibility, for instance, and facilitating an improved work-life balance—is important as well,[17] especially to limit staff turnover. It should also be possible to recruit more people by focusing upon better career prospects, by offering more training opportunities and so on. Perhaps more controversial socially and politically[18] is the option of targeted recruitment of workers from abroad for roles subject to ongoing staff shortages. Especially in long-term care for the elderly, more and more Western countries are applying this strategy.[19]

The question is whether the likely overall combined effects of these interventions would be enough to resolve the staffing sustainability challenge. Although many uncertainties are at play here, the answer is likely to be "no". Once again, the sheer scale of the challenge is too large and our potential ability to attract more human resources too small in a world where labour-market participation is already high and the total size of the workforce is stagnating.

In part, this conclusion is related to the interconnectedness of the three dimensions of sustainability discussed earlier. Even if it were feasible to recruit on a large scale to accommodate the growing demand for care, by 2060 the sector would have to employ one in three of all workers to meet that demand. Which would irrevocably strain its financial sustainability to a massive extent. Moreover, this situation would give rise to fierce competition with other sectors, private as well as public, for scarce human resources. If that were to give rise to staff shortages elsewhere, it could undermine the nation's economic competitiveness or endanger public values in other sectors. In short, yet again circumstances will ultimately force us to make tough choices.

[17] See, for example, SER (2020), RVS (2020d), and WRR (2020b).

[18] As in the case of the outcry which arose around earlier plans to address staffing problems in care through labour migration. *Financieele Dagblad* (2020) and van der Line (2020).

[19] Kruse et al. (2021).

### 9.2.6 Commitment to Efficiency and Staffing Is Important But Not Enough

Efforts to increase efficiency across the health and social care system remain hugely important. And sensible personnel and labour-market policy can help it recruit and retain more people, as well as enticing its workers to put in more hours—a point we return to later in this chapter (see Sect. 9.4). Both of these strategies are crucial in facing up to the sustainability challenge, especially in its societal dimension. Not only is there a widespread perception that care is a "wasteful" sector, people also feel that staff shortages are already affecting the quality of provision (see Chap. 3). Policy in this regard should therefore continue to explicitly tackle wastefulness with the aim of making care more efficient on an ongoing basis. Although we do not go into the specifics of those efforts in this report,[20] we have concluded that they are more likely to involve a broad palette of measures, each with a modest macro effect, than a single "magic bullet". First and foremost, though, we have to face the fact that strengthening efficiency and a commitment to staffing can never in themselves resolve the sustainability challenge. The limits of this policy model are looming increasingly large.

**Key Points—Commitment to Efficiency and Staffing Is Essential But Not Enough**

- There is no robust evidence that a system based upon substantially different principles would perform any better than the current one when it comes to the sustainability of health and social care.
- The system is bound to be complex, but we still need to be realistic about its steerability and the possibilities of improving its efficiency.
- There is some potential to accelerate productivity growth in care, but this is still very unlikely to keep up with labour productivity in the economy as a whole.
- Improving efficiency within the system is important, but on its own not enough given the scale of the sustainability challenge.
- A commitment to improved staffing, to be achieved by applying a range of strategies, is also important but again not enough in itself to resolve the sustainability challenge.

## 9.3 Choosing Sustainability

If existing policy agendas—however important and valuable—are insufficient to tackle the sustainability challenge, what else can we do? The WRR believes that better prioritization within our collective health and social care sector is also crucial.

[20] See SER (2020, 2021a, b), Menzis (2020) and ZiN and NZA (2020).

Making better choices is explicitly not a substitute for efforts to improve efficiency and staffing, but it is a necessary and urgent complementary strategy to reinforce those efforts, and as such should not be delayed. Particularly in a world of increasing scarcity, it is becoming increasingly important to make the best possible use of human and material resources. And to make the necessary decisions in a legitimate manner that enjoys broad public support. That process requires time and care, and for that reason alone it cannot wait any longer.

In short, we will have to pull out all the stops. We need to organize care more efficiently as well as recruiting and retaining staff and making better choices. To date, however, Dutch policymakers and the national discourse have paid relatively little attention to choices in care. Even those advising on sustainability issues have often focused more upon efficiency and staffing than upon choice processes. As a result, they have lagged behind as a topic of debate—certainly by comparison with the extensive discussions around system design, but also when compared with the debate in some other countries.[21] To a great extent, this report can read as a plea to catch up. And as such a continuation of the discussion triggered by the Dunning Committee[22] in its report exactly three decades ago and elaborated by the WRR in its 1997 publication on public healthcare.[23] Both of those studies pointed out the importance of making fair and equitable choices about the delineation of collective care provision—an issue that has only become even more important since, as this report demonstrates. It should therefore be read as an appeal to society to discuss the matter anew and so generate broad support for new thinking about prioritization in the care sector: thinking tailored to the challenges of our time, such as the increasing scarcity of human and material resources we have discussed.

What are the implications if we are unable to start making choices in a better way? We shall explore this question using the choice processes we have analysed previously: what impediments are already apparent and how are they affected by the impending developments we have outlined? And what does that say about the future resilience of the way we make choices about care? We then discuss what we mean by “making better choices” and explain in more detail why a different approach to prioritization is an essential response to the sustainability challenge. To make better choices, however, we will have to overcome a number of hurdles: conflicts of interest, design issues, psychological barriers, short-term thinking and issues of legitimacy. Better choices are thus about basic principles (what do make choices about?) as much as about the process (how do we make the choices?) and its final outcomes (where do we end up?). In 10.4 we provide a series of recommendations and considerations concerning each of these criteria, aligned with the three pillars mentioned earlier. As we also stated before, we do not offer ready-made policy recipes but instead outline paths within the three pillars to improve the sustainability of all aspects of health and social care by making better choices.

[21] Kruse et al. (2021).

[22] Commissie Dunning (1991).

[23] WRR (1997).

### 9.3.1 Implications of Insufficiently Futureproofed Choice Processes

Complementing an ongoing commitment to efficiency, it is important to make better choices about care. In this section we examine the implications of failing to do so, examining potential consequences both within the sector and in the wider world.

**Pressure on Public Values in Other Sectors**
We look first at the impact of—mostly implicit—choice processes on public values in sectors other than health and social care. Over the past three decades, care has been the only major public policy domain to have seen a systemic increase, relative to GDP, in the resources it has available to spend (see Chap. 3). According to all the prognoses, moreover, unless something radical changes this will remain the case for decades to come. Which inevitably means that there will be fewer resources available for other policy priorities, or to increase households' disposable incomes or businesses' scope for investment.[24] In other words, there will be little or no extra cash in the public coffers to pay for social security, poverty alleviation, sustainability, affordable housing, education and so on. As a result, public values within those domains could easily come under ever-increasing pressure. This outlook is largely a consequence of the fact that, as a result of past political decisions, the growth of the care sector has become a largely automatic process (see Chap. 7). Much of the responsibility for that lies with its budgeting system, developed by politicians over many years, that automatically accommodates any and all forecast growth in demand for care. And any deviations from the growth trajectory—even if real spending on care actually continues to rise—are easily framed in the political and public debate as "cuts", with all the negative repercussions they entail for societal sustainability. These dynamics put health and social care in a substantially different—and stronger—position than policy domains where the budgets are the product of explicit political deliberation.

Of course, politicians could explicitly choose to perpetuate this situation by continuing to increase relative spending on care in the coming decades. This, however, is unlikely to be in the long-term national economic or social interest. Indeed, its implicit displacement of investment in other policy domains may paradoxically even have a negative net impact upon public health. After all, some of those domains—such as education, poverty alleviation, housing, planning and employment—deliver significant health benefits in their own right, through their preventive effects.

[24] Studiegroep begrotingsruimte (2020) and Koolman and Wouterse (2021).

On top of that, just spending more and more on care sooner or later starts generating diminishing returns in terms of health benefits: each additional euro does less on average to improve health than the previous one, an effect that only intensifies as expenditure increases.[25] The net effect is that investing more in care can at some point actually have a negative impact on public health. When precisely that tipping point is reached cannot be stated with any certainty, but it seems to be in the interests of neither overall national wealth nor public health itself to allow spending on care to grow systematically faster in the long term than the budgets for other public policy domains.

**Pressure on Public Values in Health and Social Care**

Then there is the question of how current choice processes within health and social care affect the sector itself. Strong growth in the demand for care inevitably leads to a situation in which there are not enough human and material resources available to satisfy that demand. Staff scarcity is already a particular stumbling block in this respect, and will remain so in the future. Because we can only spend a euro once and only deploy a care worker in one place at a time, growth in one part of the sector always implicitly impacts other parts (see Chaps. 7 and 8). The key question here is where—in what aspects of care and by whom—will the displacement effects of increasing scarcity be felt if targeted choices are not made. Our analysis reveals that in recent years accessibility and quality in certain parts of the sector have not been up to par, due in large part to a lack of staff (see Chap. 4). The upshot is long waiting lists and potentially compromised quality of provision, most notably in some child and youth care services and in specialist mental healthcare, as well as in care for certain groups of elderly people—the very areas which have the highest proportions of very vulnerable patients and users.

Why quality and accessibility are under pressure in these domains in particular is a complex matter. All have been subject to major organizational and administrative reforms in recent years, in many cases accompanied by budget cuts (see Chaps. 5, 7 and 8). Sustainability issues also seem to manifest themselves more quickly in these specific areas. Meanwhile, the public and political debate only addresses their quality and accessibility problems to a limited extent or after long delays—in part because their user and patient numbers are relatively small by comparison with services like curative medicine, which almost every Dutch person uses to a greater or lesser extent. Finally, the limited availability of centralized and systematized outcome data is also partly to blame for the fact that substandard quality or accessibility is less visible in certain fields of care (see Chap. 5).

The above factors are especially prevalent in decentralized services with a large number of providers. On top of that, their situation is perceived by the public as less critical than that in curative medicine, say, especially when it comes to acute life-threatening conditions. We saw this recently during the Covid-19 pandemic, when

[25] Polder et al. (2020).

the initial focus was very much upon ICU capacity and much less upon the consequences of government-imposed restrictions for nursing homes, disability care, specialist mental healthcare and so on.[26] Yet another factor is the limited organizing power of vulnerable groups, which limits their access to decision-making processes.

Together, all of the above contribute towards the relatively major scarcity of people and resources in these fields compared with other parts of the sector. As a result, the public values of quality and accessibility come under pressure earlier and to a greater extent there than elsewhere. When a sector's growth is too much an automatic process, then, as in the case of health and social care, that has adverse consequences not only for other sectors but also within the one concerned. In a world of scarcity, expanding one form of care inevitably means that others are displaced. So the distribution of care, and of its growth, is also an important issue.

### 9.3.2 *Making Better Choices: The Basic Criteria*

The ongoing growth of the health and social care sector is putting its sustainability under pressure. How does this relate to the choices which need to be made and the priorities which need to set? In a nutshell, the sustainability challenge is an issue of scarcity. Demand is growing unabated, but financial and staffing constraints are becoming more and more restrictive. This means that the choices we make about how to allocate the scarce resources we have are becoming increasingly important—and difficult. It also makes it more and more vital that we monitor how choice processes unfold in practice. To make better choices about care, therefore, in the WRR's view three key basic criteria need to be met more than is currently the case.

1. Make choices based upon public values, both within and beyond the care sector.
2. Make choices that optimise health benefits.
3. Make choices that balance sustainability in the long term.

We elaborate on these below.

**Criterion 1: Make Choices Based Upon Public Values, Both Within and Beyond the Care Sector**

Public values, both within health and social care and elsewhere, are coming under increasing pressure. This has a lot to do with the way we as a society are dealing with the sector's growth. We are failing to use public values as much as we should as a starting point in our choice processes about care. So our first criterion for making better choices is to put public values at the heart of the process. By this we mean that society must ensure that minimum standards of quality and accessibility are

[26] For a full analysis of the Dutch response to Covid-19, see the government dossier at https://www.rijksoverheid.nl/documenten/publicaties/2020/08/31/documenten-lessons-learned-corona

observed throughout the sector—in all its services, for all its patients and users and at all stages of their lives. Moreover, the growth of this sector must not compromise public values elsewhere—as happens when, for example, care monopolizes the allocation of people and resources in a socially unacceptable way, at the expense of education, social security and so on.

**Criterion 2: Make Choices that Achieve Health Benefits**

Our second criterion is that, far more than is currently the case, we make choices with the potential to bring about health gains. In other words, that we implement policy and deploy people and resources in ways that promote health in general. Preventive interventions are a pre-eminently effective way to do this. In many cases they can also reduce or alleviate demand for care, not least in those areas where public values are already under pressure. This is explicitly not just about forms of prevention relatively closely related to healthcare, such as screening programmes, vaccinations or lifestyle interventions,[27] although these remain important. It is in fact from policy in domains like housing, problematic debt mitigation, education, employment and the environment that perhaps the greatest positive health impacts can be expected.[28] Making better choices thus means that we should focus more than we do now upon all interventions likely to improve general health. Whilst benefiting the population as a whole, moreover, the gains will be particularly great for people lower down the socio-economic ladder.

**Criterion 3: Make Choices that Balance Sustainability in the Long Term**

As mentioned earlier, too strong a focus upon one dimension of sustainability can be an impediment to better choices. Take the decentralization of social support and of child and youth care services, for example, which were accompanied by substantial budget reductions. Or the financially driven staffing cutbacks in nursing, residential and home care, child and youth care services and mental healthcare in the aftermath of the 2013–2015 financial crisis (see Chap. 3). These measures all upped the pressure on staffing sustainability in the areas concerned. More generally, overly concentrating upon any single dimension results in disequilibrium, which all too often is followed by overcompensation in the policy response intended to correct the situation. Policy consistency, in particular avoiding major outliers, is therefore essential. And all the more so if we are to take a long-term outlook, since focusing too much upon one dimension of sustainability now often simply triggers the next policy challenge.

The third criterion for making better choices, then, is all about more effective monitoring of the interaction between the three dimensions of sustainability and about maintaining the balance between them, keeping the long-term perspective particularly in mind.

[27] These include combined lifestyle interventions (CLIS) addressing overweight and obesity, as well as programmes to "reverse" diabetes (Pot et al., 2019).

[28] Polder et al. (2020). On average, that potential is especially high for people with lower socioeconomic status. See also Broeders et al. (2018).

### 9.3.3 What Does Making Better Choices Mean for the Care Sector?

The WRR has concluded that making better choices in the health and social care sector is hugely important. As is better prioritization. But what exactly do we mean by this? To avoid any misunderstandings, we first need to state as explicitly as possible what "making better choices" does not mean. It is not about reducing spending on care, for instance, either in absolute terms or as a percentage of GDP; we are not arguing for cuts. The sector will continue to grow, in terms of both its staffing and its material resources, as befits Dutch demographic and economic trends. And as the Dutch people want. For the foreseeable future, growth will therefore remain the watchword for the sector as a whole and for most of its component parts.

What making better choices does mean is that we will have to approach that growth, and those choices, in a different way. This is all about smarter prioritization and helmsmanship when, like it or not, the scope for growth is limited by factors beyond our control. Not "less" then, but "less more"—and only after better consideration. Neither overall growth nor the allocation of resources can remain automatic, as they are now. Which inevitably means that in some aspects of care we will have to do less than we would have done were the current growth trajectory to be maintained.

In our view, making better choices also means applying the three criteria outlined above. So that first of all those choices safeguard minimum standards of quality and accessibility in all aspects of health and social care, that secondly they focus more emphatically upon potential health gains and that thirdly they aim to balance financial, staffing and societal sustainability in the long term. Practically speaking, this means a shift of focus towards prevention and towards those fields in which quality and accessibility have been under the greatest pressure in recent years.

But what exactly do we make choices about, and in what way? The ability to make better choices is not just about the allocation of people and resources, but also about political, governmental and public engagement with the process. At present, that engagement is sometimes too one-sided in its focus. For instance, we discussed earlier how it took a long time for shortcomings in the quality and accessibility of mental healthcare and of child and youth care services to surface in the political and policy debate. This aspect is also about the ability to make policy choices that are not so centred on financial resources. Like a less circumspect commitment to certain forms of prevention, for example, such as stricter requirements for healthy food or air quality. When it comes to reducing the prevalence of smoking, after all, legal restrictions have had the greatest impact. Or consider the extent to which, as in other countries, recruitment abroad might be a way to overcome specific staffing shortages in a targeted way. We return briefly to aspects such as these in our recommendations at the end of this chapter. Viewed from the sustainability perspective, then, we face choices about the allocation of resources—and by extension people. But these are not the only important choices before us.

### 9.3.4 *How Does Making Better Choices Contribute to Sustainability?*

Why would better choices in health and social care help achieve a better balance between the three dimensions of sustainability? And how? If the criteria above are met, making better choices is not a solution reserved specifically for any one of the three dimensions but rather a broad strategy that benefits them all. Moreover, Dutch society, politics and our care sector itself need to learn to deal with the issue of increasing scarcity in care. Better choices in line with our criteria will improve society by enabling us to generate more health gains, to improve quality of life and to better uphold minimum standards for quality and accessibility throughout the sector. For instance, by not prioritizing care that is not scientifically proven—and therefore not appropriate. In the long run this saves on human and material resources, and so also makes a smaller claim on solidarity. And the people and assets it frees up can be redeployed elsewhere, in places where they deliver more health benefits or better safeguard accessibility and quality. Societal sustainability should also be bolstered, because a shift of this kind shows that public concerns about quality and accessibility are being taken seriously.

Such a reallocation may not always attract widespread support—because it touches on a social taboo, for example, or because the health gains lie far in the future (see Chap. 8). In some cases, then, making better choices will mean making tough choices that may be hard to digest socially and normatively. For instance, how do we deal with very expensive drugs that in some cases deliver real, albeit limited, health benefits but at very high and possibly socially unacceptable cost? Such cases are a reminder that broad public support is an indispensable precondition when making better but tougher choices about healthcare. For politicians, moreover, making better choices also means making explicit choices in all parts of the care sector. Thirdly, changes are needed at the administrative level and in implementation, especially around the delineation of collective care provision. We elaborate on these three "pillars" which support making better choices in Sect. 9.4.

**Key Points—Choosing Sustainability**

- Rising overall spending on health and social care tends to displace commitments to other policy domains. This could affect our national prosperity, and possibly even public health.
- Allowing the sector to grow automatically also favours some forms of care and displaces others, with negative effects for their quality and accessibility. The main "victims" here are child and youth care services, specialist mental healthcare and certain aspects of care for the elderly.
- Interventions that focus too much upon one dimension of sustainability without properly considering the others can harm public values.

(continued)

- To uphold the sustainability care, there is no need to cut current levels of spending but we do need to set priorities for future growth in a better, more measured way.
- Making better choices about the growth of care means applying three criteria: consider public values both within the sector and elsewhere, pursue health gains and seek balanced sustainability in the long-term.
- Better choices deliver better health and quality of life for more people.

## 9.4 Recommendations: Three Pillars to Make Better Choices

Finally, we arrive at what is perhaps the key question in this report: how do we actually make those better choices? What does that require of society, of politicians and of the responsible institutions? In search of the answer we have formulated a series of recommendations to facilitate the difficult normative deliberations around choices in health and social care.

As already stated, these rest on three pillars: (1) strengthening public support for clearer choices; (2) making clearer political choices in favour of sustainable care; and (3) strengthening the practical ability of governmental and regulatory institutions to make effective choices about the delineation of collective care provision.

The first of these pillars is all about the societal perspective: in order to make better choices, we as a society have to come to terms with the fact that better prioritization is essential and unavoidable, so we need to develop a clear understanding of the dilemmas and choices involved. The second pillar has a political perspective: where does political responsibility for choices in care lie, and how can that responsibility be borne better than is currently the case? Finally, the third pillar concerns implementation: how can the question of what we do and do not include in collective provision be answered in practical terms? How do we make good decisions—however difficult they may be—in concrete cases? And what institutions are required to achieve this?

Our three pillars are interlinked, and so must be developed and implemented in parallel. For instance, we cannot expect politicians to protect other public policy domains from displacement due to rising spending on care without also better organizing the delineation of collective responsibilities within the care sector. And that in turn only has a limited chance of success if our society does not at the same time develop a clear vision of its goals and priorities for different forms of care.

Within each pillar, we provide a number of recommendations to enable better choices and thus improve the sustainability of care. These are not ready-made policy measures, but rather directions policy should take. And whilst they are primarily tasks for government, that does not mean that it is the only actor they target. Strengthening public support for choices in care, for example, requires initiative on the part of government but also input from citizens themselves. In all three pillars it is up to the care sector and society as a whole to make moves, not just government and politicians.

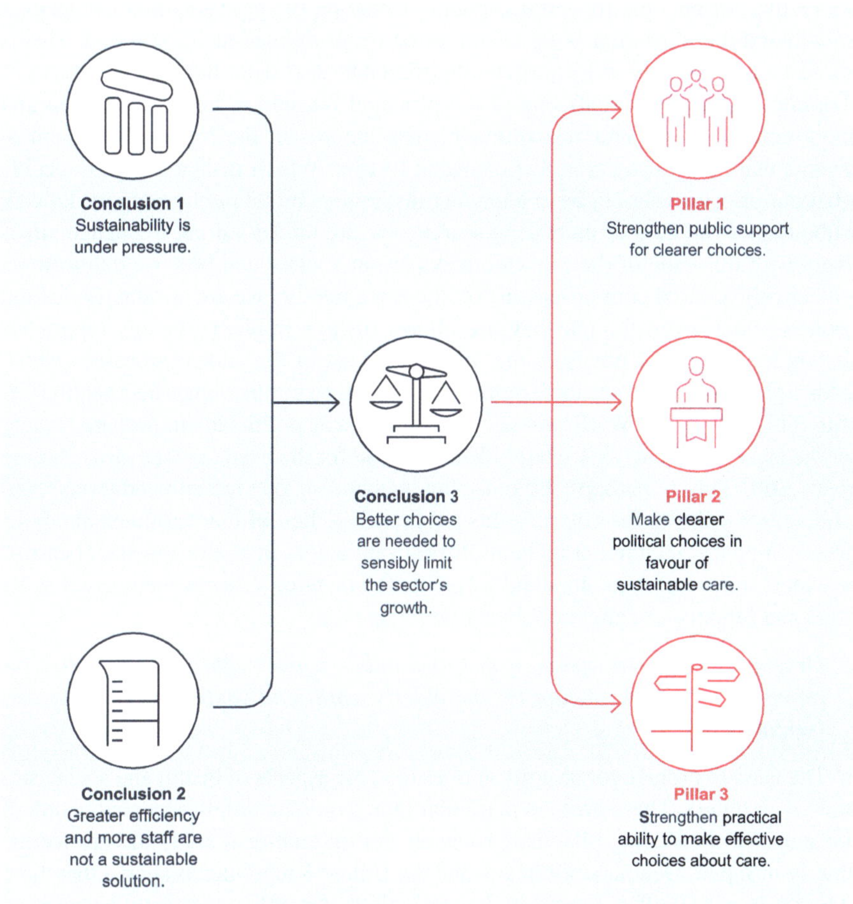


**Pillar 1—Strengthen Public Support for Clearer Choices**
Our first pillar is about the legitimacy of choices in health and social care, and public backing for them. How do we strengthen these necessities and on what major points do we need to develop a perspective with broad support in order to make choices successfully? The WRR advocates preparing citizens for and involving them in choices about care.

1. *Prepare society for increasing scarcity and the need for choices.*

It is vitally important to prepare society for an increasing scarcity of human and material resources in health and social care, and for the resulting need for better, clearer choices and prioritization. With this recommendation the WRR is explicitly not calling for cuts but for a broad public debate on the necessity that the sector's growth and the allocation of its resources be better defined and controlled. This is because our society is still insufficiently primed to deal with the issue of scarcity, a shortcoming that represents one of the principal barriers to better choices in and about care. In this sector in particular, many people in the Netherlands seem to assume that growth can continue unabated forever. Which makes it hard to decide what our priorities should be in a manner that enjoys broad public support. Indeed, without an awareness of increasing scarcity we are utterly failing to engage effectively with the issue of the role care plays in our society and how we delineate its collectively assured core provision. Yet these are matters we are constantly making choices about, even though they are almost always implicit. As this report has shown, however, it is precisely that implicit aspect of the choice processes which leads to outcomes that are undesirable with regard to public values and health benefits. This is why the WRR advises government and politicians to prepare society for the increasing scarcity we have identified, and for the need to make clear choices as a result. This is perhaps the most fundamental of our recommendations. And whilst responsibility for initiating this public debate lies with government and politicians, it is also incumbent upon all the relevant actors in health and social care—providers, insurers, regulators and so on, not to mention citizens themselves as its users and funders—to engage actively with this issue.

2. *Develop a long-term vision, with broad public support, for the core collective provision of long-term care for the elderly, child and youth care services and mental healthcare.*

The need to prepare for scarcity applies to some aspects of health and social care more than others. These areas in particular thus require a widely accepted vision of the scope of their core collective provision. An international study of care for the elderly in Japan, Denmark, Germany and the United Kingdom has shown that there is no ready-made, off-the-shelf model available that is able to perfectly balance the three dimensions of sustainability.[29,30,31] But what did maintain sustainability in a number of those countries was a long-term perspective, with broad public backing, regarding the social role of care for the elderly. The WRR extends this observation to include two further areas with deep-seated problems of quality and accessibility, namely child and youth care services and mental healthcare. In both, as in long-term care for the elderly, it is eminently important that the provision delivered align with sociocultural and normative expectations. Other factors all three have in common are the important role played by the social environment and, for the time being at least, technology's relatively limited impact. Delineating the scope of collective responsibility in these sectors should therefore be a subject for explicit public

[29] Kruse et al. (2021).

[30] In the Netherlands this form of care is governed by the Long-Term Care Act (Wlz). The other major field in size terms is curative medicine, governed by the Health Insurance Act (Zvw).

[31] Kruse et al. (2021).

debate. For example, to discuss the sometimes thin lines across which a child's upbringing becomes a matter for care services or setbacks in life become a mental health issue. In other words, when and where should collectively funded and organized provision "kick in"?

With this in mind, the WRR recommends developing a widely supported long-term vision as to what should constitute core collective provision when it comes to long-term care for the elderly, child and youth care services and mental healthcare. Such a vision is essential to support and inform the political choice process, especially when it comes to the exact scope of that collective core. Without conscious prioritization and active steering of the growth in these sectors, there is a risk that their quality and accessibility could come under pressure due to implicit (or even quite explicit) displacement. Discussions recently initiated by the Ministry of Health, Welfare and Sport around long-term care for the elderly,[32] combined with previous explorations of this theme, could form the basis for the vision we are proposing.[33,34] Similar pathways should also be set out for child and youth care services and mental healthcare.

These trajectories need to address a number of themes. The first, quite simply, is what provision we want—and do not want—to deliver and finance collectively. Then there is the question of how long-term care is funded, and in particular the role of direct charges. And a third crucial issue is staffing: all of these activities, especially long-term care for the elderly, are singularly labour-intensive with relatively limited potential for automation. The Netherlands needs to decide whether—like Germany and Japan, for example[35]—it wants to respond to this by attracting personnel from abroad to make up for specific shortages (see also recommendation 8). And whether, should it become technically possible, we are willing to commit to the large-scale delivery of care via robotics and domotics. As well as requiring wide-ranging cost-benefit analyses, such considerations also have a significant sociocultural component.

3. *Make sure that choices about care have social legitimacy through, say, a citizens' forum.*

Making better choices in health and social care means addressing tough, fundamentally normative questions. So the answers we come up with need to enjoy broad public support. To achieve that, the choices we consider—or at least the principles behind them—must be determined in consultation with society at large. As a rule, however, ordinary people have only a limited awareness of this need and are largely reluctant to think about such choices. This is why the WRR recommends that their social legitimacy be endorsed by, for instance, setting up a broad-based citizens'

[32] Ministerie van VWS (2021).

[33] Commissie toekomst zorg thuiswonende ouderen (2020).

[34] See, for example, Hussem et al. (2021) for examples of ways to organize this provision.

[35] Kruse et al. (2021).

forum on choices and priorities in care. An experiment at Radboudumc, a teaching hospital in the Dutch city of Nijmegen, has shown that—with sufficient explanation and information—even lay people are willing and able to make difficult choices about prioritization in this domain.[36] Through a forum of this kind, citizens could advise politicians on such matters as their preferred pattern of resource allocation across the care sector, including prevention. And thus help shape political decisions. In addition, initiatives like this can trigger and invigorate the broader public debate concerning the sector's sustainability.

There are many ways to arrange a citizens' forum.[37] The OECD has formulated eleven good practices based upon a broad analysis of hundreds of forms of deliberative process. These include promoting values like transparency (of purpose, design, process and follow-up), representativeness, accountability and evaluation.[38] In a general sense, it is crucial that participants be representative of the population as a whole so as to avoid organized sectional or other interests distorting the outcomes. People should thus participate as individuals, not on behalf of a particular social group. It is also important that politicians state transparently in advance what they will do with the outcomes generated, and that they account for them publicly afterwards. Another key factor is the selection procedure: it too must be transparent, well-designed and guarantee representativeness.

**Pillar 2—Make Clearer Political Choices in Favour of Sustainable Care**
Our second pillar concerns the role of politics and political choices in upholding the sustainability of health and social care. To this end, the WRR argues that political choices should be more active.

4. *Make political choices based upon all three dimensions of sustainability and with a long-term focus. Evaluate implemented policies as soon as possible and make adjustments where necessary, but avoid government impatience.*

Past political management of the health and social care sector sometimes focused too unilaterally on just one of the dimensions of sustainability. In many cases, moreover, policies were not evaluated before being succeeded by new measures.

The WRR therefore recommends that all three dimensions—financial, staffing and societal sustainability—be monitored with a long-term perspective. To achieve this it is important first and foremost that, as far as practicable, all political decision-making concerning the care sector be based upon prior assessment of the likely effects of the measures in question for all of the dimensions, as well as for the public values of quality and accessibility. Which in turn requires government and parliament to ensure that those assessments be as thorough as possible—especially in the case of radical changes such as the decentralization of child and youth care services.

[36] Baltussen et al. (2018).

[37] A recent OECD report suggests ways to address socially controversial issues through deliberative processes of this kind (OECD, 2020).

[38] OECD (2020).

Without that, legislators should be reluctant to approve new policy. Subconsciously, there is always a tendency to focus more upon financial effects than upon repercussions for the other dimensions. After all, financial sustainability is often easier to measure, is usually easier to address directly in the short term and dovetails well with existing processes of government and of political accountability. Effects for staffing and societal sustainability, on the other hand, frequently take longer to appear. As a result they are often more or less disregarded during the policymaking process, or at best not properly considered until too late a stage.

In this regard it is important to adjust new policies where necessary, but at the same time to avoid succumbing to undue political pressure. By this we are referring in particular to the launch of one programme or initiative after another without always giving each of them enough time to make any real headway. It is all too tempting for politicians to flood a sector like care with a succession of initiatives, action plans and policy agendas, often of only relatively short duration.[39] But achieving genuine change in a system this complex, with its multitude of actors and mutual dependencies, takes time. The watchword here is patience, as the system undergoes "permanent maintenance". Quick results—within the term of one government, for instance—are rarely to be expected. Tenacity and policy consistency are key.[40,41] We therefore urge politicians to be frugal in setting up programmes and initiatives, to make sure they are given sufficient time to reach maturity and to give providers the space they need to facilitate this process.

Finally, comprehensive and timely evaluation is crucial. There are always unforeseen side-effects, after all, as well as behavioural responses and other outcomes that are impossible to predict fully beforehand. This means reviewing not only performance in achieving the policy's primary goals, but also its other effects. As a result, it should be possible to make the necessary adjustments in time if unacceptable consequences for the quality or accessibility of certain aspects of care or for its sustainability are found to be occurring. And to prevent policy management descending into "incident management"—an overreaction to individual events—it is advisable to define in advance the criteria which will trigger adjustments. For example, at what point are any undesirable effects considered serious enough, and convincingly enough demonstrated, to justify corrective action? And how will this aspect be monitored systematically (see also recommendation 12)? Parliament should lay down such adjustment criteria prior to its approval of policy changes.

---

[39] The Netherlands Court of Audit, for instance, came to this conclusion in the light of the large number of initiatives aimed at promoting "appropriate care" (Algemene Rekenkamer, 2020b).

[40] This conclusion was recently reiterated in a study of Dutch child and youth care services and highlighted in a position paper by the Netherlands Youth Institute (NJI). See van Yperen et al. (2021) and AEF (2020).

[41] As also applies to quality improvement, the existing system with a covenant guaranteeing that government will contribute towards labour cost increases puts care in a unique and stronger position compared with other public policy domains when it comes to wage evolution (see Chap. 6 for more details).

5. *Strengthen political grip on collective spending on care. Restructure the budgeting system for this sector along the same lines as that in other policy domains.*

The total amount spent on health and social care should become more of a political consideration, the WRR believes. The alternative, the sector's continuing automatic growth at the expense of education and other public policy domains, is not in the national economic interest and probably not even in the interests of public health. More generally, achieving a better budgetary equilibrium between the various domains requires fundamental reconsideration of the system whereby we estimate and fund care spending to bring it more in line with the processes in those other areas (see Chap. 7). This would allow better reflection upon the importance of increasing spending on care in relation to needs elsewhere. More specifically, it might mean that whilst we automatically accommodate growth resulting from demographic developments, say, by contrast quality improvements due to technological developments or by expanding the collective health benefits package would require explicit political decision-making. A politically determined standard for expenditure growth in healthcare—possibly linked to average economic growth—could help here, as an instrument for imposing financial discipline.[42,43] Deviations from that standard would then only be permitted with cabinet approval. An arrangement of this kind would make considering and opting for growth of the care sector, and its consequences, a more visible political process. Only in the political arena, after all, is it possible to weigh up the importance of care against other policy priorities. Politicians should therefore dare to make more active choices in setting the care budget. This recommendation requires political courage, but it can also help improve societal sustainability and reduce public pressure on politicians. Presenting the current baseline as less compelling might also fend off accusations that deviations from it constitute "cutbacks" in a situation where real spending is in fact increasing.[44,45]

This recommendation is intended to contribute towards making better choices "from the top down", and in particular to help prevent spending on care displacing commitments to other policy domains. At the same time, though, we must stress that this recommendation cannot stand alone. If we only impose limits from above, after all, there is a real danger that the "bill" will be passed on to vulnerable groups lower down the ladder in the form of reduced quality of care, longer waiting lists or both. The WRR therefore interprets political responsibility more broadly: it is not just about total expenditure, but also about the equitable allocation of resources within the sector and to different groups of patients and users so as to comply with minimum standards for quality and accessibility (see recommendation 6). It is also about managing the package of collectively insured benefits in a more futureproof way (see recommendations 9–11). And all with a view to keeping the three dimensions of sustainability in equilibrium (see recommendation 4). Take the very real current

[42] Schakel et al. (2018).

[43] Studiegroep Begrotingsruimte (2020).

[44] Koolman and Wouterse (2021).

[45] AEF (2020).

constraints with to regard to staffing, for instance. As events during the Covid-19 pandemic showed, freeing up resources for more hospital beds does nothing to conjure up the personnel needed to staff them. Considerations of this kind are the subject of the remainder of our recommendations within this pillar and those in the next one.

6. *Do not allow quality and accessibility in vulnerable parts of the sector to fall below acceptable standards. Assess the effects of new policies in advance and in public.*

The public values of quality and accessibility are coming under huge strain in some aspects of health and social care (see Chap. 4). These two values are important throughout the sector, but in certain areas are at risk of falling systematically below the minimum acceptable standard. Specifically, they are child and youth care services, specialist mental healthcare and parts of care for vulnerable elderly people. This situation needs to be addressed with urgency, and its future recurrence prevented. Otherwise, in a world of increasing scarcity there is a risk that groups less well represented within the decision-making structures will increasingly be compromised (see Chaps. 7 and 8). Herein lies a political responsibility, since ultimately only politicians can weigh up and monitor the interests of various different groups. In doing that, it is also essential that the outcomes be visible (see recommendation 12).

What does this mean in concrete terms? Firstly, the government should ensure that, especially in the case of new policy concerning care for relatively vulnerable groups, the effects with regard to quality and accessibility are assessed in advance and in a transparent manner. Moreover, any changes to policy should be evaluated actively and comprehensively so that necessary adjustments can be made in good time (see also recommendation 4). This requires greater commitment to the systematic collection and accessibility of outcome data, especially in the areas mentioned above as being at risk (see also recommendation 12): where policy measures result in negative effects for the quality and accessibility of care, it has often proven difficult for their patients and users to find a hearing in the public debate—their voices are not always as loud as those of other interest groups. It is therefore essential that signals warning of inadequate quality or accessibility be detected and acknowledged in a timely fashion.

Secondly, for these vulnerable groups in particular it appears that focusing upon a single dimension of sustainability—usually the financial one—has had negative repercussions. An obvious example is how the decentralization of child and youth care services and of social support—in both cases a major transformation in itself—was coupled with far-reaching budget cuts. Such changes to the organization of care for vulnerable groups cannot be automatically assumed in advance to be a path to greater efficiency, so that they are combined from the outset with cost saving. That should only be done once the change has had the opportunity to "bed in" and it can be demonstrated convincingly that the expected efficiency gains are achievable without unacceptable consequences for quality and accessibility.

Thirdly, a greater effort to maintain minimum standards of quality and accessibility will in some cases mean that relatively more people and material resources will be needed to deliver the provision serving vulnerable groups. And also require that they be allocated carefully; for example, with a view to mitigating existing pressures on accessibility and quality. Building upon the principle that choices should be made from the perspective of safeguarding public values, this recommendation necessitates a government policy of active choices when allocating resources across the sector and when monitoring their distribution within its component parts. In the Netherlands, for instance, we find that the largest area of growth in spending on child and youth care services in recent years has been in tackling relatively straightforward indications.

7. *Focus more forcefully upon general public health and prevention, from multiple policy perspectives.*

Care, even in its broadest sense, is only one determinant of health—and probably not even one of the most important. Housing, working conditions, air quality, the environment, educational attainment and other social and contextual factors all play a more significant role.[46,47,48] The WRR therefore argues for a greater, far more systematic commitment to the promotion of good health in other public policy domains, along with structurally greater investment in preventive activities of all kinds. By this we mean that even policies in such areas as debt problems, the built environment, housing, education, agriculture, transport, the labour market and environmental issues should be developed with their likely health effects as a primary consideration, not playing second fiddle to other factors. And as far as prevention is concerned, first and foremost devoting more human and material resources to health promotion—teaching and encouraging healthy lifestyles—and protection, such as by combating harmful substances like particulate matter, soot and nitrogen oxides.

These commitments are all the more important in a world of scarcity, since in many cases the activities concerned are by far the most efficient way to generate health gains across broad swathes of the population.[49] Wide-ranging prevention, moreover, can help shore up the societal sustainability of the care sector because it averts lifestyle-related diseases (and spending on them) in particular—an area in which solidarity is coming under especial strain (see Chap. 3). It is also an effective means of curbing the influx of new "clients" in sectors such as child and youth care services and mental healthcare, where quality and accessibility are under pressure. In order to free up the necessary financial resources, in parallel with this approach it is advisable to commit to policies that convert the resulting additional health benefits into greater labour productivity and economic growth.[50]

---

46 Polder et al. (2020).

47 SER (2020) and RVS (2021).

48 Broeders et al. (2018).

49 Polder et al. (2020).

50 See also Polder et al. (2020) and de Blaeij et al. (2021) for an analysis of the potential benefits of preventive interventions for the labour market, as well as policy suggestions to turn health benefits into labour-market benefits (Sect. 5.3.1, Polder et al., 2020).

Why has this approach so far failed to gain sufficient momentum? Earlier in this report we identified a number of psychological and institutional reasons, as well as several related to economic and other interests (see Chap. 8). Examples include the so-called "wrong-pocket problem" (because the investing party is not the one reaping the benefits, it either refuses to make the necessary commitment or does not invest enough[51,52,53]) and the long delay before benefits actually occur. On top of that, those benefits tend to be statistical and diffuse in nature: the overall health of the population as a whole may improve, but we cannot identify any one individual who is healthier as a result of the measures taken. The political benefits are thus also hard to attribute. All in all, this easily leaves prevention as an "orphaned" theme—with the net effect that political and executive decision-making processes focus upon on care in its narrowest, sharply delineated sense whilst commitments to prevention remain limited and vague (see Chap. 7). Overcoming these impediments is a task only government can be expected to take on, by adopting and pursuing a wide-ranging long-term outlook that prioritizes health gains and broad-based prevention across its policy portfolio.

Bearing all this in mind, the WRR further concludes that, from the perspective of both health gains and societal sustainability, there can be no taboo on compulsion as a preventive health strategy. By this we mean legally enforced forms of prevention: the direct regulation of products or production processes with negative health effects, regulating how those products are marketed and measures to control their use. Direct regulation could include the mandatory reduction of salt percentages in foods, say, as well as stricter vehicle and industrial emission standards to improve air quality—that is, measures constraining manufacturers in the way they make their products. Examples of marketing restrictions include reducing the number of tobacco and alcohol outlets, the introduction of minimum pricing and the extension of advertising bans.[54] These again target manufacturers, but in the way they sell their products. Finally, classic examples of controls on use are sugar and fat taxes, higher excise duties on alcohol and tobacco products and higher VAT rates for unhealthy foods or lower rates for healthy foods. These aim to achieve positive health effects by changing consumer behaviour. Manufacturers may also respond to such

---

[51] This is a classic collective action problem. Investing in prevention is in the interests of society as a whole, but lags behind the optimum level as viewed from that universal perspective. Many of the benefits, moreover, are archetypal public goods: access to clean air, for instance, cannot be restricted to a paying group (it is "non-excludable") and so has no ownership and creates no private incentive to provide it. Both of these are thus perfect examples of a situation in which government intervention is desirable.

[52] RIVM (2018a, b) and Van Giessen et al. (2021a, b).

[53] Broeders et al. (2018).

[54] A recent study by the National Institute for Public Health and the Environment (RIVM) reviews possible interpretations and the likely effects of minimum unit pricing for alcohol (de Wit et al., 2021).

incentives—for instance, by changing the composition of their products to avoid or reduce its extra taxation.[55,56,57]

Normative considerations obviously play a role in this political process. For example, views on personal responsibility and the role of government in encouraging healthy behaviour. Some interventions of the type described are easily perceived as patronizing, paternalistic or infringing upon individual freedom. Conversely, potential justifications for mandatory preventive interventions include avoiding harmful effects for other people (measures to improve air quality or discourage smoking, for instance), compensating for external factors that actually drive up unhealthy behaviour (the wide availability of unhealthy food in public places, for instance[58]), protecting people from themselves (because they lack information, knowledge or the ability to act in their own interest[59,60,61]) and the fact that most of the healthcare costs resulting from unhealthy behaviour are borne collectively by society—the argument here being that society should therefore be allowed to discourage the behaviour in question in order to mitigate the associated reliance upon solidarity. How people weigh up such arguments is an intrinsically normative question, which makes this a matter that ultimately belongs in the political arena.

8. *Look to mitigate staff shortages through broad political consideration of possible fiscal incentives, improving work-life balance and targeted recruitment from abroad.*

Lack of staff is going to be one of the most urgent and severe forms of scarcity in the Dutch health and social care sector in the coming decades. This is due largely to our ageing population and to the fact that, without immigration, the size of the workforce is set to stagnate (see Chap. 3). But this does not mean that there is no potential whatsoever to increase the number of people working in the sector—or the

---

[55] Taxes on high-sugar soft drinks in countries including the UK, France and Norway have achieved a reduction in sugar intake, primarily by encouraging manufacturers to cut the sugar content of their products. See: Pell et al. (2021) and Vellinga et al. (2020).

[56] de Blaeij et al. (2021).

[57] An analysis by the Ministry of Finance has reviewed the implementation costs and side-effects of health-related taxes. Especially in the case of harder-to-operationalize systems, such as the imposition of a higher VAT rate on "unhealthy food", the implementation costs would be so high that they are considerable impracticable. Simpler measures, however, like an adaptation of the existing consumption tax on non-alcoholic beverages (the so-called "soft drinks tax"), would be easy to implement. Ministerie van Financiën (2020b).

[58] WRR (2014b).

[59] WRR (2017).

[60] RVS (2020d) and SER (2021a, b).

[61] The average marginal pressure on personal income rises very steeply from €21,000 onwards, to just below 50 per cent. From €35,000 onwards it rises to 54 per cent. For a single-income earner in a rented home with two children aged between 6 and 11, from €23,000 upwards the marginal pressure including the effects of care allowance, child budget and rent allowance amounts to 78 per cent. Ministerie van Financiën (2019, 2020a).

total number of hours they work—and thus mitigate that scarcity. The WRR recommends the political consideration of three aspects of policy outside the care sector which touch upon the issue of staffing sustainability within it. Specifically, these are: (1) fiscal measures and their effect on labour-market participation and the choice of working hours; (2) broadening options to improve work-life balance; and (3) the targeted recruitment of care personnel from abroad.

Fiscal measures affect the way the tax and benefits system encourages or discourages people from working more hours or increasing their take-home pay. Such measures affect everyone but, given that care now accounts for by far the largest part of the growth in demand for labour in the Netherlands, they are particularly relevant to workers (and potential workers) in this sector (see Chaps. 3 and 6). The marginal pressure on labour—that part of an increase in gross income that does not raise disposable income—is relatively high in our country, especially for those people we would particularly like to encourage to work more hours in care (on below average incomes, mostly in part-time jobs).

Looking to the future, a more gradual progression of taxes and fiscal allowances would create scope to encourage care workers to increase their hours. More generally, maintaining our current emphasis upon the taxation of labour is detrimental in a situation where the size of the workforce is lagging a long way behind the growth in demand for its labour.

Besides the financial hurdle to working more hours, many care workers also encounter a personal barrier: their often relatively burdensome informal care or childcare responsibilities. This obstacle could be addressed by creating better opportunities to find the right work-life balance. For example, through more accessible and generous government schemes to support parents and informal carers. The WRR has already made a number of such recommendations to strengthen people's control over their own lives in an earlier report.[62]

A third option to ease the pressure on staffing sustainability is a targeted effort to attract care personnel from abroad. OECD figures show that whilst many countries already actively recruit internationally, the Netherlands is lagging well behind in this respect (see Chap. 6). Only 0.5 per cent of nurses working in our country were trained abroad, for example, compared with an average of 7.4 per cent for the OECD as a whole.

For doctors the Dutch figure is 2 per cent; in Belgium and Germany it is 12 per cent.[63] And when it comes to long-term care for the elderly, countries where ageing is at a more advanced stage, such as Germany and Japan, use labour from abroad on a much larger scale than we do.[64] The question, then, is whether our comparatively very modest use of international personnel is sustainable—especially with staff

---

[62] WRR (2020b).

[63] OECD (2019c) and ACVZ (2021a, b).

[64] Kruse et al. (2021).

shortages in the care sector expected to worsen for several decades to come. Even now, targeted recruitment abroad could address existing shortages in some critical areas. Such a policy requires a vigilant approach, however, encompassing good professional guidance, language requirements, avoiding a brain drain in countries of origin, an eye for cultural differences and adequate monitoring of the quality of care and working conditions.

**Pillar 3—Strengthen Practical Ability to Make Effective Choices About the Delineation of Collective Care Provision**
Within our third pillar, the core question is how to better determine and delineate what health and social care is provided collectively. Sensibly limiting the sector's growth requires improvements to collective package management in the broad sense. Here we are emphatically not just referring to the basic statutory package of primarily curative healthcare provided for under the Zvw; the recommendations below relate to all aspects of care. And they also require improvements to the handling of performance and outcome data.

9. *Broaden active management of the statutory health benefits package. As well as assessing drugs for clinical and cost effectiveness, do the same for other forms of care.*

At present, 5 per cent at most of new forms of care in the Netherlands are assessed explicitly for cost-effectiveness. Only certain curative interventions aspiring to coverage under the Zwv are reviewed, primarily expensive drugs; just about everything else qualifies more or less automatically through the so-called "open" system (see Chap. 6). But this approach is simply not tenable in the long run, in part because of the many expensive—sometimes very expensive—drugs and medical devices now in the pipeline (see Chap. 2) but also due to advances in technology, medical engineering and e-health. This applies not only to curative medicine, but increasingly also to long-term care and mental healthcare.

The WRR therefore recommends broadening the scope of advance assessments of clinical and cost effectiveness as part of a more active approach to management of the statutory health benefits package, and not just in curative medicine. This means making a larger proportion of new forms of care subject to the "closed" system of authorization, creating a more strictly delineated package.

Curative care should be the first priority here, so that some medical devices, say, become subject to assessment in the same way as certain drugs already are. But we should also work explicitly towards wider express consideration of cost-effectiveness in other parts of the sector, such as the collective packages in long-term care, mental healthcare and child and youth care services.[65] Reviewing all new treatments and interventions in this way will never be practicable—it is too time-consuming, for one thing—but that does not make a more comprehensive system any less desirable.

[65] As the Netherlands Youth Institute (NJI) already does with its database of effective interventions, for example.

An analysis of the Dutch approach to package management reveals a number of practical barriers to the broadening we are proposing, however.[66] When it comes to medicines, for instance, it is always possible to identify a party (usually the manufacturer) clearly responsible for providing information on their effectiveness, safety and costs. But this is not necessarily the case with medical technology. Knowledge and information about the benefits—and to a lesser extent the costs—of an intervention are also sometimes lacking. In such circumstances our knowledge base needs to be strengthened in order to make better choices. A toolkit to assess clinical and cost-effectiveness does already exist for long-term care, for example (see Chap. 7), but we still need to develop a stronger assessment culture in this field—and provide the resources to promote it.

10. *Clearly define the roles of care buyers, politicians and regulators in management of the statutory health benefits package.*

Although the details differ across the health and social care system, different parts of which are governed by different legislation, within their respective legal parameters responsibility in practice for deciding what provision is and is not delivered collectively is divided between three actors: the relevant minister, the package manager (the Healthcare Institute of the Netherlands, ZiN) and the buyers of care.[67] As a result, package management responsibilities in the Netherlands are now overly jumbled. So, for example, a minister can be called to account in the political arena for what is in part a clinical consideration, such as a decision not to reimburse a particular treatment, and as a political actor may find it hard to remain resolute in the face of the resulting public outcry. And health insurers, in their politically assigned role as guardians of the cost-effectiveness of curative interventions under the Zwv, have to take decisions for which they lack social legitimacy. Research shows that the current apportionment of roles and incentives is undermining public trust in health insurers, which are seen as not dedicated enough to the collective interest.[68]

The WRR concludes that the current pattern of responsibilities is not sufficiently futureproof, and therefore recommends that the respective roles of politicians, regulators and buyers (health insurers, care administration bureaus and local authorities) be more clearly delineated. Politicians should set the general criteria and standards. How much is an extra year of life worth? Do we consider it legitimate—in line with the rule of rescue,[69] for example—to pay much more for some forms of health gain than others? And how much more? Or do we prefer some other criterion for fairness

[66] Enzing et al. (2020).

[67] Health insurers under the Zvw, care administration bureaus under the Wlz and local authorities under the Wmo and in child and youth care services.

[68] Maarse and Jeurissen (2019). Less is known about this factor with regard to the buyers of care in other parts of the system, such as care administration bureaus.

[69] See Chap. 7, Table 7.1. The rule of rescue states that in cases with the same potential health gain, the one with the greatest urgency should be prioritized.

in prioritization? Ultimately, these are normative questions that we must address as a society. In the end only politicians can ultimately decide what society considers desirable and acceptable, and they should make use of input from the general public (see also recommendation 3). In return, political actors should dare to keep their distance from decisions in specific cases—for instance, leaving it up to regulators like the ZiN to draw upon the general criteria when ruling (again possibly after taking public input into account—see recommendations 2 and 3) on the authorization or exclusion of specific treatments.

Indeed, it is well worth considering entirely removing such decisions from the political domain—as is already done in a number of other countries[70]—so that politicians are accountable only for the general criteria. This would also reduce the role of care buyers in determining whether a treatment falls within the collective benefits package, thus enabling them to focus more effectively upon their core task: helping to organize that package as efficiently as possible. In other words, defining the package and procurement within it are separate tasks and should therefore be entrusted to separate actors. By clearly demarcating the responsibilities of the parties involved—politicians, package managers and the buyers of care—all can better fulfil their core task (see Chap. 8).

11. *Review the clinical and cost effectiveness of current provision across the sector and prevent insurers from reimbursing inappropriate care.*

Better package management also requires active consideration of the "outflow" of old, obsolete or ineffective forms of care. In other words, systematic screening—using scientific criteria—of the provision covered. And ensuring that the results do actually lead to the exclusion of inappropriate interventions. The WRR therefore recommends more active reviews of the clinical and cost effectiveness of current provision across the sector and, where necessary, the use of independent enforcement powers to stop the delivery and reimbursement of inappropriate care.

Again, this recommendation is not confined to curative medicine but covers all aspects of health and social care. Within the curative field, we do not really know whether about half of the provision delivered through the collective package is actually appropriate.[71] More generally, we should put greater effort into the evaluation of care across the sector in order to strengthen the knowledge base underlying package-related decisions.[72,73,74,75] A risk-oriented approach might be useful here,

---

[70] See online Appendix 6.

[71] Kiers (2021).

[72] The Care Evaluation and Appropriate Use (*Zorgevaluatie en Gepast Gebruik*) programme—successor to the earlier Appropriate Care (*Zinnige Zorg*) programme—is already making an initial move in this direction. As yet, however, it makes little or no use of its power to overrule previous decisions.

[73] Algemene Rekenkamer (2020b).

[74] ZiN and NZA (2020).

[75] The relevant perspective here is that of "delegation"—regulators need to maintain a certain degree independence, not only from the political arena but also from the field they are overseeing. See Chap. 8 for more information.

informed by assessing how a new form of care will impact sustainability. And thus revealing what puts it under particularly strong pressure. Another approach to encourage the outflow of interventions proven to be inappropriate or ineffective is to work more with conditional authorization—or its mirror image, conditional exclusion. Under this model a treatment is admitted to or retained in the package on a temporary basis, but its inclusion then lapses automatically after a set period unless certain conditions are met concerning its effectiveness and the scientific evidence of that.

12. *Entrust responsibility for the systematic development, collection and dissemination of data on healthcare outcomes to a single organization.*

The Dutch care system generates an overabundance of performance and outcome data, yet at the same time fails to collate and disseminate it all in a systematic manner.[76] The resulting fragmentation makes it hard to understand performance and outcomes across the sector in a structured way (see Chap. 5 and Box 5.2). This can lead to problems with the quality and accessibility of care not permeating the public debate and policy in a timely manner, and not leading to adjustments until late in the day (see also recommendations 4 and 6). This is also an issue when it comes to proper consideration of how to delineate the collective insurance package. One of the major challenges in this respect is the fragmented nature of much of the outcome data,[77] particularly in fields with numerous providers like mental healthcare, child and youth care services and home care. For example, there is little insight into waiting times for provision of this kind.

The WRR therefore recommends that such data be systematized and that responsibility for its collection, collation and timely dissemination be entrusted to a single organization. To make this possible, it is important that that responsibility be invested for the long term, with stable funding for the body concerned. Current practice relies too much upon short-term monitoring trajectories focusing upon a single outcome variable or policy intervention. Since commercially sensitive information is involved, the organization in question should be designated as a "trusted third party" with the right to collect and process data.

## 9.5 Making Better Choices—Essential, But No Panacea

The analyses presented in this report reveal unequivocally that, given the scale of the sustainability challenge facing the Dutch health and social care sector, its current policy agendas with their focus upon greater efficiency on the one hand and a growing workforce on the other are inadequate to meet future needs. To be clear, the "making better choices" agenda being proposed by the WRR does not stand alone

[76] For an international comparison, see OECD (2015b).

[77] Koolman and Wouterse (2021).

either. It is not intended to replace the existing ones, but rather to complement and reinforce them. The three agendas are not mutually exclusive. In fact, all three are essential and they could all be improved.

That said, the existing efficiency and staffing agendas are likely to encounter less political and public resistance than our proposals, with their emphasis upon making choices and setting priorities. The former, after all, entail far fewer—if any—normative considerations. Which brings us to an important warning: making better choices is not a last resort. In other words, the fact that there is still potential to make the system operate more efficiently should not be used as an excuse to postpone better choices and prioritization in health and social care. After all, the process of making better choices also takes time and requires social and political commitment.

As a society, we find setting priorities when it comes to care deeply uncomfortable. Yet there is no alternative. In fact, not daring or wanting to make choices damages the sector's essential values—not to mention those of other public policy domains. It is vital that we face up to this reality. Ultimately, it is simply not in our own interest to avoid or evade making choices because that only undermines the overall health of the Dutch people.

The WRR's aim with this report, therefore, is to prepare our society for a future in which these dilemmas will play an ever greater role, making public and political debate about scarcity in the care sector unavoidable. At the same time, involving society in that debate must not become an excuse for politicians to avoid or delay critical decisions. Because in the final analysis they are political decisions. Not making a choice is also a choice—but it too has consequences.

# Bibliography


ACVZ [The Advisory Council on Migration]. (2021a). *Van asielzoeker naar zorgverlener. Arbeidsdeelname van asielmigranten in de zorgsector*. The Advisory Council on Migration.

ACVZ [The Advisory Council on Migration]. (2021b). *Migratie en de zorgsector. Cijfers over de arbeidsmarkt in de zorgsector en de arbeidsdeelname van migranten*. The Advisory Council on Migration.

Adang, E., Stadhouders, N., Koolman, A. H. E., Parsons, C., Wammes, J., & Govaert, P. (2018). *Verdringingseffecten binnen het Nederlandse zorgstelsel*. Rapport in opdracht van het Zorginstituut Nederland.

Adovor, E., Zaika, M., Docquier, F., & Moullan, Y. (2021). Medical brain drain: How many, where and why? *Journal of Health Economics, 76*, 102409. https://doi.org/10.1016/j.jhealeco.2020.102409. Epub 2020 Dec 30. PMID: 33465558.

AEF. (2020). *Stelsel in de groei. Een onderzoek naar financiële tekorten in de jeugdzorg*. Andersson Elffers Felix.

Alesina, A., & Perotti, R. (1995). Taxation and redistribution in an open economy. *European Economic Review, 39*, 961–979.

Alesina, A., & Rodrik, D. (1994). Distributive politics and Economic growth. *Quarterly Journal of Economics, 109*, 465–490.

Alesina, A., Ardagna, S., Perotti, R., & Schiantarelli, F. (2002). Fiscal policy, profits and investment. *American Economic Review, 92*, 571–589.

Algemene Rekenkamer [Netherlands Court of Audit]. (2015). *Basispakket zorgverzekering: Uitgavenbeheersing in de zorg deel 3*. Algemene Rekenkamer.

Algemene Rekenkamer [Netherlands Court of Audit]. (2016). *Zorgakkoorden. Uitgavenbeheersing in de Zorg deel 4*. Algemene Rekenkamer.

Algemene Rekenkamer [Netherlands Court of Audit]. (2019). *Resultaten verantwoordingsonderzoek 2018 Ministerie VWS (XVI)*. Algemene Rekenkamer.

Algemene Rekenkamer [Netherlands Court of Audit]. (2020a). *Geen plek voor grote problemen. Aanpak van wachttijden in de specialistische GGZ*. Algemene Rekenkamer.

Algemene Rekenkamer [Netherlands Court of Audit]. (2020b). *Verzekerd van Zinnige Zorg*. Algemene Rekenkamer.

Algemene Rekenkamer [Netherlands Court of Audit]. (2020c). *Resultaten verantwoordelijkheidsonderzoek 2019*. Ministerie van Volksgezondheid, Welzijn en Sport (XVI). Rapport bij het jaarverslag.

Al-Ubaydli, O., List, J. A., & Suskind, D. L. (2017). What can we learn from experiments? Understanding the threats to the scalability of experimental results. *American Economic Review, 107*(5), 282–286.




G. Werner et al., *Financial, Staffing and Societal Sustainability of Dutch Health Care*, Research for Policy, https://doi.org/10.1007/978-3-031-58564-7

Anderson, P. (1999). Complexity theory and organization science. *Organization Science, 10*(3), 216–232.

Anderson, R. A., & Mcdaniel, R. R., Jr. (2000). Managing Health Care Organizations: Where professionalism meets complexity science. *Health Care Management Review, 25*(1), 83–92.

Angelis, A., Lange, A., & Kanavos, P. (2018). Using health technology assessment to assess the value of new medicines: Results of a systematic review and expert consultation across eight European countries. *European Journal of Health Economics, 19*(1), 123–152.

Antecol, H., & Bedard, K. (2006). Unhealthy assimilation: Why do immigrants converge to American health status levels? *Demography, 43*, 337–360.

Aspalter, C. (2006). The East Asian welfare model. *International Journal of Social Welfare, 15*(4), 290–301.

AWVN [The General Employers' Association of the Netherlands]. (2021). *Beloningen in de zorg*. Algemene Werkgeversvereniging Nederland.

Baicker, K., & Chandra, A. (2005). *Labor market effects of rising Health insurance premiums*. NBER Working Paper 11160. National Bureau of Economic Research.

Baicker, K., Chandra, A., & Skinner, J. (2012). Saving money or just saving lives? Improving the productivity of US Health Care spending. *Annual Review of Economics, 4*, 33–56.

Bal, R., Wallenburg, I., & Schuurmans, J. (2019). 'De zorg moet regionaliseren'. *Medisch Contact*. Retrieved from: https://www.medischcontact.nl/nieuws/laatste-nieuws/artikel/de-zorg-moet-regionaliseren.htm

Baltussen, R., Bijlmaker, L., Van der Burg, S., Van Dijk, W., Groenewoud, S., Jansen, M., Tummers, M., Helderman, K., Boer, B., Van Exel, J., & Zwaap, J. (2018). *Draagvlak voor lastige keuzes. Eindrapport van het Burgerforum 'Keuzes in de zorg'*. RadboudUMC.

Barsom, E. Z., Van Dalen, A. S. H. M., Blussé van Oud-Alblas, M., Buskens, C. J., Van de Ven, A. W. H., Tanis, P. J., Schijven, M. P., & Bemelman, W. A. (2021). Comparing video consultation and telephone consultation at the outpatient clinic of a tertiary referral centre: Patient and provider benefits'. *BMJ Innovations, 2021*(7), 95–102. https://doi.org/10.1136/bmjinnov-2020-000512

Batenburg, R. (2019). *Zorgen voor de arbeidsmarkt. Integraal onderzoek naar de arbeidsmarkt van de gezondheidszorg, inaugurale rede uitgesproken op donderdag 19 september 2019*. Radboud Universiteit.

Baumol, W. J. (1967). Macroeconomics of unbalanced growth: The anatomy of urban crisis. *The American Economic Review, 57*(3), 415–426.

Baxter, S., Johnson, M., Chambers, D., Sutton, A., Goyder, E., & Booth, A. (2018). The effects of integrated care: A systematic review of UK and international evidence. *BMC Health Services Research, 18*, 350. https://doi.org/10.1186/s12913-018-3161-3

Beer, J., van Duin, C., van der Gaag, N., & Ekamper, P. (2020). *Eindrapport Verkenning Bevolking 2050*. The Netherlands Interdisciplinary Demographic Institute (NIDI) & Statistics Netherlands (CBS).

Begun, J. W., Zimmerman, B., & Dooley, K. (2003). Health care organizations as complex adaptive systems. In S. M. Mick & M. Wyttenbach (Eds.), *Advances in health care organization theory* (pp. 252–288). Jossey-Bass.

Bertens, R. M., & Palamar, J. (2021). *Het Nederlandse zorgbeleid in historisch perspectief, 1941–2017*. WRR Working Paper 45. The Netherlands Scientific Council for Government Policy (WRR).

Bijlmakers, L., Jansen, M., Boer, B., Van Dijk, W., Groenewoud, S., Zwaap, J., Helderman, J. K., Van Exel, J., & Baltussen, R. (2020). Increasing the legitimacy of tough choices in healthcare reimbursement: Approach and results of a citizen forum in The Netherlands. *Value in Health, 23*(1), 32–38.

Blanchard, O. (2019). Public debt and low interest rates. *American Economic Review, 109*(4), 1197–1229.

Blank, J. L. T., & Eggink, E. (2011). Productiviteitstrends in de ziekenhuiszorg. In *Een empirisch onderzoek naar het effect van regulering op de productiviteitsontwikkeling tussen 1972 en 2008. IPSE Studies Research Reeks no. 2011–2*. IPSE.

Blank, J. L. T., & Van Heezik, A. S. (2019). *Productiviteit van de overheid. Een essay over de relatie tussen beleid en productiviteit in onderwijs, zorg, veiligheid & justitie en netwerksectoren*. IPSE.

Blau, F., & Kahn, L. (2007). Changes in labor supply behavior of married women: 1980–2000. *Journal of Labor Economics, 25*(3), 393–438.

Bognar, G., & Hirose, I. (2014). *The ethics of health care rationing*. Routledge.

Böhm, K., Schmid, A., Götze, R., Landwehr, C., & Rothgang, H. (2013). Five types of OECD healthcare systems: Empirical results of a deductive classification. *Health Policy, 13*(3), 258–269.

Böhm, K., Landwehr, C., & Steiner, N. (2014). What explains 'generosity' in the public financing of high-tech drugs? An empirical investigation of 25 OECD countries and 11 controversial drugs. *Journal of European Social Policy, 24*(1), 39–55.

Booij, H. L. (1988). *Wet Voorzieningen Gezondheidszorg. Doctoraalscriptie*. Universiteit Utrecht.

Boone, J., & Remmerswaal, M. (2020a). *A structural microsimulation model for demandside costsharing in healthcare*. CPB Netherlands Bureau for Economic Policy Analysis.

Boone, J., & Remmerswaal, M. (2020b). *Eigen betalingen in de Zorgverzekeringswet. Bijlage bij het rapport Zorgkeuzes in Kaart 2020*. CPB Netherlands Bureau for Economic Policy Analysis.

Bos, A., Kruse, F. M., & Jeurissen, P. P. T. (2020). For-profit nursing homes in The Netherlands: What factors explain their rise? *International Journal of Health Science, 50*(4), 431–443.

Bosveld, M. H., van Doorn, D. P. C., Stassen, P. M., Westerman, D., Bergmans, D. C. J. J., van der Horst, I. C. C., & van Mook, W. N. K. A. (2021). Lessons learned: Contribution to healthcare by medical students during COVID-19. *Journal of Critical Care, 63*, 113–116.

Brabers, A., & De Jong, J. (2019). *Toekomst van de huisartsenzorg Het perspectief van de burger Resultaten van een enquête onder burgers*. Nivel.

Broeders, D., Das, D., Jennissen, R., Tiemeijer, W., & De Visser, M. (2018). *From disparity to potential: a realistic perspective on socio-economic health inequalities*. WRR Policy Brief no. 7. The Netherlands Scientific Council for Government Policy (WRR).

Brys, B. (2011). *Nontax compulsory payments as an additional burden on labour income*. OECD Taxation Working Papers No. 8. Organization for Economic Co-operation and Development.

Buchanan, J., & Tullock, G. (1962). *The calculus of consent. The logical foundations of constitutional democracy*. University of Michigan Press.

Bughin, J., Hazan, E., Labaye, E., Manyika, J., Dahlström, P., Ramaswamy, S., & Cochin de Billy, C. (2016). *Digital Europe: Pushing the frontier, capturing the benefits*. McKinsey Global Institute.

Buist, Y., de Bruin, S., Rijken, M., Lemmens, L., van Vooren, N., & Baan, C. (2018). *Vroegsignalering bij (kwetsbare) ouderen: wat is nodig om samenwerking te verbeteren?* National Institute for Public Health and the Environment (RIVM).

Buurman, B. M., Parlevliet, J. L., Allore, A. G., Blok, W., Van Deelen, B. A. J., Moll van Charante, E. P., De Haan, R. J., & De Rooij, S. J. (2016). Comprehensive geriatric assessment and transitional care in acutely hospitalized patients: The transitional care bridge randomized clinical trial. *JAMA Internal Medicine, 176*(3), 302–309. https://doi.org/10.1001/jamainternmed.2015.8042

Calabresi, G., & Bobbitt, P. (1978). *Tragic choices*. Norton and Co.

Callahan, D. (1973). The who definition of "Health". *The Hasting Center Studies, 1*(3), 77–87.

Carp, M., Kraal, A., de Bekker, P., Denee, L., & de Boer, A. (2018). *Effecten van het preferentiebeleid op beschikbaarheid van Geneesmiddelen*. Berenschot.

Carpenter, D. P. (2002). Groups, the media, agency waiting costs, and FDA drug approval. *American Journal of Political Science, 46*(3), 490–505.

CBS [Statistics Netherlands]. (2016). 'Gezondheid, relaties en werk belangrijker voor geluk dan geld'. Retrieved from: https://www.cbs.nl/nl-nl/nieuws/2016/11gezondheid-relaties-en-werk-belangrijker-voor-geluk-dan-geld

CBS [Statistics Netherlands]. (2018a). *Bevolkingsprognose 2017–2060*. Statistics Netherlands.
CBS [Statistics Netherlands]. (2018b). *Monitor langdurige zorg*. Statistics Netherlands.
CBS [Statistics Netherlands]. (2019a). *Jeugdhulp 2018*. Statistics Netherlands.
CBS [Statistics Netherlands]. (2019b). Aantal bewoners van verzorgings en verpleeghuizen 2019. Retrieved from: https://www.cbs.nl/nl-nl/maatwerk/2020/13/aan-tal-bewoners-van-verzorgings-en-verpleeghuizen-2019 [21th June 2021].
CBS [Statistics Netherlands]. (2020a). *De invloed van corona op onze levensverwachting, Statistische Trends, 25-9-2020*. Statistics Netherlands.
CBS [Statistics Netherlands]. (2020b). *Prognose levensverwachting 65jarigen: 20,82 jaar in 2026*'. Nieuwsbericht, 6th November 2020. Statistics Netherlands.
CBS [Statistics Netherlands]. (2020c). *Jaarrapport Integratie 2020*. Statistics Netherlands.
CBS [Statistics Netherlands]. (2020d). *Asiel en integratie 2020. Cohortonderzoek asielzoekers en statushouders*. Statistics Netherlands.
CBS [Statistics Netherlands]. (2020e). *Arbeidsmarktprofiel van zorg en welzijn. 3 Kenmerken branches zorg en welzijn, Statistische Trends 29-9-2020*. Statistics Netherlands.
CBS [Statistics Netherlands]. (2021). *Asiel en integratie 2021. Cohortonderzoek asielzoekers en statushouders*. Statistics Netherlands.
Chambers, D., Wilson, P., Thompson, C., & Harden, M. (2012). Social network analysis in healthcare settings: A systematic scoping review. *PLoS One, 7*(8), e41911.
Charlesworth, A. (2019). Measuring the productivity of the health care system. The experience of the United Kingdom. *OECD Journal on Budgeting, 19*(3), 131–150.
Coalitie Erbij. (2020). *Gevolgen van eenzaamheid*. Retrieved from: https://www.eenzaam.nl/over-eenzaamheid/83-gevolgen-van-eenzaamheid [24th August 2020].
Coast, J., Flynn, T. N., Natarajan, L., Sproston, K., Lewis, J., Louviere, J. J., & Peters, T. J. (2008). Valuing the ICECAP capability index for older people. *Social Science & Medicine, 67*(5), 874–882.
Cohen, J. T., Neumann, P. J., & Weinstein, M. C. (2008). Does preventive care save money? *New England Journal of Medicine, 358*, 661–663.
Cohen, I. G., Daniels, N., & Eyal, E. (2015). *Identified versus statistical lives. An interdisciplinary perspective*. Oxford University Press.
Commissie Dekker. (1987). *Bereidheid tot verandering*. Rapport van de Commissie Structuur en Financiering Gezondheidszorg.
Commissie Dunning. (1991). *Kiezen en delen: rapport van de commissie Keuzen in de zorg*. Ministerie van Welzijn, Volksgezondheid en Cultuur.
Commissie Toekomst zorg thuiswonende ouderen. (2020). *Advies Oud en Zelfstandig in 2030*. .
Commissie Van Dijkhuizen. (2013). *Naar een activerender belastingstelsel*. .
Commissie Werken in de Zorg. (2019). *Rapportage commissie Werken in de Zorg 2019. 'Behoud en innovatie als dé opgave'*. Commissie Werken in de Zorg.
Commissie Werken in de Zorg. (2020). *Behoud en betrokkenheid van zorgprofessionals*. Commissie Werken in de Zorg.
Commissie Willems. (1994). *Onderzoek besluitvorming volksgezondheid*. .
Companje, K. P. (2008). Verzekering van zorg 1943-2007: gezondheidszorg of sociale zekerheid? In K. P. Companje (Ed.), *Tussen volksverzekering en vrije markt. Verzekering van zorg op het snijvlak van sociale verzekering en gezondheidszorg 1880–2006. HiZ-reeks Geschiedenis Zorgverzekeringen 2*. (pp. 559–628). Aksant.
Companje, K. P., Hendriks, R. H. M., Veraghtert, K. F. E., & Widdershoven, B. (2009). Health insurance as governmental responsibility, 1850–1914. In K. P. Companje, R. H. M. Hendriks, K. F. E. Veraghtert, & B. Widdershoven (Eds.), *Two centuries of solidarity. German, Belgian, and Dutch social health insurance 1770–2008, History of Healthcare Insurance 3* (pp. 63–124). Amsterdam University Press.
Companje, K. P., Kappelhof, T., Mouton, R., & Jeurissen, R. (2018). *Vijftig jaar kostenbeheersing in de zorg. Deel I: 1966–1995*. Sdu Uitgevers.

Conrad, P. (2005). The shifting engines of medicalization. *Journal of Health and Social Behavior, 46*(3), 3–14.
Contandriopoulos, D. (2011). On the nature and strategies of organized interests in health care policy making. *Administration & Society, 43*(1), 45–65.
CPB [Netherlands Bureau for Economic Policy Analysis]. (2004). *Naar een schokbestendig pensioenstelsel*. CPB Netherlands Bureau for Economic Policy Analysis.
CPB [Netherlands Bureau for Economic Policy Analysis]. (2014). *Centraal Economisch Plan 2014*. CPB Netherlands Bureau for Economic Policy Analysis.
CPB [Netherlands Bureau for Economic Policy Analysis]. (2019). *Zorgen om Morgen, CPB Vergrijzingsstudie*. CPB Netherlands Bureau for Economic Policy Analysis.
CPB [Netherlands Bureau for Economic Policy Analysis]. (2020a). *Keuzes in kaart 2022–2025. Economische analyse van verkiezingsprogramma's*. CPB Netherlands Bureau for Economic Policy Analysis.
CPB [Netherlands Bureau for Economic Policy Analysis]. (2020b). *Zorgkeuzes in Kaart. Analyse van beleidsopties van politieke partijen voor de zorg*. CPB Netherlands Bureau for Economic Policy Analysis.
CPB [Netherlands Bureau for Economic Policy Analysis]. (2021). *Centraal Economisch Plan 2021*. CPB Netherlands Bureau for Economic Policy Analysis.
Cuijpers, P., & Beekman, A. T. F. (2018). Personaliseren van preventie van psychische stoornissen. *Tijdschrift voor Psychiatrie, 60*(3), 189–193.
Cuijpers, P., Pineda, B. S., Quero, S., Karyotaki, E., Struijs, S. Y., Figueroa, C. A., Llamas, J. A., Furukawa, T. A., & Muñoz, R. F. (2021). Psychological interventions to prevent the onset of depressive disorders: A meta-analysis of randomized controlled trials. *Clinical Psychology Review, 83*, 101955.
Damery, S., Flanagan, S., & Combes, G. (2016). Does integrated care reduce hospital activity for patients with chronic diseases? An umbrella review of systematic reviews. *BMJ OPEN, 6*, e011952. https://doi.org/10.1136/bmjopen-2016-011952
Daniels, N., & Sabin, J. E. (2008). *Setting limits fairly. Learning to share resources for health*. Oxford University Press.
de Blaeij, A., Van Gils, P., Suijkerbuijk, A., & De Wit, A. (2021). *Het potentieel van preventie*. Retrieved from: https://kosteneffectiviteitvanpreventie.nl/potentieel-van-preventie
de Blok, L., & Van der Brug, W. (2016). Beleidsevaluaties en politiek vertrouwen: wie houden burgers verantwoordelijk. In T. van der Meer & H. van der Kolk (Eds.), *Democratie dichtbij: Lokaal Kiezersonderzoek 2016, Stichting Kiezersonderzoek Nederland* (pp. 69–86). Ministry of the Interior and Kingdom Relations.
de Boer, H.-W., Jongen, E., & Kabátek, J. (2014). *The effectiveness of fiscal stimuli for working parents. CPB Discussion Paper 286*. CPB Netherlands Bureau for Economic Policy Analysis.
de Graaf, R., ten Have, M., & Van Dorsselaer, S. (2010). *De psychische gezondheid van de Nederlandse bevolking*. Trimbos instituut.
de Haan, I., & Duyvendak, J. W. (Eds.). (2002). *In het hart van de verzorgingsstaat. Het Ministerie van Maatschappelijk Werk en zijn opvolgers (CRM, WVC, VWS), 1952–2002*. Walburg Pers.
de Jong, A., & Kooiker, S. (2018). *Regionale ontwikkelingen in het aantal potentiële helpers van oudere ouderen tussen 1975–2040*. Planbureau voor de Leefomgeving.
de Klerk, M. (1997). Het gebruik van ADLhulpmiddelen door ouderen. In *Een onderzoek naar determinanten en substitutiemogelijkheden*. Dissertatie. Universiteit Utrecht.
de Klerk, M., Verbeek-Oudijk, D., Plaisier, I., & den Draak, M. (2019). *Zorgen voor thuiswonende ouderen. Kennissynthese over de zorg voor zelfstandig wonende 75plussers, knelpunten en toekomstige ontwikkelingen*. The Netherlands Institute for Social Research (SCP).
de Wit, A., Visscher, K., Over, E., van Gelder, N., Everaars, B., van Gils, P., & Voogt, C. (2021). *Minimum Unit Pricing voor alcohol. Onderzoek naar de haalbaarheid van invoering in Nederland*. RIVM-rapport 2021-0014. National Institute for Public Health and the Environment.
de Witt, S. (2019). *Solidariteit in de gezondheidszorg; opvattingen over zorgpremie en leefstijl*. Statistics Netherlands (CBS).

Dekker, P., & Den Ridder, J. (2019). *Burgerperspectieven 2019 | 1, Continu Onderzoek Burgerperspectieven*. The Netherlands Institute for Social Research (SCP).

Dekker, P., Den Ridder, J., Van Houwelingen, P., & Kooiker, M. M. V. S. (2016). *Zorg en onbehagen in de bevolking*. The Netherlands Institute for Social Research (SCP).

den Ridder, J., et al. (2019). *Continu Onderzoek Burgerperspectieven. Zorgen om Zorg*. The Netherlands Institute for Social Research (SCP).

Dethlefs, N., & Martin, B. (2006). Japanese technology policy for aged care. *Science and Public Policy, 33*, 47–57.

DNB [De Nederlandsche Bank]. (2021, June). *Economische Ontwikkelingen en Vooruitzichten*. De Nederlandsche Bank.

Dols, W. P. M., & Kerkhoff, A. H. M. (2008). De Algemene Wet Bijzondere Ziektekosten vanaf 1987. In K. P. Companje (Ed.), *Tussen volksverzekering en vrije markt. Verzekering van zorg op het snijvlak van sociale verzekering en gezondheidszorg 1880–2006, HiZ-reeks Geschiedenis Zorgverzekeringen 2* (pp. 795–880). Aksant.

Douven, R., Diepstraten, M., Kopányi-Peuker, A., Van Dulmen, S., Stadhouders, N., Wackers, E., Jeurissen, P., Wijnker, G., & Mikkers, M. (2020). *Evaluatie programma's Beatrixziekenhuis en Bernhoven. CPB Policy Brief*. Netherlands Bureau for Economic Policy Analysis.

Dowding, K. (2015). Albert O. Hirschman, exit, voice and loyalty: Responses to decline in firms, organizations, and states. In S. J. Balla, M. Lodge, & E. Page (Eds.), *The Oxford handbook of classics in public policy and administration* (pp. 256–271). Oxford University Press.

Doyle, O., Harmon, C. P., Heckman, J. J., & Tramblay, R. E. (2009). Investing in early human development: Timing and economic efficiency. *Economics & Human Biology, 7*(1), 1–6.

Elbert, N. J., van Os-Medendorp, H., van Renselaar, W., Ekeland, A. G., Hakkaart-van Roijen, L., Raat, H., Nijsten, T. E., & Pasmans, S. G. (2014). Effectiveness and cost-effectiveness of ehealth interventions in somatic diseases: A systematic review of systematic reviews and meta-analyses. *Journal of Medical Internet Research, 16*(4), E110. https://doi.org/10.2196/jmir.2790

Emanuel, E., Steinmetz, H., & Schmidt, A. (2018). *Rationing and resource allocation in healthcare*. Oxford University Press.

Enzing, J. J., Knies, S., Boer, B., & Brouwer, W. B. F. (2020, August 6). Broadening the application of health technology assessment in The Netherlands: A worth-while destination but not an easy ride? *Health Economics, Policy and Law, 16*(4), 1–17.

Érdi, P. (2008). *Complexity explained*. Springer.

Esping-Andersen, G. (1990). *The three worlds of welfare capitalism*. Princeton University Press.

Eurofound. (2019). *Quality of health and care services in the EU*. Publications Office of the European Union.

European Commission. (2010). *Commission staff working document on an action plan for the EU Health workforce*. European Commission.

Euro-Peristat Project. (2018). *European perinatal Health report. Core indicators of the health and care of pregnant women and babies in Europe in 2015*. Euro-Peristat.

FD [*Financieel Dagblad*]. (2020, February 13). D66-plan voor tijdelijke arbeidsmigratie weggehoond. *Financieel Dagblad*.

Federatie Medisch Specialisten & Koninklijke Nederlandsche Maatschappij ter Bevordering der Geneeskunst. (2020). *Draaiboek Triage op basis van nietmedische overwegingen voor ICopname ten tijde van fase 3 in de Covid19 pandemie. Criteria voor fase 3 stap C aansluitend op het NVIC Draaiboek Pandemie*.

Ferlie, E., Fitzgerald, L., Mcgivern, S., Dobson, S., & Bennett, C. (2011). Public policy networks and 'wicked problems': A nascent solution? *Public Administration, 89*(2), 307–324.

Fleck, L. M. (2009). *Just caring. Health care rationing and democratic deliberation*. Oxford University Press.

Fredriksson, M., Gustafsson, I.-B., & Winblad, U. (2019). Cuts without conflict: The use of political strategy in local health system retrenchment in Sweden. *Social Science and Medicine, 237*, 112464.

Friele, R. D., Hageraats, R., Fermin, A., Bouwman, R., & van der Zwaan, J. (2019). *De jeugdGGZ na de Jeugdwet: een onderzoek naar knelpunten en kansen*. Nivel/Nederlands Jeugdinstituut.

Gallardo, C. (2021, January 14). 8 reasons the UK leads Europe's coronavirus vaccination race. *Politico Europe*.

Garland, D. (2015). The welfare state: A fundamental dimension of modern government. *European Journal of Sociology, 55*, 327–364.

Garpenby, P., & Nedlund, A. (2016). Political strategies in difficult times – The "backstage" experience of Swedish politicians on formal priority setting in healthcare. *Science and Medicine, 163*, 63–70. https://doi.org/10.1016/j.socscimed.2016.06.046

Getzen, T. E. (2000). Health care is an individual necessity and a national luxury: Applying multilevel decision models to the analysis of health care expenditures. *Journal of Health Economics, 19*, 259–270.

Gezondheidsraad [The Health Council of the Netherlands]. (1991). *Medisch handelen op een tweesprong*. The Health Council of the Netherlands.

Gezondheidsraad [The Health Council of the Netherlands]. (2007). *Preconceptiezorg: voor een goed begin*. The Health Council of the Netherlands.

Gezondheidsraad [The Health Council of the Netherlands]. (2014). *ADHD: medicatie en maatschappij. Publication no. 2014/19*. The Health Council of the Netherlands.

Gezondheidsraad [The Health Council of the Netherlands]. (2020). *45minutennorm in de spoedzorg. advies no. 2020/17*. The Health Council of the Netherlands.

GFK. (2017). *Good life factors*. Global GfK Survey.

Gibbels, M. (2012, February 6). Zorgverzekeraars: eHealth sneller invoeren. *Zorgvisie*. Retrieved from: https://www.zorgvisie.nl/zorgverzekeraars-ehealth-sneller-invoeren-zvs013252w/

Giudici, K. V., de Souto Barreto, P., Soriano, G., Rolland, Y., & Vella, B. (2019). Defining vitality: Associations of three operational definitions of vitality with disability in instrumental activities of daily living and frailty among elderly over a 3-year follow-up (MAPT study). *Journal of Nutrition, Health and Aging, 23*(4), 386–392.

Goetzel, R. Z. (2009). Do prevention or treatment services save money? The wrong debate. *Health Affairs, 28*(1), 37–41.

Goudriaan, R., & Heida, J.-P. (2015). *Transitiekosten van stelselwijzigingen in de zorg*. Strategies in Regulated Markets b.v.

Goudswaard, C., Beetsma, R. M. J. W., Nijman, T. E., & Schnabel, P. (2010). *Een sterke tweede pijler. Naar een toekomstbestendig stelsel van aanvullende pensioenen*. Rapport van de Commissie Toekomstbestendigheid aanvullende pensioenregelingen.

Groot, W., & Van Sloten, F. (2012). Grenzen aan leefstijlsolidariteit. In F. T. Schut & M. Varkevisser (Eds.), *Een economische gezonde gezondheidszorg. KVS Preadviezen 2012* (pp. 89–107). Sdu Uitgevers.

Ham, C., & Coulter, A. (2001). Explicit and implicit rationing: Taking responsibility and avoiding blame for health care choices. *Journal of Health Services Research & Policy, 6*(3), 163–169.

Hansen, J., Arts, W., & Muffels, R. (2005). Solidair tegen (w)elke prijs? Een quasi-experimenteel onderzoek naar de voorkeuren van Nederlanders voor ruimere of beperkte pakketten in de zorgverzekering. *Sociale Wetenschappen, 48*(1/2), 61–84.

Hauck, K., Smith, P. C., & Goddard, M. (2004). *The economics of priority setting for health care: A literature review, health, nutrition and population discussion paper*. World Bank.

Haverkamp, B., Verweij, M., & Stronks, K. (2017). 'Gezondheid': voor iedere context een passend begrip? *Tijdschrift Voor Gezondheidswetenschappen, 95*(6), 258–263.

Hcaam. (2018). *Contribution à la Stratégie de transformation de notre système de santé*. Haut Conseil pour l'Avenir de l'Assurance Maladie.

Helderman, J. K., Schut, F. T., van der Grinten, T. E. D., & van de Ven, W. P. M. M. (2005). Market-oriented health care reforms and Policy learning in The Netherlands. *Journal of Health Politics, Policy and Law, 30*(1–2), 189–209.

Herrmann, F. R., Michel, J. P., & Robine, J. M. (2010). Worldwide decline in the oldest old support ratio. *European Geriatric Medicine, 1*, 3–8.

Hilbers-Modderman, E. S. M., & de Bruijn, A. C. P. (2013). *Domotica in de langdurige zorg—Inventarisatie van technieken en risico's: Handreiking voor risicobeheersing door zorgaanbieders*. National Institute for Public Health and the Environment.

Hirschman, A. O. (1970). *Exit, voice, and loyalty: Responses to decline in firms, organizations, and states*. Harvard University Press.

Holst, L., Brabers, A., & de Jong, J. (2020). *Infographic. Barometer Solidariteit – Update met cijfers uit 2019*. Nivel.

Holt-Lunstad, J., Smith, T. B., Baker, M., Harris, T., & Stephenson, D. (2015). Loneliness and social isolation as risk factors for mortality: A meta-analytic review. *Perspectives on Psychological Science, 10*, 227–237.

Honigsbaum, F., Calltorp, J., Ham, C. & Holmström, S. (1995). Priority setting processes for healthcare. . CRC Press.

Houte de Lange, S. (2021, June 29). Waarom de huidige preventieve jeugdzorg niet werkt. *Zorgvisie*. Retrieved from: https://www.zorgvisie.nl/waarom-de-huidige-preventieve-jeugdzorg-niet-werkt/

Huber, M., Knottnerus, J.A., Green, L., Horst, H. van der, Jadad, A.R., Kromhout, D., Leonard, B., Lorig, K., Loureiro, M.I., van der Meer, J.W.M., Schnabel, P., Smith, R., van Weel, C., & Smid, H. (2011). 'How should we define health?'. BMJ 343:D4163. DOI: https://doi.org/10.1136/bmj.d4163.

Hult, K. J., Jaffe, S., & Philipson, T. J. (2018). How does technological change affect quality-adjusted prices in health care? Systematic evidence from thousands of innovations. *American Journal of Health Economics, 4*(4), 433–425.

Hussem, A., Wouterse, B., & Aalbers, R. (2021). Betere risicospreiding van eigen bijdragen bij verpleeghuiszorg. *De actuaris*, June 2021, 36–38. Retrieved from: https://www.ag-ai.nl/view/48496-DA-28-5-art-Hussem%2BWouterse%2BAalbers.pdf

ICT & Health. (2021). VGZ: Zorgaanbieders nemen digitale initiatieven vaker over. Retrieved from: https://www.icthealth.nl/nieuws/vgz-zorgaanbieders-nemen-digitale-initiatieven-vaker-over/ [28 June 2021].

IGJ [Health and Youth Care Inspectorate]. (2018). *Wachttijden in de GGZ: verbeterkansen vooral in samenwerking op regionaal niveau*. Inspectie voor Gezondheidszorg en Jeugd.

IGJ [Health and Youth Care Inspectorate]. (2020a). *Meer samenhang en continuïteit in zorg nodig voor mensen met chronisch psychische aandoeningen*. Inspectie voor Gezondheidszorg en Jeugd.

IGJ [Health and Youth Care Inspectorate]. (2020b). *Verpleging, verzorging en thuiszorg tijdens de coronacrisis*. Inspectie voor Gezondheidszorg en Jeugd.

IGJ [Health and Youth Care Inspectorate]. (2021). *De coronacrisis: de zorg en de jeugdhulp blijvend onder druk. Beelden van de Inspectie Gezondheidszorg en Jeugd*. Inspectie voor Gezondheidszorg en Jeugd.

IGJ [Health and Youth Care Inspectorate] & Inspectie Justitie en Veiligheid [The Inspectorate of Justice and Security]. (2019). *Kwetsbare kinderen onvoldoende beschermd Toezicht bij de jeugdbescherming en jeugdreclassering*. Inspectie voor Gezondheidszorg en Jeugd.

IGJ [Health and Youth Care Inspectorate] & NZa [The Dutch Healthcare Authority]. (2020). *Brief IGJ en NZa over aanpak wachttijden GGZ*. Inspectie voor Gezondheidszorg en Jeugd & Nederlandse Zorgautoriteit.

ILO [International Labour Office]. (2019). *The future of work in the health sector 2018*. Working paper no. 325. International Labour Office.

ING. (2019). *Digitale ziekenhuiszorg*. Retrieved from: https://www.ing.nl/media/ING_EBZ_digitale-ziekenhuiszorg_tcm162-180669.pdf

Inspectie der Rijksfinanciën. (2020). *Naar een toekomstbestendig zorgstelsel*. Inspectie der Rijksfinanciën. Kamerstukken II 2019/2020, 32 359, no. 4.

Inspectie voor de Gezondheidszorg. (2014). *De Jeugdgezondheidszorg beter in positie*. Inspectie voor de Gezondheidszorg.

Intelligence Group. (2019). *Arbeidsmarkt Zorg in Cijfers 2019/2020*. Intelligence Group.

Ishiguro, N. (2018). Care robots in Japanese elderly care. Cultural values in focus. In K. Christensen & D. Pilling (Eds.), *The Routledge handbook of social care work around the world*. Routledge.
Jacobs, A. M. (2012). *Governing for the long term. Democracy and the politics of investment*. Cambridge University Press.
Jacobs, B. (2015). *De Prijs van Gelijkheid*. Prometheus/Bert Bakker.
Jacobs, A. M. (2016). Policy making for the long term in advanced democracies. *Annual Review of Political Science, 19*, 433–455.
Jeurissen, P. P. T. (2005). *Houdbare solidariteit in de gezondheidszorg, RVZ Signalement 05/02*. The Council of Public Health & Society.
Jeurissen, P. P. T. (2016). *Steeds meer zorg, een betaalbare oplossing?. Oratie*. Radboud Universiteit.
Jeurissen, P., Maarse, M., & Tanke, M. (2018). *Betaalbare zorg*. Sdu Uitgevers.
Jongen, E., Mastrogiacomo, M., & Ter Weel, B. (2011). *Hoe prikkelbaar zijn Nederlanders?. CPB Policy Brief 2011/14*. Centraal Planbureau.
Jongen, E., de Boer, H. W., & Dekker, P. (2015). *De effectiviteit van fiscaal participatiebeleid. CPB Policy Brief 2015/2*. Centraal Planbureau.
Jordà, Ò., Schularick, M., & Taylor, A. M. (2016). Macrofinancial history and the new business cycle facts. *NBER Macroeconomics Annual, 31*, 213–263.
Joumard, I., André, C., & Nicq, C. (2010). *Health care systems: Efficiency and institutions*. OECD Economics Department Working Papers no. 769. Organisation for Economic Co-operation and Development.
Jung, H. P., Laurant, M., & Van Asten, C. (2019). Zinnige zorg dreigt utopie te worden Limburgse Afferden zit ingeklemd tussen tegenstrijdige eisen. *Medisch Contact*. Retrieved from: https://www.medischcontact.nl/nieuws/laatste-nieuws/artikel/zinnige-zorg-dreigt-utopie-te-worden.htm [28 June 2021].
Kamerstukken II [Parliamentary papers] 1965/66, 8462, no. 1.
Kamerstukken II [Parliamentary papers] 1997–1998, 25 170, no. 6.
Kamerstukken II [Parliamentary papers] 2000–2001, 27 488, no. 1 *Actieplan Zorg Verzekerd*.
Kamerstukken II [Parliamentary papers] 2003–2004, 25 170, no. 35.
Kamerstukken II [Parliamentary papers] 2006–2007, 31 094, no. 3.
Kamerstukken II [Parliamentary papers] 2009–2010, 32 393, no. 3 Wijziging van de Wet marktordening gezondheidszorg en enkele andere wetten in verband met de aanvulling met instrumenten voor bekostiging.
Kamerstukken II [Parliamentary papers] 2012–2013, 30 597, no. 296.
Kamerstukken II [Parliamentary papers] 2013–2014, 33 841, no. 3 Memorie van toelichting Wet maatschappelijke ondersteuning 2015.
Kamerstukken II [Parliamentary papers], 2013–2014, 33 891, no. 3 Memorie van toelichting Wet langdurige zorg.
Kamerstukken II [Parliamentary papers] 2019a, 31 839, no. 730.
Kamerstukken II [Parliamentary papers] 2019b, 32 359, no. 4.
Kannampallil, T. G., Schauer, G. F., Cohen, T., & Patel, V. L. (2011). Considering complexity in healthcare systems. *Journal of Biomedical Informatics, 44*(6), 943–947.
Kappelhof, T. (2004). "Omdat het historisch gegroeid is". De Londense Commissie-Van Rhijn en de ontwikkeling van de sociale verzekeringen in Nederland (1937–1952). *Tijdschrift voor Sociale en Economische Geschiedenis, 1*(2), 71–91.
Kennedy, S., Kidd, M. P., McDonald, J. T., & Biddle, N. (2015). The healthy immigrant effect: Patterns and evidence from four countries. *Journal of International Migration and Integration, 16*, 317–332.
Kersten, K., van Dijk, T., Hogervorst, W., Muselaers, N., & Nissen, R. (2021, January 26). Niet kiezen in de begroting, is kiezen voor meer zorg en minder onderwijs. *ESB*.
Kiers, B. (2019, February 20). Zorgverzekeraars moeten congruent gedrag vertonen. *Zorgvisie*. Retrieved from: https://www.zorgvisie.nl/zorgverzekeraars-moeten-congruent-gedrag-vertonen/

Kiers, B. (2021, January 27). Politiek gaat bij de arts op schoot. *Zorgvisie*. Retrieved from: https://www.zorgvisie.nl/politiek-gaat-bij-arts-op-schoot/

Killingsworth, M. R., & Heckman, J. J. (1987). Female labor supply: A survey. In O. Ashenfelter & R. Layard (Eds.), *Handbook of labor economics* (Vol. 1, pp. 103–204). North Holland.

KNMP Farmanco Geneesmiddelentekorten 2017.

Kooijman, M., Brabers, A., & de Jong, J. (2018). *Solidariteit in de Zorg. Een onderzoek naar de bereidheid om voor anderen te betalen onder de algemene bevolking in 2013, 2015 en 2017*. Nivel.

Kooiker, S. (2011). *Nederlanders aan het woord over gezondheid en gezond leven, achtergrondrapport bij de Volksgezondheid Toekomst Verkenning 2010. Van gezond naar beter*. National Institute for Public Health and the Environment (RIVM)/The Netherlands Institute for Social Research (SCP).

Kooiker, S., de Klerk, M., ter Berg, J., & Schothorst, Y. (2012). *Meebetalen aan de zorg. Nederlanders over solidariteit en betaalbaarheid van de zorg*. The Netherlands Institute for Social Research (SCP).

Kooiker, S., de Jong, A., Verbeek-Oudijk, D., & de Boer, A. (2019). *Toekomstverkenning mantelzorg aan ouderen. Een verkenning van de regionale ontwikkelingen voor de komende 20 jaar*. The Netherlands Institute for Social Research (SCP).

Koolman, X., & Wouterse, B. (2021, June 15th). 'Bezuinigen' op de zorg, een verwarrend begrip. *Zorgvisie*. Retrieved from: https://www.zorgvisie.nl/bezuinigen-op-de-zorg/

KPMG & Vektis. (2018). *Monitor generalistische basis GGZ*. KPMG & Vektis.

Kromhout, M., van Echtelt, P., & Feijten, P. (2020). *Sociaal Domein op koers. Verwachtingen en resultaten van vijf jaar decentraal beleid*. The Netherlands Institute for Social Research (SCP).

Kruse, F. (2018). Focusklinieken en betaalbaarheid. In P. Jeurissen, H. Maarse, & M. Tanke (Eds.), *Betaalbare Zorg* (pp. 259–276). Sdu Uitgevers.

Kruse, F., Jeurissen, P., Abma, T., Bendien, E., Wallenburg, I., & van de Bovenkamp, H. (2021). *Houdbare ouderenzorg. Ervaringen en lessen uit andere landen*. WRR Working paper no. 42. The Netherlands Scientific Council for Government Policy (WRR).

Landwehr, C. (2016). Strategic institutional design: Two case studies of non-majoritarian agencies in health care priority-setting. *Government and Opposition, 51*(4), 632–660.

Landwehr, C., & Bohm, K. (2011). Delegation and institutional design in health-care rationing. *Governance: An International Journal of Policy, Administration, and Institutions, 24*(4), 665–688.

Lee, S., & Kim, C. (2018). Estimation of association between healthcare system efficiency and policy factors for public health. *Applied Sciences, 8*(12), 2674.

Leenen, J. P. L., Leerentveld, C., van Dijk, J. D., van Westreenen, H. L., Schoonhoven, L., & Patijn, G. A. (2020). Current evidence for continuous vital signs monitoring by wearable wireless devices in hospitalized adults: Systematic review. *Journal of Medical Internet Research, 22*(6), e18636.

LHV. (2021). *Handreiking Meer Tijd voor de Patiënt*. Landelijke Huisartsenvereniging.

Licher, S., Heshmatollah, A., van der Willik, K. D., Stricker, B. H. C., Ruiter, R., de Roos, E. W., Lahousse, L., Koudstaal, P. J., Hofman, A., Fani, L., Brusselle, G. G. O., Bos, D., Arshi, B., Kavousi, M., Leening, M. J. G., Kamran Ikram, M., & Arfan Ikram, M. (2019). Lifetime risk and multimorbidity of non-communicable diseases and disease-free life expectancy in the general population: A population-based cohort study. *PLoS Medicine, 16*(2), E1002741.

Lipsitz, L. A. (2012). Understanding health care as a complex system: The foundation for unintended consequences. *Journal of the American Association, 308*(3), 243–244.

Looman, W. M., Huijsman, R., & Natalina Fabbricotti, I. (2019). The (cost-)effectiveness of preventive, integrated care for community- dwelling frail older people: A systematic review. *Health & Social Care in the Community, 27*, 1–30.

Lubbers, M., & Gijsberts, M. (2019). Changes in self-rated health right after immigration: A panel study of economic, social, cultural, and emotional explanations of self-rated health among immigrants in The Netherlands. *Frontiers in Sociology, 4*, 1–13.

Maarse, H., & Jeurissen, P. (2019). Low institutional trust in health insurers in Dutch health care. *Health Policy, 123*(3), 288–292.
Maarse, H., Jeurissen, P., & Ruwaard, D. (2016). Results of the market-oriented reform in The Netherlands: A review. *Health Economics, Policy and Law, 11*, 161–178.
Mackenbach, J. (2020). A history of population health. *Rise and fall of disease in Europe*. Clio Medica Online (ebook).
Marino, A., & Lorenzoni, L. (2019). *The impact of technological advancements on health spending*. OECD Health Working Papers no. 113. Organisation for Economic Co-operation and Development.
Martínez-García, M., & Hernández-Lemus, E. (2013). Health systems as complex systems. *American Journal of Operations Research, 3*, 113–126.
Masic, I., Sivic, S., Toromanovic, S., Borojevic, T., & Pandza, H. (2012). Social networks in improvement of health care. *Materia Sociomedica, 24*(1), 48–53.
Mastrogiacomo, M., Bosch, N., Gielen, M., & Jongen, E. (2011). *Estimating labour supply responses in The Netherlands using structural models. Achtergronddocument bij CPB Policy Brief 2011/14*. Netherlands Bureau for Economic Policy Analysis (CPB).
Maybin, R., & Klein, J. (2012). *Thinking about rationing*. The King's Fund.
Mckie, J., & Richardson, J. (2003). The rule of rescue. *Social Science and Medicine, 56*(12), 2407–2419.
McKinsey Global Institute. (2016). *Digital Europe: Pushing the frontier, capturing the benefits*. Retrieved from: https://www.mckinsey.com/~/media/mckinsey/business%20functions/mckinsey%20digital/our%20insights/digital%20europe%20pushing%20the%20frontier%20capturing%20the%20benefits/digitaleurope-full-re-port-june-2016.ashx
McKinsey Global Institute. (2018). *Het potentieel pakken: de waarde van meer gelijkheid tussen mannen en vrouwen op de Nederlandse arbeidsmarkt*. Retrieved from: https://www.mckinsey.com/~/media/McKinsey/Featured%20Insights/Europe/The%20power%20of%20parity%20Advancing%20gender%20equality%20in%20the%20Dutch%20labor%20market/MGIPower-of-Parity-Nederland-September-2018-DUTCH.ashx
Medisch Contact. (2018). Administratielast: Laat dokters dokteren. Retrieved from: https://www.medischcontact.nl/nieuws/laatste-nieuws/artikel/administratielast-laat-dokters-dokteren.htm
Meersma, K., Roozendaal, B., & Rijken, J. (2021). *Juridisch onderzoek naar de overstap van vrijgevestigde medisch specialisten naar loondienst*. Akd Benelux Lawyers.
Menzis. (2020). *Nota 'Samenwerken aan gezonde regio's'. Een nieuw ontwerp voor de rol van de regio en preventie in het gezondheidszorgstelsel*. Menzis.
Meurs, M., Keuper, J., Sankatsing, V., Batenburg, R., & van Tuyl, L. (2020a). *De rol van ehealth in de organisatie van zorg op afstand in coronatijd. Perspectieven van huisartsen, consumenten en patiënten*. Nivel.
Meurs, M., Sankatsing, V., de Jong, J., & van Tuyl, L. H. D. (2020b). *Perceptie van de Nederlandse bevolking op digitale toepassingen in de zorg tijdens de coronapandemie. Organisatie van zorg op afstand in coronatijd*. Nivel.
Minister van Volksgezondheid, Welzijn en Sport [The Minister of Health, Welfare and Sport]. (2018a, April 9th). *Brief Verzoek WRR—onderzoek naar betaalbaarheid zorg*. Retrieved from: https://www.wrr.nl/adviesprojecten/houdbarezorg/documenten/brieven/2018/04/09/adviesaanvraag-toekomst-zorgkosten
Minister van Volksgezondheid, Welzijn en Sport [The Minister of Health, Welfare and Sport]. (2018b). *Brief aan de Voorzitter van de Tweede Kamer, d.d. 19-07-2018*. The Ministry of Health, Welfare and Sport.
Ministerie van Financiën [The Ministry of Finance]. (2019). *Marginale druk: op het randje van de mogelijkheden*. The Ministry of Finance.
Ministerie van Financiën [The Ministry of Finance]. (2020a). *Syntheserapport Bouwstenen voor een Beter Belastingstelsel*. The Ministry of Finance.
Ministerie van Financiën [The Ministry of Finance]. (2020b). *Gezondheidsgerelateerde Belastingen*. The Ministry of Finance.

Ministerie van Volksgezondheid, Welzijn en Sport [The Ministry of Health, Welfare and Sport]. (2002). *Geconcentreerd dereguleren? Onderzoeksnotitie naar bestaande concentraties en machtsposities in de zorg*. The Ministry of Health, Welfare and Sport.

Ministerie van Volksgezondheid, Welzijn en Sport [The Ministry of Health, Welfare and Sport]. (2020). *Stand van zaken geboortezorg 2020 – aanbevelingen voor de toekomst*. The Ministry of Health, Welfare and Sport.

Ministerie van Volksgezondheid Welzijn en Sport [The Ministry of Health, Welfare and Sport]. (2021). *Dialoognota Ouder Worden 2020–2040*. The Ministry of Health, Welfare and Sport.

Mistry, H. (2012). Systematic review of studies of the cost-effectiveness of telemedicine and telecare. Changes in the economic evidence over twenty years. *Journal of Telemedicine and Telecare, 18*(1), 1–6.

Mori, A. R., Dandi, R., Mazzeo, M., Verbiaro, R., & Mercurio, G. (2012). *Technological solutions potentially influencing the future of longterm care*. ENEPRI Research Report no. 114. CEPS.

Mueller, M., Hagenaars, L., & Morgan, D. (2017). *Administrative spending in OECD health care systems: Where is the fat, and can it be trimmed?* Organisation for Economic Co-operation and Development.

NCJ. (2012). Richtlijn: Overgewicht. Retrieved from: https://www.ncj.nl/richtlijnen/alle-richtlijnen/richtlijn/?richtlijn=10&rlpag=675 [21 June 2021].

Nederlandse Vereniging voor Intensive Care. (2020). Draaiboek Pandemie Deel 1, Versie 1.2, March 2020.

NFK (2018). 'Agenda Oncologische Netwerkzorg 2019–2022'. Nieuwsbericht Nederlandse Federatie van Kankerpatientenorganisaties. Retrieved from: https://nfk.nl/nieuws/agenda-oncologische-netwerk-zorg-2019-2022 [28 June, 2021].

NFU. (2020). Raamplan Arstenopleiding. Nederlandse Federatie van Universitair Medische Centra. Retrieved from: https://www.nfu.nl/sites/default/files/202008/20.1577_Raamplan_Artsenopleiding_-_maart_2020.pdf

Nictiz & Nivel. (2019). *Samen aan zet: eHealthmonitor 2019*. Nictiz/Nivel.

NIDI [The Netherlands Interdisciplinary Demographic Institute] & CBS [Statistics Netherlands]. (2020). *Bevolking 2050 in beeld: drukker, diverser en dubbelgrijs*. Nederlands Interdisciplinair Demografisch Instituut & Statistics Netherlands (CBS).

NIDI [The Netherlands Interdisciplinary Demographic Institute] & CBS [Statistics Netherlands]. (2021). *Bevolking 2050 in beeld: opleiding, arbeid, zorg en wonen*. Nederlands Interdisciplinair Demografisch Instituut & Statistics Netherlands (CBS).

Nielsen, S. S., & Krasnik, A. (2010). Poorer self-perceived health among migrants and ethnic minorities versus the majority population in Europe: A systematic review. *International Journal of Public Health, 55*, 357–371.

Nieuwenhuis, D. (2018). *Rapport meldactie 'Gemeenteraadsverkiezingen'*. Patiëntenfederatie Nederland/Ieder(in)/Mind, Landelijke Platform Psychische Gezondheid.

Nivel & Prismant. (2019). *Zicht op regionale capaciteit en arbeidsmarktvraagstukken huisartsenzorg. Factsheets*. Nivel, Prismant.

NJI [Netherlands Youth Institute]. (2021). *Overgewicht Probleemschets Risicofactoren*. Retrieved from: https://www.nji.nl/Overgewicht-Probleemschets-Risicofactoren [21 June 2021].

NOS. (2020). 'Protesterende suïcidale vrouw spreekt met Blokhuis, maar zet actie door'. Retrieved from: https://nos.nl/artikel/2319473-protesteren-de-suicidale-vrouw-spreekt-met-blokhuis-maar-zet-actie-door.html [28 June 2021].

NZA [The Dutch Healthcare Authority]. (2016). *Kwantitatief onderzoek naar risicoselectie en risicosolidariteit op de zorgverzekeringsmarkt*. Nederlandse Zorgautoriteit.

NZA [The Dutch Healthcare Authority]. (2018a). *Monitor zorg voor ouderen 2018*. Nederlandse Zorgautoriteit.

NZA [The Dutch Healthcare Authority]. (2018b). *Monitor Zorgverzekeringen 2018*. Nederlandse Zorgautoriteit.

NZA [The Dutch Healthcare Authority]. (2019a). *Monitor Transformatiegelden medisch-specialistische zorg*. Nederlandse Zorgautoriteit.

NZA [The Dutch Healthcare Authority]. (2019b). *Monitor Taakherschikking*. Nederlandse Zorgautoriteit.
NZA [The Dutch Healthcare Authority]. (2020a). *Stimuleren van passende zorg en digitale zorg*. Nederlandse Zorgautoriteit.
NZA [The Dutch Healthcare Authority]. (2020b). *Monitor geneesmiddelen in de medisch-specialistische zorg 2020*. Retrieved from: https://puc.overheid.nl/nza/doc/PUC_305909_22/1/
NZA [The Dutch Healthcare Authority]. (2021). *Kerncijfers GGZ*. Retrieved from: https://www.nza.nl/zorgsecto-ren/geestelijke-gezondheidszorg-ggz-en-forensische-zorg-fz/kerncijfers-geestelijke-gezondheidszorg-ggz [3 June 2021].
OECD. (2010). *Health care systems: Getting more value for money*. OECD Economics Department Policy Notes, No. 2. Organisation for Economic Co-operation and Development.
OECD. (2015a). *Fiscal sustainability of health systems: Bridging health and finance perspectives*. Organisation for Economic Co-operation and Development.
OECD. (2015b). *Health data governance privacy, monitoring and research*. Organisation for Economic Co-operation and Development.
OECD. (2017). *Health at a glance. OECD indicators 2017*. Organisation for Economic Co-operation and Development.
OECD. (2018). *Health at a glance: Europe 2018. State of Health in the EU cycle*. Organisation for Economic Co-operation and Development.
OECD. (2019a). *Health division projections*. OECD Health working paper no. 110 Health spending projections to 2030. Organisation for Economic Co-operation and Development.
OECD. (2019b). *Health at a glance 2019: OECD indicators*. OECD Publishing. Retrieved from: https://doi.org/10.1787/4dd50c09-en
OECD. (2019c). *Recent trends in international migration of doctors, nurses and medical students*. OECD Publishing. Retrieved from: https://doi.org/10.1787/5571ef48-en
OECD. (2019d). *Digitalisation and productivity: A story of complementaries*. OECD Publishing. Retrieved from: https://www.oecd.org/economy/growth/digitalisation-productivity-and-inclusiveness/
OECD. (2020). *Innovative citizen participation and new democratic institutions catching the deliberative wave*. Organisation for Economic Co-operation and Development.
OECD. (2021). *Taxing wages, 2019–2020, nontax compulsory payments as an additional burden on labour income in 2020*. Organisation for Economic Co-operation and Development.
OECD, Eurostat, & WHO. (2017). *A system of Health accounts*. Organisation for Economic Co-operation and Development.
Okma, G. H. (1997). *Studies on Dutch Health politics, policies and law* (diss. Universiteit Utrecht 1997).
Olson, M. (1971). *The logic of collective action: Public goods and the theory of groups*. Harvard University Press.
Omtzigt, P. H., & Slootweg, E. J. (2018). *Kamervragen een brede open studie naar het zorgstelsel en de zorgkosten*, 2018Z03565. The Hague.
Oosterkamp, H., de Bekker, P., Carp, M., & Koppers, G. (2021). *Een sluis voor toelating van MedTech middelen: een goed idee? Onderzoek naar de toegevoegde waarde van een sluis voor toelating van (dure) MedTech middelen*. Berenschot.
Pammolli, F., Riccaboni, M., & Magazzini, L. (2008). *The sustainability of European Health Care systems: Beyond income and aging*. Working paper no. 52/2008. University of Verona.
PBL, & CBS. (2019). *Regionale bevolkings en huishoudensprognose 2016–2040*. Netherlands Environmental Assessment Agency (PBL) & Statistics Netherlands (CBS).
Pell, D., Mytton, O., Penney, T. L., Briggs, A., Cummins, S., Penn-Jones, C., Rayner, M., Rutter, H., Scarborough, P., Sharp, S. J., Smith, R. D., White, M., & Adams, J. (2021). Changes in soft drinks purchased by British households associated with the UK soft drinks industry levy: Controlled interrupted time series analysis. *BMJ, 372*, n254. https://doi.org/10.1136/bmj.n254
Pickhardt, M. (2006). Fifty years after Samuelson's "the pure theory of public expenditure": What are we left with? *Journal of the History of Economic Thought, 28*, 439–460.

Plomp, E. (2011). *Winst in de zorg. Juridische aspecten van winstuitkering door zorginstellingen.* Dissertatie. Universiteit van Amsterdam.

Polder, J. J. (2018). Zorguitgaven. In P. Jeurissen, H. Maarse, & T. Tanke (Eds.), *Betaalbare zorg* (pp. 29–52). Sdu Uitgevers.

Polder, J. J., Hoekstra, J., & Vonk, R. A. A. (2020). *Gezondheidseffecten en maatschappelijke baten van de gezondheidszorg: Kwantitatief vooronderzoek in opdracht van de Wetenschappelijke Raad voor het Regeringsbeleid. Deel 2: maatschappelijke baten.* RIVM-rapport 2020-0060. National Institute for Public Health and the Environment (RIVM).

Pommer, E., van Kempen, H., & Sadiraj, K. (2011). *Jeugdzorg in groeifase. Ontwikkelingen in gebruik en kosten van de jeugdzorg.* The Netherlands Institute for Social Research (SCP).

Pomp, M. (2010). *Een Beter Nederland. De gouden Eieren van de Gezondheidszorg.* Uitgeverij Balans.

Pomp, M., & Vujic, S. (2008). *Rising health spending. New medical technology and the Baumol effect.* CPB Discussion Paper 115. Netherlands Bureau for Economic Policy Analysis (CPB).

Porter, M. E., & Teisberg, E. O. (2006). *Redefining health care: Creating value based competition on results.* Harvard Business School Press.

Pot, G. K., Battjes-Fries, M. C. E., Patijn, O. N., Pijl, H., Witkamp, R. F., de Visser, M., van der Zijl, N., de Vries, M., & Voshol, P. J. (2019). Nutrition and lifestyle intervention in type 2 diabetes: Pilot study in The Netherlands showing improved glucose control and reduction in glucose lowering medication. *BMJ Nutrition, Prevention & Health.* https://doi.org/10.1136/bmjnph-2018-000012

PWC. (2017). *What doctor? Why AI and robotics will define new health.* Retrieved from: https://www.pwc.com/gx/en/industries/healthcare/publications/ai-robotics-new-health.html

Raju, T. N. K., Buist, A. S., Blaisedell, C. J., Moxey-Mims, M., & Saigal, S. (2017). Adults born preterm: A review of general health and system-specific outcomes. *Acta Paediatrica, 106*(9), 1409–1437. https://doi.org/10.1111/apa.13880

Razenberg, I., Kahmann, M., & de Gruijter, M. (2018). *'Mind the gap'. Barrières en mogelijkheden voor de arbeidsparticipatie van vluchtelingenvrouwen.* Verwey Jonker Instituut/ Kennisplatform Integratie & Samenleving.

Reckers-Droog, V. T., van Exel, N. J. A., & Brouwer, W. B. F. (2018). Looking back and moving forward: On the application of proportional shortfall in healthcare priority setting in The Netherlands. *Health Policy, 122*(6), 621–629.

Reckers-Droog, V., van Exel, J., & Brouwer, W. (2019). Equity weights for priority setting in healthcare: Severity, age or both? *Value in Health, 22*(12), 1441–1449.

Regioplan. (2020). *Quickscan arbeidsparticipatie van hoogopgeleide vluchtelingen. Een vergelijking tussen Nederland en andere Europese landen.* Regioplan.

Rhodes, A., Ferdinande, P., Flaatten, H., Guidet, B., Metnitz, P. G., & Moreno, R. P. (2012). The variability of critical care bed numbers in Europe. *Intensive Care Medicine, 38*, 1647–1653.

Rijksbegroting 2019.

Rijksjaarverslag. (2019). Retrieved from: https://www.rijksoverheid.nl/onderwerpen/verantwoordingsdag/rijksjaarverslag-2019-inkomsten-en-uitgaven

RIVM [National Institute for Public Health and the Environment]. (2015). *Kosten van Ziekten 2015.* Rijksinstituut voor Volksgezondheid en Milieu.

RIVM [National Institute for Public Health and the Environment]. (2018a). *Volksgezondheid Toekomst Verkenning 2018.* Rijksinstituut voor Volksgezondheid en Milieu.

RIVM [National Institute for Public Health and the Environment]. (2018b). *Quickscan mogelijke impact Nationaal Preventieakkoord.* Rijksinstituut voor Volksgezondheid en Milieu.

RIVM [National Institute for Public Health and the Environment]. (2019). *Vaccinatiegraad en jaarverslag rijksvaccinatieprogramma 2019.* Rijksinstituut voor Volksgezondheid en Milieu.

RIVM [National Institute for Public Health and the Environment]. (2020a). *Volksgezondheid Toekomst Verkenning 2020. Verder kijken dan corona, over de toekomst van onze gezondheid.* Rijksinstituut voor Volksgezondheid en Milieu.

RIVM [National Institute for Public Health and the Environment]. (2020b). *Prevalentie multimorbiditeit naar aantal chronische aandoeningen*. Retrieved from: https://www.volksgezondheidenzorg.info/onder-werp/chronische-aandoeningen-en-multimorbiditeit/cijfers-context/huidige-situatie#node-prevalentie-multimorbiditeit-naar-aantal-chronische-aandoeningen [21 June 2021].

RIVM [National Institute for Public Health and the Environment]. (2020c). *Integrale bekostiging van de geboortezorg: ervaringen na drie jaar en de eerste zichtbare effecten*. Rijksinstituut voor Volksgezondheid en Milieu.

RIVM [National Institute for Public Health and the Environment], Trimbos-instituut and Amsterdam UMC. (2019). *Mentale gezondheid van jongeren: enkele cijfers en ervaringen*. Rijksinstituut voor Volksgezondheid en Milieu.

Rli [The Council for the Environment and Infrastructure]. (2014). *Langer zelfstandig, een gedeelde opgave van wonen, zorg en welzijn*. Raad voor de leefomgeving en infrastructuur.

RN4CAST. (2012). *Nurse forecasting: human resources planning in nursing. 12 European countries*.

ROB [The Council for Public Administration]. (2020). *Herijking van het uitkeringsstelsel*. Raad voor het Openbaar Bestuur.

Rocks, S., Berntson, D., Gil-Salmerón, A., Kadu, M., Ehrenberg, N., Stein, V., & Tsiachristas, A. (2020). Cost and effects of integrated care: A systematic literature review and meta-analysis. *The European Journal of Health Economics, 21*(8), 1211–1221. https://doi.org/10.1007/s10198-020-01217-5

Roseboom, T. (2018). *De eerste 1000 dagen. Het fundamentele belang van een goed begin vanuit biologisch, medisch en maatschappelijk perspectief*. Uitgeverij de Tijdstroom.

RTL Nieuws. (2019). Kinderrechters luiden noodklok: kinderen in gevaar door gebrek jeugdzorgwerkers. Retrieved from: https://www.rtlnieuws.nl/nieuws/nederland/artikel/4804141/kinderrechters-gebrek-jeugd-zorg-wachtlijsten-noodklok-kinderen [28 June, 2021].

Ruhs, M., & Anderson, B. (2010). *Who needs migrant workers? Labour shortages, immigration, and public policy*. Oxford Scholarship Online.

Ruijsbroek, A., Wijga, A. H., Kerkhof, M., Koppelman, G. H., Smit, H. A., & Droomers, M. (2011). The development of socio-economic health differences in childhood: Results of the Dutch longitudinal piama birth cohort. *BMC Public Health, 11*, 225.

Russell, L. B. (2009). Preventing chronic disease: An important investment, but don't count on cost savings. *Health Affairs, 28*(1), 42–45.

Ruwaard, S. (2018). *Purchasing healthcare: Beyond getting the financial incentives right*. Dissertatie. Tilburg University.

RVS [The Council of Public Health & Society]. (2017a). *Recept voor maatschappelijk probleem. Medicalisering van levensfasen*. Raad voor Volksgezondheid en Samenleving.

RVS [The Council of Public Health & Society]. (2017b). *Implementatie van ehealth vraagt om durf en ruimte*. Raad voor Volksgezondheid en Samenleving.

RVS [The Council of Public Health & Society]. (2019). *De B van Bekwaam. Naar een toekomstbestendige big*. Raad voor Volksgezondheid en Samenleving.

RVS [The Council of Public Health & Society]. (2020a). *Acute zorg: van deelbelangen naar gedeeld belang*. Raad voor Volksgezondheid en Samenleving.

RVS [The Council of Public Health & Society]. (2020b). *Digitale dialoog: vervolgstappen voor waardevolle digitale zorg*. Nieuwsbericht 12 December 2020. Raad voor Volksgezondheid en Samenleving.

RVS [The Council of Public Health & Society]. (2020c). *Zorg op afstand dichterbij? Digitale zorg na de 'coronacrisis'*. Raad voor Volksgezondheid en Samenleving.

RVS [The Council of Public Health & Society]. (2020d). *Applaus is niet genoeg*. Raad voor Volksgezondheid en Samenleving.

RVS [The Council of Public Health & Society]. (2021). *Wissels omzetten voor een veerkrachtige samenleving*. Raad voor Volksgezondheid en Samenleving.

RVZ [The Council of Public Health & Society]. (1998). *Tussen markt en overheid*. Raad voor de Volksgezondheid en Zorg.

Saez, E., Slemrod, J., & Giertz, S. (2012). The elasticity of taxable income with respect to marginal taks rates: A critical review. *Journal of Economic Literature, 50*(1), 3–50.

Samuelson, P. E. (1954). The pure theory of public expenditure. *The Review of Economics and Statistics, 36*(4), 387–389.

Sanyal, C., Stolee, P., Juzwishin, D., & Husereau, D. (2018). Economic evaluations of eHealth technologies: A systematic review. *PLoS One, 13*(6), e0198112.

Schakel, C. (2018). Budgettaire processen en de betaalbaarheid van de zorg. In P. Jeurissen, H. Maarse, & M. Tanke (Eds.), *Betaalbare zorg* (pp. 143–160). Sdu Uitgevers.

Schakel, H. C., Wu, E. H., & Jeurissen, P. (2018). Fiscal rules, powerful levers for controlling the health budget? Evidence from 32 OECD countries. *BMC Public Health, 18*, article 300. https://doi.org/10.1186/s12889-018-5198-y

Schellingerhout, R. (2004). *Gezondheid en welzijn van allochtone ouderen*. The Netherlands Institute for Social Research (SCP).

Schonewille-Rosman, A. N., Steegers-Theunissen, R. P. M., & Steegers, E. P. (2019). Preconceptiezorg anno 2018. Nog steeds te veel gemiste kansen. *Nederlands Tijdschrift voor Geneeskunde, 162*, D3076.

Schularick, M., & Taylor, A. M. (2012). Credit booms gone bust: Monetary policy, leverage cycles and financial crises, 1870-2008. *American Economic Review, 102*(2), 1029–1061.

Schut, F. T. (2003). *De zorg is toch geen markt? Laveren tussen marktfalen en overheidsfalen. Oratie*. Erasmus Universiteit Rotterdam.

Schut, E., van de Ven, M., & Varkevisser, M. (2010). Prijsconcurrentie gaat niet samen met macrobudget ziekenhuizen. *Economisch Statistische Berichten, 95*, 4587.

Schuurman, M. (2018). *Met meer kennis werken aan kwaliteit*. Kalliope Consult.

SER [The Social and Economic Council]. (2020). *Zorg voor de toekomst. Over de toekomstbestendigheid van de zorg*. Sociaal-Economische Raad.

SER [The Social and Economic Council]. (2021a). *Aan de slag voor de zorg. Een actieagenda voor de zorgarbeidsmarkt*. Sociaal-Economische Raad.

SER [The Social and Economic Council]. (2021b). *Jeugdzorg: van systemen naar mensen. Tien aanbevelingen voor de korte termijn*. Sociaal-Economische Raad.

Sheiner, L., & Malinovskaya, A. (2016). *Measuring productivity in healthcare: An analysis of the literature*. Brookings Institute. Retrieved from: https://www.brookings.edu/wp-content/uploads/2016/08/hp-lit-review_final.pdf

Snyder, J., & Caulfield, T. (2019). Patients' crowdfunding campaigns for alternative cancer treatments. *The Lancet, 20*(1), 28–29.

Soeters, M., & Verhoeks, G. (2015). *Financiering van preventieanalyse van knelpunten en inventarisatie van nieuwe oplossingen*. ZorgmarktAdvies.

Stadhouders, N., & Kruse, F. (2018). Welke maatregelen kunnen de zorgkosten bedwingen? In P. Jeurissen, H. Maarse, & M. Tanke (Eds.), *Betaalbare Zorg* (pp. 73–92). Sdu Uitgevers.

Stadhouders, N., Koolman, X., Tanke, M., Maarse, H., & Jeurissen, P. (2016). Policy options to contain healthcare costs: A review and classification. *Health Policy, 120*(5), 486–494.

Steegers, E. A. P. (2017). Sociale verloskunde: Gelijke kansen op een gezonde start. *Nederlands Tijdschrift voor Geneeskunde, 161*(5), 1–4.

Steegers, E., van der Meer, L., Ernst, H., & Blanchette, L. (2020). Een kwetsbare zwangere, wat is dat eigenlijk?. *Medisch Contact*. Retrieved from: https://www.medischcontact.nl/nieuws/laatste-nieuws/artikel/een-kwetsbare-zwangere-wat-is-dat-eigenlijk.htm

Steventon, A., Bardsley, M., Billings, J., Dixon, J., Doll, H., Beynon, M., Hirani, S., Cartwright, M., Rixon, L., Knapp, M., Henderson, C., Rogers, A., Hendy, J., Fitzpatrick, R., & Newman, S. (2013). Effect of telecare on use of health and social care services: Findings from the whole systems demonstrator cluster randomised trial. *Age and Ageing, 42*(4), 501–508.

Stichting Het Potentieel Pakken. (2020). *Het potentieel Pakken in de zorg, de kansen rondom grotere deeltijdbanen*. Retrieved from: www.hetpotentieelpakken.nl

Stigler, G. (1971). The theory of economic regulation. *Bell Journal of Economics and Management Science, 3*, 3–18.
Stolk, E. A., Pickee, S. J., Ament, A. H. J. A., & Busschbach, J. J. V. (2005). Equity in health care prioritisation: An empirical inquiry into social value. *Health Policy, 74*(3), 343–355.
Stronks, K., & Gunning-Schepers, L. (1993). Should equity in health be target number 1? *European Journal of Public Health, 3*(2), 104–111.
Studiegroep begrotingsruimte. (2020). *Koers bepalen. Kiezen in tijden van budgettaire krapte*. Rijksoverheid.
Sturmberg, J. P., O'Halloran, D. M., & Martin, C. M. (2012). Understanding health system reform—A complex adaptive systems perspective. *Journal of Evaluation in Clinical Practice, 18*(1), 202–208.
Tanke, M. (2018). Een doelmatig zorglandschap, basis voor betaalbare zorg. In P. Jeurissen, H. Maarse, & M. Tanke (Eds.), *Betaalbare Zorg* (pp. 235–258). Sdu Uitgevers.
Taskforce Juiste Zorg op de Juiste Plek. (2018). *De Juiste Zorg op de Juiste Plek—Wie Durft?* van de Taskforce.
Taylor, A. M. (2012). *The great leveraging*. NBER Working Paper 18290. National Bureau Of Economic Research.
ter Heide, H. (1984). Ervaringen met het COZ als ordeningsmodel. In L. de Wolff (Ed.), *De Prijs voor Gezondheid* (pp. 47–64). Het Centraal Orgaan Ziekenhuistarieven.
Tetlock, P. E. (2003). Thinking the unthinkable: Sacred values and taboo cognitions. *Trends in Cognitive Science, 7*(7), 320–324.
Tetlock, P. E., Mellers, B. A., & Scoblic, S. P. (2017). Sacred versus pseudo-sacred values: How people cope with taboo trade-offs. *American Economic Review, 107*(5), 96–99.
Thaler, R., & Rosen, S. (1976). The value of saving a life: Evidence from the labor market. In N. E. Terleckyj (Ed.), *Household production and consumption* (pp. 265–302). National Bureau of Economic Research.
Thatcher, M., & Sweet, A. S. (2002). Theory and practice of delegation to non- majoritarian institutions. *West European Politics, 25*(1), 1–22.
Thatcher, M., & Sweet, A. S. (2003). *The politics of delegation*. Frank Cass Ltc.
Thoenes, P. (1984). *De crisis als uitdaging: opstellen over heden en toekomst van de verzorgingsstaat*. Kobra.
Timmermans, J., van Campen, C., & Hessing, J. (2002). Zorg. In *SCP, Sociaal en Cultureel Rapport 2002. De kwaliteit van de quartaire sector* (pp. 273–337). The Netherlands Institute for Social Research (SCP).
Timmins, N., Rawlins, M., & Appleby, J. (2016). *A terrible beauty. A short history of NICE*. HITAP.
TNO. (2019). *Arbobalans 2018. Kwaliteit van de arbeid, effecten en maatregelen in Nederland*. TNO.
Toirkens, J. (1988). *Schijn en Werkelijkheid van het Bezuinigingsbeleid, 1975–1986*. Kluwer.
Transform. (2019). *Inzet personeel uit het buitenland. Oplossingen voor arbeidsmarktvraagstukken binnen zorg en welzijn in Nederland?* Transvorm.
Trappenburg, M. (2005). *Gezondheidszorg en democratie. Oratie*. Erasmus Universiteit.
Trimbos & Wetenschappelijk Onderzoek- en Documentatiecentrum Ministerie van Justitie en Veiligheid [The WODC (Research and Data Centre) The Ministry of Justice and Security. (2020). *Nationale Drug Monitor. Jaarbericht 2019*. Trimbos/WODC.
Tuohy, C. H., & Glied, S. (2011). The political economy of health care. In S. Glied & P. C. Smith (Eds.), *The Oxford handbook of health economics* (pp. 58–77). Oxford University Press.
Tweede Kamer. (2017). Algemene Financiële Beschouwingen 2018.
van Ark, B., & De Jong, H. (1996). *Accounting for economic growth in The Netherlands since 1913*. Universiteit Groningen.
van Ark, B., De Haan, J., & De Jong, H. J. (1996). Characteristics of economic growth in The Netherlands during the postwar period. In N. Crafts & G. Toniolo (Eds.), *Economic growth in Europe since 1945* (pp. 290–328). Cambridge University Press.

van Campen, C., Kooiker, S., & De Boer, A. (2016). Zorgen. Hoe gaan we als samenleving zorgen voor de groeiende groep ouderen? In A. van den Broek et al. (Eds.), *De toekomst tegemoet. Leren, werken, zorgen, samenleven en consumeren in het Nederland van later. Sociaal en Cultureel Rapport 2016* (pp. 108–141). The Netherlands Institute for Social Research (SCP).

van Campen, C., Vonk, F., & Van Tilburg, T. (2018). *Kwetsbaar en eenzaam? Risico's en bescherming in de ouder wordende bevolking*. The Netherlands Institute for Social Research (SCP).

van Dam, F., Daalhuizen, F., De Groot, C., Van Middelkoop, M., & Peeters, P. (2013). *Vergrijzing en ruimte. Gevolgen voor de woningmarkt, vrijetijdsbesteding, mobiliteit en regionale economie*. PBL Netherlands Environmental Assessment Agency.

van den Berg, M. J., Kringos, D. S., Marks, L. K., & Klazinga, N. S. (2014). The Dutch healthcare performance report: Seven years of health care performance assessment in The Netherlands. *Health Research Policy and Systems, 12*, 1.

van den Brakel, M. (2020). In W. Portegijs & B. Hermans (Eds.), *Emancipatiemonitor 2020*. The Netherlands Institute for Social Research (SCP).

van den Brink, G. (2017). *Moderne liefdadigheid*. WRR Working Paper 27. The Netherlands Scientific Council for Government Policy (WRR).

van der Erf, S., & Strijbosch, F. (2020). *Initiatieven toegankelijkheid geboortezorg. Inventarisatie bij geboortezorgconsortia, ROAZ'en en landelijke partijen*. SiRM.

van der Geest, M. (2019, September 13). Duizenden ouderen wachten op verpleeghuisplek of thuiszorg—'Er is een dramatische situatie aan het ontstaan'. *de Volkskrant*.

van der Grinten, T., & Vos, P. (2004). Gezondheidszorg. In H. Dijstelbloem, P. L. Meurs, & E. K. Schrijvers (Eds.), *Maatschappelijke dienstverlening. Een onderzoek naar vijf sectoren. WRR-Investigations no. 6*. The Netherlands Scientific Council for Government Policy (WRR).

van der Horst, A., van Erp, F., & de Jong, J. (2011). *Trends in Gezondheid en Zorg. CPB Policy Brief 2011/11*. Netherlands Bureau for Economic Policy Analysis (CPB).

van der Jagt-Jobsen, J. A. E., Rijken, J. J., & Verduijn, M. A. M. (2014). Van AWBZ naar Wlz: een trendbreuk met het verleden? *Tijdschrift voor GezondheidsRecht, 38*, 7.

van der Kaaden, A. M. (2021, May 27). Rijk moet miljarden bijleggen voor de jeugdzorg, oordeelt arbitragecommissie. *NRC Handelsblad*.

van der Line, I.. (2020, February 26). Wie staat er straks aan ons ziekenhuisbed?', *Groene Amsterdammer* 114(9).

van der Meer, L., Ernst, H., Blanchette, L., & Steegers, E. (2020). Een kwetsbare zwangere, wat is dat eigenlijk? *Medisch Contact, 22*, 34–36.

van der Meulen, M. (2020). *Zorgrobot kan mantelzorger ondersteunen in coronacrisis Vilans*. Retrieved from: https://www.vilans.nl/artikelen/zorgro-bot-kan-mantelzorger-ondersteunen-in-coronacrisis [28 June 2021].

van der Vliet, N., Suijkerbuijk, A. W. M., de Blaeij, A. T., de Wit, G. A., van Gils, P. F., Staatsen, B. A. M., Maas, R., & Polder, J. J. (2020). Ranking preventive interventions from different policy domains: What are the most cost-effective ways to improve public health? *International Journal of Environmental Research and Public Health, 17*(6), 2160.

van der Werff, S., Kok, L., Vervliet, T., & Luiten, W. (2019). *Ontwikkelingen op de Arbeidsmarkt voor Medisch en Verzorgend Personeel*. SEO Economisch Onderzoek.

van der Wilt, G. J., Adang, E., Baltussen, R., & Oortwijn, W. (2018). De waarde(n) van pakketbeheer. In P. Jeurissen, H. Maarse, & M. Tanke (Eds.), *Betaalbare zorg* (pp. 109–123). Sdu Uitgevers.

van Dijk, W., Faber, M. J., Tanke, M. A. C., Jeurissen, P. P. T., & Westert, G. P. (2016). Medicalisation and overdiagnosis: What society does to medicine. *International Journal of Health Policy Management, 5*(11), 619–622.

van Dijk, W., Meinders, M. J., Tanke, M. A. C., Westert, G. P., & Jeurissen, P. P. T. (2020). Medicalization defined in empirical contexts—A scoping review. *International Journal of Health Policy Management, 9*(8), 327–334.

van Doorn, J. A. A., & Schuyt, C. J. M. (Eds.). (1978). *De stagnerende verzorgingsstaat*. Boom.

van Echtelt, P. (2020). *Werk, zaligmakend of ziekmakend? De relatie tussen arbeid en gezondheid.* Working Paper no. 39. The Netherlands Scientific Council for Government Policy (WRR).
van Ewijk, H. (2006). De WMO als instrument in de transformatie van de welvaartsstaat en als impuls voor vernieuwing van het sociaal werk. *Journal of Social Intervention: Theory and Practice, 15*(3), 5–16.
van Ewijk, H., Van der Horst, A., & Besseling, P. (2013). *Tussen keuze en solidariteit. Toekomst voor de Zorg. CPB-boek 7.* Netherlands Bureau for Economic Policy Analysis.
van Giessen, A. (2020). *Voortgangsrapportage Nationaal Preventieakkoord 2019.* National Institute for Public Health and the Environment (RIVM).
van Giessen, A., Douma, E., Kuijpers, T., Nawijn, E., van Gestel, I., Pees, S., Koopman, N., de Pon, E., & Boer, J. (2021a). *Inventarisatie aanvullende maatregelen Nationaal Preventieakkoord Mogelijke vervolgstappen richting de ambities voor 2040. RIVM-rapport 2021-0053.* National Institute for Public Health and the Environment (RIVM).
van Giessen, A., Boer, J., van Gestel, I., Pees, S., Douma, E., Kuijpers, T., de Pon, E., Nawijn, E., & Koopman, N. (2021b). *Voortgangsrapportage Nationaal Preventieakkoord 2020.* National Institute for Public Health and the Environment (RIVM).
van Gils, P. F., Suijkerbuijk, A. W. M., Polder, J. J., de Wit, G. A., & Koopmanschap, M. (2020). Nederlandse preventie-uitgaven onder de loep. *Tijdschrift voor Gezondheidswetenschappen, 98*, 92–96. Retrieved from: https://mijn.bsl.nl/nederlandse-preventie-uitgaven-onder-de-loep/17942430
van Greuningen, M. (2016). *Health workforce planning in The Netherlands: How a projection model informs policy regarding the general practitioner and oral health care workforces.* Nivel.
van Herwerden, M. C., van Steenkiste, J., el Moussaoui, R., den Hollander, J. G., Helfrich, G., & Verberk, I. J. A. M. (2021). Thuisbehandeling van COVID-19-patiënten met zuurstof en telemonitoring. Veiligheid, patiënttevredenheid en kosteneffectiviteit. *Nederlands Tijdschrift voor Geneeskunde, 165*, D5740.
van Horst, H., & Ter Rele, A. (2013). *De prijs van gelijke zorg, achtergronddocument bij CPB Policy Brief 2013/01.* Netherlands Bureau for Economic Policy Analysis (CPB).
van Klaveren, K. J. (2016). *Het onafhankelijkheidssyndroom. Een cultuurgeschiedenis van het Nederlandse zorgstelsel.* Wereldbibliotheek.
van Lettow, B., Wouters, M., & Sinnige, J. (2019). *Ehealth, wat is dat?* NICTIZ.
van Liempt, I., & Staring, R. (2020). *Nederland papierenland. Syrische statushouders en hun ervaringen met participatiebeleid in Nederland.* The Netherlands Institute for Social Research (SCP).
van Oorschot, W. (1998). Deservingness and conditionality of solidarity. *Sociale wetenschappen, 41*(3), 54–78.
van Oorschot, W. (2000). who should get what, and why? On deservingness criteria and the conditionality of solidarity among the public. *Policy & Politics, 28*(16), 33–48.
van Rhijn, A. A. T. (1945–1946). *Rapport van de Commissie, ingesteld bij Beschikking van den Minister van Sociale Zaken van 26 Maart 1943, met de opdracht algemeene richtlijnen vast te stellen voor de toekomstige ontwikkeling der sociale verzekering in Nederland.* s-Gravenhage.
van Tuyl, L., Batenburg, R., Keuper, J., Meurs, M., & Friele, R. (2020a). *Toename gebruik ehealth in de huisartsenpraktijk tijdens de coronapandemie. Organisatie van zorg op afstand in coronatijd.* Nivel.
van Tuyl, L., Vis, E., Bosmans, M., Friele, R., & Batenburg, R. (2020b). *Visies op taakherschikking: een inventariserend onderzoek naar de diversiteit, kansen en belemmeringen van taakherschikking in Nederland.* Nivel.
van Yperen, T., van de Maat, A., & Prakken, J. (2019). *Het groeiend jeugdzorggebruik. Duiding en Aanpak.* Netherlands Youth Institute.
van Yperen, T., Hofstede, K., Hageraats, R., Kraak, A., & van der Maat, A. (2021). *Vasthoudend transformeren. Reflecties op de stelseldiscussie jeugdzorg. Position Paper.* Netherlands Youth Institute.

van Zanden, J. L. (1997). *Een Klein Land in de 20e Eeuw. Economische Geschiedenis van Nederland 1914–1995*. Het Spectrum.
Veerbeek, M., Knispel, A., & Nuijen, J. (2012). *GGZ in tabellen 2011*. Trimbosinstituut.
Velez Lapao, L., & Dussault, G. (2017). The contribution of eHealth and mHealth to improving the performance of the health workforce: A review. *Public Health Panorama, 3*(3), 357–536.
Vellinga, R., Steenbergen, E., Nawijn, E., & van Bakel, M. (2020). *Suikertaks: een vergelijking tussen drie Europese landen*. RIVM-briefrapport 2020-0112. National Institute for Public Health and the Environment.
Verbeek-Oudijk, D., & Putman, L. (2016). *Verzorgd in Europa: kerncijfers 2013. Een vergelijking van de zorg en ondersteuning voor 50plussers in 13 Europese landen*. The Netherlands Institute for Social Research (SCP).
Verbeek-Oudijk, D., & van Campen, C. (2017). *Ouderen in verpleeghuizen en verzorgingshuizen*. Sociaal en Cultureel Planbureau.
Verest, W., de Veer, A., de Groot, K., & Francke, A. (2019). *Kwaliteit en veiligheid van zorg aan cliënten: Verpleegkundigen, verzorgenden, begeleiders en praktijkondersteuners over wat ze nodig hebben voor goede zorg*. Nivel.
Verhelst, K. (2021, January 26). Denemarken vaccineert snel met dank aan korte keten. *Financieel Dagblad*.
Vermaat, M. F. (2006). Wet Maatschappelijke Ondersteuning: Alles mag, niets moet? *Tijdschrift voor GezondheidsRecht, 30*(1).
Victoor, A., van den Akker-van Marle, M. E., van den Berg, B., Hansen, J., van den Hout, W. B., & de Jong, J. D. (2011). *Preferentieonderzoek PakketAdviezen. De geschiktheid van drie waarderingsmethoden om de preferenties van verzekerden voor de samenstelling van de basisverzekering te meten*. Nivel.
Victoor, A., Hansen, J., van den Akker-van Marle, M. E., van den Berg, B., van den Hout, W. B., & de Jong, J. D. (2014). Choosing your health insurance pack- age: A method for measuring the public's preferences for changes in the national health insurance plan. *Health Policy, 117*, 257–265.
Vilans. (2020). *Regeldruk in de langdurige zorg boosdoeners blootgelegd*. Vilans.
Vlaanderen, F., & Klink, A. (2018). Betaalbaarheid en bekostiging van curatieve zorg: Combinaties van bekostigingsvormen en kwaliteitsmeting. In P. Jeurissen, H. Maarse, & M. Tanke (Eds.), *Betaalbare Zorg* (pp. 357–372). Sdu Uitgevers.
Vlaanderen, F. P., de Man, Y., Tanke, M. A. C., Munneke, M., Atsma, F., Meinders, M. J., Jeurissen, P. P. T., Bloem, B. R., Krijthe, J. H., & Groenewoud, S. (2021). Density of patient-sharing networks: Impact on the value of Parkinson Care. *International Journal of Health Policy and Management*. https://doi.org/10.34172/ijhpm.2021.15
VNG [The Association of Dutch Municipalities]. (2020). *De kracht van wijd reiken: advies om de transformatie van de jeugd hulp te laten slagen*. The Association of Dutch Municipalities, Expertiseteam Reikwijdte Jeugdhulpplicht.
Vonk, R. (2012). Een taak voor de staat? De Duitse bezetting en de invoering van de verplichte ziekenfondsverzekering in Nederland, 1939–1949. *BMGN – Low Countries Historical Review, 127*(3), 3–28.
Vonk, R. (2013). *Recht of schade. Een geschiedenis van particuliere ziektekosten verzekeraars en hun positie in het Nederlandse zorgverzekeringsbestel, 1900–2006*. Amsterdam University Press.
Vonk, R., & Schut, F. (2019). Can universal access be achieved in a voluntary private health insurance market? Dutch private insurers caught between competing logics. *Health Economics, Policy and Law, 14*(3), 315–336.
Vonk, R., Hilderink, H., Plasmans, M., Kommer, G., & Polder, J. (2020). *Toekomstverkenning zorguitgaven 2015–2060: Kwantitatief vooronderzoek in opdracht van de Wetenschappelijke Raad voor het Regeringsbeleid (WRR). Deel 1: toekomstprojecties, RIVM-Rapport 2020-0059*. National Institute for Public Health and the Environment.

Vreman, R. A., Mantel-Teeuwisse, A. K., Hövels, A. M., Leufkens, H. G. M., & Goettsch, W. G. (2020). Differences in Health technology assessment recommendations among European jurisdictions: The role of practice variations. *Value in Health, 23*(1), 10–16.

Waelput, A. J. M., Sijpkens, M. K., Lagendijk, J., van Minde, M. R. C., Raat, H., Ernst-Smelt, H., de Kroon, M. L. A., Rosman, A. N., Been, J. V., Bertens, L. C. M., & Steegers, E. A. P. (2017). Geographical differences in perinatal health and child welfare in The Netherlands: Rationale for the healthy pregnancy 4 all-2 program. *BMC PREGNANCY AND CHILDBIRTH, 17*(1), 254. https://doi.org/10.1186/s12884-017-1425-2

Waldrop, M. M. (1992). *Complexity: The emerging science at the edge of order and chaos*. Viking.

Wammes, J. J. G., Tanke, M., Jonkers, W., Westert, G. P., van der Wees, P., & Jeurissen, P. P. (2017). Characteristics and healthcare utilisation patterns of high-cost beneficiaries in The Netherlands: A cross-sectional claims database study. *BMJ Open, 7*(11), e017775.

Weaver, K. (1986). The politics of blame avoidance. *Journal of Public Policy, 1986*(6), 371–398.

Weinstein, M. C. (1998). A QALY is a QALY is a QALY—Or is it? *Journal of Health Economics, 7*, 289–290.

Weinstein, M. C., Torrance, G., & McGuire, A. (2009). QALYS: The basics. *Value in Health, 12*(S1), S5–S9.

Weisz, J. R., Sandler, I. N., Durlak, J. A., & Anton, B. S. (2005). Promoting and protecting youth mental health through evidence-based prevention and treatment. *American Psychologist, 60*(6), 628–648.

Went, R., Kremer, M., & Knottnerus, A. (2015). *De robot de baas. De toekomst van werk in het tweede machinetijdperk [Mastering the Robot. The future of work in the second machine age]*. WRR-Investigation no. 31. The Netherlands Scientific Council for Government Policy (WRR).

Whitehead, S. J., & Ali, S. (2010). Health outcomes in economic evaluation: The QALY and utilities. *British Medical Bulletin, 96*(1), 5–21.

WHO. (2005). Constitution of the World Health Organization. In *WHO basic documents fortyninth edition 2020* (pp. 1–20). World Health Organization.

Williams, G. A., Jacob, G., Rakovac, I., Scotter, C., & Wismar, M. (2020). Health professional mobility in the who European region and the who global code of practice: Data from the joint oecd/eurostat/who-Europe questionnaire. *European Journal of Public Health, 30*(4), IV5–IV11.

Wismar, M., Maier, C. B., Glinos, I. A., Dussault, G., & Figueras, J. (2011). *Health professional mobility and health systems. Evidence from 17 countries*. World Health Organization; European Observatory on Health Systems and Policy.

Woittiez, I. B., Putman, L., Eggink, E., & Ras, M. (2014). Zorg beter begrepen: verklaringen voor de groeiende vraag naar zorg voor mensen met een verstandelijke beperking. *The Hague: The Netherlands Institute for Social Research (SCP).*

Woittiez, I. B., Eggink, E., Putman, L., & Ras, M. (2018). *An international comparison of care for people with intellectual disability*. The Netherlands Institute for Social Research (SCP).

Wolfe, M. K., McDonald, N. C., & Holmes, G. M. (2020). Transportation barriers to Health Care in the United States: Findings from the National Health Interview Survey, 1997–2017. *American Journal of Public Health, 110*(6), 815–822. https://doi.org/10.2105/AJPH.2020.305579

Wong, A., Bakx, P. L. H., Wouterse, B., & van Doorslaer, E. K. A. (2018). Thuiszorg is niet altijd goedkoper dan verpleeghuiszorg. *ESB Gezondheid.*

Woolf, S. H. (2009). A closer look at the Economic argument for disease prevention. *JAMA, 301*(5), 536–538.

Wouters, M., Huygens, M., Voogdt, H., Meurs, M., de Groot, J., de Bruin, K., Brabers, A., Hofstede, C., Friele, R., & van Gennip, L. (2019). *Samen aan zet! eHealthmonitor 2019*. Nictiz & Nivel.

Wouterse, B. (2020). 'Preventie is belangrijk, maar verlaagt zorgkosten nauwelijks', blog *ESB*. Retrieved from: https://esb.nu/blog/20060501/preventie-is-belangrijk-maar-verlaagt-zorgkosten-nauwelijks

WRR [The Netherlands Scientific Council for Government Policy]. (1997). *Volksgezondheidszorg* [Public Health Care. Priorities and a Sound Financial Basis for Health Care in the 21st Century]. Reports to the government no. 52. The Netherlands Scientific Council for Government Policy.

WRR [The Netherlands Scientific Council for Government Policy]. (2014a). *Met kennis van gedrag beleid maken* [Policymaking Using Behavioural Expertise]. Reports to the government no. 92. The Netherlands Scientific Council for Government Policy.

WRR [The Netherlands Scientific Council for Government Policy]. (2014b). *Naar een voedselbeleid* [Towards a Food Policy]. Reports to the government no. 93. The Netherlands Scientific Council for Government Policy.

WRR [The Netherlands Scientific Council for Government Policy]. (2016). *Samenleving en Financiële Sector in Evenwicht* [Finance and Society: Restoring the Balance]. Reports to the government no. 96. The Netherlands Scientific Council for Government Policy.

WRR [The Netherlands Scientific Council for Government Policy]. (2017). *Weten is nog geen doen. Een realistisch perspectief op redzaamheid* [Why Knowing What To Do Is Not Enough. A Realistic Perspective on Self-Reliance]. Reports to the government no. 97. The Netherlands Scientific Council for Government Policy/ Springer Nature.

WRR [The Netherlands Scientific Council for Government Policy]. (2020a). *Samenleven in verscheidenheid. Beleid voor de migratiesamenleving* [Migration Diversity and Social Cohesion. Reassessing the Dutch Policy Agenda]. Reports to the government no. 103. The Netherlands Scientific Council for Government Policy/Springer Nature.

WRR [The Netherlands Scientific Council for Government Policy]. (2020b). *Het betere werk, de nieuwe maatschappelijke opgave* [Better Work. The Impact of Automation, Flexibilization and Intensification of Work]. Reports to the government no. 102. The Netherlands Scientific Council for Government Policy/Springer Nature.

WRR [The Netherlands Scientific Council for Government Policy], ROB [The Council for Public Administration] & Gezondheidsraad [The Health Council of the Netherlands]. (2021). *Verwerven, waarderen en wegen. De inzet van kennis bij beleidsadvisering in crisistijd* [Acquiring, assessing and weighing. The use of knowledge in policy advice in times of crisis]. The Netherlands Scientific Council for Government Policy (WRR), The Health Council of the Netherlands (GR) & the Council for Public Administration (ROB).

Zeilstra, A., den Ouden, A., & Vermeulen, W. (2019). *Middellangetermijnverkenning zorg 2022–2025*. Netherlands Bureau for Economic Policy Analysis (CPB).

Zorginstituut Nederland [National Health Care Institute]. (2016a). *Horen vitaminen, mineralen en paracetamol (1000 mg) (nog) thuis in het te verzekeren pakket?* Zorginstituut Nederland.

Zorginstituut Nederland [National Health Care Institute]. (2016b). *Passend Onderzoek effectiviteit Langdurige Zorg*. Zorginstituut Nederland.

Zorginstituut Nederland [National Health Care Institute]. (2017). *Pakketadvies in de praktijk. Wikken en wegen voor een rechtvaardig pakket*. Zorginstituut Nederland.

Zorginstituut Nederland [National Health Care Institute]. (2019). *Verbetersignalement 'Zorgtraject van mensen met COPD'*. Zorginstituut Nederland.

Zorginstituut Nederland [National Health Care Institute]. (2020a). *Pakketadvies herbeoordeling osimertinib*. Retrieved from: https://www.zorginstituutnederland.nl/publicaties/adviezen/2020/09/21/pakketadvies-herbeoordeling-osimertinib-tagrisso

Zorginstituut Nederland [National Health Care Institute]. (2020b). *Advies Digitaal waar mogelijk en wenselijk*. Zorginstituut Nederland.

Zorginstituut Nederland [National Health Care Institute], & NZA [The Dutch Healthcare Authority]. (2020). *Adviesrapport Samenwerken aan passende zorg: de toekomst is nú. Actieplan voor het behoud van goede en toegankelijke gezondheidszorg*. Zorginstituut Nederland/Nationale Zorgautoriteit.

*Zorgvisie*. (2019). Europa investeert jaarlijks tientallen miljoenen in ehealth voor ouderen. Retrieved from: https://www.zorgvisie.nl/europa-in-vesteert-jaarlijks-tientallen-miljoenen-in-ehealth-voor-ouderen/ [21 June 2021].

Zweifel, P., Felder, S., & Meiers, M. (1999). Ageing of population and health care expenditure: A red herring? *Health Economics, 8*(6), 485–496.

MIX
Papier aus verantwortungsvollen Quellen
Paper from responsible sources
FSC® C105338

If you have any concerns about our products,
you can contact us on
**ProductSafety@springernature.com**

In case Publisher is established outside the EU,
the EU authorized representative is:
**Springer Nature Customer Service Center GmbH**
**Europaplatz 3, 69115 Heidelberg, Germany**

Printed by Libri Plureos GmbH
in Hamburg, Germany